CONTEMPORARY
Black
Biography

ISSN-1058-1316

CONTEMPORARY

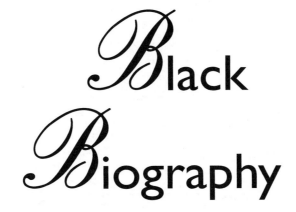

Black

Biography

Profiles from the International Black Community

Volume 46

THOMSON

GALE

Detroit • New York • San Francisco • San Diego • New Haven, Conn. • Waterville, Maine • London • Munich

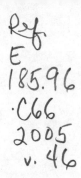

Contemporary Black Biography, Volume 46
Sara and Tom Pendergast

Project Editor
Pamela M. Kalte

Image Research and Acquisitions
Robyn V. Young

Editorial Support Services
Nataliya Mikheyeva

Rights and Permissions
Susan J. Rudolph, Ann Taylor, Edna Hedblad

Manufacturing
Dorothy Maki, Rhonda Williams

Composition and Prepress
Mary Beth Trimper, Gary Leach

Imaging and Multimedia
Lezlie Light, Dan Newell

ISBN 0-7876-6734-X
ISSN 1058-1316

Printed in the United States of America
10 9 8 7 6 5 4 3 2 1

Contemporary Black Biography
Advisory Board

Contents

Introduction ix

Cumulative Nationality Index 175

Cumulative Occupation Index 189

Cumulative Subject Index 211

Cumulative Name Index 269

Introduction

Contemporary Black Biography provides informative biographical profiles of the important and influential persons of African heritage who form the international black community: men and women who have changed today's world and are shaping tomorrow's. *Contemporary Black Biography* covers persons of various nationalities in a wide variety of fields, including architecture, art, business, dance, education, fashion, film, industry, journalism, law, literature, medicine, music, politics and government, publishing, religion, science and technology, social issues, sports, television, theater, and others. In addition to in-depth coverage of names found in today's headlines, *Contemporary Black Biography* provides coverage of selected individuals from earlier in this century whose influence continues to impact on contemporary life. *Contemporary Black Biography* also provides coverage of important and influential persons who are not yet household names and are therefore likely to be ignored by other biographical reference series. Each volume also includes listee updates on names previously appearing in *CBB*.

Designed for Quick Research and Interesting Reading

- *Attractive page design* incorporates textual subheads, making it easy to find the information you're looking for.

- *Easy-to-locate data sections* provide quick access to vital personal statistics, career information, major awards, and mailing addresses, when available.

- *Informative biographical essays* trace the subject's personal and professional life with the kind of in-depth analysis you need.

- *To further enhance your appreciation* of the subject, most entries include photographic portraits.

- *Sources for additional information* direct the user to selected books, magazines, and newspapers where more information on the individuals can be obtained.

Helpful Indexes Make It Easy to Find the Information You Need

Contemporary Black Biography includes cumulative Nationality, Occupation, Subject, and Name indexes that make it easy to locate entries in a variety of useful ways.

Available in Electronic Formats

Diskette/Magnetic Tape. Contemporary Black Biography is available for licensing on magnetic tape or diskette in a fielded format. Either the complete database or a custom selection of entries may be ordered. The database is available for internal data processing and nonpublishing purposes only. For more information, call (800) 877-GALE. *On-line. Contemporary Black Biography* is available online through Mead Data Central's NEXIS Service in the NEXIS, PEOPLE and SPORTS Libraries in the GALBIO file and Gale Group's Biography Resource Center.

Disclaimer

Contemporary Black Biography uses and lists websites as sources and these websites may become obsolete.

We Welcome Your Suggestions

The editors welcome your comments and suggestions for enhancing and improving *Contemporary Black Biography*. If you would like to suggest persons for inclusion in the series, please submit these names to the editors. Mail comments or suggestions to:

The Editor
Contemporary Black Biography
Thomson Gale
27500 Drake Rd.
Farmington Hills, MI 48331-3535
Phone: (800) 347-4253

50 Cent

1976—

Musician

50 Cent, photograph. © Reuters/Corbis.

Rapper 50 Cent, who emerged from one of the bleaker neighborhoods in New York City's outer boroughs, found himself an overnight millionaire with the 2003 release of his debut record, *Get Rich or Die Tryin',* on Eminem's Shady/ Aftermath label. It sold six million copies, finished the year as the top-seller of 2003, and set the record for top-selling debut in American chart history.

50 Cent's success seems doubly remarkable given his origins in Queens, New York. Unlike some rap artists, who grew up in middle-class households but adopted a more streetwise persona to gain credibility in the urban music marketing game, his background was indeed rough. He was born in 1976 and grew up in Queens's South Jamaica neighborhood as Curtis James Jackson III. His mother, Sabrina, was just 15 when he was born, and lived out the rest of her 23-year life as one of the most feared drug dealers in Queens. He never knew his father, and was raised by his grandparents following his mother's mysterjious, likely drug-related death in which an assailant drugged her and then turned on the gas in her home.

Riddled with Nine Bullets

50 Cent found it hard to resist the lure of drug money himself, and began selling drugs when he was 12 years old. He was periodically arrested, dropped out of high school, and in 1994 served time in prison. He had been running several profitable crack houses by the time his son was born in 1997 and he decided to quit the business. "I was going to jail every other summer," he told *Entertainment Weekly*'s Evan Serpick. After changing his street name from Boo-Boo to 50 Cent, which he explained was "a metaphor for change," as he told *Ebony* writer Zondra Hughes, he tried to earn money as a boxer, but found a more promising avenue in music. He had long idolized rappers like KRS-One, and tried writing his own rhymes. Some made their way onto underground mix tapes, in which he rapped over others' songs, and one of the tapes caught the ear of legendary Run DMC member Jam Master Jay. Around 1997, Jay signed 50 Cent and began working with him. "He was really patient with me," the rapper told *Time* journalist Josh Tyrangiel about his mentor. "I would come in with rhymes, almost free verse, and he

At a Glance . . .

Born Curtis James Jackson III on July 6, 1976, in New York, NY; son of Sabrina Jackson; children: Marquise.

Career: Columbia Records, recording artist, 1999-2000; Shady Records, recording artist, 2002–.

Addresses: *Office*—c/o Shady Records, 151 Lafayette St. #6, New York, NY 10013-3124.

explained that they had to fit 16 bars of music. Once he said it, I got it."

Jay produced a demo of rap songs by 50 Cent that got him signed to Columbia Records in 1999. The record label paid a $65,000 advance, but just $5,000 was left after the majority went to Jay and the rest to lawyers who brokered the deal. 50 Cent recorded 36 songs, but Columbia seemed leery about the release of the full LP, *The Power of a Dollar.* In response, the rapper issued a bootleg single, "How to Rob," that was a comic take-down of a roster of famous names, from Jay-Z to Whitney Houston's troubled spouse Bobby Brown. It generated a certain amount of street buzz, and also a fair amount of ill will toward 50 Cent. He had an altercation with a member of the Wu-Tang Clan, but worse was to come: in May of 2000, just days before the record was set to hit stores, he became the victim of a shooting that put nine bullets into his body. He had been sitting in a car near his grandmother's home when his assailant shot him, but miraculously drove himself to the hospital, tossing his own weapon down a sewer along the way. Doctors saved his life, but one bullet fragment remained lodged in his tongue.

50 Cent asserted on several occasions that the shooting was the result of some lingering ill will over his drug-dealing days, not any payback over the bootleg single. But Columbia dropped him, and his career seemed over before it had even begun. He returned to making his own bootlegs, and gained another dose of notoriety for "Wanksta," in which he took fellow New York City rapper Ja Rule to task. A feud between the two arose when Ja Rule was robbed of several thousand dollars' worth of jewelry, and the suspect was later seen in the company of 50 Cent. There were two altercations, one in which 50 Cent was stabbed in a Manhattan recording studio. The wound required just a few stitches, and only heightened the tensions between the two. 50 Cent's primary contention with Rule was his crossover to R&B and duets with J. Lo and Ashanti. "That kid is a fraud," 50 Cent claimed in the *Entertainment Weekly* interview. "Ja Rule grew

up a Jehovah's Witness. While we were selling crack, he was knocking on people's doors every Saturday."

"Wanksta" found its way to rap superstar Eminem, who put it on the soundtrack to his hit biopic *8 Mile* and signed 50 Cent to his label, Shady, for $1 million in June of 2002. 50 Cent said he was grateful for the chance that the white Detroit rapper took on him when other companies were interested in his musical talent, yet fearful of 50 Cent's violent reputation. "Eminem was all about the music," he told *Entertainment Weekly*'s Serpick. "He signed me knowing there was a possibility he was purchasing a problem." Some cynics, however, asserted that by bringing a bullet-scarred former crack seller into his stable, Eminem gained a priceless measure of credibility that could yield an entirely new audience of hard-core rap enthusiasts.

Debut Set New Chart Record

It did. Eminem and Dr. Dre produced 50 Cent's debut, *Get Rich or Die Tryin',* which sold 872,000 copies during its first week out and 1.6 million after just 11 days in the stores. The songs steered clear of verbal attacks on other musicians, instead focusing on 50 Cent's rough times. "Many Men (Wish Death)" chronicled the attempts on his life, but the more jubilant "In Da Club" became a dance-floor favorite. The advance buzz for the record was so great that even the austere *New York Times* published a thousand-word profile upon its debut. Writer Lola Ogunnaike revealed herself a fan of *Get Rich or Die Tryin'.* "Filled with macho tales of drugs, murder and firearms, 50's debut celebrates life in a morally bankrupt world," she wrote.

Most reviewers were also unapologetically enthusiastic. *New Statesman* writer Ted Kessler found 50 Cent's record possessed of "something for everybody," with the Dre/Eminem production team giving it "a dense, clubby soundscape featuring enough moody pop bounce to keep him in the singles chart until Christmas. To this, 50 Cent adds a slurred, stoned vocal style that sounds as casual as if he's just ordering a pizza on the telephone." A journalist for London's *Observer* newspaper, Kitty Empire declared it "something of a street opera. The jousting match between the themes of life and death, of mortality and survival, in hip hop is an intricate and mesmerising one–and one that has found an especially absorbing performer in 50 Cent."

50 Cent spent much of the summer of 2003 touring with Jay-Z, and the year ended with *Get Rich or Die Tryin'* beating out Norah Jones as the top-selling release of the year. It also earned him five Grammy nominations. He moved into his new home, a 48,000-square-foot Connecticut mansion once owned by boxer Mike Tyson. He claims there is still a contract out on his life, and both he and his young son wear bulletproof vests in public and travel in armor-plated vehicles. He

was also romantically linked with actress Vivica A. Fox, several years his senior. Despite his newfound fame and fortune, the gulf between his former life as a Queens high-school drop-out and the new, immensely rich music-industry player became apparent sometimes at upscale business meetings in posh Manhattan eateries. "I'm used to restaurants that sell french fries, you know what I mean?," he said in an interview with *Entertainment Weekly*'s Rob Brunner. "Some of this stuff on the menu, I'm like, 'What's this?' I'm experiencing different things. It's all new to me."

Selected discography

Albums

Get Rich or Die Tryin', Shady/Aftermath, 2003.
P.I.M.P., Universal, 2003.

Singles

"How to Rob," Sony, 1999.
"Thug Love" (CD), Sony, 1999.
"Your Life's on the Line," Sony, 1999.

Sources

Daily Variety, February 13, 2003, p. 6.
Ebony, August 2003, p. 52.
Entertainment Weekly, February 21, 2003, p. 148; February 28, 2003, p. 42; May 30, 2003, p. 26; December 26, 2003, p. 24.
Jet, October 20, 2003, p. 32.
New Statesman, March 31, 2003, p. 43.
New York Times, February 6, 2003, p. E1.
Observer (London, England), February 23, 2003, p. 5.
Teen People, May 1, 2003, p. 140.
Time, February 17, 2003, p. 68.

—Carol Brennan

Carmelo Anthony

1984—

Professional basketball player

In any year but 2003, basketball player Carmelo Anthony would have been the biggest story in the game. But 2003 was the year of LeBron James, the high school player who made the cover of *Sports Illustrated* and was acclaimed as the heir apparent to National Basketball Association (NBA) great Michael Jordan. In the NBA draft held in the summer of 2003, Anthony was selected third by the Denver Nuggets, behind James and Serbian center Darko Milicic. And in Rookie of the Year balloting that followed the 2003-04 NBA season, Anthony came in second to James. Constantly playing second fiddle to his friendly rival might have been difficult, save for one thing: Carmelo Anthony was a winner. He led Syracuse University to a national championship in his freshman year, and he helped turn the league-worst Denver Nuggets into a playoff team in his first season. Despite falling just short of the top honors in professional basketball, Anthony performs at the highest levels and in the views of most observers is destined for a bright career in the NBA.

Anthony was born on May 29, 1984, in Brooklyn, New York, to Carmelo Iriarte and Mary Anthony. He was the youngest of four children, and his father died of liver failure when his namesake was just two years old. His mother's work as a housekeeper did not provide much money for the family, and when Anthony was eight they moved to a crime-ridden neighborhood in Baltimore, Maryland, known as "The Pharmacy" for the ready availability of illegal drugs. Mary Anthony did not let her family's difficult circumstances stand in the way of her expectations for her children. She de-

manded that Carmelo keep his grades up, even as he began to show signs of becoming a basketball talent in his early teen years.

Anthony entered high school at Baltimore's Towson Catholic High School as a talented but undisciplined player, but he quickly grew more serious about the sport when he was cut from the team as a freshman. In his sophomore and junior seasons in high school Anthony worked hard at improving his game and he grew physically, reaching 6' 5" by his sophomore year. He was soon identified as a rising star, which brought a new set of problems. Anthony told *Sports Illustrated*: "As a good player in the inner city, you're always hearing people saying that you're better than you really are and that you don't have to do things like everybody else. When I was in Baltimore I took all that talk and ran with it. It distracted me from my schoolwork. I started getting suspended." Backed by his strong-willed mother, Anthony made the decision to leave Towson Catholic and get serious about school and his game.

Before his senior year in high school, Anthony transferred to Oak Hill Academy, a Baptist boarding school in rural Mouth of Wilson, Virginia. Oak Hill was a basketball power, known for producing players who went on to successful college and professional careers. But it was also demanding academically. Before Oak Hill would even take Anthony, he had to attend five weeks of summer school. Steve Smith, the coach of Anthony's Amateur Athletic Union (AAU) team, told *Sports Illustrated:* "He had to give up a lot of the

At a Glance . . .

Born on May 29, 1984, in Brooklyn, NY. *Education:* Attended Syracuse University, 2003-04.

Career: Denver Nuggets, professional basketball player, 2003–.

Selected awards: *USA Today,* First Team High School All America, 2002; *Parade,* First Team High School All America, 2002; NCAA Final Four, Most Valuable Player, 2003; *Sporting News* All-American Team, 2003; ESPN, ESPY Award for Best Male College Athlete, 2003; NBA All-Rookie Team selection, 2004.

Addresses: *Office*—c/o Denver Nuggets, 1000 Chopper Circle, Denver, CO 80204. *Web*—www.carmeloanthony.net.

summer basketball camps and events that players love to attend [to get ready for Oak Hill.] He would go to classes from 7 a.m. to noon, six days a week, and then at 2 p.m. each day he had to meet me in the gym." The discipline paid off, for Anthony succeeded academically while leading the Oak Hill basketball team to a 32-1 record and a ranking of third in the nation from *USA Today.* Anthony averaged 21.7 points and 7.4 rebounds per game. The highlight of his senior season was a victory over Akron, Ohio's St. Vincent-St. Mary, which was led by LeBron James.

Though some encouraged Anthony to go straight from high school to the NBA—following the example of stars like Kobe Bryant and Kevin Garnett—his mother knew better. "I didn't want him to go to the NBA," Mary told *Sports Illustrated.* "When you get all that fame and fortune, honey, you become a man, right then and there. I wanted my son to have a chance to be 18 years old." Instead, Anthony chose to attend Syracuse University, where coach Jim Boeheim was building a team of young and capable players. But no one predicted that Syracuse would have the season that followed.

From his very first college basket—a dunk against Memphis—Anthony showed that he was a star-caliber college player. During the regular season he led the Syracuse Orangemen with 22.2 points and 10.0 rebounds per game while playing 36.4 minutes per game. Then Anthony led his team to six straight victories in the NCAA tournament, culminating in a 20-point, 10-rebound performance as they defeated the University of Kansas 81-78 to take the national championship. The *Sporting News* summed up Anthony's remarkable season by noting that "Anthony played the college game better than any freshman in NCAA basketball. Ever." Coach Boeheim echoed these sentiments, telling *Sports Illustrated* that Anthony is "the best player I've ever coached," both on and off the court. "There was never a problem with him. In the admissions office they're always looking for that kid who acts like he's from the suburbs, nice and well-mannered, but when it comes to basketball [we] want him to be tough as hell and banging people. Carmelo is all of those things."

Anthony's freshman season at Syracuse banished any doubts about whether he was ready for the NBA, and he was selected as the third pick in the 2003 NBA draft by the Denver Nuggets, who had won just 17 games in the previous season. From the moment he was selected, Anthony endeared himself to Denver fans, praising the beauty of the city and promising that he would work his hardest to bring quality basketball to the city. Then he timed his contract signing—valued at $8.67 million over three years—so as to help the franchise free up money to sign free agents. The crowning glory came when Anthony led to the Nuggets to a season-opening win over the NBA champion San Antonio Spurs.

Anthony enjoyed a spectacular rookie season with the Nuggets. He started in all 82 regular season games, posting an average of 21.0 points, 6.1 rebounds, 2.8 assists, and 1.2 steals per game while averaging 36.5 minutes of playing time. Nuggets general manager Kiki Vandeweghe told *Sports Illustrated:* "Carmelo is more than a scorer. He's going to be a very good rebounder and a great passer." He helped lift the Nuggets to a 43-39 overall record and into a first round playoff berth against the Minnesota Timberwolves. Though the Timberwolves won the series 4-1, all of Denver recognized that their team had taken huge steps forward. Anthony's season was capped when he came in second to LeBron James in NBA Rookie of the Year voting.

For Carmelo Anthony the future looks very bright. Not only a solid player, he is widely viewed as a likeable player who gives back to his family, his team, and his city. One of his first acts on signing with the Nuggets was to buy his mother a home in Baltimore, and he is a big supporter of the Family Resource Centers, a Colorado organization dedicated to family and children's support services. On his personal Web site, *CA15,* he explained his support for the charity: "I came from an area where I saw poverty and hardship, and Family Resource Centers makes a big impact in helping people in those situations. If I can make a difference in my community to help people who are struggling, then in the long run, it will make my career more fulfilling." Anthony will become even more of a household name in 2004, when he plays for the U.S. national team at the Summer Olympics in Athens, Greece.

Sources

Books

Carmelo Anthony: It's Just the Beginning, Positively for Kids, 2004.

Periodicals

Denver Post, April 4, 2004; June 23, 2004.
New York Times, July 27, 2004, p. D7.
Sports Illustrated, April 16, 2003, p. 24; June 23, 2003, p. 86; November 17, 2003, p. 64.
Sporting News, April 14, 2003, p. 1; November 17, 2003, p. 22.

On-line

CA 15, www.carmeloanthony.net (July 27, 2004).
"Carmelo Anthony," *NBA,* www.nba.com/playerfile/carmelo_anthony/index.html?nav=page (July 27, 2004).
"Carmelo Anthony," *USA Basketball,* www.usabasketball.com/biosmen/carmelo_anthony_bio.html (July 27, 2004).
"Carmelo Anthony Signs with Nuggets," *Inside Baltimore,* www.insidebaltimore.com/sports/nba/carmelo-anthony0718.shtml (July 27, 2004).
"Prospect Profile: Carmelo Anthony," *NBA,* www.nba.com/draft2003/profiles/AnthonyCarmelo.html (July 27, 2004).

—Tom Pendergast

Amy Du Bois Barnett

1969—

Journalist

In 2003, Amy Du Bois Barnett became editor in chief of *Teen People,* making her the first African American to lead a major consumer publication of the Time, Inc., print-journalism empire. The company includes its flagship namesake weekly, *Time,* as well as the publications *People, In Style, Entertainment Weekly,* and *Sports Illustrated.* The year before Barnett came on board, *Teen People* was 46th on the list of the top-selling magazines in the United States, just a few notches below *Entertainment Weekly.* "I'm very aware of the responsibility that it carries," she said of her new job in an interview with the *Sister 2 Sister* Web site's Karen Halliburton. "I know that I'm [representing] a whole lot of journalists of color out there. And I want to make sure that I'm opening doors for them to come in along with me."

Barnett was born in 1969 in Chicago, where her mother, Marguerite Ross Barnett, was earning her Ph.D. in political science at the University of Chicago. The elder Barnett would go on to a distinguished career as a professor, author, and then university administrator before her death from cancer in 1992. Barnett's father, Stephen, had a similarly accomplished career as

Barnett, Amy, photograph. AP/Wide World Photos.

a business anthropologist and expert on consumer spending patterns. Because of her parents' various academic posts, Barnett moved several times during her childhood. By the time she finished high school she had lived in eight different places, including India.

Barnett's college years were spent at Brown University in Rhode Island, where she studied French and political science. When she graduated, she took a job on Wall Street, but soon realized that number crunching was just not a creative enough job for her. She began taking classes in fashion merchandising at Parsons School of Design, and eventually wound up an assistant buyer for the Lord & Taylor department store chain. She also earned a master's degree in creative writing from Columbia University. By the time she was 30, she had worked in three different career fields. "I always put myself in situations that are a little bit beyond what I can comfortably do," she admitted in the interview with Halliburton for *Sister 2 Sister.* "I'm always making sure that I challenge myself in every way."

After working for *Essence* magazine for a few years, in the summer of 2000 Barnett was hired as editor in

At a Glance . . .

Born in September, 1969; daughter of Steven (a business anthropologist) and Marguerite Ross (a professor and university president) Barnett. *Education:* Brown University, Providence, Rhode Island, bachelor's degree in French and political science; Columbia University, New York, MFA; also studied fashion merchandising at Parsons School of Design.

Career: Held a financial industry job on Wall Street, New York; Lord & Taylor, New York, assistant buyer; *Essence* magazine, editor, until 2000; *Honey* magazine, editor in chief, 2000-03; *Teen People,* New York, editor, May 2003–.

Addresses: *Office*—c/o *Teen People,* Time & Life Bldg., 35th Floor, Rockefeller Center, New York, NY 10020-1393. *Home*—New York, NY.

chief of *Honey.* The hip-hop influenced publication aimed at female readers had been launched in 1999 as a quarterly, but new owners Vanguarde Media felt that it had great potential as a more fashion and lifestyle-oriented magazine. They provided funds for putting out ten issues annually, and hired Barnett to lead the charge. During her nearly three-year tenure at *Honey,* circulation doubled from 200,000 to 400,000. Barnett felt the magazine satisfied its readers' needs and filled a particular niche in mainstream consumer journalism. "Urban culture drives popular culture, and many companies are recognizing the need to market toward a 'minority population,' especially in the current economic climate," she said in an interview with *PR Week* in 2001. "But there are still very few places to market to this demographic. *Honey* really has its ear to the ground."

Barnett was hired by Time, Inc., to edit *Teen People* in 2003. Following its launch in 1998, *Teen People* had captured the number-one spot in newsstand sales in its category, but circulation numbers for this junior version of the immensely successful celebrity-profile magazine had begun to slump. Barnett was brought on board to revive its fortunes. When she was under consideration for the job, senior executives at the company asked her how she would redesign it, and she delivered a confident pitch that included revamping the cover and layout. Executives liked her ideas, and Barnett took over in May of 2003. She became the first African American in Time, Inc., history to edit a mainstream consumer publication.

Two months later, a management shakeup at *Teen People*—in which several editors who had worked under Barnett's predecessor were let go—prompted a headline in the *New York Post,* "Bloodbath at Teen People." Barnett was also following through on her redesign plan. "It's not so much a structural change as a complete visual change," she told Lisa Granatstein of *MediaWeek.* "We're trying to make sure the aesthetic reflects what teens are surrounded by—urban culture, MTV, the Web and video games." The transformation also included the use of more contemporary language in editorial copy. *Teen People* had been one of the few magazines in its category not to adopt contemporary slang, but as Barnett pointed out to *MediaWeek,* "'Bling' is in the dictionary. To not use colloquialisms makes us look staid."

Barnett was featured in a *New York Times* style section profile in 2004 for the spectacular Chelsea apartment she had bought a few months earlier. She shares it with partner Jeff Brown, a marketing executive. The minimalist, subdued look of the apartment was enlivened by some Indian statues she had inherited from her mother. "I am very much my mother's daughter," she told *New York Times* journalist Penelope Green. "More and more my life parallels hers. She wouldn't have expected my life to have turned out the way it did, but I know she would be extremely proud of me."

Barnett writes the "Letter from the Editor" in every issue of *Teen People,* and often recounts her own experiences. In her private life, however, she is as subdued as the minimalist palette of her apartment. When asked by Green how she met Brown, Barnett explained that she had known him only peripherally, as a friend of a friend, but he once lived near her job at *Honey.* "He said he'd tried many times to talk to me on the street, but I always ignored him," Barnett told the *New York Times.* "I guess that might be true. I don't remember because I don't talk to men on the street."

Sources

Periodicals

Essence, April 2000, p. 124.
MediaWeek, July 14, 2003, p. 29.
New York Post, July 18, 2003, p. 32; August 4, 2003, p. 30.
New York Times, December 28, 2003; April 11, 2004, p. 6.
PR Week, October 29, 2001, p. 16.
WWD, April 2, 2003, p. 3.

On-line

"Who Does She Think She Is?," *Sister2Sister Online,* www.s2smagazine.com/content/content.asp?issue id=200312&listid=05 (July 8, 2004).

—Carol Brennan

Marguerite Ross Barnett

1942-1992

College president

Marguerite Ross Barnett was the first African-American woman to lead a major American university. Appointed president of the University of Houston in 1990, her dynamic life and career were cut short by cancer just two years later. Prior to taking the Texas job, Barnett had made significant improvements while overseeing the University of Missouri-St. Louis, and had also worked for the City University of New York as a vice chancellor. Hailed as "a new generation of educational leader" in her *New York Times* obituary by Anthony DePalma, Barnett "urged that urban universities play a dominant role in spurring economic growth and solving social problems in the same way that land-grant colleges of a century ago did in developing America's agricultural economy."

Barnett was a native of Charlottesville, Virginia, where she was born on May 22, 1942, to Dewey and Mary Ross. She grew up in Buffalo, New York, and after finishing high school in 1959 she entered Antioch College in Yellow Springs, Ohio, with the goal of becoming a scientist. That course was altered when she read about modern India's political history, in which native leaders like Mohatmas Gandhi and Jawaharlal

Barnett, Marguerite Ross, photograph. AP/Wide World Photos.

Nehru successfully negotiated with British colonial authorities to secure their country's independence. Barnett became a political science major at Antioch and earned her undergraduate degree in 1964. She went on to the prestigious University of Chicago, which granted her an M.A. in 1966 and a Ph.D. in 1972. During her time at Chicago she met and married business anthropologist Stephen A. Barnett. Some of her doctoral research involved spending long stretches of time in India, and Barnett took her husband and infant daughter along.

Began Academic Career

Barnett's first job after leaving the University of Chicago was as an assistant professor of political science at Princeton University, in Princeton, New Jersey. She taught at the Ivy League school for six years, and went on to a stint at Howard University in Washington, D.C., which offered her a full professorship. She chaired Howard's political science department from 1977 to 1980. In 1980, Barnett moved back to the Ivy League, teaching at New York City's Columbia University for the next three years. At Columbia she was a professor

At a Glance . . .

Born May 22, 1942 in Charlottesville, VA; died February 26, 1992, in Wailuku, HI; daughter of Dewey and Mary Ross; married Stephen A. Barnett (divorced); married Walter Eugene King (a politician and professional golfer), June 30, 1980; children: (with Barnett) Amy. *Education:* Antioch College, Yellow Springs, OH, AB, 1964; University of Chicago, MA, 1966, PhD, 1972.

Career: University of Chicago, Chicago, IL, lecturer, 1969-70; Princeton University, Princeton, NJ, assistant professor of political science, 1970-76, and James Madison Bicentennial Preceptor, 1974-76; Howard University, Washington, DC, professor of political science, 1976-80, and chair of political science department, 1977-80; Columbia University, New York, professor of politics and education, professor of political science, and director of the Institute for Urban and Minority Education, 1980-83; City University of New York, New York, professor of political science and vice-chancellor for academic affairs, 1983-86; University of Missouri-Saint Louis, chancellor and professor of political science, 1986-90; University of Houston, Houston, TX, president, 1990-92.

Memberships: Overseas Development Council; Council on Foreign Relations; Cleveland Council.

Awards: American Political Science Association book prize, 1981, for *The Politics of Cultural Nationalism in South India*; Bethune-Tubman-Truth Woman of the Year Award, 1983; Association of Black Women in Higher Education Award for Educational Excellence, 1986; American Political Science COBPS Award for Excellence in Scholarship and Service to the Profession, 1986; Project on Equal Education of the NOW Legal Defense Fund, Golden GAZELLE Award, 1987.

colleges. She was also able to launch a pet project: a program that worked with high schools in low-income communities to help prepare their graduates for college.

In 1986, Barnett moved to the Midwest to become chancellor and professor of political science at the University of Missouri-St. Louis (UMXL). Her accomplishments there were so impressive that she was the subject of a 1989 *New York Times* profile titled, "Chancellor Turns a Campus Around." UMSL had a largely part-time commuter student body, and was hard pressed for funds when Barnett came on board. It had long been overshadowed by it's the University of Missouri's main campus in Columbia. During her first weeks on the job, Barnett battled a future U.S. Attorney General, John Ashcroft, who was then Missouri governor at the time. Ashcroft vetoed a bill in the state legislature that would have given UMSL money for a badly needed new library building. He told Barnett if she raised $1.2 million, he would sign off on the other $4.8 million. "Apparently there was an expectation in the state that we would not be able to raise that kind of money," Barnett noted dryly in an interview with Amy Stuart Wells in the *New York Times,* and indeed school had never raised more than $30,000 at one time in its history. But Barnett raised the money, and the library was built.

Though Barnett raised money from the traditional sources like alumni ranks, she also went after the heavy-hitters: St. Louis-area Fortune 500 companies. Linking their involvement in the school to a sense of civic duty and pride, she culled donations from Anheuser-Busch, Monsanto, and other major employers in the city and surrounding suburbs, and her efforts brought $6 million in donations to UMSL and funded some of first new construction on campus since the early 1960s. Enrollment increased ten percent in just a few short years.

Took Helm in Houston

Barnett also founded Partnerships for Progress at UMSL, a program that linked urban high schools with the University's education department. Her commitment to urban education was well articulated and, with her proven track record, her name was even mentioned as possible New York City public schools chancellor in 1989. But in 1990 Barnett left St. Louis for a job as president of the University of Houston. She was the first woman and the first African American to head the four-campus system, and also the first black of either gender to lead a major research university. At the time, she was just one of three female university presidents in the United States who presided over campuses with 30,000 students or more. Interviewed by *Essence* a month later, Barnett asserted her goal in Texas was "to increase the pool of minority youngsters attending college," she told journalist David Thigpen,

of politics and education and professor of political science, and also served as director of Columbia's Institute for Urban and Minority Education. City University of New York (CUNY) invited her to become professor of political science and vice-chancellor for academic affairs in 1983, and she eagerly took the job. She was part of an administration team that oversaw 180,000 students enrolled in the CUNY system's 21

"and to get them to enter the burgeoning technological fields of the twenty-first century."

The University of Houston had 33,000 students and a budget of $240 million when Barnett started on the job. It also conducted $45 million in research annually, some of it in the field of superconductivity, its specialty. Not surprisingly, Barnett undertook another fundraising campaign there with great success: the school received a $50 million gift from software billionaire John Moores and his wife, one of largest grants ever made to an American public university by an alumnus. Barnett also helped establish the Texas Center for Environmental Studies, and was the driving force behind the creation of the nationally recognized Bridge Program, which helped disadvantaged students make a successful transition from high school to college. As in St. Louis, Barnett was well liked on campus and among local leaders. When she was diagnosed with cancer in late 1991, the news stunned and saddened the academic community. With her second husband, Walter King, a former professional golfer and politician from the island nation of Bermuda, Barnett went to Hawaii, where the pair had once honeymooned. She died at a hospital there on February 26, 1992, from metastatic cancer and hypoglycemia, a blood disorder.

At the time of her death, the only woman to oversee a larger U.S. college campus than Barnett at Houston was Donna Shalala at the University of Wisconsin-Madison, who was appointed Secretary of Health and Human Services in 1993 by President Bill Clinton. A collection of Barnett's papers is held at the University of Houston library, and the university established a memorial scholarship in her honor.

Selected writings

(With others) *Electoral Politics in Indian States: Party Systems and Cleavages,* Manohar Book Service, 1975.

Politics of Cultural Nationalism in South India, Princeton University Press, 1976.

(Editor, with James A. Hefner) *Public Policy for the Black Community: Strategies and Perspectives,* Alfred Press, 1976.

Sources

Books

Encyclopedia of World Biography Supplement, Vol. 21, Gale, 2001.
Notable Black American Women, Book 1, Gale, 1992.

Periodicals

Essence, October 1990, p. 50.
New York Times, June 14, 1989, p. B9; February 27, 1992, p. B7.

—Carol Brennan

Bernard B. Beal

1954(?)—

Financial executive

Wall Street pioneer Bernard B. Beal heads M. R. Beal & Company, one of just a handful of black-owned firms in America's epicenter of finance. Founded in 1988, Beal's brokerage underwrites and trades municipal bonds, and also offers investment banking and financial advisory services. It regularly earns high marks for its fiscal results and client-service reputation, and its founder's forceful, energetic personality seems to have helped it thrive in the highly competitive world of finance.

Beal grew up in New York City, but far from the riches of Wall Street. Born around 1954, he grew up at the home of his grandparents in the Morrisania section of the South Bronx. His grandmother once put their name on a waiting list for an apartment in a nearby public-housing project, but Beal's grandfather was suspicious about the long-term benefits of federally subsidized housing. "We were in a railroad flat that wasn't nearly as nice as the apartment we would have gotten here," Beal recalled in a *New York Times* article by John Tierney as they toured the Forest Houses in 2001. "My grandmother really wanted to move in when our number came up, but my grandfather said no. He said once we went in, we'd never leave."

Shot in Robbery Attempt

Beal's grandparents eventually saved enough to buy their own place in the Soundview section of the Bronx, and they moved when he was 12. His first contact with lower Manhattan's money nexus came with a job at a shoeshine stand near Wall Street. A promising student,

he benefited from the help provided by A Better Chance, a foundation that worked with students from low-income neighborhoods to place them in top private and public schools. Beal's high-school years were spent at the Wooster School of Danbury, Connecticut, and though he had money for college lined up when he graduated in 1972, he wanted to become an entrepreneur instead. With his savings, he bought a share in a Jack in the Box fast-food restaurant in the Bronx, and worked part-time as a manager there. He soon changed his mind about college late one evening when the place was held up at gunpoint, and a bullet grazed his leg.

Beal earned his undergraduate degree from Minnesota's Carleton College and went on to Stanford University's business school. In 1979, the same year he earned his graduate degree, he began work on Wall Street at E. F. Hutton, a large brokerage firm and one of the most respected names in its day. Initially, he was given a choice of two areas to join: either corporate finance or the municipal-bond desk. Corporate finance was a much more exciting field, where large-scale deals were planned and underwritten, but Beal chose the less glamorous route. Issued by state or local governments, municipal bonds are used to finance large-scale projects, such as affordable housing, new schools, public-transit initiatives, or infrastructure improvements for sewers or highways. The interest earned on them is exempt from some types of income tax. "I wanted to go into municipal finance because it blended with my deep desire to do well and do good," Beal explained to

Black Enterprise writer Derek T. Dingle. "I saw it as an opportunity to finance housing and healthcare."

Over the next few years, Beal rose through the ranks at Hutton and gained a reputation as a sharp analyst. He moved over to corporate finance in 1985 and had reached a senior vice presidency post by the time he jumped ship in 1988 to start his own firm, M. R. Beal, with a group of partners. The initials came from the names of his children, Manning and Mae, and from Rose, his wife Valerie's middle name.

M. R. Beal began with eight employees and concentrated on winning municipal finance business. By then, minority "set-asides" were commonplace in state and local government contracts for bond deals. Set-asides specified that a certain amount of business should be given to minority or female-owned firms, and even some corporations had similar rules governing the awarding of contracts. Firms such as Beal's benefited from such practices, but he avoided becoming involved in deals with other brokerage houses that simply wanted minority representation on underwriting bids. Once, a Wall Street acquaintance at a much larger bond firm asked him to step in on a deal, but he declined. "People would have said, 'Those guys just showed up and took a check for being black,'" he told *New York Times* writer Diana B. Henriques. "We will not front for *anybody*."

Firm Emerged as Bond-Business Powerhouse

In the first three years that Beal's firm was in business, it was involved in some 167 public underwriting projects, but it also bought and sold bonds on the market for added profit. The sharp trading skills of his staff were the key to his firm's success, he argued, not winning those underwriting contracts. "There is no way that there is any advantage to being a minority firm in the buying and selling of securities," he told Henriques in 1991. "Nobody is going to sell a bond to you for one-eighth of a point less just because you're black."

By then, Beal was eager to move his firm into the much more lucrative area of corporate finance, but this was a sector dominated for generations by an old-money network. There were few women and even fewer minorities in positions of power at the top investment-banking houses at the time, and a small upstart like Beal's company faced competition from well-heeled, deep-pocketed players with a network of social and business connections to the Fortune 500 decision-makers. Though Beal had made some beneficial political contacts by then, they were no help in landing contracts to underwrite initial public offerings, or IPOs, of company's stock when it was ready to become a publicly traded one. "It's worse than a glass ceiling, because at least you can break glass," Beal reflected in the *New York Times* interview with Henriques. "This ceiling is solid Lucite."

Henriques met with Beal again in 2003, a dozen years after he announced his intention to move into corporate finance. His firm had had a few successes in the IPO business, most notably with the AT&T Wireless Services deal in 2000, but he admitted to not having made it through the figurative Lucite barrier. "I got beat to hell trying to do that," he reflected. "Just beat to hell." Beal & Company was still doing a solid municipal bond business, however, and had even survived an industry-wide upheaval in the mid-1990s when new Securities and Exchange Commission rules went into effect that prohibited municipal-finance professionals from making campaign donations to elected officials in jurisdictions where they had contracts. Because of the new rules, municipal bond volume plummeted 50 percent, and many of the other minority-owned firms doing business in the sector lost crucial business; many had to reorganize, and some went under. Beal's firm had survived the upheaval, however, and by 2003 had taken senior underwriting jobs on some $5 billion in bond issues since its founding. It regularly appeared near the top of the *Black Enterprise*'s annual list of leading black-owned financial firms.

Began Planning for Long-Term Viability

Beal's company even ventured into film production at one point, helping to finance the 2002 movie *Morvern Callar*. It starred Samantha Morton as a woman who gains fame as an author with a manuscript she found on her late boyfriend's computer. But he also hired a Wall Street veteran, Stanley E. Grayson, to become the chief operating officer. Grayson, who had served as New York's deputy mayor for finance at one point, was installed to ensure the long-term prospects of Beal's firm, and one of his duties, Beal told Henriques, was to remind him of the firm's mission. "I've got somebody who can say, 'You don't want to be in the movie business—you want to go to the movies,'" Beal joked in the *New York Times* article.

Beal has been involved in several civic initiatives, including a board seat on New York's Metropolitan Transportation Authority, where he worked to improve conditions in New York subway system. He also worked with the New York City Housing Authority in a privatization scheme that encouraged residents of housing projects Forest Houses to turn their buildings into co-operative units, in which the apartments were owned outright by the tenants. "When people own, it changes their perspective on life," Beal told Tierney of the *New York Times*. "They take better care of their property and care more about the neighborhood. They demand more services. They make plans.... When they have a stake in the future, they pay more attention to educating their kids."

Beal also serves as board chair of A Better Chance (ABC), the foundation responsible for placing him in the private Connecticut school when he was a teenager. He was one of 11,000 middle and high school students that ABC had helped since its inception in 1963, and television personality Oprah Winfrey had joined its mission as well, donating a large sum and becoming its national spokesperson. When the foundation executives first contacted him about helping out with ABC fundraising efforts back in the late 1990s, he was not eager to add another job to his already-busy work schedule at the time, he told Henriques. But on the day of their scheduled meeting, "I ran into a kid from my old neighborhood," he recalled. "He'd gotten into the program, too, but his parents wouldn't let him go. We talked. He had done some time in prison, but he'd gotten himself straightened out and was working as a runner for one of the firms down here.... Now, that's a good job, no doubt about that, and I wish him well. But meeting him, it really made me think about what made a difference for me, about giving something back."

Sources

Black Enterprise, June 2001, p. 220.
Bond Buyer, August 31, 1992, p. 2.
New York Times, August 11, 1991, p. 96; June 19, 2001, p. B1; June 29, 2003.
Wall Street Journal, August 28, 1992, p. B1.

—Carol Brennan

Cecil M. Brown

1943—

Author

Cecil Brown is best known for his 1969 novel *The Life and Loves of Mr. Jiveass Nigger*. His writings focus on the black man's search for respect and identity in a racist white society. An angry and provocative writer, Brown uses humor to inform his social protest. Brown has written both fiction and nonfiction; he is a poet, playwright, screenwriter, filmmaker, commentator, and critic.

In his personal and poignant memoir *Coming Up Down Home*, Cecil Brown recounted his life as a sharecropper's son in the small farming community of Bolton in southeastern North Carolina. Born on July 3, 1943, Cecil Morris Brown spent a very short time with his real parents, Cecil Culphert "Cuffy" and Dorothy Brown. He and his younger brother Cornelius, or "Knee," were raised by their loving aunt and uncle. Though Brown would not learn the details of his family's history until he was grown, he knew, even as a small child, that it was both sad and violent.

After living for ten years with their aunt and uncle, whom they cherished as their own mother and father, the boys' birth father was released from prison. That event changed their lives dramatically. With their real parents, the boys moved to their grandfather's swamp. Under their father's abusive rule, the boys worked the land and sharecropped tobacco to support their family, which soon included four younger siblings.

Brown worked hard, but developed other interests. At age 13 he perfected his magic skills. His attempt to show off his magic on a local television talent show led to his first encounter with racism; he was denied air

time. Brown's enthusiasm for his own interests sometimes brought the wrath of his father upon him. When Brown would read or play music instead of working in the fields, his father would punish him. But his father recognized that his son had talent and bought him a saxophone. By age 16 Morris headed his own rhythm and blues band—the Bebop Kings. That summer he ran off to New York City. He dreamed of becoming a jazz musician until a heroin addict stole his sax. "Even when Culphert beat me, I didn't feel this way…Why had a black man done this to me? My saxophone was a symbol of my effort to escape the oppression of my father…I let an old black man rip my magic shield from me," Brown recalled in his memoir. As Brown walked the streets of New York, he recalled that "The frustration in the faces of the black men who passed me now was the same frustration I had seen in my father's face…and I began to see and understand why he had been so mean and brutal to me. Perhaps he had not been brutal enough." With his saxophone gone, Brown returned to Bolton to finish high school.

Defying his father, who wanted him to farm, and his teachers, who said he was not "college material," Brown won a scholarship to the Agricultural and Technical College in Greensboro, North Carolina. To help him in his new endeavor, his father bought him a typewriter.

Brown had high expectations for his education. Disappointed with the state school, he transferred to Columbia University in New York City where he came under the influence of writer/activist LeRoi Jones. After

At a Glance . . .

Born Cecil Morris Brown on July 3, 1943, in Bolton, NC. *Education:* Agricultural and Technical State University, Greensboro, NC, 1961; Columbia University, BA, 1966; University of Chicago, MA, 1967; UC Berkeley, PhD, 1993; W. E. Dubois Institute, Harvard University, fellow, 2001.

Career: Writer, 1967–; Warner Brothers, screenwriter, 1977-79; University of Illinois at Chicago Circle, teacher, 1967-68; Merritt College, Oakland, CA, teacher, 1968-70; University of California Berkeley, teacher, 1969-71, 1987-90, 1993, 1998, 2001-03; San Francisco State University, teacher, 1980-82, 1994; University of Maryland European Campus in Berlin, teacher, 1984-86; St. Mary's College, Moraga, CA, teacher, 1991-94, 2001, 2003; UC Davis, teacher, 1993-98; Université Michel de Montaigne, Bordeaux, France, teacher, 1998-99; University of San Francisco, teacher, 2002.

Awards: Columbia University English Dept., Professor John Angus Burrell Memorial Prize, 1966; Before Columbus Foundation American Book Award for *Days Without Weather*, 1984; Berlin Literary Fellowship, 1985; Besonders Wertvoll Film Preises, 1986; UC Berkeley, Mentor Fellowship, 1992.

Addresses: *Home*—Kensington, CA.

earning his bachelor's degree in comparative literature at Columbia and his master's degree in English and American literature at the University of Chicago, Brown began his career as a writer and itinerant university lecturer, teaching African American studies, literature, drama, film, and creative writing throughout the country.

Brown's first novel, *The Life and Loves of Mr. Jiveass Nigger,* was a dark, funny, satirical story of a young black expatriate searching for invisibility in white society. Although reviews were mixed, it became a best-seller among young disaffected blacks and college students of the 1960s and Brown enjoyed a brief period as a literary star.

He made influential contacts and began working in the film industry. In 1968 Brown met the actor Richard Pryor, after a friend told him that the comedian was crazier than Brown. He later co-wrote the screenplay for *Which Way Is Up?* with Carl Gottlieb, which starred

Pryor. Brown's experiences as a screenwriter at Warner Brothers and Universal Studios in the mid-1970s formed the basis for his 1983 novel *Days Without Weather*. In his story of a young black comic and a screenwriter trying to make a movie about a slave revolt, only to be confronted with black stereotyping and betrayal, Brown compared the Hollywood film industry to southern plantation life. Reviews were mixed. In a 1998 story in the *Village Voice*, Ishmael Reed, calling Brown "one of the most underrated writers in the country," charged that a black critic had killed the novel because of its negativity.

On Christmas Eve of 1990, Brown returned to Bolton to conclude his memoir. His father finally told him why he had gone to prison: in the course of a drunken fight, he had killed his good friend—his wife's favorite cousin. The information added depth and insight into his life and helped him finish his memoir. *Coming Up Down Home* received excellent reviews. At the time of his death in 1995, the French director Louis Malle was planning to make a film based on the memoir.

Inspiration for his next book came from a visit with a friend. Brown told Joel Selvin of the *San Francisco Chronicle* in 2003 that while visiting a German friend's library: "I wondered why we don't have a philosophy...We don't have any books. We must have a folklore." The idea fueled Brown's imagination, and he returned to the University of California at Berkeley (UC Berkeley) where he began his PhD dissertation in African-American literature, folklore, and the theory of narrative—*Stagolee: A Study of Black Oral Narrative*. It was published as *Stagolee Shot Billy* in 2003.

The story of "Stagolee" had been a part of Brown's life for a long time. He had first heard his uncle recite a version of the Stagolee legend in a Bolton juke joint when he was about six. In his memoir he recalled that afterward one of the men said to him: "Now, boy, talking about a bad nigger. That Cuffy is a real Stagolee!" Brown wrote: "Suddenly I felt I knew more about my father than I had ever known. Their gestures, their language, their looks, and their glances told me that my father was a hero to them."

In his book, Brown traced the Stagolee legend to the fatal barroom shooting of Billy Lyon by "Stack" Lee Shelton on Christmas night of 1895. Brown vividly described the politics and culture of the 1890s St. Louis black community and the century-long influence of the Stagolee legend on literature, music, and revolutionary black politics. "Stagolee is a metaphor that structures the life of black males from childhood through maturity," wrote Brown. Stagolee was "a 'bad nigger' cultural hero" and "a defiant, angry revolutionary...a symbol of protest." Brown told Selvin: "It gets to the struggle of the Afro-American male for dignity and masculinity." Although some reviews were critical of Brown's scholarship, it was named a best book of the year by *Esquire* magazine.

Selected works

Books

The Life and Loves of Mr. Jiveass Nigger: A Novel, Farrar, Straus & Giroux, 1969; revised edition, Ecco Press, 1991.
Days Without Weather, Farrar, Straus & Giroux, 1983.
Coming Up Down Home: A Memoir of a Southern Childhood, Ecco Press, 1993.
"Go Home to Your Wife. Go Home to Your Wife," *Speak My Name: Black Men on Masculinity and the American Dream*, Beacon Press, 1995.
Stagolee Shot Billy, Harvard University Press, 2003.

Films

(With Carl Gottlieb) *Which Way Is Up?* (screenplay), Universal, 1977.
Two-fer, 2003.

On-line

"Cecil Brown on Saul Bellow: White at Last!" *Ishmael Reed's Konch Magazine*, www.ishmaelreedpub. com/brown2.html (June 3, 2004).

Sources

Books

Dictionary of Literary Biography, Vol. 51, Gale, 1987, pp. 32-35.

Periodicals

African American Review, Spring 2004, pp. 171-173.
Artforum, Summer 2003, p. 51.
Black Issues Book Review, June-August 2003, pp. 60-61.
New York Times, June 7, 2003, p. B9.
New York Times Book Review, April 27, 2003, p. 19.
San Francisco Chronicle, July 13, 2003, p. 24.
Sing Out! Fall 2003, pp 122-123.
Village Voice, October 20, 1998, p. 141.

On-line

"Cecil M(orris) Brown," *Contemporary Authors On-line, Biography Resource Center*, www.galenet. galegroup.com/servlet/BioRC (June 3, 2004).
Stagolee Shot Billy, www.stagoleeshotbilly.com (June 3, 2004).

—Margaret Alic

John M. Burgess

1909-2003

Bishop

Reverend John Burgess, photograph. © Corbis.

In 1962 the Right Reverend John Melville Burgess became the first African American to lead an Episcopalian congregation in the United States. Burgess was installed as a suffragan bishop in one of the oldest congregations in the American Episcopal Church, located in the center of Boston, and worked to bring the church's focus onto social issues and progressive causes. "I just wanted to prove that the Episcopal Church could be relevant to the lives of the poor," *Episcopal Times* writer Tracy Sukraw quoted him as saying.

Burgess was born on March 11, 1909, in Grand Rapids, Michigan. His father hailed from Ohio, and worked as a waiter in the dining cars of the Pere Marquette Railroad in Michigan. From him, Burgess inherited the Episcopalian faith. Burgess's mother was from Grand Rapids, and had been educated as a kindergarten teacher. The family attended St. Philip's Episcopal Church, a black church in the western Michigan Episcopal diocese, where Burgess served as an altar boy.

Episcopal Church Pre-Dated Nation

The Episcopal Church differed from the African Meth-

odist Episcopal (AME) church, founded in 1816 as an offshoot of the Methodist church. Burgess's Episcopal church was considered the church of the American elite for generations. It was part of the Anglican Communion of churches, along with the Church of England, and its religious rituals on North American soil dated back to 1607 and the Jamestown colony. The colonial-era American congregation split from England's Anglican church during the Revolutionary War period, and in 1789 reconstituted itself as the Protestant Episcopal Church. Well into the twentieth century, its membership ranks included the names of some of the wealthiest and well-connected American families. Eleven U.S. presidents have been Episcopalian, the largest number from any creed.

Burgess studied at Grand Rapids Junior College before following a neighbor, fellow Episcopalian and future American president, Gerald R. Ford, into the University of Michigan in Ann Arbor. Burgess earned his undergraduate degree in social work there in 1930 and a master's degree the following year. Social work attracted him because he viewed it as a way to help others, but he eventually decided that entering the

At a Glance . . .

Born on March 11, 1909, in Grand Rapids, MI; died on August 24, 2003, in Vineyard Haven, MA; son of Theodore Thomas (a railroad dining car waiter) and Ethel Inez Beverly (a kindergarten teacher) Burgess; married Esther J. Taylor, August 21, 1945; children: Julia, Margaret. *Education:* Attended Grand Rapids Junior College; University of Michigan, AB, 1930, MA, 1931; Episcopal Theological School, divinity degree, 1934. *Religion:* Episcopalian.

Career: Episcopal Church, ordained deacon, July 1934; Episcopal Church, ordained priest, January 1935; St. Philip's Episcopal Church, Grand Rapids, MI, rector, 1935-38; Mission of St. Simon the Cyrene, Lincoln Heights, OH, vicar, 1938-46; Howard University, Washington, DC, Episcopal chaplain, 1946-56; Washington Cathedral, canon, 1951–; Boston City Mission, Massachusetts, archdeacon and superintendent, 1956-62; elected suffragan bishop, September 1962, and consecrated December 1962; Diocese of Massachusetts, twelfth bishop, January 12, 1970-75. Berkeley Divinity School of Yale University Divinity School, professor.

Memberships: Union of Black Episcopalians; National Council of Churches; World Council of Churches.

Selected Awards: Recipient of honorary degrees from the University of Michigan, Boston College, Assumption College, the University of Massachusetts, Trinity College, and St. Augustine's College.

ministry would provide a more solid foundation through which to work with the poor. He journeyed to Cambridge, Massachusetts, and entered the Episcopal Theological School there. After finishing his divinity degree in 1934, he returned to St. Philip's in Grand Rapids for his ordination in July of 1934.

Burgess was also assigned to a post at St. Philip's, which he held for the next four years until transferred to a parish outside of Cincinnati. He was assigned to the Mission of St. Simon the Cyrene in Lincoln Heights, which was a racially divided town and a poor, hard-scrabble one as well. "The experience made me very, very angry," Burgess recalled in a *Grand Rapids Press* interview, according to writer Cami Reister. "I came to believe that racism like that simply could not continue

in a country as enlightened and as rich as this. I tried to give the community some moral fiber. I tried to give them more than just jobs or streetlights. I tried to raise them to a standard of living based on the Gospel." With this mission in mind, St. Simon's new vicar established a medical clinic, a social services center, and a day school; he also worked with the local labor leaders in an attempt to integrate the nascent auto unions of the area.

Relocated to District of Columbia

Burgess had found a mentor at the Episcopal Theological School in Cambridge, Angus Dunn, who became bishop of Washington, D.C., in 1942. Dunn invited Burgess to serve as an attending presbyter for services at the landmark National Cathedral there, which was a first for a black Episcopal priest. In 1946, Dunn was instrumental in helping Burgess obtain the Episcopal chaplainry at Howard University, the prominent African-American school in the nation's capital. Burgess served as chaplain for the next decade, and his concurrent directorship of the Canterbury House, the Episcopal student center at Howard, introduced him to many students from around the world who would return to become leaders in their respective African or Caribbean nations.

Burgess was a canon of the Washington National Cathedral after 1951, the first black to hold such a position there, and used his pulpit to speak on issues of racial segregation and the burgeoning civil-rights movement. His growing profile attracted the attention of elders in the Boston diocese, who made him an archdeacon and installed him as head of what was then known as the Boston City Mission in 1956. The Mission worked with the poor in the city and served not just as a spiritual beacon but as a liaison with social service agencies. It was a time when many venerable Episcopalian parishes in the heart of Boston were losing members as city dwellers moved to the suburbs, and Burgess believed it important that the older churches find new ways to appeal to people from all walks of life. "I think that any church in a poor urban area which says that they can go it alone has not developed a big enough program," Sukraw's article in the *Episcopal Times* quoted him as once saying. "Their program ought to always be bigger than their resources."

In September of 1962, a diocesan gathering of Burgess's fellow priests elected him suffragan bishop. The event even made the *New York Times,* which ran a photo of Burgess under the headline, "Negro Is Elected Episcopal Bishop." He became the first African-American priest to lead an Episcopal congregation in the United States. "Integration is part of the ordering of the community," he told the newspaper's John H. Fenton, speaking of the Episcopal Church's outreach program to increase and diversity its membership roster. "Individuals ought to be able to accept one another as people in racial, economic and nationality areas. This will be the test."

Headed Massachusetts Diocese in 1970s

For the rest of the decade, Burgess also served as assistant bishop to the head of the Massachusetts diocese, the Right Reverend Anson Phelps Stokes. When Stokes announced his retirement, Burgess was elected to succeed him. He was installed on January 17, 1970, at Boston's Cathedral Church of St. Paul. He added yet another first, as the first black to head an Episcopal diocese. His was the largest in the United States at the time, and Burgess continued to encourage his subordinates into embracing social progressivism and making the church a model of integration. After he retired in 1975, he taught pastoral theology at Yale University's Divinity School, and edited a 1982 collection *Black Gospel, White Church,* a collection of sermons delivered by black priests dating back nearly two centuries.

Since the 1960s, Burgess had served as a summer minister at the Grace Episcopal Church on Martha's Vineyard, the Massachusetts resort community. He moved there permanently in 1989 with his wife, Esther Taylor Burgess. The pair had met at a church conference in North Carolina, married in 1945, and had two daughters. Esther Burgess was also committed to civil-rights causes, even taking part in an attempt to integrate a restaurant in St. Augustine, Florida, in 1964 during which she and the mother of Massachusetts's governor were arrested.

On the occasion of Burgess's 90th birthday in 1999, a stained glass window was installed at Grace Episcopal in his honor. The window features his likeness as well as

that of his role model, Absalom Jones, the former slave and Philadelphia minister who was the first black to serve as a priest in the Methodist Episcopal Church. Burgess died at age 94 on Martha's Vineyard. He was a longtime NAACP member, and the president of the organization's Boston branch, Leonard C. Alkins, called him "a spokesperson for equal rights," as reported by *New York Times* obituary writer Eric Pace. "He gave the encouragement to so many people of color to make that next step forward and not to be afraid. He was a beacon and a drum major for all people." St. Philip's Episcopal Church—where he went from altar boy to rector—broke ground on the John M. Burgess Wellness Center in his honor in the spring of 2004.

Selected writings

(Editor) *Black Gospel, White Church,* Seabury Press, 1982.

Sources

Books

Notable Black American Men, Gale, 1998.

Periodicals

Episcopal Times, August 25, 2003.
Grand Rapids Press (Grand Rapids, MI), April 17, 2004, p. B5; August 29, 2003, p. D3.
Jet, September 15, 2003, p. 16.
Martha's Vineyard Times, September 4th, 2003.
New York Times, September 23, 1962, p. 1; August 27, 2003, p. B10.

—Carol Brennan

Benjamin Caldwell

1937—

Playwright

Deeply involved in the black arts movement of the 1960s, Ben Caldwell is known for his short satirical plays that challenged black audiences to rise up against their oppressors. One of the most prolific playwrights of the period, Caldwell chastised his audience for accepting the values of white society, thereby contributing to their own oppression. In the decades since, Caldwell has continued as an artist, playwright, and essayist.

Born on September 24, 1937, Benjamin Caldwell was the seventh of nine children. He was born in Harlem, a borough of New York City, just two years after his parents had migrated from the South. As a child he painted and wrote. Caldwell dreamed of making a living painting or writing, but had no role models to follow. He had never met a black man who made his living as a painter or a writer. With the encouragement of a school guidance counselor, he enrolled in New York's School of Industrial Arts, planning to become a commercial illustrator and industrial designer. However during his first year of high school, Caldwell's father died and in 1954 he was forced to leave school to help support his family.

Entered His "Newark Period"

Although Caldwell continued to paint and draw and write plays and essays, he did not begin seriously writing plays and seeing them produced until the mid-1960s. During this time, he lived with a group of artists and writers in Newark, New Jersey, including the author and playwright LeRoi Jones (Imamu Amiri Baraka). Together these artists contributed to the black arts movement in which artists consciously tried to create art that represented black culture as separate and unique from white culture. Caldwell's first plays portrayed the black community in a variety of different contexts. Most of Caldwell's plays were short vignettes with few characters and props and minimal sets. Most had subtitles that took on meaning only after the play had been seen or read. His goal was to resurrect black dignity and pride, and he attacked what he saw as black characteristics that aided white oppressors.

The Job, first produced in 1966, described some of Caldwell's frustrations in seeking employment in Newark. *Riot Sale; or, Dollar Psyche Fake-Out*, also first produced in 1966, was an example of Caldwell's commentary on the antipoverty programs of the 1960s that he saw as designed to subdue black militancy. In the play white authorities shoot a canon of money into a black mob that has been incited by the police-killing of a young black man. The so-called black revolutionaries begin fighting each other for the money and then spend it in white-owned stores.

Mission Accomplished, first produced in 1967, is set in late-nineteenth-century Africa. Missionaries enter an African village to convert them to Christianity. Informed that the Africans have no need of or interest in the white religion, the missionaries physically subdue them, forcibly baptize them, and steal their jewels to send to the pope.

In Caldwell's dramatic satire *Hypnotism*, a magician hypnotizes a black man and woman to rid them of the

At a Glance . . .

Born Benjamin Caldwell on September 24, 1937, in New York, NY.

Career: Artist and author of essays and numerous plays, 1965–.

Awards: Guggenheim fellowship for playwriting, 1970.

Addresses: *Office*—P.O. Box 656, Morningside Station, New York, NY 10026.

memories of exploitation, injustice, and oppression that would lead them to black militancy. He replaces these memories with the words "nonviolence" and "integration."

All White Caste; After the Separation; A Slow-Paced One-Act Play, first produced in the early 1970s, is set in the 1990s after the third world war. Blacks had been moved to Africa and their white sympathizers are "sentenced to Harlem" where they assume the lower-caste status formerly held by blacks.

Play "Prayer Meeting" Showed Refined Style

Benjamin Caldwell's best known play is *Prayer Meeting. Prayer Meeting or, The First Militant Minister* premiered at Jones's Spirit House Theatre in Newark in April of 1967, under the title *Militant Preacher*. It was highly praised and very popular. In this very short play, a burglar is looting a minister's opulent home when the minister returns unexpectedly. The minister begins to pray: "Trying to console my people 'bout brother Jackson's death at the hands of that white po-liceman. I tried, Lord, I tried to keep them from the path of violence. I tried to show them where it was really brother Jackson's fault fo'provokin' that off'cer...The mayor said if I can't stop them there'll be trouble...and more killing!" The burglar comes out of hiding and tells the minister to "shut up." Realizing that the minister believes he has been answered by God, the burglar continues the charade: "Tomorrow you'll lead a protest march to end all protest marches. I don't want this to be no damned 'sing-along.' I said a *protest* march! You'll demand justice. And if you don't get justice you'll raise hell...Tell them I don't want no more cheek turning.'"

Prayer Meeting was produced in April of 1969 at the Chelsea Theater Center of the Brooklyn Academy of Music. It was part of *A Black Quartet* that included new one-act plays by Ed Bullins, LeRoi Jones, and

Ronald Milner. *A Black Quartet* had its New York debut at Tambellini's Gate Theater on July 30, 1969. When it was published in 1970 Clayton Riley wrote in the introduction that Caldwell "pursues, at all times, his total commitment to the cause of Black Nationalism and the complete devotion to militancy that cause implies." Both *Prayer Meeting* and *A Black Quartet* were still being produced more than 30 years later.

Caldwell continued to hone his craft, writing more than 50 plays after returning to live in New York City in 1966. In his plays, Caldwell concentrated on various aspects of the black experience and portrayed the plight of blacks in an oppressive white culture. Several of his plays expressed anger at the Christian church. *Recognition*, written in 1968 and unpublished, depicted blacks as having forgotten their black God for so long that Allah no longer recognized them. *The King of Soul; or, The Devil and Otis Redding: A One-Act Musical Tragedy*, first produced in 1968, attacked the exploitation of black musicians by agents and record companies. Caldwell frequently questioned the motives of whites who professed support for blacks. In *Top Secret, or, A Few Million After B.C.*, the president and his cabinet, attended by silent black servants, devise a secret plot to promote birth-control pills ("B.C.") as a means of limiting the black population. The play was first produced by the Performing Arts Society in Los Angeles in 1969.

Caldwell poignantly captured the generational attitudes among blacks as his work often did. In *Family Portrait; or, My Son, the Black Nationalist*, Caldwell confronted the chasm between proud young blacks and their oppressed elders. In the play a middle-class father and mother are named "Farthest From Truth" and "Nowhere Near The Truth," respectively. Their angry and militant son, known as "Sunshine On Truth," is told by his father: "We've got to show the white man that we are ready and good enough to live with him." The son's frustration with his parents' integrationist attitudes percolates in the family conversations as the two generations struggle to come to an understanding of blacks' "place" in American society.

Caldwell's Black Nationalist vision tempered with the years, but his plays continued to illustrate the lingering inequalities in American society. In April of 1982 the New Federal Theater premiered *The World of Ben Caldwell: A Dramatized Examination of the Absurdity of the American Dream and Subsequent Reality*, which illustrated the vast differences between white and black expectations for life in America. A more intimate look at the black experience came in *Moms*, the story of America's first stand-up comedienne, Jackie "Moms" Mabley. *Moms* premiered off-Broadway at the Astor Palace Theater on August 4, 1987. Developed by the actress Clarice Taylor and written by Caldwell, the play told the story of this ground-breaking comedienne, known for her risqué humor. The play received mixed reviews but Taylor won an Obie for her starring role. Caldwell's *The Solution to All the World's Problems* was produced in New York in February of 2004.

Selected writings

Plays

"Four Plays" (includes *Riot Sale, Mission Accomplished, Top Secret, The Job*), *Drama Review*, Summer 1968, pp. 40-52.

Prayer Meeting or, The First Militant Minister, Jihad, 1968.

Hypnotism, Afro-Arts Anthology, Jihad, 1969.

The King of Soul, Family Portrait, New plays From the Black Theatre: An Anthology, Bantam, 1969.

The Job, Black Identity, Holt, 1970.

All White Caste, Black Drama Anthology, New American Library, 1971.

An Obscene Play (for Adults Only), Alafia, Winter 1971, pp. 14-15.

The Wall, Scripts, May 1972, pp. 91-93.

Other

(With Askia Muhammad Touré) *Juju: Magic Songs for the Black Nation* (poetry and prose), Third World Press, 1970.

Sources

Books

Riley, Clayton, "Introduction," *A Black Quartet*, New American Library, 1970.

Walker, Robbie Jean, *Dictionary of Literary Biography*, Vol. 38, Gale, 1985, pp. 61-66.

Periodicals

Bay State Beacon, February 4, 1999, p. 17.

Boston Globe, April 23, 2004, p. C18.

Callaloo, Fall 1999, pp. 808-824.

On-line

"Ben(jamin) Caldwell," *Contemporary Authors On-line, Biography Resource Center*, www.galenet.galegroup.com/servlet/BioRC (April 29, 2004).

—Margaret Alic

Benny Carter

1907-2003

Jazz musician

Carter, Benny, photograph. © Bettmann/Corbis.

Benny Carter's musical career spanned seven decades, encompassing jazz styles from big band to bebop. Primarily known for his alto saxophone work, he also mastered the tenor saxophone, clarinet, trumpet, and even piano. He was a skilled arranger, scoring music for both Fletcher Henderson and Duke Ellington, and a fine composer, penning classics like "When Lights Are Low," "Blues in My Heart," and "We Were in Love." Carter received a lifetime achievement Grammy Award in 1987, performed for three presidents (Jimmy Carter, Ronald Reagan, and George Bush), and was named Jazz Artist of the Year in 1989 by *Down Beat* and *Jazz Times*. "Benny Carter's career was remarkable for both its length and its consistently high musical achievement," wrote John S. Wilson in the *New York Times*, "from his first recordings in the 1920s to his youthful-sounding improvisations in the 1990s."

Benjamin Lester Carter was born on August 8, 1907, in New York City and grew up in the San Juan Hill neighborhood in Manhattan (near Lincoln Center). He took piano lessons from his mother as a young boy, but his musical heroes were trumpeters like his cousin,

Theodore Bennett, and Bubber Miley, who played with Duke Ellington. At 13, he bought a trumpet, but discouraged by how difficult it was to play, he traded it for a saxophone a week later. Through a great deal of practice on his own, and the occasional help of several saxophone teachers, Carter quickly grew into a fine player.

At age 15, the young Carter sat in with Harlem bands. From 1924 to 1928, Carter paid his dues as a sideman in a number of New York City jazz bands and by working for a short time for pianist Earl Hines in Philadelphia. At age 19, he received his first full-time job with Charlie Johnson's band. His parents, however, were less than thrilled. "They thought it was undignified," he told *National Public Radio*, "demeaning to the black race and at that particular time I think they even called it devil's music.... My mother wanted me to be a violinist and she would [have] liked for me also to have been a theologian."

He entered the recording studio for the first time with Charlie Johnson's Orchestra in 1927, sessions that included two pieces arranged by Carter. He would later recall that he learned to arrange by spreading the blueprints of a composition on the floor and then writing the individual parts for the trumpet, saxophone, and other instruments. His new skill allowed him to join Fletcher Henderson's band in 1928, replacing Don Redman as the orchestra's arranger. "The charts that came out of Henderson's band are arguably the most influential of the big band era," noted *All About Jazz*.

In 1931 Carter joined McKinney's Cotton Pickers and, thanks to his growing reputation as an arranger, he sold charts on the side to musicians such as Bennie Moten. He also taught himself to play trumpet during the early thirties, and was recording solos with the instrument after only two years. In 1932 Carter formed his first orchestra with a topnotch ensemble that included tenor saxophonist Chu Berry, pianist Teddy Wilson, drummer Sid Catlett, and trombonist Dicky Wells. Although he would start a number of other big bands during the thirties and forties, he never found the same level of success as Duke Ellington or Count Basie. More impor-

tantly, though, he won respect from fellow musicians. "When you made Benny Carter's band in those days," guitarist Danny Barker told Nat Shapirio and Nat Hentoff in *Hear Me Talkin' to Ya*, "the stamp was on you.... Every time Benny got a band together all the cats would want to know who was in his band because if you could make...Carter's band, that was it. It was like major-and-minor-league baseball."

Carter traveled to Paris in 1935 to play with the Willie Lewis Orchestra, and remained in Europe for the next three years, performing with bands in England, France, and Scandinavia. He worked with the BBC orchestra in 1936 and joined saxophonist Coleman Hawkins for a recording with guitarist Django Reinhardt and violinist Stephane Grappelli in 1937. After returning to the United States in 1938, Carter played various dates with Lionel Hampton and Billie Holliday before once again attempting to form his own orchestra. He relocated to the West Coast in 1943 where he found lucrative work in Hollywood. Carter appeared as a trumpet player in the film *Stormy Weather*, and soon was busy scoring music for movies like the Marx's Brothers *Love Happy* (1950) and *The Snows of Kilimanjaro* (1952). Throughout the fifties and sixties he frequently wrote scores for television, and limited his public performances to occasional tours with "Jazz at the Philharmonic" and a number of jam sessions sponsored by Norman Granz of Verve Records.

Carter returned to active performing in 1970 following an invitation by Morroe Berger to lecture at Baldwin-Wallace College. He became a visiting professor at Princeton University in 1973 and received a Doctorate of Humanities from the institution in 1974. The following year, at Berger's suggestion, Carter traveled to the Middle East under the sponsorship of the United States State Department for a lecture and concert series. After his return, he embarked on a series of three albums for Pablo in the mid-to-late seventies. "As *The King* ...proves," wrote Scott Yanow in *All Music Guide to Jazz*, "the masterful altoist had not lost a thing through the years." Carter was also booked for an engagement at Michael's Pub in New York City, his first extended work on the East Coast in nearly 35 years.

Carter remained active in the 1980s and 1990s, recording over 20 albums for Music Masters, Pablo, and Concord. He 1989 and 1990, he performed at the Lincoln Center as part of the Classical Jazz series, in 1996, he was one of five to receive Kennedy Center Honors, and in 2000, he received the National Medal of the Arts from President Bill Clinton. He traveled to Oslo on his ninetieth birthday in 1997, and then celebrated his birthday again at a two-day tribute concert at the Hollywood Bowl. Carter died on July 12, 2003, from bronchitis at Cedars-Sinai Hospital in Los Angeles. "I don't know that I've made any real contribution," a modest Carter told *National Public Radio.* "I've done what I've set out to do, that was have fun with the music, enjoy it and perform it and listen to it, to other people. And I have, to my satisfaction, achieved much that I had not even thought of."

Selected discography

The Chocolate Dandies, Parlophone, 1930.
Benny Carter—1933, Prestige, 1933.
Spike Hughes and His All-American Orchestra, London/Ace of Clubs, 1933.
Benny Carter and His Orchestra: 1940-41, RCA Victor, 1940-41.
Benny Carter, Big Band Bounce, Capital, 1945.
Benny Carter Plays Pretty, Verve, 1954.
Jazz Giant, Contemporary, 1957.
Aspects, Blue Note, 1958.
Further Definitions, Impulse!, 1961.
The King, Pablo, 1977.
A Gentleman and His Music. Concord Jazz, 1985.
In the Mood for Swing, Music Master, 1987.
Song Book, Music Master, 1995.

Sources

Books

Berger, Edward, Morroe Berger, and James Patrick, eds., *Benny Carter: A Life in American Music*, Vols. 1 and 2, Rowman and Littlefield, 1982.
Erlewine, Michael, ed., *All Music Guide to Jazz*, Miller Freeman, 1998, p. 182.

Periodicals

Down Beat, October 1, 2003, p. 14.
New York Times, July 14, 2003, p. B7.
Wall Street Journal, July 16, 2003, p. D8.

On-line

"Benny Carter (1907-2003)," *All About Jazz*, www.allaboutjazz.com (May 3, 2003).

Other

Profile, "Morning Edition," *National Public Radio*, July 14, 2003.

—Ronnie D. Lankford, Jr.

Barbara Chase-Riboud

1939—

Artist, novelist

In her massive sculptures, Barbara Chase-Riboud fuses elements from several different cultural traditions to create a transglobal art. In her fiction, she strives to give witness to history's forgotten characters, the men and women who, often, were unable to read, and thus did not leave their written stories for posterity. Though she is acclaimed for her work as both sculptor or novelist, she has attracted the greatest public attention as the woman who challenged media mogul Steven Spielberg in a court case that accused his company of plagiarizing her 1989 novel, *Echo of Lions*, for the 1997 feature film *Amistad*.

Chase-Riboud was born on June 26, 1939, in Philadelphia, Pennsylvania. Her mother, Vivian Braithwaite Chase, was from a Canadian family descended from runaway slaves. A talented child, she was given piano lessons and ballet classes by her supportive parents, and was also encouraged to develop her artistic talents, which began to display themselves early on. A gift for language skills also came easily to Chase-Riboud: at the age of ten, she wrote a poem as part of a class assignment, but her teacher accused her of copying it from another source. She was sent to the principal when she wouldn't "confess." Her mother found another, more encouraging school for her daughter–at home. As a young woman, Chase-Riboud studied art at Philadelphia's Temple University, and after graduating in 1957 went to Rome on a John Hay Whitney Foundation fellowship for further study at the American Academy. As she recalled in a 1989 *Boston Globe* interview with Marian Christy, Chase-Riboud said that it was in Italy, away from the racial tensions of the United States, that she "first tasted liberty…. That's the ultimate liberty: feeling that the space around you is expandable."

Worked as Artist, Novelist

Chase-Riboud was accepted into the prestigious Yale Graduate School of Art, where she earned her MFA in 1960. Yet she was still moving in a world that was not quite fully integrated. Once, she was mortified when she stopped at a bar with some fellow students and was refused service. Realizing that there was a more liberated world outside of the United States, with its laws against interracial marriage and refusal to extend equal rights to all citizens, Chase-Riboud began to travel. She spent time in several exotic places, and found inspiration for her early sculpture from the mix of materials used in ceremonial masks in Africa. While in London, she traveled to Paris for a weekend, fell in love, and moved there permanently after marrying photojournalist Marc Riboud in 1961. She is now a dual citizen of both France and the United States.

Chase-Riboud's work was shown at Paris galleries by 1966, and by 1970 was included in group shows such as that year's "Afro-American Artists" at Boston's Museum of Fine Arts. Her work quickly began to gain international acclaim. Chase-Riboud was fond of working with unusual, though tactilely rich materials, such as a combination of hand-knotted silk, bronze, and layers of wax, this last element shaped using a blowtorch.

Born on June 26, 1939, in Philadelphia, PA; daughter of Charles Edward (a building contractor) and Vivian May Braithwaite (a medical assistant; maiden name, West) Chase; married Marc Eugene Riboud (a photojournalist), December 25, 1961 (divorced, 1981); married Sergio G. Tosi (an art scholar and dealer), July 4, 1981; children (first marriage): David, Alexis. *Education:* Temple University, BFA, 1957; Yale University, MFA, 1960.

Career: Sculptor, poet, and novelist. Exhibited art in group and solo exhibitions, mid-1960s–.

Memberships: PEN; PEN American Center; Century Association; Yale Alumni Association; Alpha Kappa Alpha.

Selected Awards: Janet Kafka Award for Best Novel by an American Woman, 1979, for *Sally Hemings*; National Foundation for the Arts; Carl Sandburg Poetry Award for Best American Poet, 1988, for *Portrait of a Nude Woman as Cleopatra*; Van der Zee Achievement Award, 1995; Chevelier de l'Ordre des Arts et des Lettres, France, 1996; American Library Association, Best Fiction Award, 2004, for *Hottentot Venus*.

Addresses: *Agent*—Alexandra Boutin, 3, rue Auguste Compte, 75006 Paris, France. *Web*—www.chase-riboud.com.

She also began to write poetry, and by the early 1970s had found an editor at Random House, Toni Morrison, who liked her work. Her first collection, *From Memphis to Peking*, appeared in 1974. She spent the next few years researching and writing her first novel, *Sally Hemings*. Published in 1979 and a best-seller not without its share of controversy, the book was inspired in part by a 1974 biography of Thomas Jefferson that touched upon a possible romantic relationship between the third president of the United States and author of the Declaration of Independence with a slave he owned, Sally Hemings. Hemings was the half-sister of Jefferson's own wife: Jefferson's father-in-law had sired both legitimate children, such as the future Martha Jefferson, and illegitimate ones with his slaves, as was common in the era. When Martha Jefferson died, Thomas Jefferson never remarried, but Hemings moved into his house, the Virginia estate Monticello, and may have bore him several children.

"She's a woman who's been erased from American history for no good reason except that she was inconvenient," Chase-Riboud told *Los Angeles Times* writer Edmund Newton, who noted this "titillating story of sex, slavery and the President has been gossiped about, indignantly dismissed and periodically resurrected since 1802, when a Virginia newspaper reported scandalous charges of miscegenation during Jefferson's first term in the White House. It was America's first presidential character controversy." On this topic and her other works, Chase-Riboud recalled a favorite quote from eighteenth-century French philosopher Voltaire: "There is no history, only fictions of various degrees of plausibility."

Faced Controversy Over Hemings Novel

Sally Hemings was a best-seller, but Chase-Riboud was criticized by historians for using an actual personage from history, and then inventing dialogue, inner monologues, and other characteristic devices of fiction. Moreover, some scholars contended that the alleged children did not belong to Jefferson but were instead sired by a relative, and that the actual Hemings was probably far too young to have been romantically involved with Jefferson. A major network was reportedly interested in making Chase-Riboud's book into a movie, but was urged by Jefferson's official biographer to shelve it, according to Chase-Riboud.

Jefferson, who established the University of Virginia and is considered a "founding father" of the country, had also written against miscegenation, or relations—on or off the books—between blacks and whites. "Why was miscegenation ever a crime?" Chase-Riboud wondered in the *Los Angeles Times* interview. "Because it went against the myth that the races were pure." Fictitious or not, the putative romance between Jefferson and Hemings as chronicled in Chase-Riboud's book struck a chord that has endured; the biracial romance even made its way to the screen in the 1995 movie *Jefferson in Paris*. Yet Chase-Riboud was also keenly interested in showing that the American character owes much to both black and white culture and the once-covert ties between the two, and whether the events that occurred in Sally Hemings' life were real or not, such deeds and links have been an integral part of American history. "White and Black mean nothing by themselves but only in relation to each other," she pointed out to V.R. Peterson in *Essence*.

Chase-Riboud continued to write not "historical fiction," but rather "fictionalized history" in the tradition of E. L. Doctorow and others, with works such as 1986's *Valide: A Novel of the Harem*. Set during the peak of the Ottoman Empire in Eurasia, it presents a "biography" of a Martinique woman sold by pirates to an actual sultan for his harem. Renamed Naksh-i-dil

(Embroidered Tongue), she becomes a favorite of the ruler's, gives birth to a son, is made one of his official wives, and when her son becomes sultan in 1807, is elevated to "Valide," the highest achievement for a woman in such a society. As such, she was given charge of the harem, and Chase-Riboud interweaves into the narrative discussions of feminism, women as chattel, and the impossibility of true romantic love in a society where women and men remain inequals legally and economically. *New York Times Book Review* writer Wendy Smith faulted the "baroque trimmings" garnishing Valide's prose in some passages but termed Chase-Riboud's themes "provocative." "Particularly intriguing is Ms. Chase-Riboud's analysis of the harem, a much more vivid character than any of the book's individuals."

Chase-Riboud penned a continuance of sorts to the Sally Hemings tale with a 1994 novel, *The President's Daughter*. In it, she presents a fictionalized biography of Harriet, daughter of Hemings, whom Jefferson had arranged to be sponsored in Philadelphia by a French émigré. He gave Harriet $50 when she left Monticello, but actual history loses her at this point; Chase-Riboud recreates what might have occurred since Harriet was allegedly fair-skinned enough to pass as a white. In *The President's Daughter*, she does pass and receives a college education, marries a wealthy man—then his brother—and is able to witness some great historical events of the mid-nineteenth century.

Courted Controversy

Chase-Riboud took great pride in her work and acted vigorously to protect it from copyright infringements. She proved that Philadelphia playwright Granville Burgess's 1987 play entitled *Dusky Sally* infringed on her historical novel, *Sally Hemmings*. In 1991 a judge agreed that *Dusky Sally* shared too many similarities to passages from *Sally Hemings*, and barred the play from further production or publication. "When you make a big leap of imagination based on historical events, it is not fair that this kind of imaginative effort pass into the public domain just because historical figures are involved," she told *New York Times* writer Roger Cohen.

Though by now a well-respected visual artist and acclaimed writer, it was Chase-Riboud's 1989 novel *Echo of Lions* that would catapult her to the front pages in the late 1990s. The work chronicles the actions of one Joseph Cinque, the real-life leader of a slave rebellion on board a Spanish ship in 1839. After he and several other captives broke from their chains and killed the officers of the slave ship *L'Amistad* (Spanish for "friendship"), one surviving officer tricked them into sailing to America, where they were arrested and tried. John Quincy Adams argued the case before the United States Supreme Court on behalf of the Africans and won it. Cinque and the others received

their manumission. As Chase-Riboud explained to Paula Giddings in *Essence*, she felt the story had too long been "just a footnote in history," and merited greater notice.

Prior to its publication, Jacqueline Kennedy Onassis, then an editor at Doubleday, liked Chase-Riboud's work so much that she sent the manuscript to film director Steven Spielberg and his Amblin Entertainment production company. Amblin flew Chase-Riboud from Paris to Los Angeles, met with her, then declined to offer her a deal for the movie rights. Chase-Riboud said they never returned the actual manuscript. Dustin Hoffman later legally optioned *Echo of Lions* from Chase-Riboud and hired a screenwriter to adapt it, David Franzoni, who asserted he never read it, wishing to fictionalize the story himself. Several years later, after Hoffman's option expired, an executive at Spielberg's new studio, Dreamworks SKG, met with Debbie Allen, who had long known about the Amistad incident and had been trying to drum up financing for a fictionalization of it. Spielberg eventually committed to directing a film version of Franzoni's screenplay after another writer improved its first draft's dialogue and scenes. Like *Echo of Lions*, the screenplay's story was told through the voice of Cinque.

Chase-Riboud learned of the movie's production in late 1996 and hired a prominent attorney who had won Art Buchwald's plagiarism case against Paramount Studios for the Eddie Murphy movie *Coming to America*. She obtained the script and found several similarities, including the wholly fictional character of a black abolitionist printer (in the movie played by Morgan Freeman), a discussion between Adams and Cinque that has no historical basis for fact, and a line where a prisoner on the ship compares its mast to the shape of a Christian cross. In response, Dreamworks SKG hired a prominent entertainment lawyer Bert Fields, who claimed that Chase-Riboud had lifted passages from a 1953 book on the Amistad rebellion, William A. Owens' *Black Mutiny*. Chase-Riboud argued that the similarities were based on passages from John Quincy Adams's journals, a valid historical document. Copyright law allows the creation of characters and events based on actual historical fact, but to use fictional characters or elements from one work in another, without giving due credit, is a violation of the law. There was no historical evidence, for instance, that Adams and Cinque ever spoke privately, yet both *Echo of Lions* and *Amistad* had such scenes.

Chase-Riboud made headlines when she filed suit trying to block the distribution of *Amistad* just before Christmas of 1997. "Scratch any screenwriter, that perennial victim of intellectual-property rape, and you'll hear cries of 'Go girl!' for Barbara Chase-Riboud," noted *New York Times* editorial columnist Frank Rich. This time, a Federal judge failed to find sufficient cause to block the release of the film, but did set a hearing on the dispute—Chase-Riboud also asked for $10 million in damages—for January of 1998, noting that "serious questions" were raised by a reading of both texts. Rich pointed out in his column that the credited screenwriter for *Amistad*, David Franzoni, gave "differing recollections...of just how little he knew about Ms. Chase-Riboud's novel (which he says he's never read) and when exactly he didn't know it."

Several days later, the *New York Times* then ran a story alleging that Chase-Riboud had taken passages from a 1936 book about harems for her novel *Valide*, and an African studies major in New York City came forward with similarities she found in *The President's Daughter* and a 1929 book titled *Passing*. In her defense, Chase-Riboud explained once more that she had borrowed from historical documents, not copyrighted creations from other artists. "My quarrel with Dreamworks is that they used my fictional events—my vision of Cinque and John Adams, my sequence of events. And they plagiarized them," Chase-Riboud told Margarett Loke of the *New York Times*. Loke's article contained two factual errors—one terming Chase-Riboud the plaintiff in the 1991 suit against *Dusky Sally*—which were corrected in the December 25 edition of the paper. In February it was announced that Chase-Riboud had settled with Spielberg's Dreamworks SKG for an undisclosed sum.

Continued Her Creative Output

In the meantime, Chase-Riboud continued to write, publishing *Hottentot Venus* in 2003. The historical novel tells the fictionalized story of an aboriginal South African woman named Sarah Baartman whose physical shape—enlarged buttocks and genitalia—intrigued freak show and circus audiences throughout Europe in the late eighteenth century. Upon her death, a French scientist studied her body in an effort to "scientifically prove" the racial superiority of whites. ALA honored *Hottentot Venus* with the best fiction award in 2004.

Chase-Riboud still pursues her art from abroad. She divides her time between an apartment in the Montparnasse section of Paris, a house on the island of Capri, and a Renaissance-era palazzo in Rome. She married for the second time in 1981 to Sergio Tosi. She has two children from her first marriage. In 1996 she participated in a group show at the Studio Museum of Harlem, "Explorations in the City of Light: African-American Artists in Paris, 1945-65." After the *Amistad* case, she was working on winning approval for a planned work of monumental scale: *Harrar*, a proposed work commemorating the eleven million victims of the Middle Passage. Chase-Riboud conceived the work as two massive bronze obelisks with a chain wheel of bronze between them; eleven million links would make up the chain, and the obelisks would be engraved with the geographic place-names and African clans from where people were captured for transport as slaves. In 1998 she was commissioned to create a monument, titled *Africa Rising*, for the African Burial Ground Memorial at the U.S Federal Building in New York.

In 1999 Chase-Riboud became the first African-American woman to have a solo exhibition of drawings at the Metropolitan Museum of Art. Chase-Riboud's work in the permanent collections of, among others, the Centre Georges Pompidou (Paris), Metropolitan Museum of Art (NY), and Museum of Modern Art (NY).

Selected writings

From Memphis and Peking (poetry), Random House, 1974.
Sally Hemings (novel), Viking, 1979.
Albin Michel, 1981.
Valide: A Novel of the Harem, Morrow, 1986.
Portrait of a Nude Woman as Cleopatra (poetry), Morrow, 1987.
Echo of Lions (novel), Morrow, 1989.
The President's Daughter (novel), Crown, 1994.
Egypt's Nights (poetry), 1994.
Hottentot Venus (novel), Doubleday, 2003.

Sources

Books

Black Writers, first edition, Gale, 1989.
St. James Guide to Black Artists, edited by Thomas Riggs, St. James Press/Schomburg Center for Research in Black Culture, St. James Press, 1997.
Barbara Chose-Riboud: Sculptor. Harry N. Abrams, 1999.

Periodicals

Art Journal, Vol. 59, No. 3, Fall 2000.
Boston Globe, April 2, 1989, p. B13.
Critique, Vol. 4, Summer 1995, p. 258.
Entertainment Weekly, December 12, 1997, p. 18.
Essence, February, 1989, p. 30; December, 1994, p. 56.
Los Angeles Times, August 30, 1994, p. E1; October 24, 1997, p. D5.
New York Times, August 15, 1991; December 13, 1997, p. A15; December 19, 1997, p. A1; December 25, 1997, p. A2; February 10, 1998, p. A10.
New York Times Book Review, August 10, 1986, p. 22.
New Yorker, December 1, 1997.
Publishers Weekly, February 16, 1998, p. 105.
School Arts, February, 1996, p. 31.
Smithsonian, March, 1996.
Washington Post, February 26, 1989, p. X8; March 9, 1989, p. C3; December 25, 1994, p. X7; December 20, 1997, p. F2; December 21, 2003.

—Carol Brennan and Sara Pendergast

Mary Coleman

1946—

State politician, organization leader

"I've always just wanted to do things to make people happy and that is how I spent my life: doing things for others," Mary Coleman told *Contemporary Black Biography* (*CBB*). That desire took her from small-town Mississippi to a position in the administration of President Jimmy Carter to the presidency of the National Black Caucus of State Legislators (NBCSL). Her rise to this post prompted *Ebony* magazine to name Coleman one of the "100 Most Influential Black Americans of 2003." The praise did not phase Coleman, who takes her own phone calls and calls constituents by name. Instead she pressed on, doing things for others, armed not only with her lifelong convictions, but also with legislative power.

Born Mary Hoskins on July 25, 1946, Coleman grew up in the tiny town of Noxapater, Mississippi, located in the northeast corner of the state. Her parents, Harvey and Mable Hoskins, both worked full-time to raise Coleman, her two sisters, and five brothers. "My father was a factory worker and my mother worked in the local school cafeteria," Coleman told *CBB*. Though that school was just a few minutes walk from the family's front door, Coleman couldn't attend. "When I was growing up schools were still segregated, so we rode a total of 18 miles round trip to school everyday, rode a bus," she told *CBB*. Despite this indignity, Coleman found inspiration in school. She told *CBB* that the biggest influence on her young life was "my elementary school teacher, Leonora Welch. She took an interest in me and encouraged me when I was the little poor girl. Back when I was growing up, if you were light-skinned and had long hair you would be the

teacher's pet. Well, I wasn't light-skinned and didn't have long hair. That wasn't me. But she took an interest in me because I was a smart child." Coleman was also influenced by the Baptist church. "My mother also was very, very active in the church," Coleman told *CBB*. That activism filtered down to Coleman. "I have a strong commitment to helping to others, always have," she told *CBB*.

After graduating from Louisville Colored High School in 1965, Coleman went on to Tougaloo College, a historically black college located in Tougaloo, Mississippi. She enrolled as an English major with plans to become a teacher. "But that never happened," Coleman told *CBB*. "When I went to Tougaloo, my first year there wasn't what I expected, so I left and went to California and went to Los Angeles Trade Technical College in 1966." At the time, one of Coleman's sisters was living in California and the state offered free tuition at community colleges. "I got my degree there for next to nothing," Coleman told *CBB*. After earning an associate's degree in business in 1968 Coleman returned to Mississippi and her grade school sweetheart, Cayle Coleman. "I knew him all my life. We went to school together since the fifth grade," she told *CBB*. The couple were married later that year. Coleman also returned to Tougaloo College, both as a student and as an employee. "I started off in 1968 as a secretary, and then in 1972 I moved to book store manager and purchasing agent for the entire campus. It was a small school so everyone did more than one job," Coleman told *CBB*. Meanwhile she finished her education, earning a bachelor's degree in English in 1970.

At a Glance . . .

Born on July 25, 1946, in Noxapater, MS; married Cayle (Casey) Coleman, 1968; children: Marcus, Crystal, Arqullas. *Education:* Los Angeles Trade Technical College, AA in business, 1968; Tougaloo College, MS, BA in English, 1970. *Politics:* Democrat. *Religion:* Baptist.

Career: Tougaloo College, Tougaloo, MS, secretary, 1968-72; Tougaloo College, Tougaloo, MS, purchasing agent and bookstore manager, 1972-78; White House Advance Team, Carter Administration, 1977-80; Democratic Party, Jackson, MS, office worker, 1980-87; self-employed political consultant, Jackson, MS, 1980-94; Mississippi House of Representatives, elected representative, 1994–.

Selected memberships: National Black Caucus of State Legislators, vice president, 1998-2002, president, 2002–; Girl Scouts of America, Jackson, MS, board member; General Missionary Baptist State Convention, board member; National Association for the Advancement of Colored People, member.

Addresses: *Office*—Mississippi State Capital, Basement B-NC, PO Box 1018, Jackson, MS 39215. *Home*—308 Lynnwood Lane, Jackson, MS, 39206.

Got Politics in Her System

Coleman got her first taste of politics in 1976. "I went to a meeting of a group called Human Rights Coalition in Jackson, Mississippi," she told *CBB*. There she met an attorney who worked with the Democratic Party. "He asked me to volunteer for the Jimmy Carter campaign, so I did. I didn't know what I was doing, but I volunteered and helped out any way I could." When Carter won the presidency, Coleman joined the celebration. "I rode a bus from Jackson to Washington, D.C., for the inauguration," she recalled to *CBB*. Soon after, Carter planned a visit to Mississippi, one of the key states in his election victory. "Because of my volunteer work on the campaign, I was asked to work with his advance team on his visit," said Coleman. An advance team precedes the arrival of president by several days and works closely with the secret service and local contacts to plan every detail of the visit from who is in the receiving line at the airport to seating arrangements at luncheons to hotels and meals. After Carter's visit to Mississippi, his administration offered Coleman a full-time position on the White House

advance team. She accepted and from 1977 to 1980 Cooper worked on Vice President Walter Mondale's advance team. "It was a very exciting and interesting time for me," Coleman told *CBB*. It was also a very active time as Coleman, who crisscrossed the country preparing for official vice presidential visits. "I remember I was in Texas with Mondale and eight months pregnant. The team kept saying I would have that baby on the plane," she told *CBB*. Meanwhile, her husband Cayle worked for a large company in Mississippi. "We're a one-politician family," joked Coleman.

In 1980 Coleman joined the Carter reelection campaign in Mississippi. When he didn't win, she began to work for the Democratic Party in Mississippi. "I did lots of jobs from office assistant to campaign work," she told *CBB*. "I also began to work as a political consultant to Democrats, helping them to get elected. By that time I had politics in my system."

Coleman made her own way into the political system through a chain reaction. In 1994, Democratic President Bill Clinton appointed a Mississippi congressman to the agriculture department, leaving a seat open in Congress. The then-Mississippi state supervisor ran for the seat and won, leaving his seat open. A state senator ran for that post, leaving his own vacant. Finally a state representative ran for and won the senate seat. "Suddenly there was an opening in the Mississippi House of Representatives. And people began to tell me, 'you always help everyone else get elected, why don't you run yourself?' So I did," Coleman told *CBB*. A special election was held and Coleman spent a month campaigning. "I really enjoyed campaigning. I knew many of the people in politics at that time but I wasn't part of any political machine. I just believe in working directly with the people. When I ran I didn't have a machine behind me, I had the people."

Coleman won the election and took office in 1995. "I'd say being elected to the House of Representatives for the State of Mississippi is the proudest moment of my career," she told *CBB*. After the election she took over one of 122 seats in the House. Her district was the 65th, covering the city of Jackson and including 28,000 residents. Coleman sat on several committees in the house, including Ways and Means, Public Health, County Affairs, Insurance, and Public Property. She also served as vice chair of the Interstate Cooperation Committee. Though she enjoyed her work immensely, she also found it frustrating at times. "You look for revenue and it is really difficult," she told *CBB*. "We have had a hard session this year [2004] with the budget crisis and the economy shot. We are really feeling it at the state level. We don't even have the money for the absolute necessities."

Ascended the Ranks at NBCSL

While Coleman's political career in Mississippi blossomed, so did her profile on the national level with the

National Black Caucus of State Legislators (NBCSL). On the NBCSL website, Coleman describes the group, made up of over 600 black state legislators, as "a clearinghouse of information [which] works with legislators on a number of policy issues." The group also fosters a unified front among its members on issues of concern to Africans Americans, particularly those of poor and underserved communities. These concerns include social areas such as education, employment, health care, and racism, as well as business concerns such as energy, telecommunications, and international affairs. It also sponsors seminars and reports and produces a weekly radio show. Coleman became involved with the group in 1995. "As a member of the Mississippi House of Representatives you are automatically a member, so I started attending the meetings after I got elected," she told *CBB*. At the time Mississippi had the highest number of black state legislators in the country, yet was not represented on any of NBCSL's executive committees. "We didn't hold one bit of power," Coleman recalled to *CBB*. "I remember at one meeting there was a lot of discussion about this but no one would volunteer to do anything. I said, 'Well I haven't been in office long, but I'll try.'"

In 1998 Coleman was elected to the vice presidency of NBCSL, becoming the first Mississippian to hold one of the group's top offices. "I held that post until 2002 when I ran for president and won," she told *CBB*. As president, Coleman is the official representative of the group. She meets with political and industry leaders and attends numerous meetings and conferences around the nation. "We have an office in Washington, D.C., in the Hall of State building. I am there at least once a month. We meet in various sessions and once a year have a yearly meeting," she told *CBB*. Coleman does all of this while also maintaining a full schedule with the Mississippi legislature. "It's a whirlwind, but I enjoy it," she told *CBB*.

Coleman added to her busy schedule with volunteer work for several civic and religious organizations in Jackson, including the Girl Scouts, the Mississippi Children's Home Society, Leadership Jackson, and the General State Baptist Woman's Convention. She has also been very active in her church, Cade Chapel Missionary Baptist Church. As of 2004, Coleman's busy schedule showed no signs of letting up soon. She was planning a 2004 reelection campaign to the presidency of NBCSL and looking forward to another term in Mississippi's House of Representatives. She was even planning ahead for the day she retires. "Young people in Jackson have no place to go for recreational activities," she told *CBB*. "I would love to open up a community place for young people when I leave the legislature. I think about it often and think of ways to do it. It is something that needs to be done. I figure eventually I will get it done." Considering how much she has achieved just by following her desire to help people, there is no reason to doubt that the future youth of Jackson will one day spend idle afternoons at the Mary H. Coleman Community Center.

Sources

Periodicals

Ebony, May 2003.

On-line

"Mary Coleman," *Black Mississippi,* www.blackmississippi.com/biography.html?id=39&page=2 (May 27, 2004).

"Mary H. Coleman, Democrat," *Mississippi House of Representatives,* www.ls.state.ms.us/house/coleman_(65th).htm (May 27, 2004).

Other

Additional information for this profile was obtained through an interview with Mary Coleman on June 30, 2004.

—Candace LaBalle

Margaret J. Cooper

194(?)—

Organization leader

In 2002 Margaret Johnson Cooper became the 26th president of the National Association of Colored Women's Clubs (NACWC). Dedicated to civic and social service, education, and philanthropy, the NACWC is the oldest African-American women's group in the nation. As president Cooper oversees 45,000 members, 1000 local groups, and 38 state groups.

Born Margaret Johnson in Wadesboro, North Carolina, Cooper was part of a family that included four brothers and five sisters. After her father was killed in World War II, Cooper's mother, Mary Johnson Ellerbe married a local Baptist deacon and became a housewife. Meanwhile, Cooper went to live with her grandparents, though it was as if she had never left home. "My whole family lived in a really small community so I spent a lot of time at my mother's house too. When I was with my grandparents I was at home, when I was at my mom's I was at home," Cooper told *Contemporary Black Biography* (*CBB*.) Her grandfather was a skilled brick layer who opened up a construction building business in the town. He was also a Baptist pastor.

"My family always valued education so they always encouraged us to do our best," Cooper told *CBB*. In addition to family support, Cooper and her siblings lived in a community that also expected them to do well. "My family was an outstanding family in the community so there was no question that we would excel," Cooper added. Noting that she had the same teachers that her parents had had in school, Cooper felt a little extra pressure to succeed. "My parents did well in school so it was just expected that I would do

well too," she told *CBB*. Cooper did not disappoint, graduating second in her class with the title of salutatorian from Anson County High School. Following graduation she moved to Washington, D.C., and enrolled in Federal City College. She continued to excel academically. "I majored in sociology and psychology and had a 4.0 average," she told *CBB*. She earned her bachelor's degree in 1972 with the distinction of summa cum laude. "One of the proudest moments of my life was when I received my bachelor's degree and was able to give it to my grandmother. She hadn't gone to college, but it was dream she had always held for me," Cooper told *CBB*.

At the age of 19, while still a student at Federal City College, Cooper joined the National Association of Colored Women's Clubs (NACWC). Founded in 1896, the NACWC is the oldest African-American women's organization in the country. Now as then, its mission is to promote the interests of African-American women, children, and family and strive for the political and civil rights not only for African Americans, but for all Americans. The mission of the organization impressed Cooper, and she wanted to be a part of the group's efforts. Cooper explained to *CBB* that, "we believe in peace and justice for all people." Her talents were quickly recognized at NACWC, and she was hired to work in the organization's headquarters as a secretary to the president. The demands of her paid position made it difficult to focus on her education, however, so she left her job in order to finish her studies, but she continued on with the organization as a volunteer. "I've

At a Glance . . .

Born Margaret Johnson in 194(?) in Wadesboro, NC; married Aubrey Cooper; children: one daughter. *Education:* Federal City College, BA, sociology and psychology, 1972; Bowie State University, MA, counseling psychology, 1997; Bowie State University, post-master certificate, marriage and family counseling, 1997. *Religion:* Baptist.

Career: National Association of Colored Women's Clubs, Washington DC, secretary, early 1970s; Department of Veterans Affairs, Washington DC, personnel management, 1976-89; Family Intervention Center, Washington DC, site coordinator, 1992-97; United Planning Organization, Washington DC, case manager, 1997-2000; Department of Veterans Affairs, Washington DC, personnel management specialist, 2000–.

Memberships: National Association of Colored Women's Clubs, vice president, 1996-2002; National Association of Colored Women's Clubs, president, 2002–.

Addresses: *Office*—National Association of Colored Women's Clubs, 1601 R St. NW, Washington, DC 20009.

been with [NACWC] ever since that first job," she told *CBB*.

After graduating, Cooper started to develop solid leadership skills. She became a personnel management specialist in the human resources division of the Department of Veterans Affairs (VA) in 1976, and eventually moved up to a supervisory role. "My job was to supervise other specialists in recruitment and placement for the department," Cooper told *CBB*. Though she was very successful in her job, Cooper decided to take some time off. "Starting in 1989, I stayed at home for a few years and did volunteer work with the NACWC and Emmanuel Baptist Church," she told *CBB*. At the church she volunteered with the Family Intervention Center, a social service organization that provided various services to families and individuals in the community. In 1992 Cooper accepted a full-time position with the center. "I became a site coordinator, supervising counselors and other staff and managing the center," she told *CBB*. The position prompted Cooper to continue her education and she enrolled in Bowie State University located in Bowie, Maryland, just a few miles outside of Washington, D.C. In 1997 she

earned a master's degree in counseling psychology, again with academic honors. She followed that with a post-master's certificate in marriage and family counseling, also from Bowie.

With her new knowledge, Cooper began to work as a case manager for the United Planning Organization, a private, non-profit social service agency in Washington, D.C. "I worked directly with clients and supervised one of the offices," Cooper told *CBB*. Not long after she began working with the organization, the Department of Veteran's Affairs contacted Cooper. "They said they needed my services," Cooper recalled to *CBB*. They offered her another position as personnel management specialist, again in recruitment and human resources. They also asked her to lead special projects within her department. Cooper accepted and rejoined the VA in 2000.

Meanwhile Cooper's role within the NACWC grew. "While I was at the VA the first time, I was still a volunteer [with NACWC] and served as an officer in the local chapter," she told *CBB*. "I grew to love the organization for its history, for the women involved, for its mission and programs. I really admire what it does." She continued, "Having come from a family that was very active in the community, I guess it was only natural that I should gravitate to an organization like this." Cooper's dedication to the group resulted in her being elected to various posts. "Over time I moved through a series of elected offices on the local, state, and regional level," she told *CBB*. "I was national first vice president from 1996 to 2002. In 2002, after running an election campaign, I was elected the 26th national president at the national convention in Birmingham, Alabama."

Cooper's role as president of the NACWC has kept her very busy. "I run the day-to-day operations; I lead the board of directors; and I represent the group at a myriad of other collaborations with civic and political groups," she told *CBB*. "Though we are not a political action committee, we do have interest in a lot of things that go on on Capital Hill, so sometimes I go to Capital Hill to lobby for certain issues with other organizations." Meanwhile she maintained her position with the VA. "It is a lot of work, but the VA is very supportive. They [encourage] all their employees to be involved in civic and charity organizations. So there is no conflict at all," Cooper told *CBB*. Despite her busy schedule, Cooper was happy to serve the NACWC. She told *CBB*, "It is difficult to point to one particular proudest moment, but being elected national president of NACWC is definitely one of them."

Sources

On-line

"National Association of Colored Women's Clubs," African Americans, www.africanamericans.com/NationalAsscofColoredWomen.htm (May 29, 2004).

Other

Additional information for this profile was obtained through an interview with Margaret Cooper on July 3, 2004.

—Candace LaBalle

Léon-Gontran Damas

1912-1978

Poet

Together with fellow writers Léopold Senghor and Aimé Césaire, the Caribbean-born French poet Léon-Gontran Damas is recognized as one of the founders of *Négritude,* a French-language literary movement of the twentieth century that explored the use of African themes in literature and urged African-descended peoples to struggle for independence from European domination and influence. Less well known than the other two (Senghor eventually became president of the African nation of Senegal), Damas was nevertheless deemed highly influential by other black poets; he was one of the first poets writing in a language other than English to express a distinct black consciousness. Damas was heavily influenced by African-American poetry and music, and he moved to the United States in his later years.

Born March 28, 1912, in the Caribbean coastal city of Cayenne in what was then the colony of French Guyana, Damas grew up in a middle-class household of varied ethnic background. He excelled in school early and was sent to a French government school, the Lycée Schoelcher, on the island of Martinique to complete his primary education. There he met Aimé Césaire in a philosophy class, and the two became lifelong friends.

Exposed to Jazz and Blues

Winning admission to law school in Paris, Damas seemed set for a life of financial success. The law career, however, had been his parents' idea, and he took courses on the side at the University of Paris in subjects ranging from anthropology and history to Oriental languages. He also began to develop an interest in left-wing politics. Damas felt out of place in France and began to turn to his own cultural roots for sustenance. He came under the sway of various ideas, absorbing the anticolonialist manifesto *Légitime Défense,* acquainting himself with surrealist art, and becoming fascinated with the African-American culture that was sweeping Paris at the time. The productions of the Harlem Renaissance that Damas would have encountered included not only jazz and blues music but also distinctively African-American poetry by Langston Hughes and other authors.

Damas's parents cut off his financial support when they heard about the turn his interests had taken, and he was forced to work at a series of odd jobs in the early 1930s to support himself. He won a scholarship and managed to stay in school. In 1934 he had his first poems published and joined with Césaire and Senghor to found a journal called *L'étudiant noir,* with the general goal of promoting black cultural awareness. Césaire coined the term "Négritude" to describe the movement that was taking shape in the work the three were doing, but Damas was the first to publish a book of poetry that reflected their new ideas.

That book, *Pigments,* had a political orientation. For an opening epigraph Damas used a line by the African-American poet Claude McKay: "Am I not Africa's son, Black of that black land, where black deeds are done?" One poem, "Et cetera," urged black Africans to liberate Senegal from French domination and to resist the French military draft; the book was banned in France's

African colonies as a result, but Damas's poems circulated in African-language translation among anticolonial activists. Other poems in the book were less political and were structured in emulation of American jazz rhythms.

Served in French National Assembly

Despite his dissatisfaction with the French regime, Damas served in the French army during World War II and later took part in the anti-Fascist Resistance. He continued to live in France after the war, winning a term in the French National Assembly as a deputy from his homeland of Guyana. Later he worked for the overseas department of Radio France and United Nations agency UNESCO, and he became a member of the editorial board of the influential French-African literary journal *Présence Africaine.* He traveled extensively, through Africa, the Caribbean, South America, and the United States.

Damas published essays and translated Guyanese folktales from Creole into French before and during the war years, and in 1947 he edited an anthology of poetry from around the black French-speaking world. He published three more volumes of his own poetry in the 1940s and 1950s, including *Black-Label* (1956), an 84-page poem in four parts. He became friends with Langston Hughes and translated some of his poetry into French as well. In 1961 one of Damas's books was translated into English under the title *African Songs of Love, War, Grief, and Abuse.*

Hughes became one source of influence upon Damas's poetry, which sometimes proceeded in seemingly simple, everyday language that took up the lamenting tone of blues music. "Nights with no name // nights with no moon // no name // no moon // no moon // no name // nights with no moon // no name no name," Damas wrote in one poem. Repetition of language was a common trait of Damas's poetry, and one that was borrowed in a general way from African traditions. In the introduction to *African Songs of Love, War, Grief, and Abuse,* Damas listed several traits of African traditional verse that he hoped to emulate. These included an improvised, sung quality, colloquial language, and "antitheses and parallelisms of ideas"—the construction of a poem in such a way that ideas might be restated or placed in sharp contrast with one another.

Beyond these African and African-American influences, though, another primary characteristic of Damas's poetry was anger at European domination. Unlike the writings of some of his colleagues in the *Négritude* movement who looked to a cleansing revolution in the future, Damas was often terse, ironic, and sarcastic. He flirted with Communism in his younger years and was a lifelong adherent of socialism, but as revolutionary fervor faded he became pessimistic. His book *Nèvralgies,* published in 1966, reflected this darker mood.

In 1970 Damas, together with his Brazilian-born wife Marietta, moved to Washington, D.C., to take a summer teaching position at Georgetown University. During the last decade of his life he taught at Howard University in Washington and served as acting director of the school's African Studies program. He died on January 22, 1978, in Washington and was buried in Guyana. Although the political aspect of his poetry held somewhat less appeal in the later years of the twentieth century, Damas's reputation was on the rise. His poems, which sometimes experimented with typography and with the sheer sound of words, were strikingly modern for their time, and they seemed to anticipate the black poetry, both French and English, of a much later era.

Selected works

Poetry

Pigments, 1937; revised as *Présence Africaine,* 1962.
Poètes d'expression françaises d'Afrique Noire, Madagascar, Réunion, Guadeloupe, Martinique, Indochine, Guyane: 1900-1945, Seuil, 1947.
Poèmes nègres sur des airs Africains, Guy Lévis Mano, 1948.
Graffiti, Seghers, 1952.
Black-Label, Gallimard, 1956.
African Songs of Love, War, Grief, and Abuse, Mbari Publications, 1961.
Nèvralgies, Présence Africaine, 1966.

Other

(Translator) *Veillées noires*, Stock, 1943.

Sources

Books

Herdeck, Donald, ed., *Caribbean Writers: A Bio-Bibliographical-Critical Encyclopedia,* Three Continents Press, 1979.

Racine, Daniel L., ed., *Léon-Gontran Damas, 1912-1978: founder of Negritude, A Memorial Casebook,* University Press of America, 1979.

Tucker, Martin, ed., *Literary Exile in the Twentieth Century,* Greenwood, 1991.

Warner, Keith Q., comp. and ed., *Critical Perspectives on Léon-Gontran Damas,* Three Continents Press, 1988.

Wordworks, Manitou, ed., *Modern Black Writers,* St. James, 2000.

On-line

"Léon-Gontran Damas," *Biography Resource Center,* www.galenet.galegroup.com/servlet/BioRC (June 10, 2004).

"Léon-Gontran Damas: Poet of Negritude," *Emory University,* www.emory.edu/ENGLISH/Bahri/Damas.html (June 10, 2004).

—James M. Manheim

Jeff Donaldson

1932-2004

Artist and educator

A leader of the movement to create an African-American art based on black cultural experience, Jeff Donaldson imbued his work with racial consciousness and political commitment. Through his paintings and in his teaching, he communicated the rhythms of jazz, struggle, color, and "shine" that defined, for him, the vibrancy and resiliency of the African-American spirit. As Shola Adenekan explained in a *Guardian* obituary of the artist, Donaldson "celebrated the roots of black culture during an era when 'black is beautiful' and 'black power' were echoing through the African diaspora."

Helped to Create Wall of Respect

Jeff Richardson Donaldson was born and raised in Pine Bluffs, Arkansas. At the age of three, he loved to watch his older brother draw; soon he was drawing his own cartoons and comic books. As a studio art major at the University of Arkansas, he studied with John Howard, who had been a student of Harlem Renaissance painter Hale Woodruff. Howard helped to nurture Donaldson's growing interest in Afrocentric art, which Donaldson expanded through travel in Africa and study of African art history. Donaldson earned a master's degree from the Illinois Institute of Technology, and later earned a Ph.D. in African and African American art history from Northwestern University.

Donaldson came of age at a time of rapid social change, as African Americans demanded both civil rights and respect for a black culture that refused to compromise itself to mainstream white values. Soon

after beginning his academic career, he became involved in the Organization of Black American Culture (OBAC). Through its visual art workshop, which Donaldson organized, its member artists created the "Wall of Respect" in Chicago. This mural, which 12 artists painted on an abandoned brick corner building in 1967, depicted more than 50 individuals who personified black pride, including Thelonious Monk, Charlie Parker, Billie Holiday, Stokely Carmichael, H. Rap Brown, Malcolm X, and Muhammad Ali. *Washington Post* critic Paul Richard later described the wall as a "black-is-beautiful piece, a rough guerrilla mural, part hall of fame, part billboard, pridefully depicting black figures who took pride in being black." Pointedly omitting the image of Martin Luther King, Jr., whose integrationist message was at odds with OBAC's more militant approach, the mural emphasized art that, in Richard's words, "would be vigorous and colorful and African at root. And purposefully political. Dazzling and new, it would shine out like a flower on the African family tree." The Wall of Respect, which was destroyed after it was damaged by fire in 1971, became an icon of the black pride movement. It is credited with spawning an urban mural movement throughout the country in the 1970s which included Detroit's "Wall of Dignity."

Known for his militancy, Donaldson admired the revolutionary message of such leaders as Malcolm X. According to Adenekan, Donaldson argued that African Americans' social gains after the 1960s came "more as the consequence of the threat of revolution than by all the praying by Martin Luther King." Indeed,

At a Glance . . .

Born on December 15, 1932, in Pine Bluff, AR; died on February 20, 2004, of prostate cancer; divorced; two children. *Education:* University of Arkansas, Pine Bluff, BA, studio art, 1954; Institute of Design, Illinois Institute of Technology, MS, art education and administration, 1963; Northwestern University, PhD, art history, 1974.

Career: Lamer High School, Jackson, Mississippi, art instructor, 1954-55, Chicago Public Schools, art instructor, 1957-59; Marshall High School, Chicago, art department chair, 1959-65; Northeastern Illinois University, Chicago, assistant professor, 1965-68; Northwestern University, Evanston, IL, visiting professor, 1968-70; Gallery of Art, director, 1970-76; Department of Art, Howard University, Washington, DC, chair, 1970-76; World Black and African Festival of Art and Culture, Lagos, Nigeria, director, 1975-80; Jazz America Marketing Corporation, Washington, DC, art director, 1978-82; Department of Art, Howard University, Washington, DC, professor, 1980-85; Howard University, Washington, DC, associate dean, 1985-90; College of Fine Arts, Howard University, dean, 1990-2004.

Selected awards: University without Walls, Distinguished Service Award, 1971; National Conference of Artists, Catlett Award of Excellence, 1977; Midwest Theatre Alliance, Bryant Recognition Award, 1984; University of Arkansas, Outstanding Arkansans Award, 1985; African Heritage Studies Association, African American Leadership Award, 1985; Mt. Sinai Hospital Medical Center, Spirit of Sinai Award, 1994.

Donaldson's outspokenness caught the attention of filmmaker Haskell Wexler, who cast the young artist as a black radical in his film *Medium Cool* (1968), set during the protests at the 1968 Democratic national convention in Chicago. It also attracted less favorable notice; the artist claimed that he received an anonymous death threat because of his role in creating the Wall, and that the FBI had placed him and the Wall's other artists under surveillance.

Co-founded AfriCobra

In 1968 Donaldson co-founded the African Commune of Bad Relevant Artists, known as AfriCobra. In the commune's 1970 manifesto, published just after the painter arrived at Howard University to chair its department of art, Donaldson wrote that the group's objectives were to develop a new African American aesthetic and to emphasize artists' role in effecting social change through community engagement and development of black pride. Indeed, Richard credited the artist with "demanding [the] existence" of this new African American art. "You should have seen him," wrote Richard. "He was warrior-erect...dashiki-clad, commanding and sternly on a mission." Donaldson's art, as AfriCobra member Murry DePillars told *Washington* Post writer Yvonne Shinhoster Lamb, was not simply a protest. "It was developmental. He was stimulating growth and looking inside of the black culture to develop an art that was universal."

AfriCobra attracted considerable critical notice. When its *AfriCobra* show opened in Washington, D.C. in 1972, Richard hailed it as a "knockout" with bold, vibrant, sometimes militant pieces that looked to African themes and aesthetics rather than European models. As Donaldson explained to Richard, AfriCobra's qualities included "*The expressive awesomeness* that one experiences in African Art...the Holiness church...the demon that is the blues, Jabbar's dunk and Sayer's cut, the Hip walk and the Together talk." AfriCobra's art celebrated "*Shine*...the rich luster of a just-washed 'fro, of spit-shined shoes" and "Superreal color for Superreal images...Coolade colors for coolade images for the Superreal people."

Donaldson's own paintings deal directly with themes of race, political awareness, and cultural pride. In one of his early works, "Aunt Jemima and the Pillsbury Doughboy" (1963), he shows a violent confrontation between a black woman and a white policeman. The woman, dressed as a domestic servant and wearing a headscarf, looks nothing like the docile black "mammy" who smiled out at consumers from boxes of pancake mix; by conveying the woman's strength and dignity, Donaldson subverts the racist image of "Aunt Jemima." Similarly, Donaldson's Pillsbury Doughboy is not a jolly piece of anthropomorphic biscuit dough but an oppressing figure, with stick raised to subdue the unarmed woman. As Brandi Hughes explained in her on-line study *Perceptions of Black: African American Visual Art and The Black Arts Movement*, the painting conveys the artist's belief that African Americans would have to engage in direct confrontation to win their rights, and that, like the Jemima in the painting, they would not concede defeat.

Similarly political, Donaldson's "Victory in the Valley of Eshu" (1971) was inspired by the story of an elderly couple who refused to sell their home to make way for a highway. A contributor to *St. James Guide to Black Artists* noted that "several layers of meaning are ascribed to the painting through the use of symbols and designs borrowed from African visual references, such as the six-pointed stars framing the photograph [of the couple], which symbolize the sign of Ifa in the Yoruba divination system." The woman also wears an ankh, the ancient Egyptian symbol of life, and the man wears suspenders that are colored red, green, and black—the colors of the African liberation movement. Though humble, these figures are painted with consummate dignity; in Richard's view, they are portrayed as "gods."

In other paintings, Donaldson uses a more strikingly geometric and jazz-influenced style. Among the best-known is "Jam Packed and Jelly Tight" (1988), which was painted as an homage to the Association for the Advancement of Creative Musicians, a Chicago-based jazz group. This painting, according to *St. James Guide to Black Artists*, "transcends the direct adaptation of specific African symbolism seen in the earlier work by creating colorfully rich visual patterns that convey a jazzlike rhythm, a visual 'syncopation.'" Though organized symmetrically, the painting conveys the improvisational structure of jazz. Its myriad brilliantly-colored shapes suggest forms that slap bass strings, play piano keys, or hold microphones; faces sing. As Richard put it, "Donaldson's geometry...is that of the star-burst, the halo and the shivering brass cymbal. His subject is jazz. Immersed, almost dissolved, in his ruled-out parallels and radial expansions are the performers of AACM."

Promoted "TransAfrican" Art

Donaldson came to use the term "TransAfrican" to describe the forms of expression that grew out of independence movements in Africa and the Caribbean and out of the Black Power movement in the United States. These art forms drew inspiration from African symbols and images, including kente cloth, masks, and cowrie shells, and from African music and dance. Yet this new art was informed by current ideas and images of contemporary concern. As Donaldson explained in an article by Richard, "African art—the art of Dogon masks, Kasai axes, Akan goldweights—is not art of isolated objects. Everything's together, religion and tradition, oration, dancing, song. James Brown doesn't just stand up there and sing. You can't see Africobra unless you're in the struggle, unless you hear the music, unless you really know." Working with art movements in many parts of Africa during the 1970s, Donaldson served as vice-president of the international committee and chair of the USA-Canada zone of the Festac festival. He was also director of the World Black and African Festival of Art and Culture in Lagos, Nigeria, from 1975 to 1980. Through these activities, as Washington painter Akili Ron Anderson observed to Lamb, Donaldson "was responsible for getting people on the cutting edge in their aesthetics and their philosophy."

In addition to his work as teacher and as head of Howard University's art museum, Donaldson served as president of the Barnes Foundation, an art education organization based in Philadelphia. His work is included in several major collections, including the Afro-American Art and Culture Museum in Philadelphia, Cornell University, ETACA Foundation, Howard University, Schomburg Center in New York City, and Studio Museum in Harlem, New York.

Selected works

Collections

Afro-American Art and Culture Museum, Philadelphia.
Arizona State University, Tempe.
Atlanta University, Georgia.
Cornell University, Ithaca, NY.
ETACA Foundation, Chicago.
Fisk University, Nashville.
Howard University, Washington, DC.
Musee Dynamique, Dakar, Senegal.
National African American Museum, Wilberforce, Ohio.
National Center of Afro-American Artists, Boston.
Schomburg Center, New York.
Southside Art Center, Chicago.
Studio Museum in Harlem, New York.
University of Arkansas, Pine Bluff.

Selected group exhibitions

Afro-American Museum, Wilberforce, Ohio.
Corcoran Museum, Washington, DC.
Howard University, Washington, DC.
Museo d'Arte Contemporanea, Palermo, Italy.
Museum of Contemporary Art, Chicago.
Parish Gallery, Washington, DC.
Southside Art Center, Chicago.
Steinbaum Gallery, New York, NY.

Sources

Books

St. James Guide to Black Artists, Gale, 1997.

Periodicals

Guardian, March 13, 2004.
Jet, March 22, 2004.
Washington Post, February 27, 1972; May 20, 2000; March 7, 2004.

On-line

"The Wall of Respect on the Web," *Block Museum,* www.blockmuseum.northwestern.edu/wallofrespect /main.htm (May 7, 2004).
"Perceptions of Black: African American Visual Art & The Black Arts Movement," http://xroads.virginia. edu/~UG01/hughes/blackart.html (May 7, 2004).

"Transatlantic Dialogue: Contemporary Art in and out of Africa," *Smithsonian National Museum of African Art,* www.nmafa.si.edu/exhibits/dialogue/donald.htm (May 5, 2004).

—E. Shostak

Jermaine Dupri

1972—

Record producer

In May of 1995, *Newsweek* reported on four young black record producers it called "flashy, streetwise and entrepreneurial"—young men raised on street talk and hip-hop and now working with R&B and rap superstars ranging from Michael Jackson and Bobby Brown to Boyz II Men and Kriss Kross. The four producers, according to the news magazine, were "shaping pop music the way the songwriters and producers at Motown and Stax [record labels] did three decades ago"—and selling plenty of albums, some 70 million among the four of them. Remarkably, not one of the four producers described was over the age of 30. The youngest, then just 23, was Jermaine Dupri.

Although Dupri's name may not be readily familiar, his work is: the 1992 Kriss Kross debut multi-platinum *Totally Krossed Out*, which sold eight million copies; Kriss Kross' follow-up platinum LP, *DaBomb*; the 1994 platinum *Funkdafied* by Da Brat; and the platinum *Hummin' Comin' at'Cha* by Xscape. Dupri has also been responsible for such individual songs as Mariah Carey's "Always Be My Baby," TLC's "Baby, Baby, Baby," and Toni Braxton's "Breathe Again," plus the hit "Keep On Keepin' On," by MC Lyte, from the *Sunset Park* movie soundtrack.

As he approached his 24th birthday in September of 1996, Dupri paused in his busy studio schedule to reflect, in a phone interview with *Contemporary Black Biography* (CBB) from his base in Atlanta, about his fame and considerable fortune—the same month *Vibe* magazine dubbed him a multimillionaire—as well as So So Def Recordings, the record label he acquired in a 1993 deal with Columbia Records. Speaking in the

profanity-laden street talk with which he identifies, Dupri described the harsh upbringing his artists have had, and spoke of his own love for rap and appreciation of R&B.

Speaking about his early start in the music business, and vigorously defending gangsta rap, Dupri tried to explain his success. Marketing is his secret. "I always watch each market and see what time it is—if it's time for stuff to change," he said. "I think the big major labels, not to dog them out [but] their ears are not to the streets anymore, because all the old-fashioned ways of music have changed. Like, all the underground records are above- ground. And all underground records be big records right now. Snoop's [Snoop Doggy Dogg] record "Doing It Doggie Style" is underground, Tupac [Shakur] same thing." He paused and then remarked, "Yo, the streets is where it's at right now."

Although Dupri has looked to the streets for his inspiration, his origins are from rather more fortunate circumstances. Born Jermaine Dupri Mauldin in Asheville, North Carolina, on September 23, 1972, he was the only child of Tina (Mosely) Mauldin and Michael Mauldin, a road manager for groups like Brick, the S.O.S. Band, and Cameo. "I'd go to rehearsals with him. Then I'd try to do what they did," Dupri told *Vibe*.

Dupri received his own drum set at age three—the same year the family relocated to Atlanta for better opportunities. Music was his destiny. Skeptical about reports, which his publicist has confirmed, that he was named for Donny Hathaway's guitarist Cornell Du-

At a Glance . . .

Born Jermaine Dupri Mauldin on September 23, 1972, son of Tina (Mosely) and Michael (a Columbia Records executive) Mauldin.

Career: So So Def Recordings label, president and CEO, 1993–2003; So So Def Recordings distributed by Columbia Records, 1993-2003; Arista Records, senior vice president, 2003–; So So Def Recordings distributed by Arista, 2003–.

Awards: American Society of Composers, Authors and Publishers, rhythm and soul music's songwriter of the year, 1997, 1999, 2000, and 2001; National Academy of Recording Arts and Sciences, Heroes Award, 2003.

Addresses: *Office*—c/o So So Def Recordings, Inc., 685 Lambert Drive, Atlanta, GA 30324-4125.

pree, and for Cal Dupree, a local DJ, Dupri believed that the spelling was changed because it looked more French and his parents thought that was cool. Whatever the reality, he later dropped his surname to differentiate himself from his father, who is in the same business. In fact the professional lives of father and son are closely linked; Michael Mauldin—now executive vice president of Columbia Records Group's black music division—would later manage Kriss Kross and Xscape. Although his parents separated when Jermaine was only ten, Michael Mauldin played an active role in his son's upbringing, and the two men remain close.

As a child, Jermaine was a firecracker on the keyboards and drums. He also loved to dance. He was ten years old when he made what might be called his professional debut. He recalled being at a massive Diana Ross concert with his mother: "Diana Ross wanted kids to come on stage and perform with her. My mom went to the bathroom; I went on stage." And he was such an unabashed performer he was featured in the morning papers the next day.

At age 12, with his father's connections, Dupri had a chance to tour as a dancer with the rap bands Whodini and Run-D.M.C. during their "New York Fresh Festival." His first nationwide rap and dance tour gave Dupri his own invaluable connections in the business. The Whodini link was especially telling; years later, Dupri would find a way to repay the opportunity they gave him.

Dupri soon dropped out of school, though, where he was already making and selling his own tapes on a

do-it-yourself label he called "So So Def." He was assigned a tutor, but his schooling ended in the eleventh grade. "I was into all musical aspects, more than the hip-hop, more musical aspects. I was taking piano lessons, playing drums. I was more into the musical side of the situation than the rap side. I was heading more towards musicianship."

Determined to be the "ultimate Atlanta B-boy," Dupri told *Vibe*: "I was wearing shell toes with no laces, Lee's with the crease." His aim, he said, was to be "a person that's just totally down with everything about rap, whether it be the graffiti aspect, the popping [dance] aspect, the rapping and DJ. I used to want to do all that." He got his wish, but in a way he had not anticipated when, at age 14, he met a new girl rap group called Silk Tymes Leather.

"There were these two girls who were my friends, and they wanted to make a record, and I had this little energy within myself that I could be the person to make these records," Dupri recalled in *Vibe*. "I really had no equipment. I just felt like I had the energy and half the knowledge to go into the studio." In 1987, he produced the album *It Ain't Where Ya From*, which was released in 1990 to modest success; but the teenager had attracted attention, and he was making strong contacts. He managed to get Silk Tymes Leather into Geffen Records, where he himself had been paired with Joe "the Butcher" Nicolo, who had already produced songs for DJ Jazzy Jeff and the Fresh Prince.

The association with Nicolo served them both well when, in 1989, Dupri made a major addition to his stable of artists—Kriss Kross. He had spotted the two 11-year-old boys, Chris Smith and Chris Kelly, leading around a pack of adoring little girls in a local mall and was intrigued. "I just saw them, and I just thought they should be doing something that they needed to, and I was the person to make them do something. They had some glow about themselves no other kids had." Nicolo had just started RuffHouse Records. Kriss Kross was Dupri's housewarming gift. *Totally Krossed Out*, released in 1992, was written, arranged, and produced by Dupri; it went multiplatinum. *Da Bomb*, Kriss Kross' next album, also went platinum.

Suddenly, at age 19, Dupri was a name in the industry. Audiences loved his ability to marry hip hop to melody. "Unlike the gangsta- inclined George Clinton/Roger Troutman boogie that defines Suge Knight's electrifying Death Row Records (at least when Dr. Dre was there) or Puffy Comb's notoriously smooth aural fashion show," *Vibe* wrote, "Dupri's sound is down-home, basically bassy, and lusciously—marketably—bubble-gum."

Dupri was anxious to prove himself in R&B as well as rap. At his 19th birthday party, he met his next big group, Xscape, a female group out of traditional R&B. *Hummin' Comin' at'Cha*, the album he produced for the foursome, went double platinum and included the gold single "Understanding." In 1993 Columbia offered the 20-year-old Dupri his own label deal.

In an interview with *CBB*, Dupri described how R&B artists value his rap background. "R&B artists always want somebody who's hip to know what's going to do good in the rap world as well as do right for the music they do," he said. That's why he has worked so well with Mariah Carey, he noted. "I keep my head level enough to be able to tell her, 'If you sing over the top of this beat, my rappers are going to fill it,' and 'If we put this melody here, your audience ought to be able to get with it too."

Still, gangsta rap remains his first love. "That's all I listen to," Dupri told *CBB*, listing some of his favorite groups: 2Pac, Snoop, Dr. Dre, Notorious B.I.G. "I think people don't like gangsta rap because it's like the second phase of rap. It's the phase where the rappers realize, 'We're like news people now....' They're giving you the news of what's going down in the streets.... People in Georgia, where I'm from, aren't exposed to the things you'll see in the ghettos. So, when groups like Wu Tang Clan come out talking about the projects, and Biggie and Snoop came out, all they're telling you is what's going on, where they're from. I mean, it's stories."

As for rap's misogynistic message, Dupri defended the use of the word "bitch" as a part of scenery of the ghetto and therefore its music. "They got to be true to themselves...." remarked Dupri during his *CBB* interview. "All they know is this hard lifestyle in the 'hood, and that's all they can talk about." This was his belief when he met another of his label's major artists at a Kriss Kross concert—Shawntae Harris, professionally known simply as Da Brat. Her rap sound was rougher than that of previous women rappers.

"I saw realism from Da Brat," Dupri told CBB. "There are a lot of female MCs out there, and I just felt like it was time.... And I felt there wasn't a solo female out there that had had production time put into her. And I think I like challenges, and one of my biggest challenges was to make Brat be the first female rapper to go platinum." Brat's 1994 *Funkdafied* went platinum-plus, but Dupri did not seem surprised. "Within me and Brat, we built a star. We built someone that once you see her, you never forget her. And that's the same with Kriss Kross."

Although Dupri's clients have had some cross-over success Dupri joked to *CBB*: "I think 'cross-over' every once in a while, when I ain't had no big records in a long time. But if you sit in the studio and try to put a label on your music, it don't never come out right.... I try to characterize my stuff as universal, not just for black people." Dupri has enjoyed quiet competition with those three other black producers profiled by *Newsweek*—Sean (Puff Daddy) Combs, Dallas Austin, and Teddy Riley. And he has made two new albums—*Six* with Whodini, who helped him on his way up, and

Anutha Tantrum with Da Brat. Bubblegum rap, he says, is out of the picture; and gangsta is now giving way to a cleaner, cooler rap.

Dupri's sense of the music business provides a strong foundation for his success. He concentrates his keen eye on the voids in the music and continues to fill them. He told *Jet* the "You can see the gaps and see where gaps are. It's like being at a football game. Those up in the box seats can see the field better than the coach. That's what I consider myself, as someone in the box. I can see what's going on." His special talent has been finding young men for black girls to "scream for," as he told *Jet*. After Kriss Kross, he spotted Usher Raymond and produced Usher's hit album *My Way,* which became one of the best-selling albums of 1997. He then became the mastermind behind teen heartthrob Bow Wow.

But Dupri does not confine himself to the talents of others. He too aspires to the spotlight. He performed with Mariah Carey on 1998's *Sweetheart.* For his first album as a performer, 1998's *Jermaine Duprie Presents Life in 1472* and the album's single, "Money Ain't a Thang," Dupri earned Grammy nominations. The album went platinum to further establish Dupri's dominance in the music industry. He followed these with *Instructions* in 2001, and *Green Light* in 2004.

By 2003 Dupri had created the most celebrated teen heartthrobs in the black music industry for a decade, including Jagged Edge, Anthony Hamilton, and J-Won, and produced some of the best talents in the industry, including Mariah Carey, TLC, Aretha Franklin, Ludacris, Alicia Keys and Janet Jackson, to make the So So Def one of the most successful independent music labels in the industry. And the more established record companies took notice. Arista Records made an exclusive production agreement with Dupri, naming him senior vice president. Under the agreement Dupri's So So Def label would be distributed by Arista and Dupri would find and develop new talents for Arista. One of the first talents Dupri signed under the new agreement, Bone Crusher, signaled his continued success.

Selective discography

Albums

Jermaine Dupri Presents Life in 1472, So So Def, 1998.
Instructions, So So Def, 2001.
Green Light, Arista, 2004.

Sources

Periodicals

Jet, May 21, 2001, p. 38; March 3, 2003, p. 21.
Newsweek, May 8, 1995, p. 64.
R & B Airplay Monitor, June 7, 1996.

Time, July 20, 1998, p. 63.
Vibe, September 1996, p. 136.

Other

Additional information for this profile was obtained through an interview with Jermaine Dupri on September 5, 1996, and from publicity materials from So So Def Recordings.

—Joan Oleck and Sara Pendergast

James A. Emanuel

1921—

Poet, scholar

In his half century as a poet, James A. Emanuel's poetry has evolved from traditional forms to free verse, and from traditional themes of childhood, love, and black manhood to expressions of black rage and black pride. His poems are both personal and political. During the 1990s Emanuel developed a poetic form that he called the "jazz haiku," using the language and rhythms of jazz to broaden the subject matter of the traditional Japanese poetic form. Underappreciated as a poet, Emanuel may be better known as a literary critic and an early revivalist of the literary heritage of black Americans.

Entered College after World War II

James Andrew Emanuel was born on June 15, 1921, in Alliance, Nebraska, the fifth of seven children. He listened to his mother read stories from the Bible and the *Saturday Evening Post*, the poetry of Paul Laurence Dunbar, and Booker T. Washington's autobiography. Emanuel knew from early in life that he wanted to be a writer. He memorized popular poetry and wrote poems and mystery and detective stories. He graduated from high school as valedictorian.

During his teenage years Emanuel worked at a variety of jobs throughout the Midwest. At the age of 20, he moved to Washington, D.C., as confidential secretary to the assistant inspector general of the U.S. Army. In order to attend college he joined the army in 1944, serving in the South Pacific.

Emanuel graduated from Howard University and worked at the Chicago Army and Air Force Induction Station while pursuing his master's degree at Northwestern University. While working toward his Ph.D. at Columbia University, Emanuel taught English and commercial subjects at the Harlem YWCA Business School. He taught English at the City College of New York (CCNY) while writing his dissertation on the black author and poet Langston Hughes.

Became a Poet

Emanuel's earliest poems appeared in college publications and in *Ebony Rhythm* in 1948. By the late 1950s he was deeply involved in verse, writing traditional poems in the styles of English masters. As Emanuel's friendship with Langston Hughes developed, he gained a critical reader for his early drafts. From Hughes he learned to write with the consciousness of black experience. With a goal of reaching the largest possible audience, Emanuel wrote in clear and simple language. In 1958 his poetry began appearing in various periodicals, including the *New York Times*, *Negro Digest*, *Midwest Quarterly*, and *Freedomways*. By 1964 Emanuel was giving public poetry readings.

Emanuel loved and respected the energy and passion of youth. His son James, Jr., inspired numerous poems including "A Clown at Ten:" "We should have known // His pull-ups on the closet pole, // His swimming in the kitchen zone, // His pugilistic body roll // On the church pew // And museum queue // Were ways to storm the pass // For the smallest in his class." *The Treehouse and Other Poems* included many of

At a Glance . . .

Born James Andrew Emanuel on June 15, 1921, in Alliance, NE; married Mattie Etha Johnson; divorced; children: James Andrew, Jr. (died 1983). *Education:* Howard University, Washington, DC, BA (summa cum laude), 1950; Northwestern University, Evanston, IL, MA, 1953; Columbia University, New York City, PhD, 1962. *Military Service:* U.S. Army, 93rd Infantry Division, staff sergeant, 1944-46.

Career: Poet and author, 1948—; City College of New York, instructor, 1957-62; City College of New York, assistant professor, 1962-70; City College of New York, associate professor, 1970-72; City College of New York, professor, 1972-84. University of Grenoble, Fulbright professor, 1968-69; Broadside Critics Series, general editor, 1969-75; University of Toulouse, visiting professor, 1971-73, 1979-81; University of Warsaw, Fulbright professor, 1975-76.

Memberships: Fulbright Alumni Association.

Awards: U.S. Army Commendation Ribbon; John Hay Whitney Found Opportunity fellowship, 1952-54; Eugene F. Saxton Memorial Trust fellowship, 1964; Black American Literature Forum, special distinction award for poetry, 1978; American Biographical Institute, Notable American, 1979.

Addresses: *Home and Office*–B.P. 339, 75266 Paris Cedex 06, France.

Emanuel's early reflective works. It received little critical attention.

Acutely aware of his heritage as a black poet, Emanuel became increasingly interested in other overlooked black writers. In 1966 he initiated CCNY's first course on black poetry, leading to several essays and the book version of his dissertation on Hughes. In 1968 he co-edited *Black Symphony*, the first major anthology of black American writing in 30 years. Emanuel judged his writings on Hughes and in *Black Symphony* to be among his best prose.

Turned Militant

In 1966 Emanuel became embroiled in racial politics when he ran for the Mount Vernon, New York, school board. Conducting an all-black campaign, he called for curriculum reforms, including the teaching of black literature, and he organized a black boycott of local merchants. Emanuel and his family were publicly attacked and investigated, as described in the poem "For 'Mr. Dudley,' a Black Spy." The experience radicalized Emanuel. His marriage began to deteriorate.

Emanuel's poems from this period were collected in *Panther Man*. In the preface he described them as "a reflection of personal, racially meaningful predicaments," stemming from "my feelings about the most abysmal evil in the modern world: American racism." The title poem referred to the 1969 murders of Black Panthers Mark Clark and Fred Hampton by Chicago police: "Wouldnt think // t look at m // he was so damn bad // they had t sneak up on m, // shoot m in his head // in his bed // sleepin // Afroed up 3 inches // smilin gunpowder." Like *The Treehouse*, *Panther Man* garnered scant critical notice.

Between 1970 and 1975 Emanuel was general editor of five volumes on black American poets, part of the Broadside Critics series. In his analysis of the poetic process, *How I Write/2*, he analyzed his own poems and those of other black poets.

Found Love in France

Emanuel spent several years teaching at French universities in the late 1960s and early 1970s. By 1973 he was back in New York, in the midst of a bitter divorce and completely cut off from his son. Emanuel had met Marie-France Bertrand in Toulouse in 1972, and she became his companion and the focus of his love poems. Her mother's home, Le Barry, France, became the poet's retreat.

The poems in *Black Man Abroad* describe Emanuel's personal struggle to rise above heartbreak and poetic stagnation. These poems were longer, more personal, and more complex, often dealing with parental, racial, and romantic love. Emanuel began receiving some recognition and *A Chisel in the Dark* included 22 poems from *The Treehouse* and *Panther Man* which had become unavailable. Returning to the University of Toulouse, France, Emanuel taught courses on his own poetry and directed theses on black literary figures. *A Poet's Mind* was an anthology including Emanuel's poems with text and exercises, for use by foreign students of English.

Following his retirement from CCNY, Emanuel traveled and lived in Europe. The 215 poems in *Whole Grain* represented the many broad themes that Emanuel had developed throughout his career.

Invented "Jazz Haiku"

During the 1990s Emanuel invented a form he called "jazz haiku," combining the musical expression of black

Americans with the strict structure of Japanese haiku. In the process he transformed haiku from a single, simple expression, to include narrative, rhyme, and vastly expanded subject matter. "Dizzy Gillespie (News of His Death)" reads: "Dizzy's bellows pumps // Jazz balloon inflates, floats high // Earth listens, stands by." Critic Brian Gilmore described Emanuel's work in *Black Issues Book Review:* "Emanuel is not afraid to blend poetry's traditions and innovations onto the canvas in a seemingly endless series of haikus paying tribute to the first 'world music' and, in effect, producing jazz riffs on the page for the reader."

Emanuel's essays, poems, and other writings have appeared in numerous periodicals and more than 120 anthologies. He wrote two unpublished autobiographies: *From the Bad Lands to the Capital (1943-44)* and *Snowflakes and Steel: My Life as a Poet, 1971-1980.*

Selected writings

Poetry

The Treehouse and Other Poems (includes "A Clown at Ten"), Broadside Press, 1968; recording, Broadside Voices, 1968.
At Bay, Broadside Press, 1969.
Panther Man (includes "For 'Mr. Dudley,' a Black Spy"), Broadside Press, 1970; recording, Broadside Voices, 1970.
Black Man Abroad: The Toulouse Poems, Lotus Press, 1978.
A Chisel in the Dark: Poems, Selected and New, Lotus Press, 1980.
The Broken Bowl: New and Uncollected Poems, Lotus Press, 1983.
A Poet's Mind, Jean McConochie, ed., Regents, 1983.
Deadly James and Other Poems, Lotus Press, 1987.
The Quagmire Effect, American College, Paris, 1988.
Whole Grain: Collected Poems, 1958-1989, Lotus Press, 1991.
Reaching for Mumia: 16 Haiku, L'insomniaque éditeur, 1995.

JAZZ from the Haiku King (includes "Dizzy Gillespie (News of His Death)"), Broadside Press, 1999.
The Force and the Reckoning, Lotus Press, 2001.

Nonfiction

"Emersonian Virtue: A Definition," *American Speech*, May 1961, pp. 117-122.
"Langston Hughes' First Short Story: 'Mary Winosky,'" *Phylon*, Fall 1961, pp. 267-272.
"The Invisible Men of American Literature," *Books Abroad*, Autumn 1963, pp. 391-394.
Langston Hughes, Twayne, 1967, 1995.
(With Theodore L. Gross) Editor, *Dark Symphony: Negro Literature in America*, Free Press, 1968.
(With MacKinlay Kantor and Lawrence Osgood) *How I Write/2*, Harcourt Brace, 1972.
"The Challenge of Black Literature: Notes on Interpretation," *The Black Writer in Africa and the Americas,* Hannessey & Ingalls, 1973.

Sources

Books

Emanuel, James A. "A Force in the Field," *Contemporary Authors Autobiography Series*, Vol. 18, Gale, 1994.
Fabre, Michael, "James Emanuel: A Poet in Exile," *From Harlem to Paris*, University of Illinois Press, 1991.
"James A(ndrew, Sr.) Emanuel," *Contemporary Poets*, 7th ed., St. James Press, 2001.
Watson, Douglas, *Dictionary of Literary Biography,* Vol. 41, Gale, 1985, pp. 103-117.

Periodicals

African American Review, Winter 2001, p. 681-684.
Black Issues Book Review, March 2001, p. 38.

On-line

"James A(ndrew, Sr.) Emanuel," *Biography Resource Center,* www.galenet.com/servlet/BioRC (June 29, 2004).

—Margaret Alic

Calvin Forbes

1945—

Poet

A poet in the tradition of Langston Hughes and Gwendolyn Brooks, Calvin Forbes evokes African-American speech, music, and experience in his works. At the same time, like that of Brooks, his language is compact, sometimes difficult, and generally far removed from everyday forms of expression. Some of his best-known poems are based on the figure of Shine, a hero of traditional African-American storytelling who was said to have survived the wreck of the Titanic by swimming to safety. Yet Forbes's Shine poems are not like folktales; instead they place Shine in a contemporary context and turn him into something of an alter ego for Forbes himself. Forbes has had an academic career that has often found him teaching at prestigious institutions, but he has been restless, moving from place to place in search of new experiences and artistic influences.

The seventh of eight children, Calvin Forbes was born in Newark, New Jersey, on May 6, 1945. After going to public schools in Newark he enrolled at New Jersey's Rutgers University but soon transferred to the more unconventional and arts-oriented New School for Social Research in New York City to study poetry. He also taught himself a good deal about the art of poetry, reading books of poetry before shelving them while working at the New York Public Library and the New School's library.

Traveled Widely as Hitchhiker

Before finishing his undergraduate degree, Forbes left the university to explore the world. He hitchhiked through much of the United States, lived in Mexico for a while, and spent time in Hawaii. It was during his travels that Forbes began writing poetry seriously. Some of his work was published in a Hawaiian collection, and in 1968 his poems appeared in *Poetry* and *American Scholar,* both prestigious publications aimed at academic audiences and serious poetry enthusiasts.

Those publications got the attention of university writing programs that were trying to add African-American faculty members after the explosion in black artistic creativity that accompanied the ferment of the 1960s. Forbes was hired as an assistant professor of English by Emerson College in Boston in 1969. He continued to teach at Emerson for four years, meanwhile writing the poems that would be collected in his first book, *Blue Monday.* That book was published by Wesleyan University Press in 1974, and in that academic year Forbes moved from Emerson to Boston's Tufts University.

Forbes's early poetry covered a variety of subjects. Like many other African-American poets of his time, he often wrote about his own experiences and feelings and set those experiences against the broader black experience. "Child // Of the sun look out: as you get black you // Burn. Is everything in its place except me?" he asked in "The Other Side of the World" (1974). The title *Blue Monday* linked Forbes's poetry to the tradition of the blues, but unlike Langston Hughes, Forbes rarely, if ever, cast his poems in the actual form of a blues lyric. Instead his references to the blues were indirect. He often wrote about the general history of African-American oppression using highly unusual

At a Glance . . .

Born on May 6, 1945, in Newark, NJ. *Education:* Attended Rutgers University, New Brunswick, NJ, and New School for Social Research (now New School University), New York, NY; Brown University, MFA, 1978.

Career: Emerson College, Boston, MA, assistant professor of English, 1969-73; Tufts University, Medford, MA, assistant professor of English, 1973-74, 1975-77; Denmark, France, and England, lecturer, 1974-75; Howard University, Washington, DC, writer-in-residence, 1982-83; University of the West Indies, guest lecturer, 1982-83; Washington College, Chestertown, MD, assistant professor of creative writing, 1988-89; School of the Art Institute of Chicago, associate professor, 1991–.

Awards: Fulbright Fellowship, 1974.

Memberships: Modern Language Association, College Language Association.

Addresses: *Office*—Art Institute of Chicago, 37 S. Wabash Ave., Chicago, IL 60603.

imagery, and his poems were densely woven little nets in which each individual part often encapsulated or was tightly connected to the poem as a whole.

Lectured in Europe

A year after being hired at Tufts, Forbes took a year off and visited Denmark, France, and England, spending the 1974-75 academic year giving lectures with the financial support of a Fulbright fellowship. He returned to Tufts from 1975 to 1977, moving on to a position as writer-in-residence at Howard University in Washington, D.C. It was during this period that Forbes began writing poems featuring the figure of Shine, sometimes trying them out on audiences at live poetry readings. Forbes returned to school in the late 1970s and was awarded a Master of Fine Arts degree by Brown University in 1978.

In 1979 he published some of the Shine poems in a volume entitled *From the Book of Shine.* Over the years, poems by Forbes appeared in a variety of

magazines, and his works began to show up in anthologies of new American poetry. These included *Messages: A Thematic Anthology of Poetry,* edited by X.J. Kennedy, and *The Garden Thrives: Twentieth-Century African American Poetry,* edited by Clarence Major. In the 1980s, Forbes continued his peripatetic ways, spending the 1982-83 academic year teaching at the University of the West Indies in Jamaica on a National Endowment for the Arts fellowship. He then moved on to a teaching post at Washington College in Chestertown, Maryland, and finally, in 1991, to an associate professorship at the Art Institute of Chicago. He has taught courses there in poetry, literature, and jazz history.

The total number of poems Forbes has written in small in comparison with other poets, and when *The Shine Poems* was published by Louisiana State University Press in 2001, it was his third book. The character of Shine appeared in only the last quarter of the book, with some of the other poems dealing with Forbes's own experiences. At one point, the poet converses with Shine: "Shine, Shine where you been— // Back and around the world again. // I've seen things that best remain unsaid. // One sure thing I learned: KISS // ASS and you shall receive."

"Simplicity Shacked Up with Complexity"

Forbes' poetry is "simplicity shacked up with complexity," according to publicity materials on the LSU Press Web site. His new poems had the same kinds of dense structures that he had long cultivated, and, perhaps influenced by jazz music, he reveled in the chance to make language and ideas take unexpected 90-degree turns. Yet a basic human emotion lay at the root of many of his poems "Picture of a Man," from *The Shine Poems,* depicted fatherhood in direct terms: "And I know then what another man // meant when he said // maybe I could have loved // better // but I couldn't have loved more. // I thought of a woman/like that once. // This child is all I have left."

Shine, as recreated by Forbes, was not the boasting, superhuman figure of legend but a modern African American. He has a girlfriend, Glow, and a child, Shade, and he, like his creator perhaps, is uncertain of his place in the world: "For he's the witness // To the confusion and perceives evil, anger // As folly: // His fate's a nuisance. // He goes home gloomy, moaning // About moonlit rain // Falling // Falling— // How he could be alive // and nobody know it." In the words of *Washington Post* reviewer Lorenzo Wellington, "Forbes's crestfallen Shine is nobody's hero, everybody's fool and a rather depressed dude. He spends most of his time longing for visions of Eden, and barely scraping by."

Wellington's review of *The Shine Poems* was mixed, contending that in the book's opening sections "the author skips around too much to satisfy the rhythmic and imagistic possibilities he slyly initiates." Elsewhere, however, the book received some strongly positive reviews. Commenting that Forbes's poems "possess a strong sense of voice, cultural presence, and necessity," William Doreski observed in the *African American Review* that in Forbes's work "blues rhythm isn't just a question of beat: It requires syntax that is compressed and truncated to raise the emotional level of the lyric and underscore the emotional as well as the physical rhythm of both words and music." In the slight output and spare works of Calvin Forbes, the African-American tradition found a mode of expression that encompassed both grassroots black culture and the complex art of poetry.

Selected writings

Blue Monday, Wesleyan University Press, 1974.
From the Book of Shine, Burning Deck Press, 1979.
The Shine Poems, Louisiana State University Press, 2001.

Sources

Books

Harris, Trudier, and Thadious M. Davis, eds., *Dictionary of Literary Biography, Volume 41: Afro-American Poets Since 1955,* Gale Group, 1985.

Periodicals

African American Review, Summer 2002, p. 349.
Chicago Review, Fall 2001, p. 151.
Library Journal, November 1, 2000, p. 103.
Washington Post, April 8, 2001, p. T10; June 17, 2001, p. T12.

On-line

"Calvin Forbes," *Academy of American Poets,* www.poets.org/poets/poets.cfm?prmID=467 (June 10, 2004).
"Calvin Forbes," *Biography Resource Center,* www.galenet.com/servlet/BioRC (June 10, 2004).
"The Shine Poems," *Louisiana State University Press,* www.lsu.edu/lsupress/catalog/spring2001_books/spring2001/forbes.html (June 10, 2004).

—James M. Manheim

Willie E. Gary

1947—

Lawyer

Willie E. Gary is one of the most successful and visible personal injury and medical malpractice lawyers in the United States. The multimillion-dollar awards that he regularly wins for his clients frequently make newspaper headlines. Viewers across the country have glimpsed his posh oceanfront house on television's *Lifestyles of the Rich and Famous*. Unlike many others who are equally rich and famous, however, Gary's life has been a true rags-to-riches story. Throughout his career, Gary has continued to use the combination of determination and skill that made possible his rise from abject poverty to a position of wealth and influence.

Gary, the sixth of Turner and Mary Gary's eleven children, was born on July 12, 1947, in Eastman, Georgia. His father was a sharecropper who managed a 200-acre farm. Gary's complicated birth generated steep hospital bills, forcing his father to sign over the farm in 1948. The family then moved to Silver City, Florida, where all 13 members lived in a tiny wooden shack. They became migrant workers, traveling with the seasons between the corn, sugar cane, and bean fields of Florida, Georgia, and the Carolinas. Gary began working alongside his parents and older siblings at the age of nine, attending school in the morning and hitting the fields in the afternoon.

Persevered in Sports and Business

An eager student, Gary was often frustrated by the long gaps in his education that the family's itinerant lifestyle caused. From an early age, Gary showed a strong aptitude for business. While still in junior high, he started his own lawn-mowing business, eventually saving enough money to buy a truck for his father. When the family moved to Indiantown, Florida, in 1960, Gary and his father started a business together, selling produce from the back of the truck that his lawn-mowing profits had purchased.

In high school, Gary began playing football. Although he was only five feet seven inches tall, he saw that an athletic scholarship was his best hope of attending college. After graduating from high school, Gary tried out for football scholarships at a number of Florida colleges during the summer of 1967. He made it to the final cut at one of them, Bethune-Cookman College in Daytona Beach, but ultimately failed to catch on with any of those schools. On the advice of his high school coach, Louis Rice, Gary made a final desperate attempt at landing a football scholarship by traveling to Shaw University in Raleigh, North Carolina, a traditionally black school whose football coach was an old friend of Rice's.

Earned a Scholarship Despite Hardships

Gary arrived in Raleigh with $13 in his pocket and no return ticket. The Shaw football coach immediately informed Gary that there were no more spots open on the football team, especially for such a small man. Lacking money to get home, Gary hung around the university, sleeping in dormitory lounges and surviving

At a Glance . . .

Born Willie Edward Gary on July 12, 1947, in Eastman, GA; son of Turner (a sharecropper) and Mary Gary; married Gloria Royal; children: Kenneth, Sekou, Kobie, Ali. *Education:* Shaw University, BA, 1971; North Carolina Central University, JD, 1974. *Politics:* Democrat. *Religion:* Baptist.

Career: Gary, Williams, Parenti, Finney, Lewis & McManus (law firm), Stuart, FL, senior partner, 1975–; Gary Enterprises, co-owner; Gary Foundation, cofounder, 1994–; Major Broadcasting Network, coowner, c.2000–.

Selected Memberships: American Bar Association; American Board of Trial Advocates; American Trial Lawyers Association; National Bar Association; National Bar Institute, Board of Directors; Sigma Delta Tau Legal Fraternity.

Selected Awards: Black College Alumni Hall of Fame, 1993; United Negro College Fund, National Alumni Council Achievement Award, 1993; NAACP Image Awards Key of Life, 1994; National Bar Association, C. Francis Stradford Award, 1995; Turner Broadcasting Company, Trumpet Award, 1997; Horatio Alger Award, 1999.

Addresses: *Office*—Gary, Williams, Parenti, Finney, Lewis & McManus, Waterside Professional Building, 221 W. Osceola St., Stuart, FL 34994. *Web*—www. williegary.com.

on food smuggled out of the cafeteria by members of the football team. He cleaned the locker room and helped out the football program in other ways. The coach was duly impressed with Gary's determination, and when a player was injured, Gary was offered a spot on the roster. His hard work was further rewarded when school officials eased the admission process, waived the enrollment fee, and gave him a scholarship.

Gary's years at Shaw were busy ones. In addition to his role as defensive captain of the football team, he found time to marry his high school sweetheart, Gloria Royal, and have the first of their four children, son Kenneth. He also launched a successful business–lawn care once again–while still a student. By bidding on large landscaping jobs and hiring others to do the work, Gary was bringing in about $25,000 a year by the time he

graduated from Shaw. In 1971 he received his degree in business administration. Rather than make a full-time career of lawn care, Gary decided to study law. He enrolled in law school at North Carolina Central University in nearby Durham. Gary's second child, Sekou, was born during his stay in Durham.

Gary graduated from law school in 1974, then moved with his growing family back to Florida. The following year, at age 27, he opened Martin County's first black law firm. Gary was the firm's only attorney, and Gloria Gary handled its secretarial and administrative duties on top of her regular job as a junior college instructor in West Palm Beach. Success as a lawyer came quickly for Gary. Two high-profile cases established his reputation as a talented courtroom battler. First, he successfully defended a school bus driver accused of rape in a highly publicized criminal case. Just a few months later, Gary won his first personal injury case, earning a $250,000 settlement for the widow of a truck driver killed trying to avoid a woman who had pulled into his path. Gary's success in those early cases brought a steady flow of new clients to the firm.

Achieved Courtroom Successes

Gary's firm quickly began to land eye-popping settlements one after another. In 1976 the firm added two full-time secretaries and opened a second office in Fort Pierce, Florida. By the mid-1980s, the firm was grossing over $100 million a year. Gary received national attention in 1985, when he successfully sued Florida Power & Light Co. over the electrocution death of seven members of a Jupiter, Florida, family. Although the precise amount of that settlement was not disclosed, it has been estimated at $100 million, of which the law firm received about 40 percent. In 1995, Gary won a verdict of $500 million, one of the largest jury verdicts in U.S. history, and has since continued to win multi-million dollar verdicts and out-of-court settlements.

In spite of the huge sums his cases often involve, Gary's acquaintances firmly and unanimously agree that it is concern for others, not money, that motivates his work. In a 1987 *Ebony* article, Gary was quoted as saying, "I don't take pride in having good cases. Usually, a good case is a tragic situation and nobody likes to see anyone get hurt or lose their lives." As his personal wealth grew, Gary became almost as well-known for his generosity as for his courtroom skills. Before the end of the 1980s, he had already contributed hundreds of thousands of dollars to a variety of causes in his old hometown of Indiantown, Florida. In 1992, Gary gave his alma mater Shaw University a gift of $10 million.

By 1993 the law firm of Gary, Williams, Parenti, Finney & Lewis had 70 employees. Within ten years, the firm had expanded to 130 employees, including attorneys, accountants, doctors, paralegals, a full-time investigator, and others. In addition to the law firm, Gary and his wife also operate Gary Enterprises, a company organized to manage their many ventures in real estate—including the buildings that house the law firm's Stuart and Fort Pierce offices—and other areas, with the couple's oldest son, Kenneth, serving as president and CEO. Although the people who have known him for a long time swear that money has not changed him, Gary is not bashful about his wealth. He lives in a $5 million oceanfront palace and drives, among many other luxury cars, a Rolls Royce, and often travels in a customized Boeing 737 jet named "Wings of Justice."

Gary's fame has been enhanced by his many television appearances. He was featured in a 1992 episode of *Lifestyles of the Rich and Famous.* Other appearances have included spots on the *Oprah Winfrey Show* and *CBS Evening News*'s Eye on America with Dan Rather. He was also featured as "Person of the Week" on *ABC World News Tonight* with Peter Jennings. Gary counts among his personal friends celebrities from the worlds of politics, business, and entertainment. He has served for several years as General Counsel to the Reverend Jesse Jackson, and in 1994 he received the 26th Annual NAACP Image Award "Key of Life."

In August of 1995, Gary was selected from among 25,000 lawyers for the C. Francis Stradford Award, the National Bar Association's highest honor. In choosing Gary for the award, his peers recognized that his contributions to law and to society extend far beyond the multimillion-dollar settlements he wins for his clients. As Gary stated upon accepting his Stradford Award, "I do what I do, not for the money or publicity, but because I love my profession and people. The only way our children will believe that they can attain their goals is for us to encourage them and provide a path for them to follow."

Invested in Helping Children and Families

Gary has continued to blaze a path and to inspire others to follow. He told *Black Collegian Magazine* that "No one person is an island. Regardless of how successful you become, you will need someone to lean on, someone to inspire you, someone who will say 'you can.'" And Gary lives his words. In addition to practic-

ing law, Gary established the Gary Foundation, an organization committed to education and drug prevention. The Foundation, co-created with his wife in 1994, offers scholarships and other support to help children achieve their academic goals. Gary's son Kenneth serves as the president and CEO of the Foundation. Gary himself travels the country to speak at schools to encourage children to seek higher education and to shun drugs. He also created a television campaign to broadcast his message "Education is Power," to a wider audience. Gary also owns the Major Broadcasting Cable Network, based in Atlanta, Georgia. As chairman and CEO of the network, Gary devotes the programming of the 24-hour cable channel to family-friendly, positive shows for urban black viewers. Gary himself hosts *Spiritual Impact,* a weekly talk show on the network which features discussions with nationally prominent guests about the spiritual perspectives of education, economics, and politics. In 2001 Gary began offering free advertising to historically black colleges and universities on the network. Although his shoes are hard to fill, Gary is dedicated to helping others strive to. Gary summed up his philosophy on the Gary Foundation Web site: "Don't just be another member of society; be a living example of your dreams and goals."

Selected works

Spiritual Impact (television talk show), 2001–.

Sources

Periodicals

Black Enterprise, August 1993, p. 68.
Columbus Times, September 19, 1995, p. B5.
Ebony, October 1987, p. 127; October 1992, p. 106.
New York Times, February 5, 1992, p. B7.
People Weekly, April 13, 1992, p. 65.

On-line

"Willie Gary: Rises from Migrant Farmer to Multi-Millionaire Attorney," *Black Collegian Magazine,* www.black-collegian.com/issues/1stsem01/williega ry2001-1st.shtml#top (July 22, 2004).
Willie Gary, www.williegary.com (July 22, 2004).

—Robert R. Jacobson and Sara Pendergast

Helene D. Gayle

1955—

Epidemiologist, researcher

"Sometimes it gets to me," confessed Dr. Helene D. Gayle, one of the nation's top scientists in Acquired Immune Deficiency Syndrome (AIDS) research, in *Black Enterprise.* "The demands are great because the disease is overwhelming. The virus is so difficult to prevent that it gets frustrating. But we just have to keep working."

For more than two decades, first as head of international AIDS research at the U.S. Centers for Disease Control and Prevention (CDC) in Atlanta, Georgia, and then as director of the HIV, TB, and Reproductive Health division at the Bill and Melinda Gates Foundation, Gayle has devoted herself to efforts to treat and prevent the epidemic spread of the human immunodeficiency virus or HIV—the cause of AIDS. Her work has taken her to cities throughout the world, including Kinshasa, Zaire; Abidjan, Ivory Coast; and Bangkok, Thailand. At the CDC, Gayle oversaw the efforts of more than three hundred scientists who interpreted and published data covering all facets of the HIV infection. Commending her as "a study in diplomacy," Renee D. Turner wrote in *Ebony* that colleagues consider Gayle "one of the most effective professionals working in AIDS research because of her solid scientific background and because she is a physician with a heart."

Born on August 16, 1955, in Buffalo, New York, Gayle is the third of five children. Her father, Jacob Gayle, Sr., was an entrepreneur. Marietta, her mother, was a psychiatric social worker. In the *Ebony* profile, Gayle's brother Jay characterized her as the family's "free spirit." (Jay is also a doctor affiliated with CDC, serving

as director of Minority HIV Policy Coordination.) Gayle was greatly influenced by her parents' attitude toward hard work, responsibility, and noble aspirations. She told Turner, "Both of my parents felt strongly that to make a contribution to the world around us is one of the greatest things you can do."

While in school in Buffalo, Gayle was head of a black student group. Affected by the civil rights movement as an adolescent, she pursued a study of psychology at New York's prestigious Barnard College. While still an undergraduate, Gayle heard a speech by Dr. D. A. Henderson on the efforts made worldwide to eradicate smallpox, a highly contagious and deadly virus that devastated the human population until a vaccination against it became available. That speech helped encourage Gayle to train for a medical degree at the University of Pennsylvania, because it afforded her the "opportunity to be involved in the social and political aspects of medicine." She also pursued a master's degree in public health from Johns Hopkins University, and she served her pediatric internship and residency at Children's Hospital National Medical Center in Washington, D.C.

In 1984 Gayle was selected to enter the renowned epidemiology training program at the CDC. Her preventive medicine residency at the CDC Epidemic Intelligence Service focused on the AIDS virus. Between 1984 and 2001, Gayle rose through the ranks at the CDC, eventually becoming the director of the National Center for HIV, STD, and TB Prevention. In her various positions at the CDC, Gayle concentrated on the effect of AIDS on children, adolescents, and families. In the early 1990s, she began investigating the global ramifications of the illness. While at the CDC, she also served as medical researcher in the AIDS Division of the U.S. Agency for International Development, which allowed her to combine her commitment to public health service with an opportunity to further examine the effects of the virus throughout the world. According to CDC director Dr. David Satcher, quoted on the CDC Web site, "Dr. Gayle exemplifies the best in public health leadership. For over a decade, she has made significant contributions to the international and domestic study, control, and prevention of HIV and AIDS and other infectious diseases."

The author of numerous reports on the risk factors involved in the disease, Gayle published information that showed the devastating effect of AIDS on the black community. By the late 1980s, although only 11 percent of American women were black, black women constituted 52 percent of the female AIDS population across the country. Among children stricken with the AIDS virus in the same time frame, 53 percent were black. The World Health Organization estimated eight to ten million cases of the HIV infection existed on all continents in the early 1990s, yet five million cases were reported in Africa alone. "AIDS presents a challenge to deal with problems we've been twiddling our thumbs over," Gayle told *Black Enterprise*. "We haven't talked about important issues like sexually transmitted diseases, teenage pregnancy and drug abuse in recent years. It's important that we have equitable health care. AIDS has pushed that need to the limit."

Laboring to make clear to the public how the virus is contracted, Gayle studies societies and age groups around the globe. Her work involves teaching people about the ways in which human beings are infected and how related diseases occur. Gayle told Turner that "personal behaviors, which are culturally influenced and which societies are not very comfortable in facing," contribute significantly to the spread of the disease. To counter cultural factors in certain areas, such as parts of southeast Asia where adolescent prostitution is widespread, Gayle has championed the development of female condoms and vaginal virucides.

Substance abuse contributes greatly to the growing number of AIDS cases, especially among poverty-stricken communities where drug abuse is rampant and the practice of sharing needles provides a direct route for the virus. Gayle told Turner that "sex for drugs clearly plays a role. And alcohol use, while it doesn't directly cause AIDS, decreases people's ability to make rational choices." As the doctor pointed out in a *New England Journal of Medicine* article on the incidence of HIV among college students, many people "still do not understand how the HIV infection is transmitted, and even those who do may not consider themselves at risk when they engage in high-risk behaviors."

In 2001, Gayle seized the opportunity to further her work with AIDS prevention when she took the position of director of the HIV, TB and Reproductive Health Program with the Bill and Melinda Gates Foundation, a non-profit health organization funded by Microsoft cofounder Bill Gates and his wife. At the Gates Foundation, Gayle worked with a $300-million dollar budget. At the same time, Gayle was named Assistant Surgeon General and Read Admiral in the United States Public Health Service. With the financial support of the Gates Foundation, and with her connections in the government and the medical community, Gayle set her sights on working with governments throughout the world to increase AIDS awareness and prevention.

Gayle has chosen advocacy on public health over a more lucrative career in private practice, and she remains unmarried. But Gayle revealed to Turner, "I don't regret having placed a high priority on a career that enables me to make a contribution to humankind. At some point there may be reasons why I would want to shift those priorities. In the meantime...my life [is] very full."

Selected writings

Books

Editor, *Global Mobilization for HIV Prevention: A Blueprint for Action,* Kaiser Family Foundation, 2002.

Other

Contributor to professional journals, including the *New England Journal of Medicine.*

Sources

Periodicals

Black Enterprise, October 1988.
Clinical Infectious Diseases, July 1, 2001, p. ii.
Current Biography, January 2002, pp. 48-53.
Ebony, November 1991.
Health Care Financing Review, Summer 2001, p. 208.
New England Journal of Medicine, November 29, 1990.
New York Times, August 28, 2001, p. 6.
Wall Street Journal, August 31, 2001, p. A5.

On-line

"AIDS in America," *Online NewsHour,* www.pbs.org/newshour/bb/health/july-dec99/aids_8-31.html (July 23, 2004).
"CDC Honors Dr. Helene Gayle," *CDC,* www.cdc.gov/nchstp/od/gayle.htm (July 23, 2004).
"Helene Gayle, M.D., M.P.H., Director, HIV, TB, and Reproductive Health," *Gates Foundation,* www.gatesfoundation.org/AboutUs/LeadershipStaff/BioGHGayle.htm (July 23, 2004).

—Marjorie Burgess and Tom Pendergast

Marshall Gilmore

1931—

Minister, religious leader

As Presiding Bishop of the Dallas-based Eighth Episcopal District of the Christian Methodist Episcopal (CME) Church, Marshall Gilmore is a top leader in one of the largest African-American denominations in the United States. That position of leadership has encompassed more than simply overseeing what goes on within the walls of CME churches. Bishop Gilmore has been a leading voice on several social issues, a liaison between the church and the promoters of outside social programs, and a key figure in ongoing attempts to foster cooperation between the CME Church and other Methodist denominations, both historically black and predominantly white. In light of these varied activities, *Ebony* magazine named Bishop Gilmore to its list of 100-plus Most Influential Black Americans in 2003.

Marshall Gilmore was born on January 4, 1931, in Hoffman, North Carolina, and was raised in the local Pleasant Hill CME Church. After graduating from West Southern Pines High School in 1949, he entered the U.S. Air Force and served for four years, reaching the rank of airman 1-C. Toward the end of his stint in military service, Gilmore felt the call to preach and was licensed by Pleasant Hill CME as an exhorter in September of 1953, and then as a preacher on January 2, 1954. That fall, Gilmore entered the Methodist-affiliated Paine College in Augusta, Georgia. Attending summer school at Paine and at several other area schools, Gilmore finished his B.A. degree a year early and graduated in 1957.

Became Religious Leader

By that time, Gilmore had already been an ordained CME deacon for two years and had been assigned as pastor of the Hudson Memorial CME Church in Augusta. Later he became pastor of Atlanta's West Mitchell CME Church. Ordained a CME Elder in 1956, he enrolled at the Theological School of Drew University in Madison, New Jersey, in 1957, receiving his Master of Divinity degree in 1960. He moved on to preach and lead churches in Illinois and Michigan before entering the United Theological Seminary in Dayton, Ohio, where he was awarded a Doctor of Divinity degree in 1974. While in Dayton, Gilmore was the pastor of Phillips Temple CME Church, where he stimulated fundraising that permitted the construction of a new parsonage and paid off its mortgage. He also served as leader of the Dayton chapter of the National Association for the Advancement of Colored People (NAACP). His educational credentials have been rounded out by several honorary degrees.

In 1982, at the church's general conference in Memphis, Gilmore became the 41st Bishop of the CME Church. That year, he became Presiding Bishop of the church's Fourth District, covering churches in Louisiana and Mississippi. Gilmore has served on a host of church committees and administrative bodies, including the departments of Evangelism and Personnel Services, both of which he chaired. He is the author of several books and pamphlets, including *Discipleship in Principle and in Practice, The Local Church, its*

Pastor, Officers and Their Ministries, A Larger Catechism: For Members of the Christian Methodist Episcopal Church, and *Pulpit and Pew.*

In 1994, Gilmore was given the assignment of Bishop of the Eighth District, overseeing 313 churches in Texas. Interviewed by the *Dallas Morning News,* Gilmore was philosophical about the challenges of administration. "When I was pastoring one church, I always had problems I could solve," he said. "I've felt as a bishop that I've had to live with some problems.... But it keeps you really trying to find ways to improve your own capacity for resolving issues and working with people." In the bosom of his own church, Gilmore (as quoted on the CME church's Web site) was more emotional. It was only to an "accident," he said, that he owed his high-flying church career—to his having been elected bishop first in his class in 1982. Since then, he said, God "allowed my golden moments to roll on. He

has kept me clothed and in my right mind. I know I have no reason to think more highly of myself."

Chaired Mortgage Financing Program

Gilmore's activities as bishop have gone far beyond pastoral issues. As chairman of the CME Community Development Corporation (CMECDC), he joined with the giant home mortgage finance source Fannie Mae to expand home ownership opportunities among African Americans. "Homeownership is the cornerstone of long-term financial security," Gilmore stated in a Fannie Mae news release announcing the start of a pilot program covering the greater Memphis, Tennessee, area. "The CMECDC is dedicated to helping families who have been eagerly waiting for the opportunity to own their own homes, to raise their children in a safe environment, and build a solid future." The CMECDC under Gilmore's leadership provided homebuyer education programs and financial counseling, referring potential homebuyers to partner banks that in turn offered low-cost loan programs.

Another issue that occupied Gilmore's time was a much-discussed potential merger of the CME Church with the African Methodist Episcopal Zion (AME Zion) Church. Both denominations were founded when black congregations split off from white-dominated Methodist churches as a result of discriminatory treatment, and they shared some features of their liturgy (religious rites). Gilmore pointed to the benefits of such a merger for denominations whose churches were often located in small towns and duplicated their evangelical and educational efforts. Discussions leading to a possible 2008 merger were set for the 2006 AME Zion general meeting.

Gilmore also was involved with CME groups investigating a possible rapprochement with predominantly white Methodist congregations. Among white Methodists, the ideas of repentance and atonement for the denomination's historical treatment of African American worshippers were gaining currency. In 2003 Gilmore addressed a South Indiana Methodist Annual Conference covered by the Methodist *Reporter Interactive* Web site. "God desires unity and oneness," he told the group. "We are willing to seek the common path within the Methodist family, striving for oneness in the future."

Though much of Gilmore's energy was devoted to church matters, he spoke out on wider social issues as well. He campaigned against the bid of former Ku Klux Klansman David Duke to become governor of Louisiana in 1991, and in 2002 he was one of 51 signatories, from various faiths, to a letter urging President George W. Bush to reconsider his plans to invade Iraq. On another contentious issue, Gilmore raised eyebrows by using the pronoun "She" to refer to God in a 2002 sermon.

Bishop Gilmore is married to the former Yvonne Dukes. The couple has two adult children and two grandchildren. Gilmore's son, the Rev. John Marshall Gilmore, has served as pastor of the Mount Olive Cathedral CME Church in Memphis.

Selected writings

Discipleship in Principle and in Practice, CME Church, 1993.
(With others) *Discipleship: Creation, Covenant, Community,* CME Church, 1994.
The Local Church, its Pastor, Officers and Their Ministries, CME Church, 1995.
A Larger Catechism: For Members of the Christian Methodist Episcopal Church, CME Church, 1995.
Pulpit and Pew, CME Church, 1997.

Sources

Periodicals

Atlanta Journal-Constitution, July 4, 2002, p. B4.
Dallas Morning News, December 17, 1994, p. G1.

Dayton Daily News, May 17, 1995, p. Z.7.1.
Ebony, May 2003.
Forerunner, June 2002.
Philadelphia Tribune, December 13, 1991, p. C7.
Washington Post, July 13, 2002, p. B9.

On-line

"Conferences Repent of Past Racism," *Reporter Interactive,* www.reporterinteractive.org/news/062503/repent.htm (June 17, 2004).
"51 Protestant, Orthodox, Catholic, Evangelical Leaders Petition President Bush to Reconsider Iraq Invasion," *NEWS from the National Council of Churches,* www.ncccusa.org/news/02news83.html (June 17, 2004).
"News Release," *Fannie Mae,* www.fanniemae.com/newsreleases/2002/1758.jhtml (June 17, 2004).
"Senior Bishop Marshall Gilmore," *Christian Methodist Episcopal Church College of Bishops,* www.c-m-e.org/core/bios/Bishop_Gilmore.htm (June 17, 2004).

—James M. Manheim

Jean-Luc Grand-Pierre

1977—

Professional hockey player

Voyons donc!—the idiomatic Quebecois expression meaning "Oh, come on!"—likely runs through Jean-Luc Grand-Pierre's mind as the powerful National Hockey League (NHL) checking dynamo finds himself again cited for a penalty. The Montreal native, one of only roughly 20 black NHL players, began his active pursuit of acquiring English during the late 1990s, when he set off on his journey to become an NHL skater.

The role of the six-foot-three, 223-pound skater is one of bumping and knocking opponents off balance—using physical play to challenge the opposing team. Though he prefers playing defense, Grand-Pierre finds that his coaches frequently play him forward, where his hard checking has made him a formidable right-winger. This flexibility has earned Grand-Pierre distinction in the NHL as a utility player. He can fill a defenseman void on a roster or bring checking strength to a forward line. Whether on defense or offense, Grand-Pierre is an enforcer. In the 269 NHL games he had played by end of the 2004 season, Grand-Pierre had spent 311 minutes in the penalty box.

Grand-Pierre, Jean-Luc, photograph. AP/Wide World Photos.

Grew into a Tenacious Skater

Born on February 2, 1977, in Montreal, Quebec, Grand-Pierre grew up with hockey all around him, a sport that was certainly unfamiliar to his parents. Though they both had been raised in Haiti, Grand-Pierre's parents first met at the University of Montreal. His mother, Michelene, became a nurse, and his father, Allaix, pursued further study at the University of Quebec to become a radiologist.

Grand-Pierre's parents first enrolled him in youth soccer. Later they tried figure skating. He traded in the figure skates for hockey skates by the time he was eight. Hockey crazy, like many other Montreal kids, Grand-Pierre rooted for Quebec's Nordiques and looked forward to watching his favorite player, NHL defenseman Chris Chelios. Grand-Pierre told the *Atlanta Journal Constitution*'s Guy Curtright, "Soccer is big in Haiti, but not really in Canada. Although I had to make a decision at 15, it really wasn't hard. I knew I wanted to play hockey. It is huge in Montreal where I grew up."

Grand-Pierre said that his mother had her sights on his becoming a doctor. "My dad figured it out that I had no

At a Glance . . .

Born on February 2, 1977, in Montreal, Quebec. *Education:* Attended Cégep College, Val d'Or, Quebec, c. 1992-96.

Career: Beauport (Quebec) Harfangs, amateur hockey player, 1993-94; Val d'Or (Quebec) Foreurs, amateur hockey player, 1994-97; Rochester (New York) Americans, minor-league professional hockey player, 1997-98, 1998-99, 1999-2000; Buffalo Sabres, professional hockey player, 1998-99, 1999-2000; Columbus Blue Jackets, professional hockey player, 2000-02, 2003-04; Syracuse (New York) Crunch, minor-league professional hockey player, 2002-03, 2003-04; Atlanta Thrashers, professional hockey player, 2003-04; Washington Capitals, professional hockey player, 2003–.

Addresses: *Office*—Washington Capitals, Market Square North, 401 9th St., NW, Ste. 750, Washington, DC 20004.

interest in that," Grand-Pierre explained to the *NHL* Web site's John McGourty. "But he was just as adamant that I get an education." He told the *Atlanta Journal Constitution,* "With my parents, it was always school first. My mom always wanted me to go into medicine. She hates hockey." Grand-Pierre pursued a bachelor's degree at Cégep College while playing in the juniors. His concentration was mastering spoken English, a practical skill for a young hockey player with aspirations of one day entering the NHL.

At 16, he proved his dedication to hockey, playing for the Beauport Harfangs of the Quebec Major Junior Hockey League (QMJHL). Grand-Pierre told McGourty that Harfangs coach Joe Canale helped him develop as a player. "[He] was so different from any other coach I ever had," Grand-Pierre said. "I learned a lot from him." After a year with the Harfangs, Grand-Pierre played for the QMJHL's Val d'Or Foreurs. During four seasons of junior hockey, Grand Pierre spent 548 minutes in the box during 230 games. Describing Grand-Pierre's years in the junior, the *NHL* Web site reported, "This aggressive defenseman would do anything to keep the puck out of his team's zone."

Played All Over the Ice

Grand-Pierre was picked up by the NHL's St. Louis Blues in 1995 as a seventh-round entry draft pick, making him the 179th overall pick. In 1996 he was acquired by the Buffalo Sabres with their second-round

entry-draft pick to play for the Sabres or its American Hockey League (AHL) affiliate team, the Rochester Americans. Still, Grand-Pierre continued with the semi-pro Foreurs until the end of the 1996-97 season.

Grand Pierre played the entire 1997-98 season with the Americans, and on December 3, 1997, he scored his first goal as a professional. Grand-Pierre enjoyed a remarkable first season in the AHL, earning a spot in the league's All-Star game. He won the event's fastest-skater challenge and came in second for the hardest shot, blasting the puck in the net at 95 mph. After 75 games the defenseman tallied four goals, six assists, and 211 penalty minutes for the Americans.

During the 1998-99 season, Grand-Pierre skated in 55 games for the Americans, contributing five goals, four assists and 90 minutes in the box. The Sabres moved him from the Americans' roster for his debut in the NHL on February 19, 1999. He recorded his first NHL point, an assist, on March 23, 1999. Finishing out the season as a Sabre, he registered 17 penalty minutes in 16 games. Though he was added to the Sabres' playoff roster as a kind of defenseman injury-insurance, he did not skate any playoff minutes and did not contribute ice-time to the Sabres' win of the Eastern conference title. The Sabres lost to the Dallas Stars in the Stanley Cup finals. Grand-Pierre admitted to McGourty, "I wished I could have helped [the Sabres] out or helped the Americans."

The following season, 1999-2000, Buffalo management split him between the Sabres and Americans. In 15 Sabres' contests, he was scoreless with 15 penalty minutes. In 55 Americans games, he recorded five goals, four assists, and 90 minutes in the box. His defensive checking and enforcing played a part in the Americans earning its spot at the Calder Cup finals.

Before the 2000-01 season, Grand-Pierre was acquired by the expansion team the Columbus Blue Jackets. On November 9, 2000, against the San Jose Sharks, Grand-Pierre scored his first points for the Blue Jackets, tallying one goal and one assist. He ended the season with one goal, four assists, and 73 box minutes in 64 games. Blue Jackets coach Dave King told McGourty in February of 2001, " [Grand-Pierre]'s a young player with very good work ethic.... He gives us a strong physical presence on the ice and is very aggressive when he goes after the puck."

Grand-Pierre continued to improve his game with the Blue Jackets during the 2001-02 season. On January 16, 2002, against the New York Rangers, he skated 25:09 minutes, his pro-career high. In 81 regular season games, he tallied two goals, six assists, and 90 penalty minutes. Grand-Pierre faced injuries during the 2002-03 season, missing seven games in December for a sprained knee and another 15 games the following month for an orbital fracture. That year he registered one goal and 64 penalty minutes in 41 games as a Blue Jacket. After his injuries, he was moved to

Columbus's minor-league team, the AHL's Syracuse Crunch, for which he played two games, scoring one goal and sitting in the box six minutes.

The 2003-04 season was eventful for Grand-Pierre. He entered the season as a Blue Jacket with 213 NHL games under his belt, and a reputation as one of the league's most ardent enforcers. Yet the defenseman was moved to forward, playing right-wing for the first 22 games of the season. On December 5, 2003, he was sent down to the Crunch, then recalled to the Blue Jackets by December 16. He had only registered 12 penalty minutes in 16 games as a Blue Jacket and one assist and eight penalty minutes in four games with the Crunch before he was put on waivers and acquired by the Atlanta Thrashers on December 31, 2003. He made his Thrashers debut playing against his home-town Montreal Canadiens on January 3, 2004. Moved back to defense, he scored a goal against the Boston Bruins on February 3, during a game in which he set his career high in ice-time, 27 minutes.

The Thrashers put him on pre-trade-deadline waiver, and Grand Pierre was acquired by the last-place Washington Capitals on March 9, 2004. Moved to forward, he played in every game for the rest of the regular season. Capitals head coach Glen Hanlon called the move of Grand-Pierre to forward an "experiment" to see how to fit the team together for the 2004-05 season.

The *TSN* Web site's scouting report concluded that by the end of the 2004 season, Grand-Pierre's greatest assets were his size, speed, and ability to "play either along the blueline or as an imposing winger." However, the report suggested that Grand-Pierre "Needs to fine-tune his overall game. Must gain more experience and improve his hockey sense in order to earn more ice time."

Encouraged Youth Hockey

In 2002, Grand-Pierre served as the honorary host for the seventh-annual Willie O'Ree All-Star Weekend, a youth hockey event that promotes diversity in ice hockey and honors the NHL's first black player, Willie O'Ree. "I think there will be more black players coming to hockey," Grand-Pierre told Curtright. "It's a great sport to play."

During his professional career, Grand-Pierre has also donated time and energy to Ice Hockey in Harlem (IHIH), a non-profit, after-school program for kids in Harlem, New York. IHIH's free services include ice and classroom sessions. While centered on ice hockey, the training is also designed to fine-tune their skills in math, social studies, and literacy, as well as to promote responsibility and discipline. Participants develop ice hockey dexterity while growing up with the program and at age 14 are invited to try out for the Harlem Rangers travel team.

In 2004, Grand-Pierre was engaged to be married to Roseann Koch. In an online forum on the *NHL* Web site, he told fans that he shared his home with his pet cat, Minnie. He also told fans that the player he would most like to see as a spectator and most like to play against is Jaromir Jagr. Asked which superpower he'd like to have, Grand-Pierre responded, "The ability to fly." As one of the NHL's speediest skaters, Grand-Pierre has already enjoyed a high-flying NHL career.

Sources

Periodicals

Atlanta Journal-Constitution, January 4, 2004; January 20, 2004.
Sports Illustrated, October 4, 1999; December 15, 2003.
Washington Post, March 22, 2004.

On-line

"Columbus Blue Jackets: Fan Center," *Blue Jackets,* www.bluejackets.com/fans/qa/index.php?guest_id=17 (May 4, 2004).
Ice Hockey in Harlem, www.icehockeyinharlem.org/site/document.php?id=3 (May 6, 2004).
"Jean-Luc Grand-Pierre," *TSN.ca: Canada's Sports Leader,* www.tsn.ca/nhl/teams/player_bio.asp?player_name=Jean-Luc+Grand-Pierre&hubName=WSH (May 4, 2004).
"Jean-Luc Grand-Pierre," *Washington Capitals,* www.washingtoncapitals.com/team/plyrbio.cfm?player_id=81424 (May 4, 2004).
NHL.com, www.nhl.com (May 4, 2004).

—Melissa Walsh

Cecil N. Hayes

1945—

Interior designer

Florida-based interior designer Cecil N. Hayes has been hailed in the pages of *Architectural Digest* as among the leading 100 architects or designer in the world. Hayes's work reflects her deep appreciation for African art forms and their link to contemporary design aesthetics. Her client list includes several high-profile people, for whom she has created modern but warm interiors with elements symbolizing a respect for earth, water, fire, and air in traditional African cultures.

Hayes was born on April 25, 1945, in Malone, a small town in Florida's Panhandle, but went to high school in Fort Lauderdale. Artistically gifted, she knew little about interior design as a profession while growing up, and saw teaching as her only career option. Upon graduating with a degree in art education from Florida A&M University in 1967, Hayes took a job as a high school art teacher in Alma, Georgia, as part of a federal program to integrate the schools and their staff. She lived in the nearby southeast-central Georgia community of Waycross, but there were no apartments for rent there, and so her first lodging was a rented room in a house owned by an older woman. "I asked her to see the closet and she pointed to the penny nail in the door," Hayes recalled in an interview with *Knight Ridder/Tribune News Service* journalist Audra D.S. Burch. Hayes eventually moved into a tiny house located behind the town Dairy Queen, and deployed her artistic skills to redecorate it on her less-than-opulent salary. It turned into a pleasing, warm space, and Hayes began to consider a career change.

In 1971, Hayes quit teaching and enrolled at the Art Institute of Fort Lauderdale to study interior design.

She was one of the first black students at the school, and graduated at the top of her class in 1973. Hired by a Plantation, Florida, interior-design firm for $80 a week, Hayes gained enough experience in two years to strike out on her own. Cecil's Designers Unlimited opened for business in Plantation with a Small Business Administration loan of $6,000. The space had a storefront window which Hayes used to display her own drawings and accessories, and during her first year in business she landed a wealthy client from the posh Jacaranda section of the city. Hayes outfitted a 4,500-square-foot home on a budget of just $1,400, a feat that was so impressive that she earned local media coverage.

Hayes's business found new clientele and won bigger budgets over the next few years, but a black woman in the world of interior design was still a relative rarity. As a member of the American Society of Interior Designers, the professional organization with a rigorous qualifying examination, Hayes had access to fabric, furniture, and flooring showrooms open only "to the trade." When she took her clients to such places, the reception was sometimes a cool one, and she eventually went into the custom-furniture business with her husband, Arzell Powell. "I started doing more custom designs out of fear of the design center," she explained to Burch in the *Knight Ridder/Tribune News Service* profile. "People would meet me at the door and ask, 'May I help you?' Translation: Are you in the wrong place? Or I would walk in with my client and they would begin talking to him or her, never considering that I was

Hayes, Snipes asserted, proved herself up to the challenge. "She didn't know what I was talking about at first," he told *Ebony,* "about having the spirit and the vibe correct, and how they affect the emotions. But as it progressed, she started to really dig it, and you can tell that she put her heart and soul into it." Snipes's home includes a waterfall fountain in the foyer, an aquarium filled with African cichlids on the way to the patio, and many African and Asian elements. Hayes found Nigerian carvings, Haitian contemporary art, and copper accessories, and covered some walls in grass cloth. The spectacular result helped put her on *Architectural Digest*'s top 100 list of designers and architects. The list is an international one, but in both 2000 and 2002 she was the sole African-American professional included on it. Her fellow listees included Getty Museum architect Richard Meier and Michael Graves, whose mass-market line is carried by Target Stores.

Hayes's business is located in Coconut Creek, near Pompano Beach, and several employees among the dozen there are family members. The firm does both residential and commercial interiors, but she won a plum commission for the interior of a new African American Research Library and Cultural Center in Fort Lauderdale. The archives and research facility was only the third of its kind in the United States, and was destined to become a cultural landmark for Broward County.

In 2002, Hayes created an exhibit for a textile fair at Florida's Design Center of the Americas (DCOTA). Her installation, "Influences of African Legacy Revealed," was a walk-through lesson on the ties between contemporary design and traditional African elements, such as rich, dark specialty woods, earth-tone palettes, and vibrantly patterned textiles. "I really wanted people to see that the African art form is not 'ethnic,' that it is stronger, deeper than that. Ethnic is insular, within a culture; African forms extends far beyond the culture," Hayes told Burch, the *Knight Ridder/Tribune News Service* writer. "Beyond the influence, the exhibit also shows ways in which African art and furnishings can mix with other kinds of decor."

actually the designer. It was very uncomfortable." Started in 1983, Powell's Interiors, Inc. functions as the manufacturing division for Cecil's Designers Unlimited.

Hayes's impressive mix of custom pieces and African art and patterns began winning her a roster of well-known clients from the world of sports and entertainment. She has created interiors for actors Wesley Snipes and Samuel L. Jackson, as well as professional athletes Ty Law, Penny Hardaway, and Derek Brown. Hayes's work on Snipes's 7,000-square-foot home made the cover of *Ebony* magazine in 1997. Hayes met Snipes through his mother, Marion Snipes, but won the commission only when she presented him with a plan that met with his approval: unlike many who hire a design professional, Snipes had a very specific vision of what he wanted his Mediterranean-style home to become. Hayes worked for months on the design plan, after a two-day meeting in which the actor presented his elaborate philosophies on the subjects of light, angles, and mood for living spaces. Snipes disliked squares, for example. "Squares create 90-degree angles, and 90-degree angles create dust and positive ions," he explained to *Ebony* writers Lynn Norment and Vandell Cobb. "It messes with our sinuses, messes with your clothes. So you change the angles and the air can move the dust particles from stagnation in the corners."

Sources

Periodicals

Ebony, November 1997, p. 194; September 2003, p. 94.
Jet, March 25, 2002, p. 33.
Knight-Ridder/Tribune News Service, April 29, 2002.
Palm Beach Post, February 17, 2002, p. 1K.

On-line

Cecil's Designers Unlimited, www.cecilsdesigners. com (June 29, 2004).

"Cecil Hayes: Biography," *The History Makers*, www.thehistorymakers.com/biography/biography. asp?bioindex=226&category=artMakers (May 10, 2004).

—Carol Brennan

Clarence "Frogman" Henry

1937—

Musician

With a voice that croaked and a theme song that declared "I sing like a frog," Clarence Henry soon became known as "Frogman." Through a series of singles recorded for Chess Records in the 1950s and 1960s, he established himself as a rhythm and blues powerhouse. Like many singers of his era, however, his brand of music went out of style following the British Invasion during the mid-1960s, leaving Henry and his peers to make a living as best they could. These "hard times" were complicated by the fact that record companies often neglected to pay proper royalties to artists. "I don't mind them stealing a little," Henry told John Wirt in the *Batan Rouge Advocate*, "but don't steal it all." Far from washed up, the Frogman made a dramatic comeback in the early 1990s. "You'll likely find him joyously reviving his classics at the New Orleans Jazz & Heritage Festival every year come spring," noted Bill Dahl in *All Music Guide*, "and his croak remains as deep and melodious as ever."

Henry was born in New Orleans, Louisiana, on March 19, 1937, and moved with his family to nearby Algiers when he was 11. He learned about music from his father, who liked the blues, and his brother, who played

Clarence "Frogman" Henry, photograph. © Jack Vartoogian.

trombone. He also tagged along when his sister took piano lessons, eventually taking her place when she dropped out, and made a habit sneaking into clubs to hear other players perform. "When I was going to school I wanted to be Fats Domino, Professor Longhair, and I would wear a wig with two plaits and call myself Professor Longhair," Henry told Cain Burdeau of the *Associated Press*. "I like the Fats Domino rhythm, but I play my own chords and my own style." While attending L.B. Landry High School, he learned to play trombone and soon joined Bobby Mitchell and the Toppers. Although he recorded an album on Imperial with the Toppers, he was fired for missing a performance.

Henry quickly regained his footing, playing at a number of New Orleans clubs, including the Chicken Shack, the Joy Lounge, and the Fatman. It was at the Joy Lounge in 1955 that he penned his most famous song, less out of inspiration than the fact that the band had run out of material. While the band normally played until 2:00 a.m., one night the band manager insisted that they continue to play until all the customers had gone. Henry began to adlib, "Ain't got no home, no place to roam...I can sing like a frog, rivet, rivet." A disc jockey

At a Glance . . .

Born on March 19, 1937 in New Orleans, Louisiana; married five times.

Career: Musician, 1952–; joined Bobbie Mitchell and the Toppers, 1952-55; signed to Chess Records, 1956; toured with the Beatles, 1964.

Addresses: *Home*—New Orleans, Louisiana.

at WJMR later took the joke one step further, bestowing the "Frogman" label on Henry, and the audience began requesting the song.

Henry liked his new song, but knew it needed work. He added a high vocal section—his other specialty—to offer contrast, and auditioned the song to Paul Gayten at Chess Records. Gayton liked what he heard and asked Leonard Chess to fly down to catch Henry's show. Having passed the audition, Chess quickly signed the teenager and brought him into the studio to record "Ain't Got No Home" along with "Troubles, Troubles." Chess decided to promote "Troubles, Troubles," though, and the initial response was lukewarm. "Finally," Henry told Jeff Hannusch in *Off Beat*, "... Poppa Stoppa [Clarence Hayman] at WWEZ flipped the record over and started playing 'Ain't Got No Home.' Right away people started calling the station asking for the frog song by the frog man." The young singer came to national attention as "Ain't Got No Home" rose to number three on *Billboard's* R&B chart and number 30 on the pop charts. Henry embarked on package tours with the Teenchords and others, traveling as far as Jamaica.

Although Henrys' star faded with his first song, it rose again in 1961 with "Lonely Street," which reached number 19 on *Billboard's* Black Singles chart. He toured nationally, and followed the hit with strong versions of "You Always Hurt the One You Love" and "On Bended Knees." "Henry's vocals were consistently warm and humorous," wrote Richie Unterberger in *All Music Guide*, "his recordings always polished." Henry's string of hits also placed him the position of opening 18 dates for the Beatles in 1964. However, the British Invasion represented a new style of music that made 1950s R&B sound old fashioned. In the wake of changing musical tastes, Henry and many of his musical peers would be left to survive the best they could.

When Henry quit recording hits, Chess dropped his contract, and he started recording for smaller labels like Dial, Parrot, and Roulette. Although the quality of his work remained high, it lacked the necessary distribution to gain attention outside of his base in New Orleans.

He continued to earn a living by performing locally. "I played on Bourbon Street for 19 years...," he told Hannusch. "I played nearly every club on the strip. Six hours a night, six nights a week. I had the best band in town." The work was grueling, though, and by 1981 Henry needed a change. In 1982 he embarked on a tour of England and returned again the following year to tape a series of appearances for a popular British television program. He also recorded *The Legendary Frogman Henry* for Silvertone records while in England.

Henry's career received a boost in the 1980s when talk show host Rush Limbaugh began using "Ain't Got No Home" on his syndicated radio program. Unfortunately, Henry suffered from a ruptured disc in his neck around the same time, temporarily paralyzing him. A successful operation, however, returned Henry to the performing stage. Explaining his return, Henry told Wirt: "Well, it's a miracle, and determination, motivation. I was determined that I would pull through. I had to have faith." In 1994 Henry's career got yet another new lease on life when "(I Don't Know Why) But I Do" was included on the *Forest Gump* soundtrack, which subsequently sold eight million copies. Although the New Orleans-based singer continues to perform at Jazz Fest, he now reserves much of his time for his many grandchildren. "I don't jump because of money," Henry told Burdeau. "I like friendship more than money. Some people let success go to their head, but I don't. I know where I come from and I haven't forgotten where I come from: down there in the ghettos."

Selected discography

You Always Hurt the One You Love, Argo, 1961.
Alive and Well and Living in New Orleans, Roulette, 1969.
The Legendary Frogman Henry, Silvertone, 1982.
But I Do, Charly, 1994.
Ain't Got No Home: The Best of Clarence "Frogman" Henry, Chess, 1994.

Sources

Periodicals

Associated Press, October 3, 2003.
Baton Rouge (Louisiana) *Advocate*, July 12, 1996.
New Orleans Times-Picayune, April 23, 1999, p. 1A.

On-line

"Clarence 'Frogman' Henry," *All Music Guide*, www.allmusic.com (May 13, 2004).
"Clarence 'Frogman' Henry," *Off Beat*, www.offbeat.com (May 13, 2004).

—Ronnie D. Lankford, Jr.

Harold Hurtt

1947(?)—

Law enforcement executive

Hurtt, Harold, photograph. AP/Wide World Photos.

Harold Hurtt became the chief of police in 2004 of Houston, Texas, the fourth-largest city in the United States. He brought to the job an impressive record of success in the Phoenix, Arizona, police department, where he had spent much of his professional life. "Perhaps Hurtt's best recommendation is the desire of Phoenix's citizenry and police force for him to stay," noted the *Houston Chronicle* after the announcement of Hurtt's new appointment. While other big-city police departments struggled with conflicts between citizens and police, and between police leadership and officers' unions, Hurtt had engendered goodwill in both areas. He seemed well prepared to take on a daunting set of challenges in Houston.

Many of Hurtt's accomplishments could be grouped under the heading of community policing; as chief he met frequently with community organizations, and he opened new offices in neighborhoods where the police had long been seen as outsiders. But for Hurtt, community policing was more than a textbook idea; in his early days on the force it had been a method of survival on the streets where he began his career. Born around 1947, Hurtt joined the Phoenix police as a patrol officer in 1968 after military service at Arizona's Luke Air Force Base.

Started Career on Projects Beat

"I worked a walking beat in a housing project," Hurtt told the *Chronicle*. "For eight hours you lived there. You went to family fights, you went to the child abuses, and the homicides. You had to sell yourself every day, and when you made a promise, you had to carry it through. You had to make sure you treated people fairly, and that still stands today. Nothing has changed." Coping successfully with the pressures of working in a predominantly black housing project during the unrest of the 1960s, Hurtt rose through the ranks in Phoenix. Along the way he furthered his education, earning a bachelor's degree in sociology from Arizona State University in 1977 and later a master's degree in organizational management from the University of Phoenix.

Hurtt left Phoenix for the first time in his professional life in 1991, when he was named police chief in Oxnard, California. There he encountered an issue that

At a Glance . . .

Born in 1947(?); married; children: three. *Education:* Arizona State University, BS, sociology, 1977; University of Phoenix, MA, organizational management, 1991; Valley Leadership Program, graduate; University of California at Los Angeles, School of Public Policy and Social Research, senior fellow. *Military service:* U.S. Air Force.

Career: Police department, Phoenix, AZ, officer, 1968-91; Oxnard, CA, chief of police, 1991-98; Phoenix, chief of police, 1998-2004; Houston, TX, chief of police, 2004–.

Selected memberships: Major Cities Chiefs of Police, past president; International Association of Chiefs of Police, member; National Organization of Black Law Enforcement Executives, member; Police Executive Research Forum, member.

Addresses: *Office*—Houston Police Department, 1200 Travis, Houston, TX 77002.

would equip him well for his later posts in Phoenix and Houston, both cities with large Latin American populations. "When I went to Oxnard, that was a city that was 67 percent Hispanic. Service levels, equity of service was always an issue," he told the *Houston Chronicle.* Hurtt managed the challenges in Oxnard well. Over the course of his seven-year tenure, crime rates in Oxnard dropped by 30 percent. When the post of police chief in Phoenix became available in 1998, Hurtt jumped at the chance to return. He even turned down a finalist slot in the competition to become police chief in San Jose, California, to live in Phoenix.

In Phoenix, Hurtt worked closely with the community. He served on the boards of directors of the Phoenix Boys choir and the Valley of the Sun YMCA among other organizations, and he was elected president of the Major Cities Chiefs of Police. Although generally a delegator in his management style, Hurtt often visited meetings of neighborhood organizations. He succeeded in reversing a homicide spike in 2003 after consulting with residents in the hardest-hit neighborhoods and determining the causes for the rash of murders—an increase in drug trafficking and in the victimization of illegal aliens. Overall, Phoenix's violent crime rate fell by more than 9 percent from 1998 to 2002, and property crime also fell.

Pioneered Issuance of Stun Guns

The biggest challenge Hurtt faced in Phoenix involved police use of force: Phoenix's rate of police shootings eclipsed that of the controversial Los Angeles police department in the early 2000s. Hurtt responded with a series of measures that included video simulation training. His most significant innovation was to issue Taser electronic stun guns to all city patrol officers. The Tasers enabled officers to subdue violent arrestees without resorting to lethal force. When Phoenix became the first major police department in the country to equip all its street officers with stun guns in March of 2003, the city's police shootings for the year dropped to their lowest level since 1990.

Successes like these got the attention of Houston's hard-charging, millionaire mayor Bill White, whose police department was faced with a host of problems, including allegations of police misconduct in the shootings of two unarmed Hispanic teenagers and questions about the competence of the department's DNA testing lab. Passing over several internal candidates and deflecting pressure to name a Hispanic chief, White named Hurtt Houston's new chief of police in February of 2004. "Harold Hurtt is a police officer's police offer….," White told the *Houston Chronicle.* "He's recognized in this nation by his peers as being a leader in policing in the United States."

In his first weeks on the job in Houston, Hurtt announced a commitment to replicate his Taser initiative in Houston. He also hoped to set in motion another program that had proven successful in both Oxnard and Phoenix—the installation of intersection cameras that could detect the license numbers of cars that ran red lights. What got the most attention was Hurtt's reshuffling of the department's top-rank command staff, which resulted in the departure of several long-time assistant chiefs but put in place a diverse young staff that gained praise from Houston journalists. New assistant chiefs included Dorothy Edwards, the department's first African-American woman to serve in that capacity. Hurtt built strong bridges to the police rank and file by meeting with all 5,400 officers and opening up lines of communication with the department's police union.

Despite his strong record, Hurtt remained an elusive figure in some ways. Described as very private, he often declined interviews and preferred to be represented in public by members of his staff. Journalists and staffers noted his frequently mangled syntax when he was speaking, referring sarcastically to his use of language as the King's English. Yet even those same individuals praised Hurtt for his overall effectiveness. Hurtt did make known that he was married, with three children and seven grandchildren. He was an enthusiastic golfer and often lamented that his professional responsibilities left him little time to pursue the sport.

Even in the face of an unexpected budget shortfall of $20 million to $30 million that confronted him during his first months on the job, Hurtt seemed well-prepared for the challenges of running Houston's enormous department and administering its budget of over $400 million annually. He continued his practice of meeting with neighborhood groups, and he started out with the respect of various constituencies in a troubled situation. Though not a headline-grabber, Harold Hurtt had become one of the most respected law enforcement leaders in the United States.

Sources

Periodicals

Associated Press, February 26, 2004; February 27, 2004.

Houston Chronicle, February 28, 2004, p. A1; February 29, 2004, Outlook sec., p. 2; March 3, 2004, p. 3; March 5, 2004, p. 25; March 18, 2004, p. 26; March 25, 2004, p. 24; March 30, 2004, p. 11; April 15, 2004, p. 5; April 28, 2004, p. 17; April 30, 2004, p. 25, May 27, 2004, p. 26.

Houston Press, March 11, 2004; May 6, 2004.

Jet, March 15, 2004, p. 18.

—James M. Manheim

Allen Iverson

1975—

Professional basketball player

Allen Iverson, perhaps the quickest player ever to play in the National Basketball Association (NBA), was born on June 7, 1975, in Hampton, Virginia. His mother Ann Iverson was a teenager and was deserted by Iverson's father. Soon after her son was born, Ann Iverson's mother died, leaving the young mother and son to fend for themselves. Iverson grew up in severe poverty in a house that sometimes had no electricity or water. Sports offered an outlet for the immensely gifted young athlete and he excelled in football, baseball, and basketball. Though he is arguably the best player in the NBA today, Iverson told Leigh Montville of *Sports Illustrated* that basketball was not his first choice: "I always figured I was going to go to one of those big football schools. Florida State. Notre Dame. Football was my first love. Still is. I was going to go to one of those schools and play both. I just loved running the option, faking, throwing the ball, everything about football. I didn't even want to play basketball at first. I thought it was soft. My mother's the one who made me go to tryouts. I thank her forever. I came back and said 'I like basketball, too.'" Iverson cruised through high school doing just well enough in the classroom to stay eligible for sports. In his senior year he led Bethel High School's football team to a state championship. He was excelling in basketball also until the night of February 13, 1993. Iverson and some friends were at a bowling alley when a fight broke out which then escalated into a brawl divided along racial lines. Of the 50 or so participants involved in the fight, only four black teenagers were charged—one of them Iverson. Though video of the incident did not show Iverson at all and he testified that he left the bowling alley when the brawl

started, two other witnesses said that he threw a chair at a woman. The 17-year-old was tried as an adult and sentenced to five years in prison for maiming by mob.

Iverson went to jail for four months before the governor of Virginia commuted his sentence under the condition that he not play organized sports until he graduated from high school. Two years later his conviction was overturned by the State Court of Appeals. Though the incident is erased from his legal record, it made him even more determined to succeed for his family. Iverson told *Sports Illustrated's* Rick Reilly about his motivation: "I knew I had to succeed for them. People would say, 'Man, that's a million-to-one shot to make it to the NBA,' but I'd say 'Not for me it ain't.' 'Cause if I didn't succeed, well, I don't wanna think about it. I thought, for all the sufferin' they've done, they need me to make it. They oughta have some satisfaction in life." Iverson suddenly became serious about school and worked all the way through the summer at a rigorous learning center to make up his lost class work.

After high school, Iverson attended Georgetown University. The freshman would earn the Big East Rookie of the Year award after leading his team with 20 points and 4.5 assists per game. His sophomore season was better. He drove the Hoyas to a 29-8 record, averaging 25 points, 4.7 assists, and 3.5 steals per game. Iverson, who started 66 of 67 games as a Hoya, was also named Big East Defensive Player of the Year in 1994 and 1995 and named an Associated Press (AP) First Team All-American in 1995. Despite his success and enjoyment of college life, after two years at

At a Glance . . .

Born Allen Ezail Iverson on June 7, 1975, in Hampton, VA; son of Allen Broughton and Ann Iverson (a factory and shipyard worker); married Tawanna; children: Tiaura, Allen II, and Isaiah. *Education:* Attended Georgetown University.

Career: Philadelphia 76ers, professional basketball player, 1996—.

Awards: Big East Rookie of the Year, 1995; Big East Defensive Player of the Year, 1995, 1996; first team AP All-American, 1996; NBA Rookie of the Year, 1997; All-NBA first team, 1999; Eastern Conference All-Star Team, 2000-2004.

Addresses: *Office*—c/o The Philadelphia 76ers, 3601 South Broad St., Philadelphia, PA 19148.

Georgetown he knew it was time to leave. His family was still living in poverty back in Hampton, and he now had a daughter Tiara to think about. His sophomore season at Georgetown would be his last in college.

Entered the NBA

On June 26, 1996, Iverson was the first player selected in the NBA draft by the Philadelphia 76ers. He signed a $9.4 million contract and set his sights on becoming the best player in the NBA. If he was not the best on the court in his first season, Iverson quickly established himself as one of the most exciting players in the league. His crossover dribble proved to be so explosive that the NBA issued a memo to referees across the league addressing one individual player's single move. Iverson had to change his crossover dribble slightly to avoid travelling but that did not diminish his achievements. He led his team and all NBA rookies in points (23.5), assists (7.5), steals (2.07), and in minutes played (40.1) per game. His coach Johnny Davis told Montville of *Sports Illustrated*: "He's as quick with the ball as anyone in the history of the league. He's a combination of Isiah Thomas and Tiny Archibald. Fast guys in this league, he makes them look as if they're slow. He has a level beyond their quickness." Iverson was named Rookie of the Year and was the Most Valuable Player (MVP) in the Rookie All-Star game during the NBA's All-Star weekend. Despite his success, Iverson came under some harsh criticism. His penchant for taking off-balanced shots, sometimes before looking for teammates, coupled with a poor shooting percentage for a point guard (.416), and his turnovers, prompted some to label him selfish—espe-

cially among the leagues old guard. Charles Barkley called him "Me-Myself-and-Iverson." His loyalty to the shoe company Reebok, which erected a 40-foot mural of Iverson in downtown Philadelphia, prompted his next coach Larry Brown to openly question his devotion to the 76ers. And then the league fretted about Iverson's image. Instead of suits and ties, the 20-year-old opted for baggy pants, mountains of jewelry, and do-rags—like many other young people of his generation. The league even questioned his choice of friends who remained with him from his days in Hampton. But Iverson told *Sports Illustrated*'s Montville that his loyalty would remain firm: "The NBA can't pick my friends. When I was struggling growing up, no running water in my house, the electric lights turned off, these were the guys who were with me. They grew up with me. I'm not going to turn my back on them now. Not many people were always angels as they grew up. These are the guys who won't always be telling me how great I am. They know me."

The league and other critics seemed to be proved correct in the off-season after Iverson's rookie year. Iverson was on his way to record a rap song at a local Richmond recording studio; a man offered to drive him there, and Iverson fell asleep around midnight on the way there. Police pulled over Iverson's car after it was clocked at 93 miles per hour and allegedly found marijuana and a handgun in the Mercedes. Iverson was arrested but all charges were dropped after he was given two years probation with monthly drug tests and 100 hours of community service. Iverson told *Sports Illustrated*'s Reilly about the incident: "That was so stupid. It was such poor judgment...If that car had crashed, I'd have put my family right back where they'd come from. From then on, I decided I gotta be smart."

Iverson vowed to put his past behind him and even hired two bodyguards to help him make better decisions socially. The 76ers brought in veteran coach Larry Brown to help tutor Iverson as a point guard. Though the two had their moments of frustration, Iverson improved his game. He led Philadelphia in every offensive category and finished eighth in the league in scoring with 22 points per game and eleventh in minutes played with 39.4 a game. He scored in double figures in 74 of his 80 games and improved his shooting percentage to .461. Though the 76ers improved in the 1997-98 season, coach Brown thought the team and its star punctured could do better. The following season, he switched Iverson from point guard to shooting guard to relieve some of the pressure of bringing the ball up court. Even though he played against taller opponents, Iverson and his team had a breakout year. Iverson led the NBA in scoring with 26.8 points per game and in minutes played. He was named to the All-NBA first team and scored in double figures in 46 of 48 games. The season was not without controversy, though, when Iverson was on the bench and Brown told him to go back in during an April second game; Iverson cursed at having been held out of the game for so long, and Brown sat him for the rest of the contest. Iverson then missed the following game citing a hamstring injury. But ironically the incident seemed to help relations between the two stubborn men. Iverson apologized and later told *Sports Illustrated's* Michael Bamberger: "Coach and myself, we've come a long way. We started off rocky. Now we're friends." More importantly the 76ers finished the lockout-shortened season 28-22 and made the playoffs. The sixth-seeded Philadelphia team proceeded to defeat the third-seeded Orlando Magic three games to one. Iverson dominated the series averaging 28.3 points a game during the first round. Though Philadelphia was swept by the Indiana Pacers in the following round, Iverson had returned playoff basketball to Philadelphia.

Developed Personally and Professionally

Iverson approached the 1999-2000 season as a seemingly different individual. Fresh off his post-season success and a new six-year multi-million dollar contract, Iverson left the bodyguards and much of the controversy behind him. He found himself more concerned with his two children, and instead of two bodyguards, he often traveled with his mother. He became fully committed to his team, telling Ken Berger of the Associated Press, "I'll do anything to help this team win, I don't care what it is. I'll do anything it takes to get a championship. I think Coach Brown knows what it takes to get there."

Iverson continued to shine in the NBA. He was selected for the All-NBA first team in both 1999 and 2001, and for the second team in 2000, 2002, and 2003. And at the 2001, All-Star game he was named the Most Valuable Player. That same year he was named the Most Valuable Player for the NBA for being the league's leading scorer and stealer for the season. Iverson was the NBA scoring champion in 1999, 2001, and 2002. He ended the longest streak of double-figure scoring in NBA history on March 20, 2003. Over 186 games from November 24, 2000, to the March 20 game against the Detroit Pistons, Iverson had averaged 32.1 points per game. The Pistons ended his streak by holding him to just five points that game. That year, the Sixers signed a multiyear contract extension with Iverson, signaling that his dream of being a Sixer would continue. Iverson announced at a press conference that "I always wanted to be a Sixer. I always wanted to finish my career as a Sixer...It just means a lot to me that I could be in a Sixers uniform for the rest of my career," according to *Sixers.com.* Sixers President and General Manager Billy King responded, saying "With this contract, we're telling him we always want him to be here as well."

In 2004, Iverson's play helped qualify the USA Basketball Men's Senior National team qualify for the Olympics. His superior play and stamina was rewarded in playing time. That year he ranked first in the NBA for playing time, averaging 42.5 minutes per game. Iverson also hit two personal records in 2004; on January 23rd, he became the tenth fastest player to score 14,000 points in NBA history and on February 19th he scored 40 points in a single game for the fiftieth time in his career.

Although a variety of injuries kept him from playing 21 games during the 2004 season, he was ready to get back in shape when he made a surprise appearance at a workout for 76er rookies and free agents in July. Iverson remarked to *Sixers.com* that it was "fun just getting back into it," adding: "When you don't play the game for a while and then you are able to play it again, it's kind of like a kid in the candy store. You kind of forget what you have been missing, not playing the game." With his body healed, Iverson was primed to start the next season as strong as ever.

Sources

Books

Platt, Larry, *Only the Strong Survive: The Odyssey of Allen Iverson,* ReganBooks, 2002.
Schmidt Jr., Charles E., *Allen Iverson*. Chelsea House Publishers: Philadelphia, PA. 1998.
Smallwood, John N., Jr., *Allen Iverson: Fear No One,* Pocket Books, 2001.

Periodicals

Basketball Digest, May 2001; Summer 2001.
Los Angeles Times, October 10, 1999.
Newsweek, July 22, 2002.
Sporting News, April 2, 1001; June 18, 2001; February 18, 2002.
Sports Illustrated, December 9, 1996; March 9, 1998; May 24, 1999; April 23, 2001; May 28, 2001; June 18, 2001; October 29, 2001; July 29, 2002.

On-line

NBA, www.nba.com (July 27, 2004).
"Allen Iverson: I Always Wanted to Be a Sixer," *Sixers.com* www.nba.com/sixers/features/iverson_030924.html (July 27, 2004).
"Workout News and Notes," *Sixers.com* www.nba.com/sixers/summer_league/workouts_040702.html#iverson (July 27, 2004).

—Michael J. Watkins and Sara Pendergast

LeBron James

1984—

Professional basketball player

No player in the history of the National Basketball Association (NBA) has received so much attention so early in his career as LeBron James, the 18-year-old who was selected as number one draft pick by the Cleveland Cavaliers in the 2003 NBA draft. For James, however, this kind of attention was nothing new: ever since his freshman year in high school, James had been hailed as the next basketball superstar—the heir apparent to Michael Jordan, the retired Chicago Bulls star who many view as the best to play the game. The expectations facing James in his rookie year were immense: in Cleveland, he was viewed as a potential savior for a franchise that had struggled for years to reach the playoffs; in the NBA as a whole, he was greeted as a potential crossover marketing phenomenon who could spur sales of licensed products and tickets, and help polish the image of a league whose best young players made news as much for their legal court appearances as their play on the basketball court.

James took his first step toward realizing the expectations of many observers when he completed a successful first season in the NBA and was crowned the 'got milk?' Rookie of the Year in April of 2004. Statistically, the 6' 8", 240-pound forward placed in the top five among rookies in all the major categories: he led in steals at 1.65 per game; was second in scoring, behind Carmelo Anthony, with 20.9 points per game; placed third in assists, with 5.9 per game; and was fifth in rebounding, with 5.5 boards per game. He became just the third rookie ever to average more than 20 points, five rebounds, and five assists per game, joining legends Michael Jordan and Oscar Robertson. James led

Rookie of the Year voting, taking 78 first place votes to 40 for fellow phenom Carmelo Anthony. Most importantly to James himself—who is adamant that he is playing for his team, not his personal stats—he helped the Cavaliers more than double their victory totals from the previous year, though their 35-47 record did not earn a playoff berth.

Found Stability in Basketball

James was born on December 30, 1984, in Akron, Ohio. He never knew his biological father, who was reputed to be a stellar street-basketball player, and remains silent about him to this day. His mother, Gloria, gave birth to James when she was just 16 years old and became his biggest fan. "My mother is my everything. Always has been. Always will be," James told Jack McCallum of *Sports Illustrated*. James's devotion is announced to the world with the large tattoo on his arm: it reads "Gloria."

By all accounts, James did not have an easy upbringing. His mother switched jobs and houses often. When James was just five, they moved seven times. Due to the unstable environment, he missed large stretches of elementary school and spent two years living with a foster family. The most stable male influence in the athlete's life as a child was Gloria James's boyfriend, Eddie Jackson, who James sometimes refers to as his father. But Jackson was sentenced to three years in prison in 2002 for mail and mortgage fraud.

Toward the end of elementary school, James found a true stabilizing influence in his life: basketball. He and

At a Glance . . .

Born on December 30, 1984, in Akron, OH; son of Gloria James.

Career: Cleveland Cavaliers, OH, professional basketball player, 2003–.

Selected Awards: Cleveland *Plain Dealer*'s Player of the Year, 2001, 2002; Gatorade National Player of the Year, 2002; *USA Today* National Player of the Year, 2002; *Parade* Magazine Player of the Year, 2002, 2003; NBA got milk? Rookie of the Year, 2003-04.

Addresses: *Office*—c/o Cleveland Cavaliers/Gund Arena Company, One Center Court, Cleveland, Ohio 44115-4001.

his mother lived with basketball coach Frankie Walker for several years. By the time he was in eighth grade, his Amateur Athletic Union team went to the finals of the national tournament, and scouts began to notice that the young player from Akron had real talent. That talent brought James to the attention of coaches at St. Vincent-St. Mary high school in Akron, a private Catholic school, and James began attending the school in ninth grade. It was his time at St. Vincent-St. Mary that launched James on the road to stardom.

Became High School Superstar

James made an instant impact as a high school player. During his freshman year he led the St. Vincent-St. Mary Fighting Irish to a 27-0 record and the Ohio state basketball championship. James averaged 18 points a game. Things only improved in the years to come. In his sophomore year (2000-01), the Fighting Irish finished with a 26-1 record and took their second state championship in a row. James averaged 25.2 points, 7.2 rebounds, 5.8 assists, and 3.8 steals per game. The next year the team finished second in the state, but James's statistics improved to 29.0 points, 8.3 rebounds, 5.7 assists, and 3.3 steals per game. By the middle of his junior year, people began to speak of the prospects of James turning pro—before he even finished high school. His team began to play its games on college campuses to accommodate the overflow crowds coming to see the rising star. Just over 17 years old, LeBron James was quickly becoming a national celebrity.

Despite the hype that built up around James in his high school years, his mother and his advisors at school helped him stay grounded. "St. V's has been very good

for him," mother Gloria James told *USA Today*. "There's no messing around there, they're on the books and [the students] have to get good grades." She continued: "He goes to movies, loves Playstation, and gets good grades. He knows school work comes first: No work, no basketball." James was no one-sport wonder: he also played football for the Fighting Irish, earning all-state honors as a sophomore and helping his team make it to the state championship semifinals in his junior year. He was also, by his own accounts, a world-class consumer of Fruity Pebbles cereal. When he was turning pro and being offered endorsement deals, he joked to *Sports Illustrated*: Fruity Pebbles is "the endorsement I really want. Somebody gave me 10 boxes of it for [high school] graduation. Best present I got."

By his senior year, however, the hype was inescapable. National sports networks ESPN and ESPN2 began to provide coverage of games in which James played, and every Fighting Irish game was a sellout. The pressures of competing at this level led James and his family to make some questionable decisions. When James turned 18 during his senior year, his mother borrowed $80,000 to buy him a Hummer H2 sport utility vehicle, leading many to believe that he was receiving money improperly. That same year, Gloria James and Eddie Jackson borrowed over $100,000 to help finance travel for Jackson to negotiate shoe contracts for James; they were later sued by the businessman who loaned them the money. Ironically, the biggest trouble came when James accepted two vintage sports jerseys, valued at $845, from a Cleveland-area sports store. James was ruled ineligible for future play because the state forbids players from accepting compensation for performance. James immediately returned the jerseys, and he missed one game, but his eligibility was reinstated on appeal.

Despite the controversy surrounding his final season, James had his best year yet, averaging 31.6 points, 9.6 rebounds, 4.6 assists, and 3.4 steals per game. He led his team to its third state championship in four years, and *USA Today* crowned the team the high school national champions. Following that spectacular season, James made the rounds of the postseason all-star games, and he earned Most Valuable Player awards at the McDonald's High School All-American Game, the EA Sports Roundball Classic, and the Jordan Capital Classic. He was named the player of the year by several national organizations, and the *Sporting News* later called him "the nation's most-watched high school athlete ever." When he declared his eligibility for the NBA draft in the spring of 2003, observers knew that whichever team selected him would be getting someone special.

Drafted by Cleveland Cavaliers

The Cleveland Cavaliers "earned" the right to select first in the 2003 NBA draft after winning just 17 games in the 2002-03 season, and they did not hesitate in selecting James. Pressure built in the off season, as observers wondered how coach Paul Silas and the rest of the Cavaliers team would handle the presence of the heralded rookie. From the very beginning, James's play was solid. He scored 25 points in his debut, and on March 27, 2004, became the youngest player in NBA history to score more than 40 points in a game when he lit up New Jersey for 41 points. By season's end he averaged 20.9 points per game while playing forward and sometimes guard.

Fans, coaches, players, and sportswriters loaded James with accolades for his rookie performance. Indiana Pacers coach Rick Carlisle told the *Sporting News:* "Some of the things he is doing out there are just breathtaking. He makes plays we have not seen anybody make since Jordan in terms of pure strength and athletic ability and hanging and seeing things and finishing." Numbers produced by the Cavaliers bear out this observation. Strength and conditioning coach Stan Kellers told *Sports Illustrated* that the team tests players on vertical jump, strength, agility, body fat and speed, and rates them on a scale of one to five. But, says Kellers, "LeBron's a six." Teammate Carlos Boozer lauded James for unselfish play, noting that James often gives up a basket to feed the ball to his teammates. "When he gets the ball," Boozer told the *Sporting News,* "you better have your hands up and ready and make yourself available because he is going to find you." Such praise helped earn James the Eddie Gottlieb Trophy as the got milk? Rookie of the Year in for the 2003/04 season.

There are those who have been more cautious in their estimation of the rookie sensation. Michael Jordan told *Ebony* that James has "unbelievable potential, but he hasn't played against the competition consistently in college or the pros.... Five years from now,...he can definitely be a good pro." James himself seems to recognize that he has to pay his dues before he can raise to the top ranks of the NBA. "I don't want to be a cocky rookie coming in trying to lead right off the bat," James told *Sports Illustrated.* "I'm going to lead more by example.... If there's one message I want to get to my teammates it's that I'll be there for them, do whatever they think I need to do."

Already, James has become a marketing phenomenon. His $10.8 million, three-year contract with the Cavaliers amounts to peanuts besides the more than $100 million in endorsement contracts he has signed with Nike, Sprite, Powerade, Upper Deck cards, and Bub-

blicious bubble gum (his agent is still working on Fruity Pebbles). Assessing the rush to get James to endorse their products, Cavaliers coach Paul Silas told *Sports Illustrated:* "I've been around the game for 40 years, and I've never seen anything like it. It's scary." For the corporations, however, James seems like a good risk. Unlike some of his fellow NBA players, James appears to be a solid citizen. He speaks well of teammates, takes time to sign autographs, is respectful of the history of the game, and—most importantly—has not had any brushes with the law like high profile players Kobe Bryant and Allan Iverson. Even more importantly, he appears to have unlimited potential as an athlete. For now, his team, his fans, and some major corporations are all invested in the idea that LeBron James is the next big thing.

Sources

Books

Jones, Ryan, *King James: Believe the Hype,* St. Martin's Press, 2003.
Morgan, David Lee, *LeBron James,* Gray & Co., 2003.
A Tribute to LeBron James, Beckett/Statabase, 2003.

Periodicals

Basketball Digest, March-April 2004, p. 26.
Ebony, June 2003, p. 174; January 2004, p. 124.
Sporting News, July 23, 2001, p. 60; February 10, 2003, p. 72; June 2, 2003, p. 60; July 14, 2003, p. 16; October 20, 2003, p. 40; November 17, 2003, p. 22.
Sports Illustrated, February 18, 2002, p. 62; February 10, 2003, p. 37; October 27, 2003, p. 68.
USA Today, November 28, 2001, p. 3C; December 13, 2002, p. 3C; May 7, 2002.

On-line

"LeBron James," *NBA,* www.nba.com/playerfile/lebron_james/ (July 21, 2004).
LeBron James, www.lebronjames.com (July 21, 2004).
"LeBron Watch," *Cleveland.com,* www.cleveland.com/lebron/ (July 21, 2004).

—Tom Pendergast

Marianne Jean-Baptiste

1967—

Actress

In 1997 Marianne Jean-Baptiste became the first black British actor nominated for an Academy Award. Her performance in 1996's *Secrets and Lies* earned her the nomination for best supporting actress, and though she did not take an Oscar home, her performance in the film by renowned director Mike Leigh brought glowing critical accolades and assured her future success. Jean-Baptiste, however, does not limit her career to acting alone; she is also an accomplished singer and composer.

Jean-Baptiste was relatively unknown even in England when she was named an Oscar contender, partly because *Secrets and Lies* was one of her first film roles. Until that point, her career as an actress had been spent mainly in the theater. The youngest of the four Jean-Baptiste children, she was born in London on April 26, 1967, and grew up in the city as well. An aptitude for music surfaced at a young age, and she began playing the guitar at the age of eight. As a youngster, she was told that she could pursue any career choice she wished, as long as she excelled. "My parents taught me to place importance on family," Jean-Baptiste told *Women's Wear Daily* reporter Elizabeth Gladfeller. "Appearances weren't emphasized necessarily, but they did make an impression," she added. For a time, she considered studying for a law degree and becoming a barrister.

Instead Jean-Baptiste became sidetracked by her love of the performing arts. She earned a degree from the prestigious Royal Academy of Dramatic Arts in London, and began appearing in roles on the stage of London's Royal National Theater; she also was cast in productions in the English cities of Manchester and Yorkshire. For a time Jean-Baptiste was a member of the Cheek by Jowl Company, and once played two roles in one work, both Mariana and Mistress Overdone in *Measure for Measure*. Other stage credits include *Running Dream* at the Theater Royal Stratford, and *Ave Africa*, which Jean-Baptiste both wrote and performed.

Jean-Baptiste's first screen role was in the 1991 Hanif Kureishi film *London Kills Me*, the story of homeless teens living in London's subway system. In 1993 she appeared back on the London stage in *It's a Great Big Shame*. The play was written by stage and screen director Mike Leigh—known for his quirky, intense portraits of modern England and its class differences—and collaboration with his cast plays an integral part in Leigh's oeuvre. In the play, Jean-Baptiste played Faith, the sister in a lower-middle-class family in *London's East End*; the play contrasted the modern-day lives of her family with their apartment's nineteenth-century inhabitants. Her character, wrote Ian Buruma in the *New York Review of Books*, "clucking with disdain and parroting the language of advertising brochures, was the perfect example of a developed Leigh character."

For her next project with Leigh, Jean-Baptiste was asked to consider this premise: a black woman looks into her adoption records and discovers her birth mother was white. She then seeks her out, and her biological parent is equally astonished. Jean-Baptiste's development of this character into *Secrets and Lies*'s Hortense Cumberbatch centered around the tragicomic possibilities that surface when the lives of a

At a Glance . . .

Born on April 26, 1967, in London, England; married Evan Williams; children: one. *Education:* Royal Academy of Dramatic Arts, London, England.

Career: Actor, singer, composer, 1991–.

middle-class, educated black woman and a vulgar, chain-smoking factory worker connect. The concept behind Jean-Baptiste's first major screen role was something that had been in the works for some time, she said in an interview with *Cinemania Online's* Sheila Benson. "Mike Leigh was sort of saying, every year, 'Would she look for her mother?' And I would say, 'No,'" the actress said, referring to her Hortense character. "So he killed her father off, and he asked again. And I said, 'Of course not, because her mum's on her own, it would be even worse.' So he killed her off as well, and said, 'Now, would she look?' And I said, 'All right, now she'd look,'" she continued.

Secrets and Lies's Hortense Cumberbatch is an optometrist and the epitome of the sleek and fashionable young urban European woman. When she begins thinking about having a child of her own after her foster parents pass on, she becomes curious about her real heritage. She tracks down her birth mother—whom she already knows is of a different race—and by telephone arranges to meet with her. Leigh's actors work with just a skeleton of the script, then develop the characters in workshop-type rehearsals. Initially they work one on one with Leigh, and later move to an ensemble format, but Jean-Baptiste and Brenda Blethyn, the actress who played her birth mother, had not met until the day shooting was scheduled for their first scene together outside a London Underground station. Blethyn had noticed Jean-Baptiste's name on the cast list, but did not know she was black—nearly the same experience of her character Cynthia, who in the film receives a telephone call from a well- spoken young woman wishing to meet her. When the two characters met, Blethyn assumed Jean-Baptiste was part of the film crew. "So when Cynthia says there has been some mistake, that was my honest reaction," Blethyn told *Time* film critic Richard Corliss. "It wasn't acting," she added.

After the initial shock at discovery, the film tracks the unlikely mother-daughter pair as they begin to enrich one another's lives: Jean-Baptiste's Hortense remedies some of the squalor in Cynthia's life, and finds herself part of a highly dysfunctional new family; eventually Cynthia's "secret" that was the source of so many "lies" is revealed. The movie debuted to British audiences in 1995 and the following year in North America, winning laudatory reviews on both sides of the Atlantic. Critics lauded Jean-Baptiste's cool, understatedly el-

egant portrayal of Hortense, and she herself had selected the clothes that emphasized her character's educated, middle-class status, in dramatic contrast to the loud, working- class chaos of Cynthia's household. "All the actors are so convincing that *Secrets and Lies* often seems like a documentary," wrote Joseph Cuneen in the *National Catholic Reporter.*

Secrets and Lies took home the Palme d'Or at Cannes Film Festival, and the following year Jean-Baptiste was nominated for both a Golden Globe and an Academy Award. "People are talking about the race issue in the film, of which there is none," Jean-Baptiste said in the *Cinemania Online* interview. "It's about adoption. It's about a mother and a daughter. The bigger issue here is that these people here are related. We do, sort of, judge people by the way they dress or the way they appear. But I don't think we should. Hortense doesn't. She's an optometrist and that isn't a coincidence. It's somebody who looks deep into other people, who has real insights, who helps other people see clearly," she continued.

Jean-Baptiste followed the success of *Secrets and Lies* with a steady stream of work. She told *Essence* that "In the States it's much easier to get work once you have an Oscar nomination." Although none of the works she appeared in matched the critical acclaim of *Secrets and Lies,* Jean-Baptiste has drawn more praise for her individual work. "Superior," *Library Journal* reviewer Danna Bell-Russel said of Jean-Baptist's portrayal of Stephen Lawrence's mother in *The Murder of Stephen Lawrence,* a fictionalized account of an actual murder. Although *Variety* critic panned *Women in Film* as an "overwritten, patronizing piece of pseudo-feminist flatulence," he praised Jean-Baptiste's performance for being "better than the material." For her work as part of the dramatic ensemble in the television series "Without a Trace," she was nominated for a Screen Actors Guild Award in 2004. In addition to her acting work, Jean-Baptiste is a talented musician. She wrote and sang four songs on British jazz musician Jason Rebello's 1993 album, *Keeping Time,* and composed the score for Michael Leigh's 1997 film, *Career Girls.*

Selected works

Films

London Kills Me, 1991.
Secrets & Lies, 1996.
Mr. Jealousy, 1997.
How to Make the Cruelest Month, 1998.
Nowhere to Go, 1998.
The 24 Hour Woman, 1999.
28 Days, 2000.
The Cell, 2000.
Women in Film, 2001.
New Year's Day, 2001.
Spy Game, 2001.
Don't Explain, 2002.

Television

The Wedding, 1998.
The Man, 1999.
The Murder of Stephen Lawrence, 1999.
Men Only 2001.
"Without a Trace" (series), 2002.
Loving You, 2003.

Other

(Contributed) *Keeping Time* (jazz album), 1993.
(Wrote musical score) *Career Girls* (film), 1997.

Sources

Periodicals

America, November 9, 1996, p. 22.
Entertainment Weekly, October 18, 1996, p. 58; May 2, 1997, p. 68.

Essence, December 2003, p. 146.
Jet, March 3, 1997, p. 64.
Library Journal, September 15, 2002, p. 106.
Nation, October 7, 1996, p. 34.
National Catholic Reporter, January 17, 1997, p. 18.
New York Review of Books, January 13, 1994, pp. 7-11.
Newsweek, September 30, 1996, p. 74.
Time, September 30, 1996, p. 66.
Variety, February 19, 2001, p. 46.
Vibe, September 1997.
Women's Wear Daily, August 7, 1997, p. S2.

Other

Additional information for this profile was provided by a *Cinemania Online* interview with Sheila Benson.

—Carol Brennan and Sara Pendergast

Fergie Jenkins

1943—

Professional baseball player

Jenkins, Fergie, photograph. Rich Pilling/Getty Images.

"Pitchers are a breed apart...," wrote Eliot Asinof in a *Time* biography of pitching great Fergie Jenkins. "They are special, and they know it. Ferguson Jenkins was the perfect pitcher." Over 19 baseball seasons, the three-time All-Star finished with a record of 284 wins and 226 losses, despite pitching at home in some of baseball's hitters' ballparks, including Wrigley Field in Chicago and Fenway Park in Boston. Jenkin's unprecedented combination of 3,000-plus strikeouts and less than 1,000 walks made him one of baseball's most controlled finesse pitchers.

The six-foot-five, 200-pound right-hander joined Major League Baseball's elite early in his career and was lauded by baseball fans in the United States and Canada after his retirement in 1983. The first Canadian elected to the National Baseball Hall of Fame in Cooperstown, New York, Jenkins also became Commissioner of the newly formed Canadian Baseball League (CBL) in 2003.

Developed Pitching Talent

Ferguson Jenkins, Jr. was born in Chatham, Ontario,

on December 13, 1943. His mother went blind during the birth. His father, Ferguson Arthur Jenkins, Sr., was a talented baseball player but "born too early to break the organized-baseball color line," observed Asinof. A well-rounded athlete—he played hockey, soccer, basketball, track, and swam—the younger Jenkins adored baseball most. Asinof reported that as a youth Jenkins practiced his pitching by "throwing chunks of coal at open doors of passing freight cars 100 feet away."

Philadelphia Phillies scout Gene Dziadura took notice of Jenkins's game after watching the lanky teen play in a local Chatham league. According to a 1991 *Maclean's* article, Jenkins began "a regimen of splitting firewood...even though his parents' home had no fireplace" after Dziadura advised him to build his upper body. In 1961, Jenkins signed a $7,500 contract with Philadelphia. He worked on improving his game with the club's minor league team for three-and-a-half seasons before joining the Phillies for the first time in 1965 as a relief pitcher. He took the mound seven times that season, performing well. Nevertheless, the Phillies traded him to the Chicago Cubs early in the 1966 season.

At a Glance . . .

Born Ferguson Arthur Jenkins on December 13, 1943, in Chatham, Ontario, Canada; married Kathy Williams, 1965 (divorced); married Maryanne (died 1991); married Lydia Farrington, 1993; children: Kelly, Delores, Kimberly, Raymond (stepson), Samantha (died 1993).

Career: Philadelphia Phillies (National League), professional baseball player, 1965-66; Chicago Cubs (National League), professional baseball player, 1966-73, 1982-83; Texas Rangers (American League), professional baseball player, 1974-75, 1978-81; Boston Red Sox (American League), professional baseball player, 1976-77. Team Canada, pitching coach for Pan-Am Games, 1987; Texas Rangers (Oklahoma City 89ers minor league team), pitching coach, 1988-89; Cincinnati Reds, roving minor league coach, 1992-93; Chicago Cubs, minor league coach, 1995-96; Canadian Baseball League, commissioner, 2003–.

Membership: Major League Baseball Players Alumni Association

Awards: National League All-Star, 1967, 1971, 1972; *Sporting News* National League Pitcher of the Year, 1971; Lou March Trophy, 1971; Cy Young Award, 1971; inducted into Canadian Baseball Hall of Fame, 1987; inducted into National Baseball Hall of Fame, 1991.

Addresses: *Office*—The Fergie Jenkins Foundation Inc., 3280 Schmon Pkwy, Thorold, Ontario L2V 4Y6, Canada; *Web site*—www.cmgww.com/baseball/jenkins/index.php.

Cubs manager Leo Durocher soon made Jenkins a starter. According to *Maclean's*, Durocher called Jenkins "one of the best pitchers in baseball, ever." Durocher's hunch regarding Jenkins's pitching potential was proven when Jenkins struck out six of the American League's greatest hitters in the 1967 All-Star game, including Mickey Mantle, Harmon Killebrew, Rod Carew, Jim Fregosi, and Tony Oliva. Cubs catcher Randy Hundley praised Jenkins as "a dominant pitcher I could have caught with a pair of pliers." According to an article found on Jenkins's official Web site, written by Darl DeVault, Hundley said, "[Jenkins's] location was near perfect, and he could blow his fastball by

hitters, although sometimes we didn't agree on the sign."

Leading the National League in starts in 1968, 1969, and 1971, and in completed games in 1970 and 1971, Jenkins's talent was showcased with the Cubs, bringing his pitching prowess to the attention of baseball fans across America. DeVault wrote, "Jenkins proved to be a power-pitching, durable, consistent strikeout artist for many years to come by mentally charting batters' tendencies and devising a game plan to get them out." Jenkins led the National League in strikeouts in 1969 with 273, and he set the Cubs strikeout record in 1970 with 274.

Dominated in Two Leagues

Jenkins told DeVault that he never considered pitching work. The competition was a thrill for him. "From '67 through '75 there were a lot of premier pitchers performing in the major leagues, such as Don Drysdale, Jim Palmer, Juan Marichal, Bob Gibson, and Tom Seaver," Jenkins told DeVault. "Beginning a series I always wanted to start against the number-one pitcher on the opposing ball club, even if it meant pitching with only two or three days rest."

Jenkins began a streak of more than 20 wins a season for six consecutive years. He would have seven total 20-win seasons. While with the National League Cubs, Jenkins proved an effective batter. In 1971, the year Jenkins became the first Cub to capture the Cy Young award for best Major League pitcher, he batted .243, including six homers and 20 RBIs. DeVault speculated in his 2004 biographical article on Jenkins, "Since today's pitchers start fewer games with five-man rotations, and managers depend on their bullpens more, Jenkins will likely be the last pitcher to put a six-year, 20-game win streak together." Asinof summed up Jenkins's baseball savvy this way: "Statistics have always been the sportswriters' measure of a ballplayer. But Jenkins's special talents take him beyond the stats. There was a purity to his pitching, often described as water flowing from a glass. He had pinpoint control of his 90-m.p.h. fastball and was always ahead of the count."

Jenkins was traded to the Texas Rangers before the 1974 season, after a rare losing season with the Cubs. He posted 25 wins during his first season as a Ranger, becoming the first 20-win pitcher in a Rangers' uniform. "It was an outstanding year with Billy Martin managing the Rangers and great rookies hitting the ball well," Jenkins reported to DeVault. "Fortunately for me, they also played some great defense helping me win 25 games that year." *The Sporting News* voted Jenkins the American League's Comeback Pitcher of the Year for 1974. He played two seasons with the Rangers, falling to 17-18 in 1975, before he was traded to the Boston Red Sox. After two seasons with the Red Sox, where he threw inconsistently, Jenkins was traded back to the Rangers, where he played for four more seasons.

Following the 1981 season he became a free agent and signed with the Cubs, determined to improve his game. In 1982, he became the seventh Major League pitcher to notch 3,000 career strikeouts. When he retired in 1983, Jenkins had posted 49 career shutouts.

Revered in Canada Despite Missteps

Though Jenkins played for teams in the United States, Canadian sports fans took notice of Jenkins's achievements in baseball. Canadian sports writers named him the Canadian Press Male Athlete of the Year four times between 1967 and 1974. And in 1974, Jenkins became the first baseball player to be awarded the Lou March Trophy, an annual honor recognizing Canada's top athlete.

Jenkins won more Canadian than American sports awards, a point of controversy among baseball commentators who believe that Jenkins ought to have won more than one Cy Young award. Jenkins admitted to DeVault that he felt his stats made him a terrific Cy Young candidate during several seasons, but he often pitched for mediocre teams. "I am grateful to have won my Cy Young Award, and to make the top three in balloting five times," he said, "but it was hard to figure out the voting some years. I sometimes had a better season than the guys who won in my time, but they had starred in postseason the years before. Maybe the writers voted for pitchers who had good seasons who they saw bask in the spotlight of pennant races and the World Series. Unfortunately, I never got to do that, so my Cy Young chances suffered."

In 1980, Jenkins was convicted of cocaine possession after being found with three grams in his suitcase at Toronto International Airport. Fortunately for Jenkins, a judge—who described Jenkins as "a person who has conducted himself in exemplary fashion in the community and the country"—declared his criminal record wiped-clean. But the incident became a cloud shadowing Jenkins's otherwise golden reputation as a player and person. The incident delayed Jenkins's induction into the Baseball Hall of Fame at Cooperstown, New York, which came in 1991. He had become the first unanimous inductee into the Canadian Baseball Hall of Fame in 1987. Jenkins was eligible for the Cooperstown Hall in 1989, and thought to be a shoe-in by many sports commentators, given his superior record on the mound. While some sports writers admitted to overlooking Jenkins in 1989 and 1990, perhaps unconsciously because he was a rather modest and subdued baseball hero, others charged the lack of votes to a bias against Jenkins for his conviction for drug possession. The exclusion of Jenkins and Gaylord Perry for the 1989 induction did not go unnoticed by many observers, including Peter Gammons of *Sports Illustrated,* who wrote in a January, 1989, article,

"Jenkins and Perry would have been locks for Cooperstown if they had been judged as Ruth, Drysdale and Ford were—simply on the basis of performance." Incidentally, Perry and Jenkins were, respectively, the third and fourth pitchers to win more than 100 games in both the American and National leagues.

After agreeing to a pitching coach position for the Texas Rangers minor-league team, the Oklahoma City 89ers in 1988, Jenkins sold his 100-acre farm in Blenheim, Ontario, near Chatham, and settled on a 300-acre ranch in Guthrie, Oklahoma, where he bred and raised Appaloosa horses and hunting dogs. "After playing in big cities, I found that going to the country and relaxing was good therapy," Jenkins told *Time*'s Kevin C. Bias in 2003. "As a pitcher your job is to be intimidating. When the off-season comes, you try to be laid-back." Following his retirement from pitching in 1983, Jenkins occupied himself with family and with coaching for several more clubs, including the Reds and Cubs, as well as for Team Canada in its competition in the 1987 Pan Am Games.

Endured Tragedy to Serve Baseball

Three days after Jenkins's induction into the Hall of Fame in 1991, his wife Maryanne died from injuries sustained in a car accident a few weeks earlier. "It took a while to grasp that I was left without a partner," Jenkins told *Maclean's* in July of 1991. "I had thought that Maryanne and I would be around together for a long while, and maybe have some more children." They had an infant daughter at the time, Samantha.

The tragedy did not end there. In February of 1993, only days after Jenkins accepted a pitching coach position with the Cincinnati Reds, Jenkins's girlfriend, Cindy Takieddine, took her life and that of Jenkins's three-year-old daughter by carbon monoxide poisoning. According to *Jet,* in his first public appearance since the murder-suicide, Jenkins told an audience at a Chicago Cubs convention, "There's moments when you just can't cope with (the tragedy), and you go back to your room, try to relax and try to control yourself. But I'm not the only one who had to suffer through pressures, so I don't feel like I'm alone in the situation." Jenkins likely benefited from counseling he received as a member of a bereaved parents support group, which he joined shortly after the loss of Samantha. "You have to talk these things out," Jenkins told *Maclean's* in 1998. "Life's a lot brighter for me now." Jenkins then sought reassignment to a position of minor-league roving instructor, citing his determination to remain close to his 12-year-old stepson, Raymond. Later in 1993, Jenkins married his third wife, Lydia.

During the 1990s and early twenty-first century, Jenkins frequently appeared on baseball broadcasts on American and Canadian television and radio programs for interviews. He also served as a color analyst for Major League games. In 1999, the Society for American Baseball Research selected Jenkins as one of the top 100 baseball players of the twentieth century.

Since the 1990s, Jenkins has been a committed activist for the promotion and preservation of baseball. In 1992 Jenkins helped found the Oklahoma Sports Museum. He spent hours at the museum, running clinics and speaking to youngsters about baseball and about the perils of drug and alcohol use. He also tapped into his sports-world connections to acquire items for the museum's displays. In August of 2002 he wrote a letter (which can be found on Jenkins's official Web site) to the Major League Baseball commissioner arguing against the disparities in income available to teams and about the stifling impact this has had on competition. The best players gravitate to the wealthiest clubs, Jenkins observed, leaving many teams with no chance to win a pennant. "The lack of parity is killing the game," Jenkins wrote, "because fans want to watch talented players display their skills and have a chance to win in every game they start." Jenkins urged that teams stop salary dumping and that the league cease team expansion. Jenkins also advised the league to test players for performance-enhancing drugs three times a year.

In 2003, Jenkins moved from his ranch in Oklahoma to one in Arizona. Retired from playing and coaching, Jenkins continued to dedicate himself to charitable works and to the promotion of the game he loves. The Fergie Jenkins Foundation, headquartered in Thorold, Ontario, raises money for several charitable organizations, including the Canadian Red Cross, the Special Olympics, the Canadian National Institute for the Blind, CRIED-Abused Women's Program, and several children's camps. As the first commissioner of the Canadian Baseball League (CBL), beginning in 2003, Jenkins sought to encourage young Canadians to pick up the game he has loved. "We need to get kids back into the game," he told Asinof. "The Canadian Base-

ball League offers them a chance to play a good brand of ball in a good baseball environment." The winner of the CBL championship will receive a trophy named the Jenkins Cup, after one of Canada's most beloved baseball heroes.

Selected writings

(With Dave Fisher) *Inside Pitching,* NTC Contemporary Publishing, 1972.
(As told to George Vass) *Like Nobody Else: The Fergie Jenkins Story,* NTC Contemporary Publishing, 1973.
(With Stanely Pashko) *Ferguson Jenkins: The Quiet Winner,* Putnam, 1975.
(With Dorothy Turcotte) *The Game Is Easy—Life Is Hard: The Story of Ferguson Jenkins, Jr.,* The Fergie Jenkins Foundation, 2003.

Sources

Periodicals

Jet, February 8, 1993, p. 48.
Maclean's, July 8, 1991, p. 42; September 14, 1998, p. 9.
Sports Illustrated, June 23, 1989, p. 78; January 21, 2001, p. 10; June 9, 2003, p. 12.
Time, June 20, 2003, p. 56.

On-line

Fergie Jenkins, www.cngww.com/baseball/jenkins/index.php (May 19, 2004).
"Ferguson Jenkins," *Baseball Library,* www.baseballlibrary.com/baseballlibrary/ballplayers/J/Jenkins_Ferguson.stm (May 19, 2004).

—Melissa Walsh

Bill T. Jones

1952—

Dancer, choreographer

Bill T. Jones is one of America's premiere choreographers and dancers. His innovative work has established a growing following and earned excellent reviews. Jones' esteem in the dance world is founded on his collaboration with Arnie Zane. From the early 1970s until Zane's death in 1988, Jones and Zane worked closely together, creating award-winning modern dances. Soon after Zane's death, Jones created an extraordinary dance called *Absence,* which evoked the memory of his late partner and lover, and addresses the varied feelings associated with bereavement. Zane's death is only one of the many subjects with which the choreographer and his troupe have wrestled; Jones said in *People* that "a dance can come from my fears about aging or about the betrayal of the environment. I just want this funky company to say, 'Yeah, life hurts like hell, but this is how I keep going. I have a sense of humor. I've got my brothers and sisters. I've got this ability to make something out of nothing. I can clap my hands and make magic.'"

Fell in Love with Dance

Jones was born William Tass Jones, the tenth of his parents' twelve children, on February 12, 1952. His parents were migrant workers and moved frequently between Florida and New York to find harvesting work. Jones became a star high school athlete in New York, where he also gained valuable early stage experience and became an award-winning amateur actor. As a student at the State University of New York in Binghamton, Jones began to question his artistic direction and sexual orientation. He told *People:* "A lot of things were changing in my life, one of which was meeting Arnie and starting my first relationship with a man. I didn't feel comfortable being a jock anymore, and the theater department was too conservative for me. So dance reared its beautiful head." Soon after their introduction Jones and Zane traveled together to Amsterdam, where they lived for several years before returning to New York, where they formed the American Dance Asylum with Lois Welk in 1973. That troupe performed—completely naked—to great local acclaim. Jones and Zane would manage, nonetheless, to avoid the predictability that early success often creates. Throughout the 1970s, the Jones performed throughout the world as a soloist as well as in duets with Zane and others.

In 1982 Jones and Zane formed another dance troupe; the new group, however, was immediately accused of selling out because they had created what *New York* magazine described as "big, splashy spectacles in which outrageousness or fashion, of social and political attitudes—melded blithely with earlier formalist concerns." Most critics, though, agreed that the troupe's progressiveness in both subject and execution demanded serious attention. *Interview* called the Jones/Zane troupe "one of the freshest and most innovative modern dance troupes in the world," relating how at "their breakthrough performance at the Brooklyn Academy of Music's Next Wave Festival in 1982, when they performed with jazz drummer Max Roach, [they] reinvented the language of movement."

At a Glance . . .

Born William Tass Jones in February 15, 1952, in Bunnell, Florida; raised in Florida and Wayland, NY; son of migrant laborers. *Education:* Attended the State University of New York at Binghamton, 1971(?).

Career: Dancer and choreographer, 1970–, American Dance Asylum, cofounder with Lois Welk, 1973, Bill T. Jones/Arnie Zane dance company, cofounder with Arnie Zane, 1982.

Selected Awards: New York Dance and Performance "Bessie" Award, 1989 and 2001; Dorothy B. Chandler Performing Arts Award, 1991; MacArthur Fellowship, 1994; Dance Heritage Coalition named Bill T. Jones one of America's Irreplaceable Dance Treasures, 2000; Dorothy and Lillian Gish Prize, 2003.

Addresses: *Office*—Foundation for Dance Promotion, 853 Broadway, Suite 1706, New York, New York 10003.

The dance company's future hung in the balance when Zane became ill in the mid-1980s. Jones feared that making Zane's illness public might adversely effect their funding, but Zane insisted on going public in hope of educating people about AIDS. By refiguring Zane's health issues as artistic material, the troupe began exploring the emotional and physical impact of AIDS in its dances. "Living and dying is not the big issue," Jones told the *MacNeil/Lehrer Report* in 1987, as reported in *People.* "The big issue is what you're going to do with your time while you're here. I [am] determined to perform." Zane's death in 1988 was reflected in dances of loss, grieving, anger, and ultimately, acceptance. The company encountered financial problems that year, partly because of Zane's inability to dance. *People* recounted that "the troupe toured less and less often and nearly declared bankruptcy in 1988 but was saved by a group of artist friends who sold their works to raise $100,000."

The company pulled together to support Jones emotionally after Zane's death, again using dance as a catalyst for their grief. The piece *Absence* was composed by Zane to depict the poignancy of a dancer who has lost a partner of many years. Jones called up the memory of Zane by sometimes seeming out of balance on stage, lacking a counterweight, and then pausing forgetfully for his partner's steps. Critic Robert Jones responded in *People* to a 1989 performance of *Absence;* he described "a shimmering, ecstatic quality that

was euphoric and almost unbearably moving." Tobi Tobias, dance critic for *New York,* said that the work took "its shape from Zane's special loves: still images and highly wrought, emotion-saturated vocal music." When another troupe member fell ill with AIDS soon after Zane's death, Jones choreographed *D-Man in the Waters,* which depicted dancers struggling with fateful tides.

Created Heartening Dances

Triumphs for the troupe after these painful losses included a premiere at the Houston Grand Opera in the fall of 1989 and a debut at the Munich Opera Festival in 1990. Like *Absence,* Jones's next important piece, *Last Supper at Uncle Tom's Cabin,* was inspired partly by Zane—conflict was still a theme, but not strictly as an effect of death. In the *New York Times* Jones explained the origins of *Last Supper at Uncle Tom's:* "I think of Harriet Beecher Stowe's novel as a wonderful liberal tract. Arnie Zane and I were talking about the Last Supper a couple of months before he died, and the idea of the Last Supper at Uncle Tom's Cabin sort of started as a joke. After Arnie died, I began to look more closely at the idea. There is so much about people being torn from each other and people in pursuit of each other and with the kind of robust athletic partnering that we do, I think we'll produce something quite evocative."

The subjects in conflict are meant to be resolved in the course of *Last Supper at Uncle Tom's Cabin,* which is divided into distinct parts. The opening section of the dance is a fast-paced summation of Stowe's book about slavery, using nontraditional casting, mime, and masks to emphasize the role-playing and absurdity of slavery. The next portion is a series of four solos by women, who in turn present the troubles of a slave, a battered woman, a lesbian, and a prostitute. Jones then dances a solo portrait of Job, the biblical character ravaged by misfortune as a test of his faith in God. Next, the biblical reference to Job becomes a tableau of the Last Supper. The final part of the dance is presented by an enlarged troupe—the core company, joined by others, "stages a sixties love-in," as it was termed in *New York.* "It's amazing how this sort of cheaply sentimental catharsis can still get to you," the magazine ventured.

Tobias took a broad view of Jones's choreography for *Last Supper at Uncle Tom's Cabin.* "Dance is not, primarily, what it's about. In genre, it's a multimedia extravaganza. Although there's plenty of movement—vibrant solos in an eclectic vocabulary, sternly patterned group work—someone's usually talking at the same time…. [It is a] work bristling with anger, energy, and provocative questions, but one apparently still 'in progress.'" Commenting to Tobias, Jones said of the work, "This piece must start as a fight and end as a huge song." It remains a testimony to his ongoing commitment to take life's jumbled and troubled experiences and make them meaningful and beautiful through his art.

Blended Life with Art

For some critics, Jones's art does not separate itself enough from real life. Jones, who has been HIV-positive since 1985, held a series of workshops with other HIV- and AIDS-infected people. In 1999 he created *Still Here* blending dance with commentary and video clips from the workshop participants. *New Yorker* dance critic Arlene Croce panned the piece without viewing it as "victim art." But *Still Here* captured the hearts of many; to present it to national and international audiences, Jones worked with others to make it into a television documentary. The making of it also became a television presentation entitled "Bill T. Jones: Still/Here with Bill Moyers," for the Public Broadcasting Station in 1997.

In celebration of the twentieth anniversary of the Bill T. Jones/Arnie Zane Dance Company, the troupe created The Phantom Project. The Project began as an attempt to represent the creative output of the company over its twenty-year history, however, the retrospective of Jones's and Zane's work created a unique situation because neither had concerned themselves with the lasting images or impressions of their work; they were always looking to the future, to their next creation. Jones remarked on the company's Web site that "Because our choreographic and theatrical investigation has been broad and evolutionary, any attempt to retrieve a work from the past is like trying to evoke a phantom." The phantom-like qualities came from the elusiveness of the mindset of the choreographers when they created the dances, the context of the times in which the dances were performed, and the physical presence of the dancers themselves. Recreating these qualities was difficult and sometimes impossible, especially since some of the dances had only been performed by Jones and Zane. The anniversary season performances began in New York City in 2003 and would travel throughout the country and the world in 2004.

But as the Phantom Project and documentaries, and even Jones's memoirs celebrated the collaboration between Jones and Zane, Jones has continued to create fresh, new performances for himself as a soloist and for others as well. For his artistic output as an individual, the Dance Heritage Coalition honored Jones in 2000 as an "irreplaceable dance treasure." In 2003 he won the Dorothy and Lillian Gish Award for his artistic contributions to dance. Bill T. Jones continues to dance and create dances that thrill and challenge audiences around the world.

Selected works

Books

Last Night on Earth (memoirs), Pantheon Books, 1995.
Dance (children's book), Hyperion, 1998.

Dances

Pas de Deux for Two, 1973.
Absence, 1989.
D-Man in the Water, 1989.
Last Supper at Uncle Tom's Cabin/The Promised Land, 1991.
Still Here, 1994.
The Table Project, 2001.
The Phantom Project, 2003.

Sources

Books

Body Against Body: The Dance and Other Collaborations of Bill T. Jones and Arnie Zane, Station Hill Press, 1989.

Periodicals

Interview, March 1989.
Los Angeles Times, September 23, 2001.
New York, January 5, 1987; September 10, 1990; November 26, 1990.
New York Times, December 31, 1989; January 27, 2002.
People, July 31, 1989.
Village Voice, August 5, 2002.
Washington Post, June 20, 2000.

On-line

Bill T. Jones / Arnie Zane Dance Company, www.billtjones.org (July 26, 2004).

Television

"Uncle Tom's Cabin/The Promised Land" (Great Performances television series), PBS, 1992.
"Bill T. Jones: Still/Here with Bill Moyers," PBS, 1997.
"I'll Make Me a World: A Century of African American Artists," Blackside, 1999.
"Free To Dance: The Presence of African-Americans in Modern Dance," PBS, 2001.

—Christine Ferran and Sara Pendergast

Ed "Too Tall" Jones

1951—

Professional football player

Standing six-feet, nine-inches tall, defensive lineman Ed "Too Tall" Jones came by his nickname honestly. As a boy he dreamed of becoming a basketball player, and as an adult he spent a year pursuing a career in boxing. But Jones won acclaim for his role in the Dallas Cowboys' defensive line-up during the 1970s and 1980s, playing for a record 15 years. During the course of his career, he played in three Super Bowls and three Pro Bowls, recorded 57-1/2 sacks, and appeared in 224 games with 203 starts. "In his prime, Ed 'Too Tall' Jones was known as a big hitter," wrote John Chase in the *Daily Herald*. The "Dallas Cowboys defensive lineman struck fear in those lined up on the other side of the ball just seconds before he plowed them over on his way to the quarterback."

Jones was born on February 23, 1951, in Jackson, Tennessee. In high school he played basketball and received 52 offers for college scholarships, but he decided to stay closer to home and play football for the Tennessee State Tigers. He soon discovered that he was a natural, and over the next three years he only played in one losing game. Jones also received his nickname at Tennessee State when a teammate, noting that his football pants were too short, told him he was "too tall for football." His performance at Tennessee State caught the eye of the Dallas Cowboys' recruiting staff, and in 1974 Jones became the number one pick in the NFL draft. "I heard rumors," Jones would later recall to Jean-Jacques Taylor in the *Dallas Morning News*, "but I didn't believe it because I was an underweight defensive lineman from a small school." Jones

also sang in a band at Tennessee State and helped book bands for college events.

Jones quickly found his place in Dallas's line-up as part of the Cowboys' "Doomsday Defense." During his first five years with Dallas, the Cowboys played in the Super Bowl three times, following the 1975, 1977, and 1978 seasons. The second time, Super Bowl XII against Denver, was the charm, with the Cowboy defense tying up the Broncos' quarterback, leaving him little time to pass. "Rushing the passer was the key to it, as far as we were concerned," Coach Tom Landry said in *The Super Bowl*. "We knew if we gave Craig [the Broncos' quarterback] time, he could hurt us. So we wanted a big rush." Jones, who played his part in the rush, would later recall Super Bowl XII as his best game. "It's easy to say the Super Bowl," he told Richard Durrett at the *CowboysPlus* Web site. "Just to be world champions is a good feeling."

Jones shocked his coaches and teammates at the end of 1979 when he announced he would not be returning to Dallas the following season. "One year after his greatest season in football, after he had finally met the expectations that came with being the first player chosen in the 1974 National Football League draft," wrote Malcolm Moran in the *New York Times*, "Ed Jones walked away from professional football." He had dreamed of pursuing a career in boxing since childhood, and when his contract expired, he made his move. "I'm really glad we were winning, because I was on the football field doing the best I could," Jones told the *Dallas Morning News*, "but my mind was in the ring." He planned to build his career slowly, starting

At a Glance . . .

Born on February 23, 1951, in Jackson, TN. *Education:* Tennessee State University, Nashville, TN, BS in Health and Physical Education, 1973.

Career: Dallas Cowboys, professional football player, 1974-78, 1980-89; professional boxer, 1979; Team Jones, Inc., Addison, TX, chief executive officer, c.1990–.

Awards: National Football League, Pro Bowl selection, 1981, 1982, 1983; named to All-Pro team by sportswriters, 1981, 1982; Dallas Cowboys, Most Valuable Player, 1982; Ed Block Courage Award, 1989.

Addresses: *Office*—Team Jones, Inc., P.M.B. 282 - 14232 Marsh Lane, Addison, TX 75001.

with minor fights and working his way into the heavyweight category over time. While writers openly wondered if Jones had what it took to be a world-class champion, he won his first six fights.

By the year's end, however, Jones had re-entered negotiations with Dallas, and planned to return during the 1980 season. "After fighting a year, I experienced a lot of personal problems and some family problems," he told the *New York Times*. "I took some time off to think, and now football is the No. 1 thing on my mind." Jones also played a small role in the movie *The Double McGuffin* (1979) and appeared in an episode of the television series *Diff'rent Strokes* (1978).

Jones quickly reinserted himself into the Dallas line-up in the 1980 and 1981 seasons, playing in 16 games both years. By the 1982 season, he also began to develop a reputation as a fierce opponent to the quarterbacks he sacked with increasing regularity. He reached his record high in 1985, sacking the opposition's quarterback 13 times. He was named All Pro in 1981-82, played in the Pro Bowl three times, and was named Most Valuable Player in 1982. Although Dallas failed to compete in the Super Bowl between 1980 and 1989, the team entered the playoffs five times.

Jones retired in 1989 after a record number of years in the NFL, attributing his longevity to his training as a boxer. "The game of football is very mentally and physically demanding on your body," he told the *NFL Players* Web site. "I wouldn't have been in the mental state of mind to play 15 years if I hadn't boxed." Even following retirement, he continued to be an avid Dallas supporter. "He remains a Cowboy through and through," wrote Chris Stevenson in the *Ottawa Sun*. "When asked who he thought would be in the Super Bowl this year, he replied: 'You mean other than Dallas, who will be in it?'" After his departure from Dallas, Jones went into business for himself, running Team Jones, Inc., an organization that booked entertainers for corporate events. "I've been involved in the music business since high school," he told Taylor. He also learned to love another sport, golf. "I've worked hard all my life," Jones told Taylor. "I've discovered that being on the golf course for five or six hours is the only place where my mind is truly relaxed." In 1998, he joined a number of other athlete-celebrities for a high-profile game of golf sponsored by Athletes Against Drugs. In 2002, he also lent his support to the Shoe Carnival, a store that offered athletic shoes at a discount price. "I...do it because they promote the Boys and Girls Club, a charity I've always supported since I first broke into the league in 1974," he told Christopher Mapp in the *Hattiesburg American Online* Web site. "And it gives me a chance to interact with the fans, who supported me for 15 years."

Sources

Periodicals

Daily Herald (Arlington Heights, IL), June 27, 1998. p. 5.
Dallas Morning News, April 29, 2004.
New York Times, July 9, 1980, p. D18.
New York Times, September 8, 1980, p. C4.
Ottawa Sun, July 11, 2002.

On-line

"Ed 'Too Tall' Jones: 'Everything About Dallas Was Fun,'" *Cowboys Plus*, www.cowboysplus.com (May 13, 2004).
"Former Cowboys Star Still Stands Tall," *Hattiesburg American Online*, hattiesburgamerican.com (May 13, 2004).
Team Jones, Inc., www.teamjonesinc.com (June 29, 2004).
"Where Are They Now," *NFL Players*, www.nflplay ers.com (May 13, 2004).

—Ronnie D. Lankford, Jr.

Jayne Harrison Kennedy-Overton

1951—

Actress, sports commentator

Kennedy-Overton, Jayne, photograph. Kevin Winters/Getty Images.

Jayne Harrison Kennedy-Overton became one of the first female network sports anchors in an era when hiring attractive women was merely a ratings ploy designed to lure male viewers. As co-host of *NFL Today* on CBS from 1978 to 1980, the actress and former model was the first African-American woman to anchor a network sports program.

Kennedy-Overton was born on November 27, 1951, in Washington, D.C., but her family soon moved to suburban Cleveland, Ohio, where her father worked as a machinist in a local factory. One of five children, she was a standout in her Wickliffe-area high school as a cheerleader, National Honor Society member, and three-time class president. In 1969, at a youth organization rally in Washington, D.C., she became the first black vice president of Girls State. The following year, Kennedy-Overton added another first to her resume when she became the first African American to win the crown of Miss Ohio. Most of those in her hometown of Wickliffe were thrilled, but some weren't, and a banner erected in her honor was taken down. "We got some phone calls because, after a couple of newspaper articles, some blacks thought she was bragging," her mother, Virginia Harrison, recalled in an interview with the *Washington Post*'s Jacqueline Trescott a few years later.

Kennedy-Overton went on to compete in the Miss USA beauty pageant, and was fourth runner-up. Around this time, she began dating a popular Detroit-area disc jockey named Leon Isaac Kennedy, and the two wed in a ceremony that featured Motown star Smokey Robinson as her husband's best man. The couple moved to Los Angeles, and Kennedy-Overton began working in television advertising. She even served a stint with comedian Bob Hope on his overseas tours to entertain American troops in Southeast Asia toward the end of the Vietnam War. Kennedy-Overton became a regular on *The Dean Martin Show* as a dancer, which led to episodic television work in such top-rated series as *Shaft, Kojak, Sanford & Son,* and *Starsky & Hutch.*

The Billie Holiday biopic *Lady Sings the Blues,* which starred Diana Ross as the famous jazz and blues singer of the 1930s, was Kennedy-Overton's first film role,

At a Glance . . .

Born on November 27, 1951, in Washington, D.C.; daughter of Herbert (a machinist) and Virginia Harrison; married Leon Isaac Kennedy (an actor and film producer), 1972 (divorced, 1982); married Bill Overton (an actor and entrepreneur), May 1985; children: (with Overton) daughters Savannah Re, Kopper, Zaire. *Religion:* Evangelical Christian.

Career: Actress, 1972–; *NFL Today,* co-host, 1978-80; released exercise video, *Love Your Body,* c. 1982; advisory board, Ta Life, Inc., New York City.

Awards: Miss USA beauty pageant, fourth runner-up, 1970; National Association for the Advancement of Colored People (NAACP), Image Award for Best Performance by an Actress in a Motion Picture, 1982, for *Body and Soul.*

Addresses: *Office*—c/o Ta Life, Inc., 71 W. 128th St., 3rd Fl., Ste. B, New York, NY 10027-3102. *Home*— Maine and California.

though it was a small, uncredited part. She went on to appear in a string of B-movies over the next few years, including *Group Marriage* and *The Muthers.* Her one starring vehicle, a 1977 television movie called *Cover Girls,* featured her as one-half of a top-model duo who moonlight as secret agents. Its premise was nearly a copycat of *Charlie's Angels,* the hit television series, and Kennedy-Overton was even considered for a role on the show when Farrah Fawcett left the show in 1977. Kennedy-Overton admitted to having a tough time as a black actress in Hollywood during this era. "I like it when someone says you are intelligent or pretty," she said in the interview with Trescott in the *Washington Post.* "But universal is a quality most people in Hollywood don't want to see in blacks. That's an appreciation of my talent. I did an episode of 'Police Woman' last year and I played an inmate, wore no make-up and had my hair pulled in a pony tail. And the producer said 'I like you because you want to work, you want to be good.' And that's the nicest thing anyone could say."

Kennedy-Overton was one of the more recognized faces in her day, thanks to her advertising work for Jovan fragrances and the diet soft drink Tab. Her high visibility helped her land the *NFL Today* job in 1978. She became the first black woman to host a sports show on American network television, but she was not the first female to land such a part: she was the

replacement for a former Miss America, Phyllis George, on a broadcasting team that included Brent Musburger, Irv Cross, and Jimmy "The Greek" Snyder. Some seven million viewers tuned in to the CBS show during fall football season, during which Kennedy-Overton bantered with her co-hosts on-air, interviewed players, and displayed a command of NFL statistics and team rosters. She was replaced in 1980 when she auditioned for an NBC television series called *Speak Up, America.*

Kennedy-Overton joined the celebrity-exercise bandwagon and released a how-to video, *Love Your Body,* that was a top seller in the early 1980s. She also starred in film with her husband, who had had a minor hit in 1979 with *Penitentiary,* about a boxer wrongfully incarcerated. In 1981's *Body and Soul,* Kennedy-Overton portrayed a television journalist who interviews a famous boxer, played by her husband, and the interview leads to romance. She won an NAACP Image Award for best actress for the part, but the couple called it quits in 1982.

Few film or television roles came Kennedy-Overton's way in the 1980s. She did a few episodes of the *Love Boat* and *Benson,* and wed an actor she had met on the set of *Cover Girls,* Bill Overton, in 1985. By this time, Kennedy-Overton had been suffering from endometriosis, a painful uterine-tissue condition, for a number of years. "I was in pain all the time," she recalled in an article in *USA Today* by Adele Slaughter, an interview that came about as a result of her role as a spokesperson for the National Endometriosis Foundation. "Sometimes I would be standing in the kitchen, lift the top off a pot and pains came in my stomach. They were not dull aches, they were all sharp pains. It was difficult to walk and certainly almost impossible to exercise." After other remedies had failed, Kennedy-Overton was told that having a baby seemed to relieve symptoms for many women, and her first child, Savannah Re, was born in late 1985.

Kennedy-Overton went on to have two more daughters, Kopper and Zaire, but the condition did not abate until she underwent surgery. She spent much of the 1990s raising her children, splitting time between Los Angeles and a farm property in Maine. She also conquered a weight gain that pushed the former model and dancer past the 200-pound mark. "One of the reasons being overweight was so embarrassing for me is because I used to have my own exercise video," she told *Ebony* journalist Laura B. Randolph. "So here I am, the preacher of being in shape and maintaining good habits, and I am so out of shape.... I didn't feel that I was a good example to my children because I always taught them how important it is to be in shape."

No longer active in Hollywood or on TV, Kennedy-Overton now devotes her time to community causes and to writing her memoirs. A devout Christian, she is deeply involved in her church. She has also done charity work for groups including the National Lung

Association, the Sickle Cell Anemia Foundation, and the National Endometriosis Foundation, and has served as a spokeswoman for the National Council of Negro Women and on the board of the Efficacy Institute, which offers a program that teaches motivation to college-bound students.

Sources

Books

Notable Black American Women, Book 2, Gale, 1996.

Periodicals

Ebony, October 1992, p. 66.
USA Today, July 25, 2001.
Washington Post, September 22, 1978, p. D1.

—Carol Brennan

Leon G. Kerry

1949(?)—

College sports administrator

Kerry, Leon G., portrait. Courtesy of Leon G. Kerry.

Leon G. Kerry serves as commissioner of the Central Intercollegiate Athletic Association (CIAA), the conference of sports teams for 12 historically black colleges in several southern states. Kerry is committed to making the CIAA a powerhouse in the National Collegiate Athletic Association Division II, and to promoting its well-attended annual men's basketball tournament on a larger stage. "My job is to make the CIAA so much fun and special until the only thing you think about is the CIAA and coming back next year," he told a writer for *Black Enterprise,* Hamil Harris, in an article that appeared on the magazine's Web site.

Born in the late 1940s, Kerry grew up in Hampton, Virginia, and attended Norfolk State University in Norfolk, Virginia, which had originally been founded as part of Virginia Union University, one of the CIAA schools. He studied business administration, went on to earn a degree from the American Institute of Banking, and served in the U.S. Army as well. After a stint with the Atlantic National Bank and Systems Management of America, he rose to the position of assistant vice president at Sovran Bank, which later became part of Bank of America.

Kerry first became involved with the CIAA as a volunteer in its business office in 1988. Based in Hampton, Virginia, the CIAA dates back to 1912, which makes it the oldest black-schools athletic conference in the United States. In 2004, the conference's 12 member schools were: Bowie State University, Elizabeth City State University, Fayetteville State University, Johnson C. Smith University, Livingstone College, North Carolina Central University, Saint Augustine's College, Saint Paul's College, Shaw University, Virginia State University, Virginia Union University, and Winston-Salem State University. The CIAA oversees athletic meets between the men's and women's sports teams of the schools, which mostly belong to Division II of the National Collegiate Athletic Association (NCAA).

When Kerry began working at the CIAA business office, it was badly organized and its finances were in disarray. With his years of banking experience, he was the right person for the task at hand, and it soon became clear that the CIAA's business office needed a full-time leader. He was offered the post within months, and in 1989, when CIAA commissioner Bob Moorman

At a Glance . . .

Born c. 1949, in Hampton, VA; married to Angela; children: Lisa, LeAnne. *Education:* Norfolk State University, VA, degree in business administration; American Institute of Banking, degree in banking. *Military Service:* U.S. Army, active duty, attained rank of captain.

Career: Began career with Atlantic National Bank and Systems Management of America; Sovran Bank, assistant vice president; Central Intercollegiate Athletic Association (CIAA), Hampton, VA, interim commissioner, 1989, commissioner, 1990–.

Memberships: National Collegiate Athletic Association (NCAA) Division II Commissioner's Association; National Association of Collegiate Directors of Athletics John McLendon Minority Scholarship Committee.

Awards: National Association for the Advancement of Colored People (NAACP), Leadership Award, 1992; National Collegiate Athletic Association, Fellows Award, 2002; MBC Network, Making Better Communities Award, 2003;

Addresses: *Office*—Central Intercollegiate Athletic Association, P.O. Box 7349, 303 Butler Farm Rd., Ste. 102, Hampton, VA, 23666. *Home*—Chesapeake, VA. *Web*—www.theciaa.com.

moved on, Kerry was made interim commissioner. Nine months later, in early 1990, he was named the full-time commissioner.

The CIAA runs 16 championship tournaments, in sports ranging from men's golf and track to women's volleyball and even bowling. But its annual men's basketball showdown, which dates back to 1946, remains the most popular CIAA intercollegiate event. It is held every winter in a North Carolina or Virginia city. These cities are home to a large number of CIAA alumni, and the tournament has become an annual social event and informal reunion.

One of Kerry's tasks has been to find corporate sponsorships for the CIAA tourney to help defray costs. The men's basketball tournament had just two corporate sponsors when he began in 1990, but a dozen years later there were five in all, including

Coca-Cola, Reebok, and Ford Motor Company. Attendance has increased dramatically under Kerry's tenure. Some 42,000 people came to the tournament in 1999, but in 2004 more than 90,000 tickets were sold for its games in Raleigh, which concluded with the Virginia Union Panthers defeating the North Carolina Central Eagles 80-72. The Panthers went on to the NCAA Division II playoffs two weeks later, but lost to Georgia's Columbus State University.

The CIAA men's basketball tournament has proved so successful under Kerry that there is intense bidding competition to host the event, from such cities as Raleigh, Winston-Salem, Charlotte, and even Washington, D.C.. Kerry hopes that the tournament might someday move on to an even larger venue. "We just need to market this a little better to make things happen," he told *Winston-Salem Journal* reporter John Dell, "and that's what we will continue to do.... [B]efore you start moving into a megabuck arena, you've got to gradually build it up."

Kerry has served in the U.S. Army Reserve, and was honored with an NCAA Fellows Award in 2002. He makes his home in Chesapeake, Virginia. His wife, Angela, is a kindergarten teacher. They have two grown daughters, both of whom are graduates of Hampton University, another historic black college. At age 49, in the late 1990s, he survived a bout with cancer, and he credits his staff at CIAA with carrying the torch and making the men's hoops tournament a possibility that year. "I was scared, it was a difficult time of my life," he told *Ebony.* "But the team kept the dream going. I have a pretty good team here. I found out just how good they were when I had major surgery."

In 2003, Kerry celebrated his thirteenth year on the job, which made him the longest-serving athletic commissioner among the historically black college athletic conferences, which include the Mid-Eastern Athletic Conference (MEAC) and the Southern Intercollegiate Athletic Conference (SIAC). On a television show, *Black Issues Forum,* Kerry explained why the CIAA and its motto, "CIAA for Life," were such an integral part of black life in these Southern cities: "I tell everybody that the reason the history is so rich is because, before integration, people knew they were going to college, but they knew it was going to be a CIAA school. And when you look around at most of the [historically black colleges] on the east coast, they belonged to the CIAA at one point in time."

Sources

Periodicals

Ebony, February 2003, p. 94.
Winston-Salem Journal (Winston-Salem, NC), November 9, 2001, p. C4; November 17, 2002, p. C5.

On-line

Best, Bonitta, "One-On-One with CIAA Commissioner Leon Kerry," *Onnidan's Black College Sports On-line,* www.onnidan.com/99-00/news/lkerrybb.htm (July 6, 2004).

Farrey, Tom, "Not the Kind of Place Looking to Cheat," *ESPN,* http://espn.go.com/ncf/s/2001/1126/1284955.html (July 6, 2004).

CIAA Online, www.theciaa.com (July 21, 2004).

"Fans Gear Up for CIAA," *Black Enterprise,* www.blackenterprise.com/ExclusivesEKOpen.asp?id=670 (July 6, 2004).

"Leon G. Kerry, Commissioner," *CIAA Office Staff,* www.theciaa.com/about/staff.htm (July 6, 2004).

Other

Additional information was found at a transcript of a UNC-TV television broadcast of the show *Black Issues Forum* on March 17, 2000, located at www.unctv.org/bif/transcripts/1999/bif1521.html (July 6, 2004).

—Carol Brennan

Sam Lacy

1903-2003

Journalist, newspaper editor

Sam Lacy became a pioneering sportswriter for the *Afro-American* newspaper in Baltimore and was one of the most important early forces in the integration of Major League Baseball. The sportswriter inherited his pioneering spirit from his grandfather, Henry Erskine Lacy, who was the first black detective on the Washington, D.C., police force. Perhaps the most amazing thing about Lacy's story is not that he covered all the giants of the twentieth-century sporting world—Joe Louis, Jesse Owens, Jackie Robinson, Sugar Ray Robinson, and Muhammed Ali, to name a few—but that he continued to cover sports well into his nineties. He left home for the office at the *Afro-American* at 3:00 a.m. to do three weekly columns and supervise the layout of the paper. When he became too old to drive after suffering a stroke in 1999, his son brought him to work. When his fingers became too riddled with arthritis to type, he wrote out his column longhand, continuing until shortly before his death in May, 2003. Lacy's story began with his selling peanuts to the Jim Crow section of old Griffith Stadium in Washington, D.C., and it continued until he reached a place of honor in the writers' wing at baseball's ultimate shrine, the Hall of Fame in Cooperstown, New York.

Samuel Harold Lacy was born on October 23, 1903, in Mystic, Connecticut, to Samuel Erskine Lacy, a researcher in a Washington, D.C. law firm, and Rose Lacy, a full-blooded Native American from the Shinnecock tribe. Lacy's family moved to Washington, D.C., early in his life. Lacy's father taught his son to love baseball, and Sam began hanging around the stadium. The young fan would do errands for the

players such as buying cigarettes and picking up their laundry. By the time Lacy was nine years old, he was shagging balls in the outfield before games at batting practice. Lacy got a job at the stadium selling popcorn and peanuts in the stands. He also caddied for the winning golfer at the 1921 U.S. Open. His time carrying the bag of Englishman "Long Jim" Barnes earned him $200. His tip was so enormous that the young man had a difficult time making his mother believe he had earned the princely sum by carrying around a golf bag for four days.

Advocated for Desegregation in Sports

Lacy attended Armstrong High School in Washington, D.C. and played football, baseball, and basketball. After he graduated from high school, he was good enough to play baseball in the local semipro leagues but decided he needed to further his education. He attended Howard University and earned a degree in education with the intention of becoming a coach. Little did he know that his part-time job would turn out to be his career and his crusade.

While attending school in the 1920s Lacy worked part-time at the local African-American paper, the *Washington Tribune*, earning a nickel for every inch of copy he wrote. After graduation he joined the paper full-time and soon moved into the sports department, where he began a lifelong crusade for fairness in the world of sports. The first big story Lacy wrote involved a black football player at Syracuse University. To allow the player to continue on the team, the university claimed that he was not black but a Hindu with Indian ancestry. Lacy wrote a story in 1937 proving that the player was not Indian, but born in Washington, D.C., to African-American parents. When the University of Maryland found out about the black player, it refused to play the game with Syracuse unless Wilmeth Sidat-Singh was removed from the team. The player was taken off the team and Syracuse lost, but the reaction against both universities was so strong that Sidat-Singh played against Maryland the following year.

Lacy then turned his attention to the game of baseball. He met with Clark Griffith, the owner of the Washington Senators, then the local major-league team that eventually became the Minnesota Twins. Lacy suggested that Griffith's last-place team could be turned around by an infusion of new talent from the Negro Leagues: Satchel Paige, Cool Papa Bell, and Josh Gibson were suggested to the owner. Lacy told Sam Donnellon of the *Philadelphia Daily News* about his first meeting with a major-league owner: "I used that old cliché about Washington being first in war, first in peace, and last in the American League, and that he could remedy that. But he told me that the climate wasn't right. He pointed out there were a lot of Southern ballplayers in the league, that there would be constant confrontations, and, moreover, that it would

break up the Negro Leagues. He saw the Negro Leagues as a source of revenue."

But a cause was born. Lacy became one of the earliest and most outspoken voices for desegregation in baseball. In 1940 Lacy moved to Chicago to join the *Chicago Defender*, a black paper with a national readership. On numerous occasions he sought a meeting with baseball commissioner Kenesaw Mountain Landis to talk about the integration of Major League Baseball, but Lacy never received a reply. After three years of wrangling and agitating, Lacy finally was given a place on the agenda at the 1943 baseball meetings in Cleveland to discuss the issue. At the last minute the paper decided to send noted athlete and actor Paul Robeson to make the case for the black baseball player, a decision on the part of the paper that Lacy took very personally. He told D.L. Cummings of *The New York Daily News* about his reaction to the snub: "That made me furious. All this work I had done on this, for them to send Paul Robeson, who had known Communistic leanings, I questioned the good sense of it all. I knew when the owners saw this guy who admitted to being Communist-oriented, they would simply say, 'OK, we heard you and don't call us, we'll call you.'"

Lacy immediately moved to the *Afro-American* in Baltimore and continued to press the race issue. He wrote to the owners and suggested an integration committee be formed. Lacy was named to just such a committee with Branch Rickey of the National League's Brooklyn Dodgers and Larry MacPhail of the New York Yankees. The group tried to meet, but MacPhail never attended any of the meetings, so Rickey told Lacy that he was going to be integrating baseball on his own. In April of 1945 Major League Baseball got a new commissioner who was not opposed to integration, and six months later the league got its first black ball player when Rickey signed Jackie Robinson to a contract for Brooklyn's Triple A team in Montreal.

Covered a Pioneer

The *Afro-American* allowed Lacy to cover Robinson exclusively for the next three years. The black press was unanimous in its support of Robinson, and all agreed he was the man to take the first giant step in integrating Major League Baseball. Robinson had attended UCLA, a racially mixed college, competed against white players, had served with honor in the military, and was engaged to be married. Lacy traveled with Robinson from Montreal, where Robinson played Triple A ball, to the deep south for spring training, and even to Cuba for winter baseball. Lacy witnessed all the trials that Robinson experienced and told Kevin Merida of the *Washington Post* that it was difficult for Robinson to keep all of his pain and frustration to himself: "There were a lot of things that were bothering him. He was taking so much abuse that he said to me that he didn't know whether or not he was going to be able to go through with this because it was just becoming so intolerable, that they were throwing everything at him."

Lacy endured many of the same indignities as Robinson, eating with him in separate facilities and staying at the same segregated rooming houses. Once they woke up in the middle of the night to find a cross burning in front of the rooming house where Robinson and other black journalists were staying. Lacy faced discrimination in the press box also. Lacy had to report on some Dodger games from the dugout because he was not allowed to sit with the other reporters. In New Orleans he was forced to go up on the roof of the press box, but there he was joined by some white writers from New York. As late as 1952 Lacy was denied entry into Yankee Stadium to cover the World Series, though he had been a member of the Baseball Writers of America since 1948 as the organization's first African-American member. But Lacy never dramatized his own situation; he kept the focus on the athletes. He told Merida, "It would have been a selfish thing for me to be concerned about myself and how I was treated."

After his victory in desegregating Major League Baseball, Lacy continued to press for fairness in sport. He saw that black ballplayers were having a major impact on their team's records and also on their team's bottom lines. He campaigned to increase their salaries and to have the "separate but equal" accommodations eliminated. Lacy first brought up the issue of blacks and whites staying in different hotels with the New York Giants (before the team moved to San Francisco). He told the story to *Sports Illustrated*'s Ron Fimrite: "I pointed out to Chub Feeney (then the team's general manager) that he had guys like Willie Mays and Monte Irvin and Hank Thompson holed up in some little hotel while the rest of the players, people who might never even wear a major-league uniform, were staying at the famous Palace. Chub just looked at me and said, 'Sam, you're right.' He got on the phone to (owner) Horace Stoneham, and that was the end of that."

A Legend is Born

After twenty years in the business Lacy began to be recognized as one of the best sports journalists in the profession. He received numerous offers to move on to bigger and more widely read publications—*Sports Illustrated* came calling as early as 1950—but he stayed at the *Afro-American*. He told Bill Kirtz of *The Quill* why he stayed put in Baltimore: "No other paper in the country would have given me the kind of license. I've made my own decisions. I cover everything that want to. I sacrificed a few dollars, true, but I lived a comfortable life. I get paid enough to be satisfied. I don't expect to die rich." Lacy continued to work nearly until his death at the age of 99, always striving to achieve a greater sense of fairness in the sporting world. He fought the major networks for their refusal to hire black broadcasters; he chastised major corporations for their failure to sponsor more black golfers; he fought for the inclusion of players from the old Negro Leagues into baseball's Hall of Fame in Cooperstown; and he took the National Football League to task for hesitating to hire black head coaches. In addition to his crusading, Lacy helped edit the paper and covered six different Olympic Games and some of the biggest prizefights of the twentieth century.

In 1997, the fiftieth anniversary of Robinson's integration of Major League Baseball, suddenly everyone wanted to speak to Sam Lacy. He was given an honorary doctorate at Loyola University, was honored by the Smithsonian Institute with a lecture series, and then the following year won the Associated Press's Red Smith Award and the baseball Hall of Fame's J.G. Taylor Spink Award for sports writing. In 1998 Lacy achieved the ultimate reward for a baseball writer. He was inducted into the writers' wing of baseball's shrine. Though Lacy was awestruck that he was even considered for induction into the Hall of Fame, others recognized the important role he played in the history of baseball and racial desegregation in the United States. Jackie Robinson's widow, Rachel, told Cummings of *The New York Daily News* about Lacy's contribution: "We had a great deal of respect for Sam and the other black journalists. They were really crusaders. They really paved the way for the integration of baseball because they were so persistent in their criticism of the owners. They never gave up and I don't think their efforts have ever been properly recognized or appreciated for the role they played behind the scenes." Upon his death on May 8, 2003, broadcasting great Bob Wolff told *Editor & Publisher* that Lacy was "a monument in the business."

Selected writings

(With Moses J. Newson) *Fighting for Fairness: The Life Story of Hall of Fame Sportswriter Sam Lacy*, Tidewater Publishers, 1998.

Sources

Periodicals

Editor & Publisher, May 19, 2003, p. 34.
New York Daily News, February 7, 1997.
Philadelphia Daily News, April 9, 1997.
Quill, January-February, 1999.
Sporting News, May 26, 2003, p. 60.
Sports Illustrated, October 29, 1990.
Washington Post, June 11, 1997.

—Michael J. Watkins and Tom Pendergast

Bertram M. Lee, Sr.

1939-2003

Entrepreneur

Bertram M. Lee, Sr. made history in 1989 when he became the first African American to hold a majority stake in a major-league U.S. sports franchise. Lee and his partners, who included the late U.S. Secretary of Commerce Ron Brown, acquired the National Basketball Association's Denver Nuggets team for $65 million. At the time, Lee stressed that affirmative action had played no part in the historic ownership deal. "As African Americans, in these kind[s] of transactions, one of the things we fight is the tendency for people to think we need all sorts of subsidies or crutches," *Black Enterprise* writer Patricia Raybon quoted him as saying. "There are no subsidies here. But then I've always said that if we're given a level playing field, and access to capital, we can do as much as anyone."

Lee was born on January 21, 1939, in Lynchburg, Virginia, and was raised in a public-housing project. His father, William, was a teacher, and Lee told the *New York Times'* William C. Rhoden that while his family was not an affluent one, neither were they poor, just "an average American family." After finishing high school Lee moved to Naperville, Illinois, to study at North Central College, and after earning his degree in

Lee, Bertram M., Sr., photograph. AP/Wide World Photos.

1961 he took a civil-service job with the city of Chicago. A stint in the U.S. Army between 1963 and 1965 interrupted that career, but he returned to City Hall to hold various posts in the administration of longtime Chicago Mayor Richard J. Daley.

Declared Bankruptcy

In 1967, Lee was hired as the executive director of the Opportunities Industrialization Centers of Greater Boston, which provided local African-American communities with empowerment aid. He and his wife Edith, whom he had met in college, soon moved to Boston with their infant daughter; a second daughter was born there. For a time, Lee's fortunes thrived: he had a management consulting firm, and bought what was then the largest black-owned printing company in the United States, Geneva Printing and Publishing. With two investment partners, he acquired the business for $250,000, and though it won lucrative new contracts, it proved a steady money-loser, and Lee was forced to file for bankruptcy in 1975. He had neglected his management-consulting firm, and a magazine venture in Chicago in which he had a stake also tanked when paper costs skyrocketed. "Those

At a Glance . . .

Born on January 21, 1939, in Lynchburg, VA; died of a brain aneurysm, October 7, 2003, in Washington, DC; son of William T. (a teacher) and Helen (Harris) Lee; married Edith Spurlock (died 1983); married Laura Murphy, 1989 (divorced); children: Paula, Elaine (from first marriage), and Bertram Jr. (from second marriage). *Education:* North Central College, BA, 1961; Roosevelt University, graduate work, 1963-65. *Military service:* U.S. Army, 1963-65. *Religion:* Baptist. *Politics:* Democrat.

Career: City of Chicago, IL, city bureaucrat, 1961-67; Opportunities Industrialization Centers of Greater Boston, MA, executive director, 1967-68; EG & G of Roxbury, Inc., MA, general manager and vice president, 1968-69; Geneva Printing and Publishing, MA, owner, c. 1969-75; Dudley Station Corporation, Boston, president, 1969-81; BML Associates, Inc., Boston, chair, after 1969; New England TV Corporation, Boston, senior vice president, then president, 1978-86; Albimar Management, Inc., chair after 1983; Mountaintop Ventures Inc., treasurer, 1984-2003; Kellee Communications Group Inc., president after 1986; Denver Nuggets Corporation, Denver, CO, chair, 1989-92. Rev. Jesse Jackson's presidential campaign, finance co-chair, 1984, 1988. Served on the boards of the of Pacifica Radio Network, Boston Bank of Commerce, Martin Luther King, Jr. Center for Non-Violent Social Change, Congressional Black Caucus Foundation, Reebok International Ltd., and Howard University. Director of the Jackie Robinson Foundation.

Awards: NAACP Image Award, 1982; American Heritage & Freedom Award, 1983.

were just some of the most frightening days in my life. I felt like a personal failure," he told *Black Enterprise* writer Sharon R. King. Though for a time he had to rely on his wife's salary, he remained undaunted. "I never bowed my head or stopped wearing a shirt and tie," he said in the *Black Enterprise* interview. "I never allowed bankruptcy to bankrupt me."

Despite the setbacks, Lee had already planted the seeds for what would become one of the most profitable business ventures in his career. In 1969, he formed a Boston-area media group to challenge ownership of one of the city's television stations, the ABC affiliate WNAC-TV. He and a group of fellow investors, calling themselves the Dudley Station Corporation, petitioned the Federal Communications Commission (FCC), which grants operating licenses to radio and television stations, to review the track record of the current owner, RKO, which they claimed had failed to meet its obligations to the community, according to the terms of its FCC license.

The Dudley Station group, for which Lee served as president, was actually one of two groups that was challenging the WNAC license. In 1978, Lee's group merged with the other grass-roots organization to form the New England Television Corporation (NETV). A year later, the FCC revoked the RKO license for Boston's Channel 7, and NETV was able to buy the affiliate in 1982. In the interim, the station had switched alliances and become a CBS affiliate. Lee and the other investors had spent 13 years in the courts, and were saddled with $5 million in legal fees in the end. They paid $22 million to buy the station, which was valued at $60 to $150 million. Lee, a senior vice president of the media group, had made an initial investment of $10,000.

Pioneered Black TV Station Ownership

The station's changeover to new ownership in May of 1982—heralded with new call letters, WNEV-TV—was chronicled on the pages of the *New York Times* as an historic first. The article noted that Lee's first experience with television came from watching programs through a store window in Norfolk, since his family did not own a set. The transaction represented "the largest ownership and management interest of blacks and other minority groups of any major American television station," according the *Times*'s Dudley Clendinen, who also termed it "a calendar landmark in the history of American television, and some measure of ethnic progress in this racially divided city."

Lee sold his stake in the station in 1986, cashing out with what was estimated to be a $5 million to $13 million profit. By then he was running BML Associates, Inc., which bore his initials. This Boston holding company had stakes in six enterprises; by 1988 it had posted $30 million in sales and earned a spot on *Black Enterprise* magazine's list of leading African American-owned businesses. It owned radio stations in Utah and Nebraska under the Albimar Management name, operated pay telephones as Kellee Communications Group, and acquired a stake in an Atlanta haircare company in early 1989. Lee was also involved in the Shawmut National Bank as a director, and chaired the Boston Bank of Commerce. The president of the latter, Ronald Homer, told *USA Today* writer Shelley Liles that Lee was a "very persuasive" person and formidable negotiator. "He convinced me to leave the largest and most profitable black-owned bank in the country to take over the smallest and least profitable one," Homer joked. "He said we could make a statement, and we did."

Lee had built up a network of political connections over the years that brought him to the attention of the Reverend Jesse Jackson, who tapped him to serve as finance co-chair for his campaign to win the 1984 Democratic presidential nomination; he also worked for Jackson's 1988 bid. Lee was friendly with a rising star in Democrat National Committee circles, Ron Brown, and brought the future U.S. Secretary of Commerce on board when he began a bid for another historic first: to purchase a major-league sports team. In 1986, Lee tentatively explored the possibility of acquiring the New England Patriots football team, and then moved from football to baseball when the Baltimore Orioles seemed ready to change hands. The football and baseball leagues, however, were long-entrenched operations, and such local franchises were prohibitively expensive to own and operate. Lee then looked into the National Basketball Association (NBA), which dated back to the 1950s and was thus considered a relative upstart in professional sports.

Bought Denver Nuggets

In 1988, Lee and his group lost out on a bid for the San Antonio Spurs when their $50 million tender offer proved too low. "We learned a lot in that process," Lee told *Sports Illustrated* columnist Michael Jaffe. "You learn to come back from unsuccessful challenges. We just kept our eyes on the prize." Finally, with some help from an encouraging new NBA commissioner, David Stern, Lee and his partners—which included tennis great Arthur Ashe as well as Brown—bought the Denver Nuggets for $65 million.

The announcement was made in a two-hour press conference at New York City's Waldorf-Astoria Hotel in July of 1989. The Nuggets were the first among the 27 NBA teams to be owned by a black majority interest ownership group, though about 70 percent of the NBA's player roster was African American. Lee stressed that he and his main partner on the deal, Peter Bynoe, "view this as a business venture; it had to make economic sense before it could make a social statement," *New York Times* writer William C. Rhoden quoted him as saying. "If it didn't make economic sense, believe me, we would not be sitting out there having a need to be first. To the extent that we are, and that we can be used as role models, that we can give hope and inspiration then, fine."

Though he was pleased with comparisons to Jackie Robinson, the baseball player who became the first African American to play in Major League Baseball in 1947, Lee dismissed the idea that the Nuggets deal was truly revolutionary. The real marker of progress, he noted, "would be that a year from today, there were at least two more major sports franchises that had been bought by African Americans and/or minorities," he said at the press conference, according to Rhoden.

Returned to Chicago

Lee was long active in the TransAfrica Forum, an anti-apartheid group, and in 1990 helped organize Nelson Mandela's visit to Boston in 1990 as part of the recently freed South African leader's historic North American fundraising tour. He still had ties in Chicago, however, and in the late 1980s had moved back there after his wife died. His younger daughter wanted to attend high school in same city as her late mother, and Lee told *Wall Street Journal* writer Leon E. Wynter that family took precedence over business for him. "This was my one shot at spending time with my daughter in her teen years," he told the newspaper. "I think they're critical."

Lee's ownership stake in the Nuggets ended in 1991, when he failed to meet a $5 million capital call. After moving to Washington, D.C., around 1994, he continued his involvement with media ownership, and served as an interim board member for the progressive Pacifica Radio network. But his financial troubles returned in the late 1990s, compounded by lingering health problems from a parasite he picked up while traveling in South Africa.

Lee's name was touted as a potential investor in a 1999 effort to bring a Major League Baseball franchise to Washington, but MLB executives had notoriously tough standards for potential owners, and the deal disintegrated. Lee died in October of 2003 in Washington from a brain aneurysm, though the announcement of his passing on the Pacifica Radio Web site noted that his death followed what had been a lengthy illness. Lee was imperturbable when it came to the high-risk, historic deals he had put together over the course of a 30-plus-year career. Referring to the Wall Street suicides of the Great Depression, he vowed after his first major setback that he would never again let a business reversal bring him down. "If you hear that Bert Lee jumped out of a window," he joked with *Black Enterprise,* "then you know that somebody pushed me."

Sources

Periodicals

Black Enterprise, March 1988, pp. 40-46; September 1989, pp. 17-18; December 2003, p. 28.
Chicago Sun-Times, July 30, 1989, p. 19; March 1, 1991, p. 32.
New York Times, May 22, 1982, p. 11; July 12, 1989, p. A17.
Sports Illustrated, July 24, 1989, p. 12; October 30, 1989, p. 17; February 12, 1990, p. 220.
USA Today, July 13, 1989, p. 7B.

Wall Street Journal, July 12, 1989, p. 1; September 13, 1990, p. B12.
Washington Post, April 2, 1999, p. B1.

On-line

"Bertram M. Lee, Sr. A Life Well Lived," *Pacifica Radio,* www.pacifica.org/news/031007_BertLee.html (May 12, 2004).

—Carol Brennan

Adrian Lester

1968—

Actor

Lester, Adrian, photograph. AP/Wide World Photos.

Critics have been nearly unanimous in their enthusiastic praise for British stage and screen actor Adrian Lester. American audiences remember him as the earnest young narrator of the 1998 political comedy *Primary Colors,* and he also appeared in the 2004 blockbuster global-warming film, *The Day After Tomorrow.* Yet it has been his Shakespeare roles that have garnered Lester the most enthusiastic of critical plaudits. In 2001, he starred in what was termed an electrifying new version of Hamlet in New York City. "A slim, angular, dreadlocked figure in black," noted *New York Times* theater critic Ben Brantley, "his Hamlet slices the air like a razor with every limber movement." Across the Atlantic, London's *Sunday Times* journalist Michael Wright delivered similar praise, declaring that Lester's "acting is like an open window, drawing fresh, clear air into stuffy corners."

Lester was born on August 14, 1968, in Birmingham, England; his parents were of Jamaican heritage and his father owned a cleaning company. He has one older brother, and his parents also took in three cousins who needed a home. An admittedly lackluster student, he showed early promise on the stage, and his parents encouraged his talents. He began singing in a cathedral choir at the age of nine, which led to membership in a children's opera company. At age 16, with his parents' permission, he left school and landed a walk-on role in a long-running though famously inept British television drama series called *Crossroads.* It was set in a Birmingham motel, and Lester had occasional roles like bellhop or car thief. "I remember, you did have to be very careful when opening and shutting doors, because the scenery really would shake," he recalled in an interview with James Rampton for London's *Independent.*

All-Male Cast Delighted Playgoers

Lester won a spot at London's Royal Academy of Dramatic Arts, and made his stage debut in the August Wilson play *Fences* in 1990. He appeared in the lead in the acclaimed John Guare drama, *Six Degrees of Separation,* at the Royal Court Theatre in 1992, and the following year was nominated for an Olivier Award, the British equivalent of a Tony, for his role in a revival

At a Glance . . .

Born Adrian Anthony Lester on August 14, 1968, in Birmingham, England; son of a cleaning-company owner; married Lolita Chakrabarti (an actress and screenwriter), August, 1997; children: Lila. *Education:* Studied at the Royal Academy of Dramatic Arts, London, England.

Career: Television actor, 1984–; stage actor, 1990–; film actor, 1991–.

Awards: Olivier Award for Best Actor in a Musical, Society of London Theatre, 1996, for *Company.*

Addresses: *Home*—London, England. *Agent*—William Morris Agency, 1325 Ave. of the Americas, New York, NY 10019.

of *Sweeney Todd.* He made a memorable American stage debut in an all-male production of Shakespeare's *As You Like It* at the Brooklyn Academy of Music in the fall of 1994. "Lester, a willowy black Rosalind, has the gift of breathless apprehension, ever ready to burst into tears at the folly and wonder of men," declared *Time*'s Richard Corliss.

In 1996, Lester won a plum role as the lead, Bobby, in the Donmar Warehouse revival of the Stephen Sondheim musical *Company.* The production was directed by Sam Mendes, who went on to win an Academy Award for the film *American Beauty* a few years later. Bobby is a perennial bachelor who learns about relationships—of the both solid and shaky sort—from a quintet of couples. Lester made history as the first black actor to be cast in the lead in a Sondheim work, and won the Olivier Award that year for best actor in a musical.

Lester took his first film roles in the early 1990s, beginning with a little-seen Martin Sheen drama, *Touch and Die,* set in Italy. He auditioned unsuccessfully for a role in *The Birdcage,* a 1996 Mike Nichols film, but the famed director offered him a starring role in his next work. That film was *Primary Colors,* the screen adaptation of the bestselling 1996 novel of the same name that caused a stir for its thinly veiled behind-the-scenes look at what appeared to be Bill Clinton's 1992 bid for the White House. In it, John Travolta was cast as the charismatic governor of an unnamed Southern state who is running for president, with Lester as Henry Burton, the grandson of an

American civil-rights legend whom the candidate hires as his deputy campaign manager.

Returned to Stage as Hamlet

In *Primary Colors,* Lester's narration as Burton reveals his mixed feelings about helping elect a man who appears to be a dedicated public servant, but who also has a penchant for extramarital liaisons that threatens to derail his political career. The film was released in 1998 during Clinton's second term, when revelations of his affair with a White House intern made front-page headlines for months and nearly resulted in impeachment. "The beauty of *Primary Colors,*" noted *Newsweek*'s David Ansen, "is that it forces us to grapple with the same questions of political faith that haunt its narrator." Before the film's premiere, Lester was stunned to learn that the promotional poster featured just him, Travolta, and Emma Thompson, who played the candidate's wife. As he recalled in an interview with *San Francisco Chronicle* journalist Ruthe Stein, when he first saw it, "I went, 'Oh, my God.' I had to sit down and have a cup of tea."

Pegged as a rising young name in Hollywood, Lester found instead that his career stalled. "I came home and did no paid work for a year," he told Rampton in the *Independent* interview. In 2000, he appeared in the ill-fated Kenneth Branagh film, *Love's Labour's Lost,* an all-singing, all-dancing adaptation of Shakespeare that was generally loathed by critics. He appeared in three other films that same year, but also returned to the stage as a dreadlock-sporting Hamlet in Paris. Directed by Peter Brook, the new production, retitled *The Tragedy of Hamlet,* was a revised, reenergized version that was enthusiastically received by critics on both sides of the Atlantic. It went on to successful runs at the Brooklyn Academy of Music and London's Young Vic Theater. "Like its leading man," asserted Brantley's *New York Times* review, "this *Hamlet* has wit, charm, and elegance." Brantley noted further that "if Mr. Brook has reconceived *Hamlet* as a timeless fable, then Mr. Lester is the classic cleverboots, arrogantly assured and intelligent and needing to be brought down a peg."

Lester appeared in two more film roles, *Dust* (2001) and *The Final Curtain* (2002), before returning to the National Theatre in another acclaimed Shakespeare revival in 2003: director Nicholas Hytner's modern-dress version of *Henry V.* Lester was cast in the title role of the king, and was the first black actor in a major production of the wartime saga. Rampton, writing in the *Independent,* noted that "Lester played the monarch as a charismatic, media-friendly war leader, complete with sharp suits, smooth press-conference manner, and concerned televised addresses to the nation." Again, critics dispensed superlatives in assessing his performance. "Rarely has an actor conveyed as strongly as Adrian Lester the damage both inflicted and suffered by this king," noted *Observer* critic Susannah Clapp. Once again, Lester's role dovetailed with current events, for *Henry V* opened in the spring of 2003 just as British Prime Minister Tony Blair argued in favor of joining a U.S.-led invasion of Iraq, against tremendous public opposition. As Lester told Rampton in the *Independent,* "I saw Blair doing exactly what Henry did—campaigning for war in the hearts and minds of English people and saying whatever needed to be said to convince us that we had to go to war."

Lester, who lives primarily in London, is married to a former Royal Academy of Dramatic Arts student, Lolita Chakrabarti, with whom he as a daughter. He appeared in the UPN series *Girlfriends* during its 2002 and 2003 seasons, and though he had numerous British television credits to his name, had never yet been cast in a lead role on the small screen. That changed when he debuted in the BBC1 drama, *Hustle,* in early 2004 as the leader of gang of con artists. He was attracted to the role, he told Rampton, just because it had not been specifically written for a black actor. "Some characters are written as black," he said in the *Independent* article, "and for the writer it seems the mere fact that they're black gives them an interesting character—but it doesn't! As soon as anybody ceases to see you as an individual, it's problematic, because they stop seeing you as you."

Sources

Books

Contemporary Theatre, Film and Television, Vol. 31, Gale, 2000.

Periodicals

Entertainment Weekly, March 27, 1998, p. 44.
Essence, December 2003, p. 146.
Independent (London, England), February 23, 2004, p. 12.
Jet, April 6, 1998, p. 56.
New Republic, April 20, 1998, p. 24.
New Statesman and Society, February 3, 1995, p. 34.
Newsweek, March 23, 1998, p. 63.
New York Times, April 8, 2001, p. 7; April 27, 2001.
Observer (London, England), July 22, 2001, p. 6; May 18, 2003, p. 11.
People, March 30, 1998, p. 19.
San Francisco Chronicle, March 25, 1998, p. E1.
Seattle Times, April 1, 2001, p. F6.
Sunday Times (London, England), April 27, 2003, p. 4. *Time,* December 12, 1994, p. 84; June 12, 2000, p. 82.
Variety, November 17, 1997, p. 65; March 16, 1998, p. 63; February 21, 2000, p. 36; October 9, 2000, p. 27; May 26, 2003, p. 43; July 14, 2003, p. 48.

—Carol Brennan

John Lewis

1940—

Politician, civil rights activist

A Democratic congressman from Georgia since 1986, John Lewis is perhaps best known for his prominence in the U.S. civil rights movement. As a strict follower of nonviolent social protest, Lewis was a relentless organizer and participant in numerous sit-ins, freedom rides, and protest marches throughout the South in the tumultuous years of the 1960s. "There were a lot of people who pretended they were civil rights heroes," professor Roger Wilkins told Peter Applebome in the *New York Times,* but Lewis "was a true hero, an absolute hero, a man of absolute fearlessness and total integrity." For the first half of the 1960s, Lewis served as chairman of the influential Student Nonviolent Coordinating Committee (SNCC) and later worked as a grass-roots organizer for the Field Foundation and ACTION. He shifted to mainstream politics in the early 1980s, first serving on Atlanta's City Council and later as the representative from Georgia's Fifth Congressional District. As a government official, Lewis still champions the civil rights message he once carried into the streets of the deep South. "A lot of young people who came to Mississippi or Selma or the Freedom Rides thought you could come for a summer, a semester, a year, and create something new," Applebome quoted him as saying. "But most of us knew this is not a struggle that lasts one day or one week or one month or one lifetime."

Inspired by Martin Luther King, Jr.

Lewis was born in 1940 in Troy, Alabama, the son of parents who operated a cotton and peanut farm in rural Pike County. As a young boy, he displayed a religious intensity and single- mindedness that would later characterize his unswerving dedication to civil rights. With aspirations to become a minister, he regularly preached to the chickens on his parents' farm and also conducted baptisms for them. By the time he was a teenager—and despite a stammering voice and shyness—Lewis was a regular preacher in Baptist churches throughout the area. He became inspired in his ministerial pursuits by the weekly radio sermons of Dr. Martin Luther King, Jr., whom he listened to in the mid-1950s. The first person from his family to graduate from high school, Lewis moved at the age of seventeen to Nashville, Tennessee, where he began studies at the American Baptist Seminary. Lewis's first opportunity to meet King came in the late 1950s, when Lewis enlisted the help of the civil rights leader with his plans to gain admittance to all-white, segregated Troy State College in Alabama.

When those plans failed to materialize, Lewis returned to Nashville and enrolled at Fisk University to pursue a degree in philosophy. There, influenced by theories of nonviolent forms of social protest, as well as the burgeoning efforts of blacks to protest segregation laws throughout the South, he took up the cause of civil rights. He became a student and follower of the teachings of clergyman and activist James Lawson. In 1960, Lewis and several other Nashville blacks conducted their first "sit-ins" in the city's lunch counters, taking their place in "white-only" designated areas. Despite being repeatedly arrested by police and harassed by the community, Lewis and his comrades

At a Glance . . .

Born John Robert Lewis, February 21, 1940, in Troy, AL; son of Eddie and Willie Mae Lewis; married Lillian Miles, December 21, 1968; children: John Miles. *Education:* Attended American Baptist Seminary, 1957-58(?); Fisk University, BA, 1967. *Politics:* Democrat. *Religion:* Baptist.

Career: Student Nonviolent Coordinating Committee (SNCC), cofounder, 1960, chairman, 1963-66; Field Foundation, New York City, associate director, 1966-67, Field Foundation Southern Regional Council, Nashville, TN, director of community organization projects, beginning 1967; Field Foundation Voter Education Project, Atlanta, GA, executive director, 1970-77; ACTION, director of domestic operations, 1977-80; Atlanta City Council member, 1982-86; U.S. House of Representatives, Washington, DC, Democratic congressman from Fifth District of Georgia, 1986–; chief deputy whip, 1991–; Faith and Politics Institute, co-chairman, 1997–.

Selected Memberships: Southern Coordinating Committee to End the War in Vietnam, cofounder, 1966; White House Conference on Civil Rights, member, 1966; Robert F. Kennedy Memorial Foundation, trustee; National Association for the Advancement of Colored People (NAACP); Southern Christian Leadership Conference (SCLC); American Civil Liberties Union.

Selected Awards: Eleanor Roosevelt Award for Human Rights, 1998; Martin Luther King, Jr. Non-Violent Peace Prize; Robert F. Kennedy Book Award, 1999; John R. Lewis Monument erected at foot of Edmund Pettus Bridge, Selma, Alabama, 2004; John F. Kennedy "Profile in Courage" Award, for lifetime achievement.

Addresses: *Offices*—343 Cannon House Office Building, Washington, DC 20515; The Equitable Building, 100 Peachtree Street, NW, Suite £ 1920, Atlanta, GA 30303.

Lewis—with an unwavering belief in civil rights and nonviolent protest, as well as a willingness to risk his own life—soon emerged as a foremost young leader of the civil rights movement. He was a frequent participant in the more dangerous forms of protest, including the so-called "freedom rides," which challenged racial discrimination in bus facilities throughout the South. Lewis, like other freedom riders, endured vicious physical beatings, death threats, and numerous arrests for the rides, which were predominantly conducted in the summer of 1961. Lewis also led much-publicized marches against segregated movie theaters in Nashville, again prompting numerous arrests as well as physical and verbal assaults by local whites. Lewis's staunch commitment to continue with such front-line protests—despite ever-present physical dangers—distinguished him as a role model of the early nonviolent protests. He was unanimously elected chairman of the SNCC in 1963 at the age of 23. That same year he was the youngest speaker at the March on Washington, D.C., protest, making a noteworthy speech that criticized the administration of President John F. Kennedy for not proceeding quickly enough with legislation ensuring civil rights.

Refused to Give Up on Nonviolent Protests

As chairman of the SNCC, Lewis maintained a path of nonviolence toward achieving the goals of civil rights. Eventually, however, more militant elements of the organization—espousing principles of Black Power—began to grow restless with Lewis's leadership. In 1966, he was ousted as SNCC chairman by Stokely Carmichael, and shortly thereafter resigned. Lewis went on to work for the Field Foundation, first as a director of community organization projects in the Nashville area, and eventually becoming director of the foundation's Voter Education Project (VEP) based in Atlanta. As VEP director from 1970 until 1977, Lewis led grass roots efforts to organize southern black voters, to provide political education to young people, and to offer a variety of voter-assistance programs. In 1977, he was appointed by President Jimmy Carter to be director of U.S. operations for ACTION, a federal agency that oversees various economic recovery programs on the community level. That same year, Lewis first ran for public office, finishing second in the Democratic primary for Georgia's Fifth Congressional District.

Wanting a more direct involvement with community groups, and critical of the federal government's efforts to aid the poor, Lewis became more involved in mainstream politics. In 1982, he was elected to the Atlanta City Council, a position in which he became known for his close attention to the needs of the poor and elderly. Lewis's popularity and respect among constituents became apparent in 1986, when he won a special run-off election for the Democratic nomination

continued their protests throughout Nashville. Eventually they joined forces with leaders of similar student groups across the South to form what became known as the Student Nonviolent Coordinating Committee.

for U.S. Congress. Lewis's opponent for the Democratic nomination was black Georgia state senator Julian Bond, a close SNCC ally of Lewis during the early days of the civil rights movement. Pitting two prominent civil rights figures against each other, the race captured national attention and was marked by Bond's charges of Lewis's inarticulateness, as well as Lewis's contention of Bond's drug abuse. In the end, as political observers pointed out, Lewis's reputation as a diligent listener to the needs of black, elderly, and labor groups carried him past Bond and onto victory in the general election in November of 1986.

In his role as a U.S. congressman, Lewis has maintained a position as a prominent and respected figure who fights for civil rights in the United States. Some observers in the 1990s have argued, however, that he lacks effective strategies for adapting the movement to the current needs of blacks. In particular, Lewis was been criticized for his staunch support of the 1991 civil rights bill, which some Democrats and black leaders attacked as ineffective because of its failure to address the economic needs of blacks. However, Lewis possesses, as Applebome noted, "a sense of what is missing in the civil rights debate: a sense of shared purpose, of basic morality, that speaks to blacks and whites alike." In the fall of 1991, Lewis was appointed one of three chief deputy whips in the House of Representatives. According to Harold Ford, Jr., writing in *Black Enterprise,* "The move up positions Lewis...as one of the most influential members of the House."

Developed Power in Congress

Over the next decade, Lewis continued to increase his influence in Congress and worked hard to preserve civil and other rights of citizens. At a gathering on the steps in front of the Lincoln Memorial, the same spot that Martin Luther King Jr. delivered his now famous I Have a Dream speech, Lewis and other prominent civil rights leaders applauded the efforts of the hundreds of thousands of citizens whose protests helped to pass the Civil Rights Act of 1964. Lewis summed up their effort thusly: "I think it is fitting and appropriate for us to pause to celebrate the distance we've come and the progress we have made. Because of the actions of hundreds of our citizens, and because of the response of the U.S. Congress, President John F. Kennedy and President Lyndon Johnson, we have witnessed what I like to call a nonviolent revolution, a revolution of values, a revolution of ideas. And I say today, we are a better nation, and we are a better people," according to his office press release. Lewis published a memoir of

his work during the civil rights movement in 1998 entitled *Walking with the Wind.* The book recorded his personal account of this volatile time in American history.

In his work in Congress, at the Faith and Politics Institute, and at schools and gatherings around the country, Lewis continues the work he started during the "nonviolent revolution" of the 1960s. In 2004, Lewis introduced a bill dubbed the "Civil Rights Act of 2004" by other congressmen, according to *Jet.* If passed, it would help to protect the civil rights of American workers. He noted in a press release in 2004 that the work of the civil rights movement is "far from done," adding that "There are doors that remain unopened and some that have slammed even harder shut." Lewis has committed his life to continuing the struggle for equal rights for all.

Selected works

(With Michael D'Orso) *Walking with the Wind: A Memoir of the Movement,* Simon & Schuster, 1998.

Sources

Books

Branch, Taylor, *Parting the Waters: America in the King Years 1954-63,* Simon and Schuster, 1988.

Periodicals

Black Enterprise, November 1991.
Christian Science Monitor, August 11, 1986; September 4, 1986.
Ebony, November 1, 2003.
Jet, May 8, 2000; October 2, 2000; August 11, 2003; March 1, 2004.
New Republic, November 24, 1986; July 1, 1996.
New Yorker, October 4, 1993.
New York Times, July 6, 1991.
Parade, February, 1996.
Time, December 29, 1975; August 25, 1986.
U.S. News and World Report, September 1, 2003.

On-line

"Congressman John Lewis," http://www.house.gov/ johnlewis/ (July 26, 2004).

—Michael E. Mueller and Sara Pendergast

Randall Maxey

1941—

Physician, organization leader

In 1972, with the roar of the civil rights movement still ringing loud, Dr. Randall Maxey began practicing medicine. As he launched a lifelong career in kidney disease prevention and treatment, he also fought for the rights of minority patients and doctors. Years of research and activism in minority healthcare eventually led to his being elected president of the National Medical Association (NMA), the country's largest association of African-American doctors. Dedicated to promoting the collective interests of physicians and patients of African descent, the NMA was a perfect match for Maxey. In an interview with *Contemporary Black Biography* (*CBB*) he stated, "My goals are those of NMA—to eliminate health disparities that exist between under-served Americans and the general population."

Maxey, Randall, photograph. Frank Micelotta/Getty Images.

Chose Medicine over Law

Randall W. Maxey was born on December 1, 1941, and raised in Cincinnati, Ohio along with two brothers and a sister. His mother, Laura Roberto Maxey, was an elementary school teacher and his father, Jerry Maxey Sr., was a mortician. "I lived in a middle middle-class neighborhood in Madisonville, a suburb of Cincinnati," Maxey told *CBB*. "For a while we lived in the upstairs apartment of my mother's sister's house. It was great. We had chickens, pigeons, an orchard, a goldfish pond." When his father opened the Maxey Funeral Home in Cincinnati, the family moved in and Maxey finished out his childhood there.

After graduating from high school, Maxey attended the Cincinnati College of Mortuary Science and became a licensed mortician and embalmer. "It was something my father wanted me to do, following in his footsteps," he told *CBB*. Maxey had other ideas. After earning a degree in pharmacy from the University of Cincinnati in 1966, he started thinking about graduate school. "I was torn," he told *CBB*. "I wanted to be a civil rights lawyer, because I was very into Martin Luther King and what he stood for. But I also wanted to be a physician. So, I applied to both law and medical schools and got accepted into both." Maxey chose law at the University of Cincinnati partly because he had landed a job on the campus. "I was the first black assistant dean of men at the University of Cincinnati, so that was going to pay for my law school," he told *CBB*. However, law school didn't last

At a Glance . . .

Born on December 1, 1941, in Cincinnati, OH; married Gem L. Maxey, 1979; five children. *Education:* University of Cincinnati, BS, pharmacy, 1966; Howard University, MD, 1972; Howard University, PhD, cardiovascular pharmacology, 1972.

Career: University Hospital, Downstate Medical Center, Brooklyn, NY, director ambulatory dialysis, 1976-78; Charles R. Drew University, Department of Medicine and Science, Los Angeles, CA, clinical assistant professor, 1980-88; Daniel Freeman Memorial Hospital, Inglewood, CA, director of nephrology, 1983-88; Robert F. Kennedy Medical Center, Hawthorne, CA, director of nephrology, 1983-96; DaVita Pacific Coast Dialysis Center, Inglewood, CA, medical director, 1986–; Diversified Health Care, Inglewood, CA, executive vice president, 1992–; Los Angeles Dialysis Center, Los Angeles, CA, supervising medical director, 1993-98; Pacific Dialysis Center, Dededo, Guam, supervising medical director, 1993-98; Guam Renal Care, Hemodialysis Center, Agana, Guam, supervising medical director, 1996-98. Served as attending physician at many hospitals over the course of his career.

Selected memberships: Association of Minority Nephrologists, founder and board member, 1986–; Church Health Network, founder and president, 1990–; Unity One, Anti-Gang Advocacy Program, board member, 1998–; National Medical Association, president, 2003–; Congressional Black Caucus, Health Policy Advisory Commission, member, 2004–.

Selected awards: Howard University, President's Service to Howard Award, 1972; Operation PUSH, Cincinnati Chapter, Academic Excellence Award, 1972; Minority Health Institute, Service Award, 1991; Charles R. Drew Medical Society, President's Award, 1994; Howard University, Dean's Special Service Award, Outstanding Alumni, 2002.

Addresses: *Office*—DaVita Pacific Coast Dialysis Center, 1416 Centinela Ave., Inglewood, CA 90302.

Maxey entered a dual M.D./Ph.D. program being launched by Washington, D.C.'s Howard University. "I was the very first student [in the program]," he told *CBB*. During the six-year course of study, Maxey also worked at Howard. "I was a faculty member and a department head in the college of dentistry. I also taught basic sciences and was a graduate assistant in the department of biology," he told *CBB*. After graduating with a degree in medicine and a doctorate in cardiovascular pharmacology, Maxey did three years of internships in internal medicine at Harlem Hospital Medical Center in conjunction with Columbia University in New York. This was followed by a two-year fellowship at the Downstate Medical Center and Kings County Hospital of Brooklyn, where he specialized in nephrology. Focusing on the diagnosis and treatment of kidney diseases, nephrologists often manage the long-term healthcare of patients with kidney disease, including the administration of dialysis treatment. From 1976 to 1978 Maxey served as the director of the ambulatory dialysis unit at University Hospital in Brooklyn. He also remained active in academia, serving as a clinical assistant professor at University Hospital and assistant professor of medicine at the State University of New York.

Began Medical Career

In 1978 Maxey moved to Inglewood, California, where he became an attending physician at several area hospitals including Brotman Medical Center, Cedars Sinai Medical Center, Centinela Hospital Medical Center, Daniel Freeman Memorial Hospital, Daniel Freeman Marina Hospital, and Robert F. Kennedy Medical Center. The following year he married Gem Maxey, with whom he would have five children. "My proudest moment was marriage to my wife and the birth of each of my children," Maxey told *CBB*.

In 1980 Maxey took on a position of clinical assistant professor in medicine at Los Angeles's Charles R. Drew University, a job he would hold for eight years. In the 1980s he also served as the director of nephrology at both Daniel Freeman Memorial Hospital and the Robert F. Kennedy Medical Center. In 1986 he became the medical director at the Pacific Coast Dialysis Center, later renamed DaVita. A few years later, he also assumed the title of supervising medical director at the Los Angeles Dialysis Center. In the 1990s Maxey became interested in cases of renal failure in Guam. He became licensed to practice there and in 1992 became an attending physician at Guam Memorial Hospital. From 1993 to 1998 he also served as supervising medical director at the Pacific Dialysis Center in Dededo, Guam, and from 1996 to 1998 he held the same position at the Guam Renal Care Hemodialysis Center in Agana. He also published several medical papers on renal failure among South Pacific Islanders in Guam.

In 2004 Maxey was still serving as an attending physician at several hospitals in California and Guam and

long. "After only a few weeks I realized that I was better suited to medicine," he told *CBB*.

held the title of medical director at several dialysis centers. He also continued to teach, research, lecture, and publish. According to a press release published on the NMA website, "During the course of his career, he has made outstanding contributions to research regarding the prevention and treatment of renal failure, especially in cases complicated by cardiovascular disease." He has received numerous awards for his work over the years, though they are not what Maxey reflects on when contemplating his accomplishments. "Work-wise, really my proudest moments are when a patient thanks me," he told CBB. "That is more gratification than all the money or awards in the world. And I am glad that there have been a lot of those moments. You get honors, promotions, but they are not on the same level of satisfaction as knowing that someone really means it when they thank you and tell you that you have really contributed to their life." He continued, "As a dialysis doctor, I do a lot of counseling. Not just medical, also personal. I am involved in all parts of the patient's life, family, job, personal issues. In this field you have to deal with the whole individual. Often they are depressed, they don't see the light at the end of the tunnel. I deal with that in addition to their medical needs."

Advocated for African-American Patients and Doctors

Maxey has always been a doctor concerned with more than medical needs. His early commitment to the tenets of Dr. King has pushed him to fight for medical access for all Americans, particularly underserved minority communities. As a student at Howard he started the school's Mississippi Project, which helped provide healthcare to those affected by the civil rights movement. In 1990 he founded the Church Health Network, a non-profit organization which strived to reach underserved patients through their churches and communities. In addition, he published several articles on healthcare delivery to minorities. Over the years his focus of concern has settled on the healthcare disparities that exist between minority and non-minority patients. It is an issue that he has witnessed daily in the healthcare industry and even in his own home. He recalled in an interview on the Iconoclast Web site that his young son once visited the school nurse because of a skin irritation and was told, "all little black boys have skin rashes." Maxey concluded in the interview, "Black people's [medical] problems are discounted all the time."

Since finishing medical school, Maxey has also been a strong voice for African-American doctors. He joined the NMA in 1972 and became a very active member. He served on several committees within the organization and presented papers at their national conventions. In 1996 he was elected to the board of trustees. In 1999 he served as secretary of the board, and in 2001 he moved up to chairman. In 2002, the 25,000-plus member organization elected him national president, a post he assumed in August 2003 at the group's annual convention in Philadelphia. "I think I bring a skill set of broad knowledge of clinical medicine [to the post]," he told The Philadelphia Tribune upon his inauguration. "I also bring a lot of enthusiasm and a lot of energy and a fair amount of impatience to see that things get done."

One focus of Maxey's impatience has been the ongoing health disparity that he had witnessed throughout his career. "Right now our major concern is that there are significant major health disparities that exist and these health disparities are leading to excess deaths in all categories, excess morbidity, excess hospitalization and we need to stop it," Maxey told The Philadelphia Tribune. He planned to lead the NMA in this battle on several fronts, including encouraging increased participation of black patients and doctors in clinical trials and research. "We don't know that the current therapeutic and medical recommendations that are out there now really fit African-Americans," he told The Philadelphia Tribune. He also planned on fighting on the policy level. "I see us as being a very important health policy organization that helps create and drive health policies," he continued in the interview with The Philadelphia Tribune. To that end, Maxey has spoken on Capital Hill on issues ranging from the Medicare Modernization Act of 2003 to the Closing the Gap on Healthcare Act of 2004.

Maxey and the NMA have also focused on the doctors that treat minorities. "We want to make sure that doctors are both culturally competent and health literate and can meet the needs of underserved American populations," Maxey told CBB. Related to this is the problem of a lack of African-American doctors. In a press release posted on the NMA website Maxey said, "The loss of practicing physicians in the African American community also negatively impacts patients. Patients may have to seek physicians outside of their communities; they may have to find a physician willing to take on new patients or one who has the interest or cultural competence to understand and address their special needs." The NMA hoped to combat this loss of minority physicians by exposing minority youth at a young age to the possibility of healthcare careers and also extending the NMA's already-existing mentoring program.

Maxey's presidency at the NMA was scheduled to end in August of 2004, after which he planned to open a holistic medical center, "where my approach will be a combination of so-called western medicine and other schools of knowledge, including spiritual healing," he told CBB. Planned for the center was a meditation center and several contemplative gardens. Though it seemed a new venue for a man who had spent his life fighting against kidney disease and for patients' rights, the holistic center is actually a perfect marriage of his commitment to healthcare and his belief that patients should have access to healthcare that meets their needs culturally as well as physically.

Sources

Periodicals

Jet, August 25, 2003.
Modern Healthcare, August 11, 2003.
Philadelphia Tribune, August 8, 2003.

On-line

Graham, Judith, "Black-white Health Gap Grows; Disparity Rises as Care Improves," *Iconoclast*, www.iconocast.com/H/Health1_News16_04/Health6.htm (May 28, 2004).

"Randall W. Maxey, MD, Installed as 104th president of the National Medical Association," *National Medical Association,* www.nmanet.org/pr_080703.htm (May 28, 2004).
"Statement by Randall W. Maxey, M.D., PhD," *National Medical Association,* www.nmanet.org/about_from_president.htm (May 28, 2004).

Other

Additional information for this profile was obtained through an interview with Dr. Randall Maxey on June 14, 2003.

—Candace LaBalle

James Madison McGee

1940—

Association executive, labor activist

James Madison McGee heads the oldest and largest independent black-led industrial labor union in the United States—the National Alliance of Postal and Federal Employees, NAPFE. Excluded from existing craft unions at the time, a group of black railway mail clerks formed the NAPFE in 1913 to secure the inclusion of blacks' jobs with the railway mail service. The NAPFE grew throughout the decades as a predominantly African-American organization, never relying on funding from whites. NAPFE is the fourth largest union in the postal service, with 50,000 members in 10 districts and 141 locals in 37 states. Despite the majority African-American membership the NAFPE has remained open to all people of all races, genders, and religious faiths. Elected union president in 1989, McGee continues to uphold NAPFE's mission of equality for all workers, battling against discrimination and unfair practices in the federal sector and the Postal Service.

McGee also serves as chief executive officer of the NAPFE Federal Credit Union and of the NAPFE 202 Housing Program, which provides housing for the elderly and handicapped. McGee's concern for labor issues is not limited to the United States. He is North American vice president of the World Confederation of Labor, an international labor organization, and World Confederation of Labor representative to the United Nations.

Influenced by Early Images

James Madison McGee was born on December 22,

1940, in Nashville, Tennessee, to Raymond McGee Sr. and Coma Mai McGee, his role models. He lived in the atypical mixed section of South Nashville called Trimble Bottom. It was here, among this patchwork of black and white neighborhoods whose children played together and saw first-hand that the races could coexist, that McGee grew up, the youngest of seven children. Despite being poor, McGee said in an interview with *Contemporary Black Biography*, "My family enjoyed a pretty good life. We didn't know we were poor; we got what we needed. Yet we knew Jim Crow existed; the schools were still segregated."

"The children who had a parent at the post office seemed to have everything they needed, in abundance," McGee remembered. This image from his youth of a middle-class life within the context of the segregated South would later shape his decision to seek employment with the U.S. Post Office, and seed his rise through the ranks of NAPFE.

McGee attended Fisk University in for a year starting in 1959. He joined the Marine Corps in 1961 to serve in the Vietnam War. The racism McGee experienced in the military at Camp Lejeune and nearby Jacksonville, North Carolina, was the genesis of McGee's life as an activist. Black servicemen would spend their pay in town but could not have credit at its stores or travel to some areas of the city. Seeing this, McGee and fellow marines decided to donate a portion of their $78.00 monthly salary to the NAACP. However, there was no means to get donations to the NAACP, their white paymaster informed them, as he returned their money. Prompted to action, McGee then decided, "If I couldn't

At a Glance . . .

Born James Madison McGee on December 22, 1940, in Nashville, TN; married Mary Francis Wilkins; children: Andrea, LaSandra, James Jr. *Education:* Fisk University, 1959-60; Mid-S School of Electronics, diploma, 1968-70; Mason's School of Business, diploma, accounting. *Military Service:* United States Marine Corps, 1961-65. *Religion:* Methodist.

Career: NAPFE Local 410, Nashville, TN, political action chairman, 1967-68; NAPFE Local 410, Nashville, TN, treasurer, 1968-72; NAPFE Local 410, Nashville, TN, president, 1972-78; NAPFE District Four, Washington, DC, president, 1978-82; NAPFE, Washington, DC, national first vice president, 1982-89; NAPFE, Washington, DC, national president, 1989–; World Confederation of Labor, Brussels, Belgium, vice president, 1989–.

Selected memberships: National Black Leadership Roundtable; NAACP; Tennessee Voters Council, member, 1967-80.

Addresses: *Office*—NAPFE, 1628 11th St. NW, Washington, DC 20001.

give it to the NAACP, I wouldn't give it to anyone." Other black servicemen on base followed his lead and began to boycott the businesses of Jacksonville. Their cause was aided by an unexpected source: To reduce tensions, a two-star general on base ordered Jacksonville off limits to all servicemen. Restricting 40,000 servicemen from spending their paychecks in Jacksonville had the desired effect; Jacksonville's economy suffered, and over time the city changed. Blacks were able to get credit and shop where they pleased.

Focused on the Post Office

In Nashville on a cold January day in 1965, newly discharged from the service, a revealing encounter in a local pool hall crystallized McGee's career options. Having left behind a pair of gloves his future wife had given him, McGee returned to the pool hall and found them gone. "I had left them for only a moment," McGee told CBB. "When I returned no one knew anything. And these were supposed to be my friends." He figured there were much better things to do with his life. Again he thought about the benefits and stability of employment at the post office.

The post office, McGee believed, would afford him a way to have the life he wanted. He remembered one neighbor whom he admired in particular wearing his postal uniform at school assemblies. "Many prominent blacks we knew worked at the post office. This influenced me greatly. I saw early on that they seemed to be well off. I didn't think I could get rich working there, but I believed I'd be all right." McGee decided he would take the entrance exam for the post office once it opened up, and take whatever job he could get in the meantime.

On December 2, 1965, the post office called, and McGee started work on the following Monday. On December 7, NAPFE, the only union open to blacks at the post office at the time, invited him to join. "There were people there who put their arms around you when you came into the union and taught you the ropes," McGee told CBB. "I met my best friend there, Jimmy Brown. He encouraged me to attend union meetings. Eventually I discovered what I had always suspected: Blacks could indeed lead, as well as follow. Here was this organization that was 99 percent black and doing marvelous things. I started getting more involved and people started putting their arms around me again. They brought you along and told you when you were ready for office. I called them my 'griots.'"

McGee knew he had found his niche. In 1968 he landed the treasurer's spot at Nashville local 410. During this time McGee attended his first national convention in Norfolk, Virginia. It was here that McGee decided privately that he would run for national president of NAPFE; the year, he decided, would be 1990. McGee went on to become president of Local 410 in 1972. In 1978 he was elected president of District Four, comprising the states of Alabama, Mississippi, and Tennessee. In 1982, Robert L. White, incumbent national president of NAPFE, sensing McGee's ambitions for the president's office, suggested that McGee run for the position of national vice president. "I really didn't want it, but it made sense, so in 1982 I ran and won."

A rift among the membership and executive committee ensued in 1987, and McGee thought about returning to Nashville. That notion lasted only three days, however. Instead McGee told his supporters that he would run for the national presidency in November 1988. McGee lost the election in June of 1988, but the results seemed questionable. "There were things that were not right, so we went to the national convention in August of that year in Jackson, Mississippi, and filed appeals to contest the election, and for the first time in labor union history a national convention set aside seven contested positions in a union election," McGee told CBB. A rerun was ordered in March of 1989 and McGee was the victor. But the transfer of authority would not be an easy one. The case went to court and only after a decision was rendered in his favor in October of 1989 was McGee seated as national president. He's been there ever since.

In October of 2001, two postal workers in the Brentwood Post Office in Washington, DC, which processes mail for the U.S. Senate, died from exposure to Anthrax, a deadly bacteria. Many members of NAPFE were angered over the deaths and treatment they received from postal officials during this time. "It did have an impact on us," McGee said. "We are still dealing with complaints stemming from this case. But we're pretty capable of taking care of problems that affect our members. We do a good job of using statutory laws to protect the interests of our members."

Followed His Father's Lesson

Just as McGee's father followed the "specifications" of his own plumbing work, he also expected his children to meet what he called the "specifications of life." Although McGee says he can't translate this directive literally, he knew what his father meant. "The union," he says, "taught me to leave a place better off than the way I found it. I've tried to live up to that." Nashville Local 410 and District Four were both left with sizeable increases in membership roles and bank accounts." As head of Local 410 he saw the organization through the purchase of its union headquarters. Leading NAPFE since 1989, McGee has skillfully steered his organization through court battles, financial crisis, changing technology, layoffs, the prospects of privatization and bioterrorism. Under McGee's leadership, NAPFE has also established a Labor Management Institute at Howard University, with a $1.5 million dollar grant. McGee, it seems continues to heed his father's advice.

Sources

Periodicals

National Alliance, October 1999, pp. 11-16.
Focus, June 2001, pp. 2-8.

On-line

"National Alliance of Postal and Federal Employees (NAPFE)," Associations Unlimited, www.galenet. galegroup.com/servlet/AU (May 9, 2004).
"NAPFE," National Alliance of Postal and Federal Employees, www.napfe.com/NAPFEabout.asp (May 9, 2004).
"James Madison McGee," Biography Resource Center, www.galenet.galegroup.com/servlet/BioRC (May 10, 2004).
"Officials' Response to Anthrax Riles Workers," Federal Times, www.federaltimes.com/postal/post10 2901 (May 29, 2004).
"Brentwood Postal Workers Push Lawsuit Over Anthrax," The Washington Post, www.washington post.com/wp-dyn/articles (May 29, 2004).

Other

Additional information for this profile was obtained through an interview with James M. McGee on May 26, 2004.

—Sharon Melson Fletcher

Dorothy Rudd Moore

1940—

Composer

Dorothy Rudd Moore, considered one of her generation's leading woman composers of color, has received commissions from such orchestras as the National Symphony, Opera Ebony, and the Buffalo Philharmonic. Her work, which includes chamber pieces, song cycles, orchestral music, and an opera, is admired for its high level of artistry and its seriousness of purpose.

Dorothy Rudd was born on June 4, 1940, in New Castle, Delaware. From a very early age, she loved music—an interest that her mother, a singer, actively supported. "I never knew a time when I wasn't interested in music," she observed to William C. Banfield in *Musical Landscapes in Color.* As a young girl, Moore listened to performances by the Philadelphia Orchestra, with Eugene Ormandy conducting, an experience that she cherished. She also made up songs and music for herself, as part of her play. "I didn't even know that the word 'composer' existed," she commented in *Musical Landscapes in Color.* "I just used to do the music." Her parents, who sent her to public schools in nearby Wilmington, encouraged her to explore all of her interests, and provided her with piano lessons. By her teens, Moore knew that she wanted to become a composer. Yet there were few role models in this field for a young black woman. As she noted in remarks quoted in *International Dictionary of Black Composers,* it seemed that all composers must be "male, white, and dead."

Moore's parents fully supported her ambitions. She continued her study of piano at Wilmington School of Music, and became a student of Howard High School

teacher (and later, Music Superintendent of Wilmington Public Schools) Harry Andrews. Moore learned to play clarinet so that she could join the all-male band at Howard High. In addition, she was a member of the school orchestra, studied music theory, and sang in the school choir and in her church choir. Though Moore considered attending Harvard University, she decided instead to enroll at Howard University in Washington, D.C., where she began as a music education major.

Excelled in Music as a University Student

At Howard, Moore studied with Dean Warner Lawson, Thomas Kerr, and Mark Fax, who supported her decision to change her major to composition. The mathematical aspects of music especially appealed to her; she has noted that the logical structure of Bach and the inventiveness of Duke Ellington were both major influences. In fact, Ellington inspired the young composer's first work, "Flight," a solo piano piece that Moore wrote at age sixteen. Howard University's music school had a symphonic wind ensemble contest, which Moore and six male students entered, using pseudonyms as required to eliminate any bias in judging. Her piece, "Reflections of Life," won the competition and was performed in concert. Her *Symphony Number One,* also written for a student competition at Howard, received the prize and was performed by the National Symphony.

After finishing her studies at Howard, Moore went to France to study with renowned teacher Nadia

Boulanger at Fountainebleau. She then returned to the United States, settling in New York City and studying composition with Chou Wen Chung. In New York, she met cellist Kermit Moore; they married in 1964. Their partnership has been described as one of mutual support and inspiration; indeed, Kermit Moore has commissioned and debuted several works by Dorothy Rudd Moore. In 1968 the Moores became founding members of the Society of Black Composers. "We felt that black composers didn't have any recognition," Dorothy Rudd Moore observed in *Musical Landscapes in Color.* "People now know about many of the [black] composers, and one of the reasons why people know is because of our organization."

Though Moore received a traditional musical education and admired the works of the great classical composers, she also grew up hearing rhythm and blues, jazz, and spirituals, and these have also influenced her work. Several of her song cycles are based on poems by black writers. *Weary Blues*, a piece for baritone cello and piano, is set to a poem by Langston Hughes. *From the Dark Tower*, a cycle of eight songs for mezzo-soprano, cello, and piano that was commissioned by Kermit Moore, sets to music poems by James Weldon Johnson, Arna Bontemps, Herbert Clark Johnson, Langston Hughes, and Countee Cullen. Moore has called the piece her "black power statement," in refer-

ence to the pain and anger she felt at pervasive racism and class privilege. "You want to put out positive energies," she commented. "With all the turmoil that was going on then, I knew that I wouldn't go out, pick up a gun, and kill somebody or anything like that, even though I was very sympathetic to a group like the [Black] Panthers...I made my statement in this way...I do not write music in a vacuum, but I was thinking that communicating my ideas and emotions about the world would make a difference."

Inspired by African American Creativity

The poems in *From the Dark Tower*, according to Helen Walker-Hill in *International Dictionary of Black Composers*, "are unified by the themes of affirmation of black creativity and anger at its frustration." The critic particularly admired Moore's references to spirituals in the cycle's first song, "O Black and Unknown Bard," by James Weldon Johnson: "the phrase 'Steal Away to Jesus' breaks the prevailing dissonance momentarily with the indescribably sweet consonance of traditional harmonies; 'Swing Low' echoes the rising and falling thirds of its tune; 'Nobody Knows the Trouble I See' is sung mournfully on repeated notes, while the piano softly plays the familiar melody as if from a great distance." The cycle ends with Cullen's "From the Dark Tower," which states "We shall not always plant while others sow.... We were not made eternally to weep!"

Among Moore's other vocal compositions set to texts by African American poets are *Flowers of Darkness*, a cycle of six songs; *Sonnets on Love, Rosebuds, and Death,* for soprano voice, violin, and piano; and *In Celebration*, a collage of poems by Langston Hughes. When the latter piece was performed in 1988 as part of the Smithsonian's series "Music of the Black American Composer," *Washington Post* critic Norman Middleton praised is as a "richly scored work" that was "just one of many jewels" in the program. Moore herself has also written numerous poems, but has chosen not to set her own work to music.

Moore's biggest project to date is her opera *Frederick Douglass*, commissioned by Opera Ebony. The composer worked for eight years on this piece, which is in three acts; she wrote the libretto as well as the music. The opera's premiere, in New York City, was conducted by Warren Wilson. Moore has taught at the Harlem School of the Arts, Bronx Community College, and New York University. Her works have been performed throughout the United States as well as in Europe and Asia.

Selected works

Reflections (symphonic wind ensemble), 1962.
Twelve Quatrains from the Rubaiyat (song cycle for soprano and oboe), 1962.

Symphony No. 1, 1963.
Baroque Suite for Cello (chamber piece), 1965.
Three Pieces for Violin and Piano, 1967.
Modes (string quartet), 1968.
Lament for Nine Instruments (flute, oboe, clarinet, trumpet, trombone, percussion,, violin, viola, and cello), 1969.
From the Dark Tower (mezzo-soprano voice, cello, and piano), 1970.
Dirge and Deliverance (cello) 1971.
Sonnets on Love, Rosebuds, and Death (soprano voice, violin, and piano), 1975.
Dream and Variations (piano), 1974.
In Celebration (chorus, soprano and baritone solos, and piano), 1977.
Weary Blues (baritone voice, cello, and piano), 1979.
Frederick Douglass (opera), 1981-85. Libretto also by the composer.
A Little Whimsy (piano), 1982.
Transcension (chamber orchestra), 1985-86.

Flowers of Darkness (song cycle, tenor voice and piano), 1988-89.

Sources

Books

Banfield, William C., *Musical Landscapes in Color: Conversations with Black American Composer,* Scarecrow Press, 2003.
Floyd, Samuel A., ed., *International Dictionary of Black Composers,* Vol. 2. Fitzroy Dearborn Publishers, 1999.

Periodicals

American Music, Spring, 1988.
Washington Post, February 19, 1987; May 18, 1988.

—E. Shostak

Lewis Nkosi

1936—

Writer

Described in South Africa *Sunday Times* as a "sharp and gifted writer with an irreverent take on life," Lewis Nkosi has lived in exile since 1960. He held several jobs in print and broadcast journalism before beginning an academic career that brought him to campuses in Europe, the United States, and Zambia. In his plays, fiction, and essays, Nkosi confronts issues relating to apartheid and its aftermath in contemporary South Africa.

Embraced Socially-Conscious Journalism

Nkosi was born on December 5, 1936, in Natal, South Africa, and attended a boarding school run by religious missionaries in Zululand, a region of Natal province that is the ancestral home of the Zulu people. He then enrolled in the M. L. Sultan Technical College in Durban. Nkosi's first job as a journalist was with a Zulu newspaper, *Ilanga Iase Natal*. In 1956 he joined the staff of *Drum* magazine, an influential publication by and for Africans that attempted to raise anti-apartheid consciousness. As he explained to Kerri Berney in the Brandeis University newspaper *The Justice*, "We would send reporters [in disguise] to jail or to white farms and have them write about how the prisoners were treated."

By 1959 Nkosi's work was sufficiently well-known that the young reporter was invited to apply for a Neiman Fellowship for study at Harvard University. He was accepted, but the South African government refused to give him a passport. "I figured I would just stay in South Africa," he explained in *The Justice,* "but a lawyer friend of mine got very angry about my treatment. He...found a very obscure law that let me out of South Africa." But once Nkosi left the country, he would lose his citizenship and not be allowed to return.

After completing his studies at Harvard, Nkosi flew to London, where he obtained work with the BBC. He produced the radio series *Africa Abroad* from 1962 to 1965, and interviewed major African writers for the television program *African Writers of Today*, a series for National Education Television. In London, Nkosi also served as editor of *New African* magazine from 1965 to 1968. Commenting later on his decision to live in exile, Nkosi told the South Africa *Sunday Times* that "I couldn't care about the prospect of not returning. My sense of what was wrong in South Africa at the time remained. But leaving helped me come to terms with the fact that we did not own injustice. I began to see the larger world from a perspective not limited to race," he added. "To be frank, I was relieved to be rid of the constraints placed on me."

Hailed as Important Black Dramatist

In 1963, Nkosi's stage play *The Rhythm of Violence* was produced in London. When it was published the following year, the play received significant praise. Depicting the plight of characters who are caught up in a spiral of mindless violence, the play shows that

At a Glance . . .

Born on December 5, 1936, in Durban, South Africa; married Bronwyn Ollerenshaw, 1965; children: Louise, Joy (twins). *Education:* Sultan Technical College, Durban, 1954-55; Harvard University, Nieman Fellow, 1961-62; University of London, BA English literature, 1974; University of Sussex, MA, 1977.

Career: *Ilanga Lase Natal* (Zulu newspaper), Durban, South Africa, staff member, 1955-56; *Golden City Post,* Johannesburg, South Africa, journalist, 1956-60; *Drum* magazine, Johannesburg, South Africa, journalist, 1956-60 *South African Information Bulletin,* Paris, France, writer, 1962-68; BBC Transcription Center, London, England, radio producer, 1962-64; *The New African,* literary editor, 1965-68; University of California-Irvine, visiting Regents professor, 1970; University of Wyoming, professor of English, 1991-99. University of Zambia, University of Warsaw, and Brandeis University, visiting teaching positions.

Awards: Dakar Festival prize, 1965; C. Day Lewis fellowship, 1977; Macmillan Silver Pen award, 1987.

Addresses: *Home*—Switzerland; *Agent*—Deborah Rogers, Rogers, Coleridge, and White Ltd., 20 Powis Mews, London W11 1JN, England.

understanding between human beings is an attainable goal, but that the rhythm of self-perpetuating violence prevents it. According to a contributor to *Contemporary Dramatists*, *The Rhythm of Violence* is an "outstanding first play and an important one," and caused critics to place Nkosi among the "vanguard of the new black South African theater."

Nkosi also wrote radio plays during this period, including *The Trial* and *We Can't All Be Martin Luther King.* His television play, *Malcolm,* aired in Sweden and in Britain. In addition to dramatic works, Nkosi also began writing literary criticism.

Nkoksi's most famous work for the stage is *The Black Psychiatrist,* a one-act play that toured several African countries and also was produced at the Centre Pompidou in Paris, France. In this work, a white woman visits the consulting room of a black male psychiatrist in England. In an openly seductive manner, the woman implies that she knows him from long ago, when they were lovers in South Africa. The psychiatrist vehe-

mently denies this, but as the play proceeds, it becomes clear that the woman does have intimate information about the doctor's past—enough to worry him. Though he tries to fend off the woman's sexual advances, the psychiatrist finally embraces her, but then reveals his own secret: that her father had raped his mother, a black servant on the white estate, and that he is the woman's half-brother.

Earned International Acclaim for "Mating Birds"

The subject of rape is also central to Nkosi's celebrated first novel, *Mating Birds*. Sibya, a young man who has just moved to the city from his native Zulu village, sees an attractive white woman on the segregated beach and begins a silent flirtation with her across the fence that separates white and colored areas. He begins following the woman everywhere, and eventually goes to her bungalow. Seeing him watching her, she undresses in front of him and lies down on the bed. He enters her room and they have sex, but almost immediately he is arrested and charged with rape. Sibya narrates his story from his prison cell, where he awaits the death sentence for this "rape." The novel attracted considerable attention. Some critics were disturbed by its suggestion that the woman was "asking for it," but others hailed it as a powerful indictment of apartheid. *Nation* critic George Packer wrote that the novel "attempts nothing less than an allegory of colonialism and apartheid, one that dares to linger in complexity." The novel won the Macmillan Silver Pen award in 1987 and has been translated into several languages.

Despite using the subject of interracial sex so prominently in his own work, Nkosi has been highly critical of the stereotypical treatment that many other black South African writers have given this theme. He makes this point clearly in his essay "Fiction by Black South Africans," which criticizes writers who rely on "readymade plots of racial violence, social apartheid, [and] interracial love affairs." Yet these elements are found in Nkosi's work, too; critics, however, have admired the fresh and often ironic approach that he brings to this material. His novel *Underground People,* for example, deals with apartheid-era resistance during South Africa's State of Emergency, which was declared in 1985 and gave the government wide-ranging emergency powers, including the power to imprison people without charge. Despite the gravity of this subject, Nkosi's novel focuses comic characters and situations. Cornelius ("Corny") Molapo is a dabbler in poetry and politics whose disappearance from Johannesburg is staged by the resistance movement so that he can travel to the countryside to organize an uprising there. Thinking that Corny has actually been detained by the government, a naive human rights worker from London comes to "find" him. South Africa *Sunday Times* contributor Andries Oliphant described the *Underground People* as a "mélange of irony, satire and ribald humour" that communicates a "droll attitude to history." Nkosi's use of a laughable character instead of a heroic one, in Oliphant's words, "boldly enacts the license of fiction and breaks with the dull dirges on the historical crisis in South Africa."

A prominent literary critic, Nkosi has written frequently for *New York Review of Books* and *London Review of Books* and has published several volumes of essays. He often criticizes contemporary South African fiction, as he does in the anthology *Writing South Africa: Literature, Apartheid, and Democracy, 1970-1995*, for its "formal insufficiencies, its disappointing bread-line asceticism and prim disapproval of irony, and its well-known predilection for what Lukacs called 'petty realism, the trivially detailed painting of local colour.'" This condition, Nkosi adds, is rooted in South Africa's colonial legacy and, "it is hoped, a post-apartheid condition will set it free." Nkosi has taught at several universities, including the University of California-Irvine, Brandeis University, and the University of Zambia. Retired from the University of Wyoming, where he was a tenured professor, he now lives in Switzerland.

Selected works

Novels

Mating Birds, East African Publishing House, 1983; St. Martin's Press, 1986.
The Hold-Up, Wordsmiths Zambia Ltd., 1989.
Underground People, Kwela Books, 2003.

Plays

Come Back Africa (screenplay), 1959.
Rhythm of Violence, 1963.
The Trial (radio play), 1969.
The Chameleon and the Lizard (libretto), 1971.
We Can't All Be Martin Luther King (radio play), 1971.

Malcolm (television play), 1972.
The Black Psychiatrist, c. 1994.

Other

Home and Exile (essays), Longman, 1965; revised edition, 1983.
The Transplanted Heart: Essays on South Africa, [Benin City, Nigeria], 1975.
Tasks and Masks: Themes and Styles of African Literature, Longman, 1981.
(Contributor) *Writing South Africa: Literature, Apartheid, and Democracy, 1970-1995*, Derek Attridge and Rosemary Jolly, eds., Cambridge University Press, 1998.

Sources

Books

Contemporary Authors, Gale Research, 2001.
Contemporary Dramatists, 6th ed., St. James Press, 1999.
Encyclopedia of World Biography, 2nd ed., Gale Research, 1998.

Periodicals

Justice, November 1, 1995.
Nation, November 22, 1986.
New York Times, May 18, 1986.
New York Times Book Review, May 18, 1986.
Sunday Times (South Africa), November 24, 2002.

On-line

"Arts/Culture Review: Underground People," *Mmegi*, www.mmegi.bw (June 29, 2004).

—E. Shostak

Ronald K. Noble

1957—

Law-enforcement official

Noble, Ronald K., photograph. AP/Wide World Photos.

Ronald K. Noble is the first American citizen ever to head Interpol, the prestigious international law-enforcement agency. A former Clinton Administration appointee in the Treasury Department, he authored the official report on what went wrong in the 1993 Waco, Texas, conflagration between U.S. federal law-enforcement personnel and a well-armed doomsday cult. For a time in the 1990s, Noble was the highest-ranking African-American law-enforcement official in the United States.

Noble was born in 1957 and grew up in Fort Dix, New Jersey. He grew up in a mixed-race household; his German-born mother had met his father, a master sergeant in the U.S. Army, when he was stationed overseas. Back home, his father worked two jobs—one at the military base nearby, and another as the owner and principal employee of a janitorial services company. As a youngster, Noble sometimes accompanied his father to work on the latter shift. His father had high hopes for him, Noble recalled in an interview with the *New York Times*'s Joyce Wadler. When they cleaned offices together, "my father would point at the degrees on the wall and say: 'Look. As soon as you have one of

those, you will have someone like me working for you.'"

Dismayed by Job Offers

Noble and his brother attended local Roman Catholic schools. He went on to the University of New Hampshire, where he studied economics and business administration. After he graduated in 1979, he entered the Stanford University School of Law. Though he earned good grades and even served as the articles editor for the school's *Law Review*, job offers were scarce as he neared his 1982 graduation date. His father decided to take matters into his own hand, and went to the Philadelphia home of a prominent federal judge and respected civil-rights figure, A. Leon Higginbotham, Jr. The elder Noble asked Higginbotham to hire his son as a clerk—a type of internship undertaken by law-school students around the time of graduation—and the judge agreed. Noble said that his father had promised the federal judge that his son was "going to make your career," as Noble recalled in the interview with Wadler. The son was mortified when he learned what his father had done, but Higginbotham agreed to hire him

The months that he spent working for Higginbotham certainly changed the direction of Noble's career. As his clerkship neared an end, Noble planned to enter private practice. Higginbotham recommended otherwise, advising Noble to enter public service. "My dream was to be able to pay the bills," Noble recalled in the *New York Times* interview. "I left Stanford with the idea of making as much money as I could make. The judge kept telling me, 'Ron, you do not want that kind of life.' I said, 'Yes, I do!'"

In the end, Noble acquiesced and took a job in the U. S. Attorney's office for the Eastern District of Pennsylvania. He was a federal prosecuting attorney, and he quickly made his name with a famous drug-ring bust that was known as the "Yuppie Conspiracy," as he explained to *American Banker* writer Robyn Meredith. The bust involved several University of Pennsylvania dental students who began selling cocaine as a way to finance their own drug use. It evolved into a $50 million cartel that operated in 13 states. "We ended up indicting and convicting a number of dentists and lawyers and stockbrokers and pilots," Noble told Meredith by the time the case went to court. "It was a

very wealthy, upper-class group who made tremendous amounts of money." Noble also prosecuted one of the largest public-corruption cases in history during his years as a federal prosecutor in Philadelphia, and earned high marks from his mentor. As Higginbotham told *Jet* a number of years later, Noble proved "a whiz. He's the smartest lawyer I've ever had in my courtroom."

Became Top Cop in United States

In 1988, Noble took a post with the U.S. Department of Justice, and also began teaching at New York University Law School. In 1993, newly elected President Bill Clinton nominated him to serve as assistant Treasury Secretary. It made him the highest-ranking law-enforcement official at the Treasury Department. Within a year, he was made Undersecretary of the Treasury, a newly created position. This gave him supervision of several agencies, including the Secret Service, Customs, and the Bureau of Alcohol, Tobacco, and Firearms (BATF). It also made him the highest-ranking African American in federal law enforcement.

President Clinton named Noble as the lead investigator of the disastrous BATF raid in Waco, Texas, that occurred in April of 1993. BATF agents had laid siege to a compound where a cult group known as the Branch Davidians lived. Noble had originally cautioned against storming it, but his advice was not heeded. His report on what went wrong cited several internal problems with the BATF and other law-enforcement agencies, and several resignations of Treasury Department officials followed.

Noble was an early advocate for investigating money-laundering trails in order to track down criminals, and headed a Financial Action Task Force within the Treasury Department to track down shadowy criminal groups via their bank transactions. He left the Treasury Department in 1996, returning to his teaching post at NYU. In 1999, Attorney General Janet Reno nominated him to head Interpol, an international agency dedicated to coordinating the law-enforcement efforts of different national agencies. He was officially elected secretary-general by its General Assembly and arrived on the job in the fall of 2000.

Headed Interpol

Interpol is an acronym for the "International Criminal Police Organization," a Lyon, France-based agency that dates back to 1923. Its original mission was to serve as a cooperative agency of police officials that would help track criminal rings that worked the casinos in Monte Carlo. In the years following World War II, its leadership had been dominated by French law-enforcement professionals. Noble was the first American to ever hold the post.

By the time Noble took over at Interpol, it had evolved into an international organization of some 181 member nations. Its internal mechanisms, however, were famously slow, and Noble believed that bureaucratic roadblocks kept it from reaching its full potential. He already had some experience with the ponderous bureaucracy for which Interpol had become somewhat infamous: back in 1998, he served on an executive committee for Interpol, where he authored a study that recommended its richer member-nations should pay added dues to offset the financial shortfalls when poorer countries could not meet their obligations. Some of this money would enable Interpol to provide the same advanced-technology tools used by countries like the United States to cash-strapped law enforcement agencies in other parts of the globe. The plan it was approved and implemented.

When he took over at Interpol in late 2000, Noble immediately began studying its remaining flaws and enacting changes. He recommended, for example, that the Interpol information clearinghouse become a 24-hour, seven-day-a-week office, instead of operating during standard business hours. He also instituted a practice whereby international alerts on suspected terrorists went out to law-enforcement personnel around the world within 24 hours. These new policies were scheduled to begin on September 17, 2001. Instead it began operating under the new plan in the hours immediately following the devastating September 11, 2001, attacks on the World Trade Center in New York City and the Pentagon Building in Washington.

At the Forefront of Anti-Terrorism Battle

Four days after September 11, Noble wrote an op-ed piece for the *New York Times* that outlined his goals as Interpol chief. "It's fine to talk about fighting terrorism, but the United States and other countries must invest more in law enforcement agencies outside their own countries," he wrote. "Investing in the world's police forces and Interpol is the only way to ensure that valuable intelligence can be gathered, analyzed, and shared internationally."

Noble also made Arabic one of the agency's official languages, along with English, French, and Spanish, and worked to rebut criticisms of Interpol. In 2002, Iraq and Libya belonged to the agency, and some critics argued that allowing rogue nations to participate was unconscionable. But Noble countered such talk by pointing out that it was an international cooperative agency, and the more members it had, the more

effective it could be. He also noted that Libyan officials were the first to issue an Interpol red notice for Al Qaeda head Osama bin Laden back in 1998. "If you're looking for dangerous people," he explained to *Fast Company* writer Chuck Salter, "you don't care whether it's your enemy or your friend who tells you, as long as you find out."

In 2003, Noble sounded a warning about fake consumer goods after an Interpol investigation linked them to shadowy political organizations such as Al Qaeda. He called the illegal trade in counterfeit designer wear such as shoes and purses "the preferred method of funding for a number of terrorist groups," according to an *International Herald Tribune* article by David Johnston.

Thanks to his mother, German is one of the languages that Noble speaks fluently, which is crucial for an Interpol chief. In earlier interviews, he claimed that the 16-hour days he regularly put in at his job made having a steady personal relationship impossible, but after becoming Interpol head, he began dating the professor who had been assigned to improve his Spanish. They had become parents in 2002, by the time Salter interviewed him for *Fast Company*. He recalled the important advice his father gave him and his brother early in life. "My father used to tell us, 'You're going to meet people who are better off than you. You can't change that,'" he told the magazine. "'But you don't have to meet anybody who works harder than you.'" It's a lesson Noble lives out every day.

Sources

Books

World of Criminal Justice, Gale, 2002.

Periodicals

American Banker, November 18, 1993, p. 6; June 21, 1994, p. 2.
Bond Buyer, April 29, 1993, p. 3.
Fast Company, October 2002, p. 96.
International Herald Tribune, July 18, 2003, p. 1.
Jet, May 31, 1993, p. 8; August 1, 1994, p. 36; January 8, 1996, p. 7; July 26, 1999, p. 4.
New York Times, July 13, 1999; September 15, 2001, p. A23.

—Carol Brennan

Ron O'Neal

1937-2004

Actor

For some three decades before his death from cancer in 2004, actor Ron O'Neal struggled to distance himself from his 1972 role as Youngblood Priest in the 1972 smash movie, *Superfly*. Considered one of the classics in the "blaxploitation" genre of the era, *Superfly* featured O'Neal as the iconic anti-hero of a gritty urban milieu who tries to cash out of the drug-dealing business with one final, lucrative transaction. The stage-trained actor's "interpretation of the long-haired, ultra-hip, ultra-violent cocaine dealer," noted *Guardian* journalist Ronald Bergan, "who wore tight white suits and drove a customised Cadillac, made him into an instant star, mainly among the vast urban black movie-going public."

O'Neal was born on September 1, 1937, in Utica, New York, but he grew up in a working-class black neighborhood in Cleveland, Ohio. His father was a factory worker who had been a jazz musician in the 1920s and even played in the pit orchestra for the hit revue *Blackbirds of 1929*. Yet as O'Neal told the *New York Times* in a lengthy 1972 interview, his father "kept his clarinet and saxophone up in the attic, and I

O'Neal, Ron, photograph. The Kobal Collection.

never even knew he had been a musician until after he was dead." The idea of a dream deferred became a force in O'Neal's own tenuous ambitions, he told the newspaper's Maurice Peterson. His father died when he was 16, and his son believed the hard labor was the cause of death. "I swore right then that they'd never work me to death in those factories," he told Peterson in the *New York Times*. "I told my mother that; I told everybody."

Discovered Theater

Tragedy struck the O'Neal family again just six months after the father's death, when O'Neal's brother, a truck driver, died in an accident. His mother found a job in a hospital and, after finishing high school, O'Neal spent one semester at Ohio State University in Columbus, where he preferred playing bridge and chess to attending class, and earned dismal grades as a result. Returning to Cleveland, his prospects dim, he even considered taking a dreaded factory job himself, but one day a friend took him to see a play at the Karamu House, an experimental theater group in Cleveland that dated

At a Glance . . .

Born September 1, 1937, in Utica, NY; died of pancreatic cancer, January 14, 2004, in Los Angeles, CA; son of a factory worker and a hospital employee; married; wife's name, Audrey Pool.

Career: Actor, 1956-2004. Housepainter, Cleveland, OH, c. 1956-64; Harlem Youth Arts Program, NY, acting instructor, 1964-66.

Awards: Actors' Equity, Clarence Derwent Award, 1969, *Village Voice,* Obie (Off-Broadway) Award for best performance, 1970, and Drama Desk Award, 1970, all for *No Place to Be Somebody.*

back to 1913 and featured interracial productions. "I saw *Finian's Rainbow* there and it blew my mind," he recalled in the interview with Peterson. "I had never seen a play before."

Within months, O'Neal had joined the Karamu House ensemble and spent the next eight years performing in plays like *A Raisin in the Sun* and *A Streetcar Named Desire.* He worked as a housepainter to support his acting career. "It was good training," he said of the Karamu years in the *New York Times* interview, "and, though I wasn't paid, at least I wasn't charged, as I would have been at an actor's studio." In 1964, offered a job teaching acting classes at the groundbreaking Harlem Youth Arts Program, O'Neal relocated to New York City. He taught for two years there and tried to win parts in off-Broadway productions, but found it difficult. Part of the reason was due to his appearance: with his long, straight hippie hair and lighter skin, O'Neal failed to fit the bill for standard African-American roles in theater. One day in 1970 he tried out for a play called *Ceremonies in Dark Old Men.* "As soon as I stepped into the room, the producer said, 'you won't do,'" he told Peterson. "By this time, I was getting pretty desperate, so I went out and bought an Afro wig. When I got back to the office, he took one look at me and said, 'Well, now, that's better!'"

O'Neal won the role, but was also offered another right afterward, for a play slated for a weeklong tryout at the small experimental theater at the Joseph Papp Public Theatre. The *Ceremonies* role would pay him $112 a week, while he would have to do the untested play for free. He chose the latter, and *No Place to Be Somebody,* a new drama by Charles Gordone, became a turning point in O'Neal's career. Papp, a highly regarded theater impresario, liked the unsentimental urban drama so much that he signed O'Neal and rest of the cast to a contract immediately. The play went on to enjoy a long run at the American National Theatre Academy venue, and critics applauded O'Neal's portrayal of a bar owner and part-time pimp trying to gain the upper hand over the local mob. Gordone became the first African American to win a Pulitzer Prize in drama for the work, and O'Neal racked up several honors himself for *No Place to Be Somebody,* including the prestigious Obie, Drama Desk, and Clarence Derwent awards.

Rejected for Shakespeare

O'Neal's big break was a mixed blessing, however, for he still found it difficult to win new roles. He appeared in a 1970 Elliott Gould movie called *Move,* returned to *No Place* for its run on Broadway, which lasted just three weeks, and then didn't work for seven months. Papp offered him part in his acclaimed "Shakespeare in the Park" summer series, but another director took over the project, and when O'Neal went to see him, he was cagey about whether or not there was a part for him. The director finally told him, "'Quite frankly, I really don't think Black people should do Shakespeare,'" O'Neal recalled in the *New York Times* interview. "I said, 'Well, at least you're honest about it,' and that was the end of that."

O'Neal took another film role, in a 1971 drama with Sidney Poitier called *The Organization,* but he loathed it. He was cast as a Puerto Rican "who was always upset, always angry—what they *thought* a Puerto Rican is," he told Peterson. He returned to the stage in *The Dream on Monkey Mountain* with the Negro Ensemble Company, which earned good reviews during its 1971 Los Angeles previews and again for a New York run, but it was a part he had almost not received, and he remained frustrated over the stalling of what had seemed a promising career just a year before.

O'Neal's fortunes were about to change once again, however. A friend of his, Phillip Fenty, ran a successful advertising agency, but was writing a screenplay that fell into a new and daring black film genre. Two releases from 1971 marked the onset of what became known as the blaxploitation film genre, *Shaft* and Melvin Van Peebles's *Sweet Sweetback's Baad Asssss Song.* Both portrayed urban life in America as a melting pot, a roiling mix of violence, distrust of corrupt authorities, political awakening, and streets ruled by sharp-witted characters who triumphed through sheer nerve. Fenty told O'Neal that he would write the screenplay's main character with O'Neal in mind, and the actor agreed to become *Superfly* if the project got off the ground.

Superfly built upon the box-office success of *Shaft,* the 1971 film directed by Gordon Parks Sr. The title character of *Shaft* was played by Richard Roundtree, who became an overnight star thanks to the film and its intriguing premise about who actually controlled the streets of Harlem. Parks's son, Gordon Jr., signed on to direct *Superfly,* and it became a sensation as well.

O'Neal played Harlem cocaine dealer Youngblood Priest, who has wearied of his lifestyle and engineers a deal that will net him a small fortune and enable him to get out the business forever. Corrupt cops and vicious mobsters prove more of a danger than the threat of potential jail time, but O'Neal's hero walks away unscathed, with his retirement money intact.

Movie Became Classic Blaxploitation Epic

When *Superfly* hit theaters in the summer of 1972, Warner Brothers spent little to promote it, fearing negative publicity, but the movie quickly caught on via word of mouth and became a sensation. Made by Parks on a budget of just $500,000, it grossed $5 million, and the soundtrack by Curtis Mayfield sold two million copies. "Urban audiences flocked to the cinemas, identifying with the tall, charismatic leading man and loving the gritty dialogue, locations, and situations," noted Perrone in London's *Independent*. "The film was condemned by critics and by the National Association for the Advancement of Colored People for glorifying the dealer life style, but O'Neal remained adamant that the whole point of *Superfly* was that the pusher was trying to escape his circumstances."

In interviews at the time, O'Neal argued strenuously that the Mayfield soundtrack provided the real theme behind the film, weaving a strong anti-drug message into the narrative that did not glamorize the drug trade, but instead portrayed the desperation and ambiguity of those drawn into it, both as purveyors and consumers. Even "the title is an ironic one," O'Neal explained to the *New York Times*'s Peterson. "'Fly' means hip, glamorous, together, and we show that that life is just the opposite." He also scoffed at the NAACP picketing of certain theaters in the Los Angeles area, in which protesters handed out leaflets demanding that the studio recall *Superfly* and re-shoot it with a new, more morally resounding ending. "Can you dig that?" O'Neal joked with Peterson. "Here's a picture where a Black man finally manages to beat the system and they'd rather see him dead!"

Partly in response to the storm over *Superfly*, O'Neal agreed to appear in a sequel, which also marked his directorial debut. *Super Fly TNT*, released in 1973, found Priest living in Europe, but missing the action of his former career. Inspired by the story of a group of African rebels fighting for their country's independence, he becomes involved in the illegal arms trade. The *Times* of London termed it "a bore, with Rome and Senegal seeming much less hip than Harlem in the original."

Relegated to Action Roles

O'Neal had a hard time finding solid roles after *Superfly*. He appeared in several crime and action films over the next quarter-century, including *Billy Jack* (1975), *A Force of One* (1979), and *Red Dawn* (1984). His first television role came opposite Muhammad Ali in a 1979 television miniseries, *Freedom Road,* about a slave who becomes a politician. In the 1980s and 1990s O'Neal won recurring roles on the small screen in *Bring 'Em Back Alive* and *The Equalizer,* and occasional guest roles on shows like *Hill Street Blues* and *Living Single*. He returned to directing in 1991 with *Up Against the Wall,* a little-seen drama set in a Chicago housing project, and to the theater in a 1994 Stratford Festival production of *Othello*.

In the years since the blaxploitation films came and went, a cult following has sprung up around them. Mainstream Hollywood responded with *Original Gangstas,* a 1996 film that featured all the genre's screen luminaries, including O'Neal, Roundtree ,and the original Foxy Brown, Pam Grier, in a drama set on the gang-violence-plagued streets of Gary, Indiana. O'Neal enjoyed making the film, and noted that it was the first time that all the era's names had ever appeared together in the same movie. He noted in an *Entertainment Weekly* interview that though he had been forever typecast by his Superfly role, he remembered fondly the spirit of daring and originality with which those films had been made. "I had a sense of hope, a sense of the future," he told the magazine. "I saw no reason why black films wouldn't go on, strengthen themselves, and become better."

O'Neal was diagnosed with pancreatic cancer in 2000, and made his last film, *On the Edge,* in 2002 with Ice-T. He died on January 14, 2004, at the age of 66. In the *New York Times* interview from 1972, he had predicted that *Superfly,* though somewhat controversial in its message, would prove inspirational in the end. "Black people are dying quietly without skills, motivation, or any desire to accomplish," he insisted. "If indeed 'Super Fly' does encourage young people, I'm happy. And I doubt that they'll be encouraged to become coke hustlers, because they're too intelligent. I'm hoping that the most inspiration will come from our success as filmmakers."

Sources

Books

Contemporary Theatre, Film, and Television, Vol. 37, Gale, 2002.

Periodicals

Daily News (Los Angeles, CA), May 10, 1996, p. L11.
Daily Variety, January 19, 2004, p. 9; March 8, 2004, p. 16.
Entertainment Weekly, May 10, 1996, p. 45.
Independent (London, England), January 20, 2004, p. 16.
Jet, February 9, 2004, p. 64.

New York Times, September 17, 1972, p. D11; January 17, 2004, p. B7.
Times (London, England), March 12, 2004, p. 42.

—Carol Brennan

Percy Pierre

1939—

Educator, engineer

In 1967 Percy Pierre became the first African American to earn a doctorate in electrical engineering. Within a year he had begun a very successful career that would include stints as a White House fellow, a university president, and an engineering consultant. He could have very easily focused only on his own career and enjoyed the fruits of his hard academic labors, but he was lonely. "I felt good about having made it," Pierre told *MSU Today,* "but I felt that there was something wrong being the only one." In 1973 Pierre helped outline what would become the National Action Council for Minorities in Engineering (NACME). Bringing together corporate, academic, and foundation support, NACME has provided more than $100 million to nearly 18,000 minority engineering graduate students in the days since its founding. Those students have gone on to become highly trained scientists, engineers, and business leaders, making sure that Pierre was never alone in his field again.

Percy Anthony Pierre was born on January 3, 1939, in St. James Parish, Louisiana, not far from New Orleans. His parents were Rosa Villavaso Pierre and Percy John Pierre, whose ancestry stretched back to the Maqua tribe of Mozambique, Africa. After graduating from St. Augustine High School in New Orleans, Pierre enrolled in Notre Dame University in South Bend, Indiana. While a student there Pierre helped organize the first and only civil rights march in South Bend and participated in efforts to integrate bars and restaurants in the city. In 1961 he received a bachelor's of science and in 1963 a master's of science, both in electrical engineering. He then transferred to Baltimore's Johns Hopkins

University where in 1967 he earned an electrical engineering PhD, becoming the first African American in the country to do so. He specialized in applied mathematics and signal processing in the field of communications.

After receiving his doctorate, Pierre did post-doctoral work at the University of Michigan before moving to Santa Monica, California, to take on a research position in the communications division of The Rand Corporation in 1968. In 1969 Pierre was appointed a White House Fellow for the Office of the President of the United States. Following the fellowship he returned to Rand for an additional year. During this period Pierre published several important academic papers on signal processing and detection.

In 1971 Pierre moved into the academic side of his field when he accepted the position of dean of the school of engineering at Howard University, one of the nation's most prestigious historically black colleges. At Howard he soon became involved in various programs to increase minority participation in engineering. The group Minority Engineering Education Effort asked Pierre to assist with several areas including the Minority Introduction to Engineering program. The following year, after announcing its plans to support a country-wide effort to increase the number of minority engineers, GE recruited Pierre to be a partner in this plan. On behalf of GE, Pierre approached the National Academy of Engineering (NAE) and proposed a symposium on the subject. NAE agreed and appointed Pierre chairman of the planning committee and co-chairman of the symposium. The symposium, held in

At a Glance . . .

Born on January 3, 1939, in St. James Parish, LA; married Olga A. Markham, 1965; children: Kristin Clare and Allison Celeste. *Education:* University of Notre Dame, BS, electrical engineering, 1961; University of Notre Dame, MS, electrical engineering, 1963; John Hopkins University, PhD, electrical engineering, 1967; University of Michigan, post-doctoral studies, 1968.

Career: Rand Corporation, Santa Monica, CA, systems engineer, 1968-71; White House, Office of the President, fellow, 1969-70; Howard University, School of Engineering, dean, 1971-77; Alfred P. Sloan Foundation, New York, NY, program officer, 1973-75; U.S. Department of the Army, assistant secretary, 1977-81; Percy A. Pierre & Associates, Bethesda, MD, president, 1981-83; Prairie View A&M University, president, 1983-89; Michigan State University, vice president, research and graduate studies, 1990-95; Michigan State University, professor, 1995–.

Selected memberships: The University of Notre Dame, trustee, 1973–; CMS Energy, board member, 1990–; The Aerospace Corporation, board member, 1991–; Hampshire College, trustee, 1996–; National Action Council for Minorities in Engineering, board member, 1983-89.

Awards: University of Notre Dame, honorary doctorate, 1977; U.S. Army, distinguished civilian service award, 1981; Rensselaer Polytechnic Institute, honorary doctorate, 1984; National Action Council for Minorities in Engineering, Reginald Jones Award, 1984; National Action Council for Minorities in Engineering, Founders Award, 2004.

Addresses: *Office*—Michigan State University, Electrical and Computer Engineering, 3224 Engineering Bldg., East Lansing, MI 48824-1226.

nority engineering students. Pierre credited this success to working with the private sector, particularly companies such as GE, Exxon, and Boeing who would benefit from an increased engineering talent pool. "You can always take money and give it to one student, but if we ran out of money the project would end," Pierre told *MSU Today*. "Instead, we created an institute to raise money for scholarships from industry. It's about leveraging a lot of resources to build something that would last."

Following the symposium, the Alfred P. Sloan foundation, an educational foundation started by former General Motors CEO Alfred P. Sloan, pledged 20% of its budget over a five-year period to increasing the number of minorities in engineering. They tapped Pierre to head up the program. Though still a full-time dean with Howard, he was able to work part-time with Sloan and helped institute several enduring programs. They included the National Scholarship Fund for Minority Engineering Students, developed with Sloan and NACME, and the National Consortium for Graduate Degrees for Minorities in Engineering and Science. He also funded mathematics and engineering programs at several high schools across the country. During this time Pierre published several papers on the topic of minorities in engineering. Meanwhile he maintained his academic career in engineering, earning grants and publishing academic papers on communications and systems research.

Pierre left the world of academia and joined that of defense in 1977, becoming an assistant secretary for research, development, and acquisition in the US Department of the Army. He managed nearly $10 billion annually for the research, development, and production of weapons systems including smart weapons, radar systems, and secure communications. During the first Gulf war, Pierre was credited with the success of the Patriot Missile's capabilities. In 1979 he authored "Equipping the Army," a congressional report that was cited for an Award of Merit by Senator Proxmire, who called the report one of the most readable and honest presentations that he had seen in his many years in government.

Pierre left the military sector in 1981 to open a private engineering consultancy firm. Upon his resignation he received the distinguished civilian service award from the army. Percy A. Pierre Associates of Bethesda, Maryland, assisted Morgan State University, Florida A&M, and Xavier University with their respective engineering programs. Pierre also consulted with the Washington, DC, and the Baton Rouge, Louisiana, public school systems on the creation of engineering high schools.

In 1983 Pierre returned once again to academia, accepting the post of president at Prairie View A&M University, a historically black university located in Prairie View, Texas. Overseeing a budget of $65

the summer of 1973, resulted in the creation of the NAE's National Advisory Committee on Minorities in Engineering (later changed to National Advisory Council on Minorities in Engineering after breaking off from the NAE). Thirty years later NACME stood as the nation's largest private source of scholarships for mi-

million, 950 employees, and nearly 6,000 students, Pierre led the school in major reforms including the construction of nine new buildings and the renovation of seven more. He established the College of Engineering Technology as well as an honors program. By the time he left the post in 1989, enrollment had increased by 25 percent and the school's endowment had swelled from $300,000 to over $3 million.

Pierre moved to Michigan State University in 1990 and took over the position of vice president for research and graduate studies. He oversaw 6,000-plus graduate students and research projects valued in excess of $140 million per year. In 1995 he returned to teaching as a professor of electrical engineering for the university. In 1998 he also became director of MSU's Sloan Scholars Program in Signal Processing, Communications, Computers and Controls (SPC3). The program recruits and mentors minority graduate engineering students.

In May of 2004 Pierre received the Founders Award from NACME at lavish gala held at New York's Waldorf-Astoria hotel. The gala, celebrating the group's 30th anniversary, was attended by a who's who of academia, industry, and philanthropy. Bill Cosby was even on hand to lend his support. Upon accepting his award *Business Wire* quoted Pierre as saying, "NACME, over its 30 year history, has provided direct support to thousands of minority engineering students and been the focal point for collaboration and leadership for many organizations and individuals working in this important field. I am proud to accept this award from an organization that continues to be a part of America's efforts to develop and utilize its human talent." Had Pierre not turned his own talent to developing opportunities for others, NACME might not exist at all, and though it is not likely he'd still be lonely in his field, there would be a lot fewer minority engineers working alongside him.

Sources

Periodicals

Business Wire, May 5, 2004.
People Weekly, September 25, 2000.

On-line

"Black Alumni of Notre Dame," *Notre Dame University,* http://alumni.nd.edu/groups/bio.htm (May 28, 2004).
"Founders Award," *National Action Council for Minorities in Engineering,* www.nacme.org/gala/honorees.html#pierre (May 28, 2004).
"History," *Prairie View Texas A&M University,* www.pvamu.edu/index.php?page=history (May 28, 2004).
"Percy A. Pierre, PhD," *Michigan State University,* www.egr.msu.edu/ece/fac_staff/pierre/ (May 28, 2004).
"The Faces of Science: African Americans in the Sciences: Percy Anthony Pierre: Electrical Engineer, Mathematician,"*Princeton,* www.princeton.edu/~mcbrown/display/pierre.html (May 28, 2004).
"Professor to be Honored for Creating Opportunities," *MSU Today,* www.msutoday.msu.edu/news/index.php3?article=30Apr2004-10 (May 28, 2004).

—Candace LaBalle

Iris Rideau

1940(?)—

Winery owner

Iris Rideau may be the only African-American female winery owner in the United States. Her success in the competitive world of vines and vineyards seems surprising, given that she knew nothing about wines before setting up Rideau Vineyard in the mid-1990s, and that opening a winery wasn't even her first choice when she decided to start a new business. Yet to those who knew Iris Rideau well, it was no surprise that her wines began winning prizes and garnering write-ups in magazines like *Wine Spectator.* She had a long record of success in business behind her.

And furthermore, Rideau grew up surrounded by good food and an appreciation for the pleasures of the palate. Born Iris Duplantier around 1940 in New Orleans, she lived in the city's Seventh Ward, a Creole neighborhood. Two of her uncles ran a restaurant called Little Ferd's, and food was central to her domestic life. "I'm originally from New Orleans, and I have a Creole heritage," she told *Wines & Vines.* "When you're born and raised in New Orleans, you have to cook. I grew up with this culture of good food and good wine, so starting a winery was kind of a natural for me."

Rideau and her mother moved to Los Angeles when she was 10, and as she grew up her love of food never left her. She would always, she told *New Orleans Magazine,* taste "everything I thought might be good." But it was a long time before Rideau put her good taste to work in her career. She worked in a variety of positions in the Los Angeles area, even becoming a model for Victoria's Secret catalog at one point. Though she stopped using her maiden name at some point in her adult life, little information is known about Rideau's personal life.

Headed Successful Insurance Agency

In 1967, she opened Rideau & Associates Insurance Agency and later created another business, Rideau Retirement Planning Consultants. These enterprises were tremendously successful; by the 1990s Rideau was worth an estimated $12 million, and in 1998 she was listed in an *Essence* magazine feature profiling some of the nation's wealthiest African-American female business owners. But by the late 1980s Rideau, who had grown up in neighborhood-oriented New Orleans, was tired of the stress of living in Los Angeles and its on-the-road life. Looking toward retirement, she purchased a six-acre plot of land northwest of Los Angeles near the town of Solvang in the Santa Ynez Valley.

She had two houses built on the land, one for herself and the other for her mother Olivia. Then, in 1995, she bought another 24 acres of land adjoining the plot she already owned. The new land contained a crumbling mansion built in 1884 by two English immigrants, a local landmark called the Alamo Pintado Adobe that had served as an inn at the turn of the nineteenth century. Rideau was looking for a new outlet for her considerable energies. "The closer I got to retiring, the more I realized that I wasn't ready to quit working," she told *Wines & Vines.* So she laid plans to restore the mansion as a bed-and-breakfast inn. She worked closely with an architect on the restoration.

Born Iris Duplantier in 1940(?) in New Orleans, LA.

Career: Rideau & Associates Insurance Agency, owner, 1967-89; Rideau Retirement Planning Consultants, owner, c.1960s-c.1990s; Rideau Vineyard, owner, 1997–.

Awards: Best of Show, New Orleans Wine Competition, 1998; more than three dozen awards for individual wines since 1997.

Addresses: *Office*—Rideau Vineyard, 1562 Alamo Pintado Rd., Solvang, CA 93463, *Web*—www.rideauvineyard.com.

The bed-and-breakfast plan couldn't be reconciled with local zoning regulations, but Rideau did determine that a wine tasting room would be permitted. So, with an abundance of prime Central Coast grape-growing land at her disposal, Rideau decided on a winery even though she knew little about the business. At the beginning it might have seemed like a second choice, but Rideau, with her love of good food, quickly warmed to the idea. "Once you learn how to run one business successfully, you can pretty much run any business," Rideau pointed out to *Essence*. "You just have to learn about the industry and surround yourself with experienced and talented people."

Those talented people in Rideau's case included veteran winemakers Rick Longoria, Ariel LaVie, and James Rutherford, who supervised Rideau's Rhone-style wines and who, unbeknownst to Rideau at first, had some black ancestry. Rideau Vineyard opened for business in 1997, at first buying grapes from neighboring wineries. Rideau had lots of competition in her part of California, but her wines began winning prizes almost from the start. One vintage took the Best of Show prize in the 1998 New Orleans Wine Competition, and *Wine Spectator* magazine took note of several of her wines.

Rideau's 15-acre vineyard cost about $375,000 to develop, an expense partly financed by the sale of Rideau's other businesses in 1999. By 2002 she was making wines from grapes grown on site. By that time, Rideau had learned more about her new business. She moved away from selling wine through wholesalers in favor of a direct, hands-on approach that involved making fine restaurants and high-end retailers aware of her product. Rideau also focused on her tasting room housed in the Alamo Pintado Adobe mansion. The tasting room became a popular Southern California stop for food lovers, and it helped introduce consumers to Rideau's wines.

Tapped New Customer Base

That was important for a business like Rideau's, because as an African-American winemaker she couldn't necessarily count on the African-American customer base that other black business owners enjoyed. Consumption of fine wines was historically low among African Americans, but winemakers were beginning to market their wares to a group many saw as an underserved potential market. Rideau herself didn't expect a large black customer base, but she was pleasantly surprised. "I have gotten so much support from the black community," she told *Wines & Vines*. "The people just started coming—now they come in buses! We have a bus come out from Los Angeles just about every month, either with a sorority or a club or just a group of friends. People come out with different things to present to me; they've given me awards, plaques, and books. They tell me they're so honored that I've done this."

By the first quarter of 2003, Rideau Vineyards was turning a profit; 2002 revenues of $1 million rose to $1.5 million in 2003, with annual production of 6,500 cases. And Rideau added another award to her mantelpiece with a 2004 *Black Enterprise* Business Innovator of the Year nomination. As the top-flight winemakers with whom Rideau had surrounded herself began to refine her newly planted grape stocks, connoisseurs of fine wine looked forward to new top-quality vintages from the vineyard. Rideau herself, working 10 to 12 hours a day and cooking gumbo at Alamo Pintado Adobe before every tasting, seemed further from retirement than ever. "I love what I do," she told *Black Enterprise* in 2003. "I work hard and, at the end of the day, I just burn out and crash."

Sources

Periodicals

Black Enterprise, August 2003, p. 37; May 2004, p. 48.
Essence, February 2000, p. 50.
Jacksonville Free Press, September 23, 1998, p. 3.
Louisiana Weekly, September 10, 2001.
New Orleans Magazine, September 2000, p. 50.
San Francisco Chronicle, January 2, 2003.
Wines & Vines, January 2002.

On-line

"An Interview With…Rideau Vineyards, Solvang, CA," *El Rancho Marketplace*, www.elranchomarket.com/arch_rideau.html (June 10, 2004).
"Iris Rideau," *Rideau Vineyard*, www.rideauvineyard.com (June 10, 2004).

"Passport to Wine Finds Two Distinct Destinations: New Orleans and Australia," *Taste California Travel,*Fwww.tastecaliforniatravel.com/passport -wine.htm (June 10, 2004).

—James M. Manheim

Randall Robinson

1941—

Lobbyist, foreign policy strategist, human rights activist, author

Randall Robinson is the executive director of TransAfrica, Inc., a Washington-based lobbying organization devoted to the fight for human rights for people of color throughout the world. Since its inception in 1977, TransAfrica has been at the forefront of the crusade to shape U.S. foreign policy in Africa and the Caribbean Basin. Robinson's passion, commitment, and political savvy—combined with financial support from corporate giants like Coca-Cola, Nike, Reebok, and Anheuser-Busch—have made him and TransAfrica indisputable forces in the continued fight for racial justice worldwide.

According to Robinson, it is ignorance of geopolitics that so often explains America's regrettable silence on the human rights violations of tyrannical regimes that operate all over the globe–and, in some cases, only hundreds of miles beyond U.S. borders. In addition, he charges that racism is at the root of an American immigration policy that has rejected the political asylum claims of Haitian refugees while welcoming non-blacks from other corners of the world. In order to fight these twin foes of ignorance and racism, Robinson's TransAfrica has relied on both backroom political pressure and high-profile public education campaigns.

Robinson's participation in a quiet act of civil disobedience in 1984 set in motion a radical change in American policy toward South Africa's discriminatory apartheid regime. Along with black political activists Mary Frances Berry and Walter Fauntroy, he masterminded a year-long protest of the South African embassy in Washington, D.C. So successful was he in creating the atmosphere for political change in South Africa, so influential was his voice in the chorus to end that country's institutionalized racism, that U.S. Senator Ted Kennedy of Massachusetts, as quoted in the *New York Times,* described the lobbyist as "the 101st senator in all our debates on apartheid."

The man who turned a two-person organization in a basement office into a 15,000-member national lobby that ignited the "Free South Africa Movement" was exposed to racism in his own country long before he cast his eyes on injustices around the world. Born on June 6, 1941, in Richmond, Virginia, Robinson—the younger brother of the late Max Robinson, the nation's first African American network news anchor—was educated in segregated public schools and graduated from Richmond's formerly all-black Virginia Union University in 1967. "Early on in life," he told *People* magazine, "I was taught that an unprincipled life is not worth living."

Robinson first sat next to white students at Harvard University Law School, where he earned his degree in 1970. While many of his classmates chose to follow the lucrative path of corporate law, Robinson traveled to Tanzania on a Ford fellowship and then returned to Boston to work as a civil rights attorney for a legal aid project. He went to Washington in 1975 as an aide to Missouri congressman William Clay. A year later, while an administrative assistant to Michigan Democratic representative Charles C. Diggs, Jr., took part in a congressional delegation's trip to South Africa.

At a Glance . . .

Born on July 6, 1941, in Richmond, VA; son of Maxie Cleveland (a high school history teacher) and Doris (a teacher and homemaker) Robinson; married Brenda Randolph (a librarian; divorced); married second wife, Hazel (a foreign policy adviser), c. 1987; children: (first marriage) Anikie, Jabari; (second marriage) Khalea. *Education:* Virginia Union University, Richmond, BA, 1967; Harvard University Law School, Cambridge, MA, JD, 1970. *Military Service:* Served in the U.S. Army, mid-1960s.

Career: Civil rights attorney, Boston, 1971-75; aide to U.S. representative William Clay, 1975, and to U.S. representative Charles C. Diggs, Jr., 1976; TransAfrica, Inc., executive director, 1977-95, president, 1995-2001; TransAfrica Forum, executive director, 1981-95, president, 1995-2001; writer, 2001-.

Selected awards: Ford fellowship; National Association of Black Journalists' Community Services Award; Martin Luther King Jr. Center for Non-Violent Social Change, Humanitarian Award; National Rainbow Coalition, Hope Award; Southern Christian Leadership Conference, Drum Major for Justice Award.

Addresses: *Office*—c/o TransAfrica Forum, 1426 21st Street, NW, 2nd Floor, Washington, DC 20036. *Home*—St. Kitts.

Founded TransAfrica

The dehumanizing consequences of South African apartheid—a political system that denied the country's black majority its most basic civil rights—became frighteningly clear to Robinson. In one case, a liberal South African businessman told Diggs that granting voting power to blacks would be akin to giving a gun to a five-year-old. In an interview with *Ebony*, Robinson stated that South African blacks were obliged to endure "a hate-inducing system that forces one to choose between an expression of self-dignity that puts your life at risk or a turning of that emotion inside that makes you a stooped human being." The idea for TransAfrica was born in 1976 during the annual session of the Congressional Black Caucus. Representative Diggs and former congressman and civil rights crusader Andrew Young convened a special meeting to discuss the policy of then-President Gerald Ford's administration in Rhodesia (now Zimbabwe). Calling for an end to white rule

of the 98-percent-black populace, guerrilla fighters in that African country were engaged in deadly fighting with government troops.

In articulating their opposition to Ford's policy of tolerance toward the white rulers, the meeting attendees broached an issue of much larger scope. They concluded that there was a deplorable scarcity of people of color in high-level international affairs positions and that a private advocacy organization was needed to counter the neglect of African and Caribbean needs in U.S. foreign policy-making circles. TransAfrica, the first organization of its kind, was incorporated in 1977; Robinson—with his educational and work background and his political savvy—was chosen as its executive director.

In order for the lobbying group to enjoy influence with Washington politicians, Robinson knew he needed to assemble a constituency of Americans who had overcome their ignorance of African and Caribbean issues and would provide support, in money and in their own activism, for the causes that TransAfrica would champion. In 1981 TransAfrica Forum, the research and educational affiliate of TransAfrica, was established to collect and disseminate information to help plan U.S. foreign policy in black areas of the world.

With educational programs for minorities, foreign policy conferences, and numerous publications, TransAfrica Forum undertakes the frequently challenging role of shedding light on political injustices that have not attracted sustained television news coverage. This task, Robinson has said, is complicated by the fact that most Americans of all colors care less about foreign than domestic policy, less about the cruel and barbarous conditions in which millions of non-American blacks are forced to live than about the standards of living for people within the United States.

Focused on South Africa

But as Robinson told *Black Enterprise*, "You don't change policy under the presumption that you must have a majority opinion on your side. In the final analysis, you need to organize a critical mass of people, which is not necessarily the majority of the black community. The issue is how well organized we are at a certain level and how vigorously we can apply pressure on the administration and the Congress to create the foreign policy we want." TransAfrica emerged as a potent national force in 1984, when apartheid, the official, segregationist policy of South Africa that was instituted in 1948, first began to generate heated public debate and outrage on the worldwide political scene. After a meeting with South Africa's ambassador to the United States, Robinson, former U.S. civil rights commissioner Mary Frances Berry, and former Washington, D.C., delegate Walter Fauntroy refused to leave the South African embassy in Washington until the process to dismantle apartheid had begun and Nelson Mandela, the long-jailed president of the African National Congress (ANC), was released.

This 1960s-style sit-in and the subsequent arrest of Robinson and the others prompted 53 consecutive weeks of daily protests in Washington and at South African consulates in 23 cities across the United States, as well as symbolic vigils at embassies around the world. At the American protests, more than 4,000 people were arrested, including 23 members of Congress, mayors, civil rights activists, and celebrities. Because of these demonstrations and the famous names associated with them, American scrutiny of South African political injustice reached an all-time high, and, consequently, TransAfrica's fight for political action enjoyed the fuel of public support.

Robinson and others called on Congress to enact strict economic sanctions against South Africa, claiming the suspension of U.S. trade and loans to that country would expedite the fracturing of apartheid. However, then-President Ronald Reagan continued to embrace his "constructive engagement" policy, which argued that sanctions would hurt black South African workers more than their white employers and that political reform in South Africa would more likely result from a conciliatory rather than antagonistic approach. But TransAfrica and other groups had momentum on their side. In 1986 the U.S. Senate overrode a Reagan veto to pass a series of sweeping sanctions against South Africa.

This legislation, known as the Anti-Apartheid Act of 1986, resulted in a ban on the importation of the gold Krugerrand coin (a South African currency) into the United States; a ban on the transfer of nuclear materials and technology to South Africa; a ban on the sale of computers and computer technology to South African military, police, and other agencies enforcing apartheid; and a cut-off in U.S. loans, except those providing education, housing, or health facilities on a nondiscriminatory basis. John S. DeMott wrote in *Time*, "U.S. Senators and Representatives who voted for sanctions against apartheid enthusiastically acknowledge that Robinson's cool, calm competence helped rally black and white Americans against apartheid."

Though academics and policy analysts debated the effectiveness of the sanctions, subsequent events in South Africa indicated that financial leverage, in combination with continued public pressure, contributed to the reversal of apartheid. After the release of Mandela in 1990 and his triumphant world tour, Robinson urged anti-apartheid activists not to allow the euphoria to quiet their calls for the structural dismantling of the regime. When U.S. president George Bush's administration relaxed the sanctions in 1991, responding to reform measures implemented by South African president F. W. de Klerk, Robinson argued that blacks still had no real economic or political power in that country, and that the incentive for de Klerk to continue toward

a democratic government had been unwisely lifted.

Robinson maintained his belief that the main pillars of apartheid were likely to remain in place. Responding to a 1992 referendum—in which white South Africans overwhelmingly endorsed de Klerk's increasingly dramatic reforms—Robinson was quoted as saying in the *Washington Post*: "It's important not to celebrate prematurely, but having said that, this is a watershed event in South African history. The citizens of that country were faced with a clear choice: reform that will hopefully lead to a democratic South Africa, or chaos which would likely lead to a civil war. But no one is at the finish line yet."

South Africa held its first free and fair multiracial elections in the spring of 1994. During this historic event, South African people of color finally savored the taste of freedom. Voters waited in snakelike lines for hours—some elderly black citizens actually had to be carried to the polls—to cast their ballots for the very first time in a presidential election. ANC leader Nelson Mandela emerged as the country's clear choice for president, garnering 62.65 percent of the votes; his party gained 252 of the National Parliament's 400 seats. Still, during the transition from apartheid to democratic rule in South Africa, Robinson urged the United States to assist with peacekeeping measures.

Broadened Scope of Advocacy

According to *Emerge*, "TransAfrica lost its villain with the death of apartheid in South Africa. Today, the nation is headed down the rocky road toward a multiracial democracy, and apartheid, at least the legal version, has exited. That exit has left TransAfrica without a focal point.... Now, TransAfrica is at the starting gate again, faced with [the challenge of building] a constituency for a progressive policy toward Africa and the Caribbean."

The early 1990s saw Robinson lobbying for U.S. aid to war-torn Somalia and for the establishment of a humane and just policy toward Haitian refugees. Robinson continues to speak out on global issues affecting people of color, educating Americans on the economic ills of many African countries, and urging Congress to be as generous with aid to emerging African democracies as it is to former Communist nations in Europe. Asked about the future lobbying direction of TransAfrica, Robinson told *Black Enterprise*: "We have to acquire all the muscle we need from the horn of Africa to West Africa to the smaller nations of the Eastern Caribbean to blacks in Brazil. We have to make sure that no policy is made that affects our people that we have not effectively weighed."

In April of 1994, Robinson planned a hunger strike and a demonstration on the White House grounds to protest U.S. president Bill Clinton's policy on Haiti. *Newsweek* quoted Robinson as saying that he was "prepared to die" in the fight for the Haitian boat people seeking political asylum in the United States. Beginning April 12, he refused all nourishment except for juice and water and remained in the basement of TransAfrica's Washington headquarters waiting for some action from the U.S. government.

Although an embargo on fuel and arms had been initiated against Haiti in October of 1993, it wasn't until seven months later that a near-total trade embargo was instituted by the United Nations, effectively banning all international trade except for food and medicine. Such sanctions were established in the face of increased political violence in Haiti—violence that stemmed directly from the 1991 ousting of President Jean-Bertrand Aristide and the vehement anti-democracy tactics of the nation's subsequent military regime.

Wracked by poverty and fearing for their lives under Haiti's oppressive military rule, many Haitians risked almost certain death in their attempts to escape their homeland. Boatloads of Haitian people seeking refuge on U.S. shores were returned to Haiti by the Coast Guard; passengers were then placed in police custody. As reported in *Jet* magazine, Robinson deemed this a "profoundly racist" policy that made "President Clinton complicitous in the behavior of Haitian military leaders as they murder anyone who favors democracy in that country."

But on May 8, 1994, Clinton agreed to allow asylum hearings at sea to Haitian refugees, deciding on a case-by-case basis whether to grant each one entry into the United States. According to the *New York Times*, escalating violence in Haiti throughout the spring of 1994 "made the new asylum policy necessary." The *Times* also noted that administration officials were considering the use of American military force in Haiti to restore democracy, quoting President Clinton as saying, "The United States has clear interests at stake in ending this crisis."

Although Clinton claimed that he would not allow Robinson's actions to influence the administration's decisions on Haitian immigration, many political observers felt that the 27-day-long fast, which landed Robinson in the hospital briefly for dehydration by the third week, played a key role in the policy change. Still, when all was said and done, Robinson felt that Clinton did "discernibly little" for blacks while winning their support with minor "gestures (and) no quid pro quo."

Argued for Slavery Reparations

Toward the end of the twentieth century, Robinson continued to work on human rights issues in African countries such as Ethiopia, Kenya, Zaire, Liberia, and Malawi. In 1999, he met with Pope John Paul II to discuss relieving the debt of Third World countries. In 2000, Robinson published *The Debt: What America*

Owes to Blacks, and the brought the idea of paying reparations to the descendants of black slaves to public attention. (This was followed in 2002 by *Reckoning: What Blacks Owe to Each Other*.) In the introduction to *The Debt*, Robinson wrote, "No race, no ethnic or religious group, has suffered so much over so long a span as blacks have." He added: "It is a miracle that the victims—weary dark souls shorn of a venerable and ancient identity—have survived at all, stymied as they are by the blocked roads to economic equality."

A key argument advanced by Robinson was that slavery—by making the retention or passing along of African language, religion, and history illegal—resulted in psychological damage that created an impediment to black social and economic progress. Robinson went on to argue that slavery established patterns of self-hatred, class conflict, and internal dissension that undercut collective efforts to build wealth. Though he recognized that the movement to gain reparations for the descendants of slaves would not succeed overnight, Robinson told *Black Issues in Higher Education*: "I'm very optimistic. I put no clock on these things, you see. I don't know flit will happen in my lifetime in the same way I didn't know if apartheid would end in my lifetime…. But you fight prepared to go the long term, and if your life won't cover the term of the struggle, then you hand off your progress to the next generation."

In 2001, Robinson handed part of his struggle on to the next generation when he stepped down as head of TransAfrica and TransAfrica Forum. That year, citing his persistent disgust with the enduring racism and discrimination that existed in American culture, moved his family to St. Kitts, the Caribbean island home of his second wife, Hazel. In an *Essence* interview, Ellis Cose asked Robinson why he left his native land. Answered Robinson: "America is a huge fraud, clad in a narcissistic conceit and satisfied with itself, feeling unneedful of any self-examination nor responsibility to right past wrongs, of which it notices none. It's the kind of fraud that simply wears you out." Robinson wrote of the painful decision to leave the United States in his 2004 book *Quitting America: The Departure of a Black Man from His Native Land,* which also laid out his ongoing objections to American policy in Iraq and to European exploitation of Caribbean economies. The book was a clear signal that while Robinson may no longer be knocking on the doors of Congressmen to lobby for change, he will remain a voice for progress and humanity in dealing with black nations around the world.

Selected writings

The Emancipation of Wakefield Clay: A Novel, Bogle-L'Ouverture Publications, 1978.
Defending the Spirit: A Black Life in America (biography), Dutton, 1998.
The Debt: What America Owes to Blacks, Dutton, 2000.

Reckoning: What Blacks Owe to Each Other, Dutton, 2002.

Quitting America: The Departure of a Black Man from His Native Land, Dutton, 2004.

Sources

Books

The African Americans, edited by David Cohen and Charles M. Collins, Viking Studio Books, 1993.

Periodicals

Black Enterprise, October 1985, p. 29; August 1992, p. 53.

Black Issues in Higher Education, November 8, 2001, pp. 20-32.

Boston Globe, February 21, 1990, p. 3.

Chicago Sun-Times, April 24, 1994.

Dollars & Sense, May 1994, pp. 8-15.

Ebony, July 1987, p. 108; May 1993, p. 48.

Emerge, October 1993, p. 33.

Essence, March 1993, p. 170; February 2004, p. 114.

Jet, May 2, 1994, pp. 5-6.

Library Journal, February 1, 2004, p. 113.

New Republic, July 9-16, 1990, p. 14.

Newsweek, July 29, 1991, p. 8; April 18, 1994, p. 4.

New York Times, October 5, 1989, p. A31; September 25, 1990, p. A27; August 22, 1991, p. C12; May 9, 1994; May 23, 1994.

People, May 23, 1994.

Publishers Weekly, January 12, 2004, p. 51.

Time, November 25, 1985, p. 41.

Washington Post, March 19, 1992, p. A19; August 24, 1992, p. A17.

—Isaac Rosen, Barbara Carlisle Bigelow, and Tom Pendergast

Maya Rudolph

1972—

Actor

Known for her hilarious spoofs of celebrities such as Italian fashion designer Donatella Versace, *Saturday Night Live* cast member Maya Rudolph is a versatile performer. Her strong musical skills have contributed to the success of her *SNL* skits, which frequently feature her portrayals of pop singers, including Nelly Furtado, Beyonce Knowles, and members of the hip-hop group Destiny's Child. Though she feels most at home with comedy, she has also appeared in various dramatic roles and has worked professionally as a musician.

Rudolph, Maya, photograph. Arnold Magnan/Getty Images.

"The Comedy Was Always There"

Born on July 27, 1972, in Gainesville, Florida, Rudolph grew up in a racially-mixed musical family. Her father, songwriter Richard Rudolph, is Jewish; her mother, Minnie Riperton, was a soul singer who died of breast cancer just before Maya turned seven. Maya Rudolph remembers standing backstage as a little girl, watching her mother perform. "She was such a diva in the most exquisite sense," she told *Interview* magazine. "Those are very vivid memories for me. I always had the idea of wanting to be on a stage, in these

beautiful gowns, with a microphone in my hand, and that comes from my mom."

Rudolph and her older brother, Marc, grew up in Santa Monica, California, where the family had moved when the children were young. Struggling with the loss of her mother, Rudolph found some solace in comedy. As she told *People Weekly* reporter Galina Espinoza, she inherited her mother's offbeat sense of humor and "learned quickly to laugh so I wouldn't have to deal with pain." Rudolph would stage skits about odd characters, and often starred in school plays with her friend and classmate at St. Augustine by the Sea School, Gwyneth Paltrow. "The comedy was always there," Rudolph commented in *Interview*. "There's this moment I remember from when I was seven or eight: I was with a friend and she hurt herself and started to cry, and I just started talking in a funny voice. I thought, This is much better than feeling bad; I want to make her feel good. And she started to laugh."

After graduating in 1994 from the University of California at Santa Cruz, where she studied fashion design and majored in photography, Rudolph joined the Rentals, a pop band that was successful enough to open for

At a Glance . . .

Born on July 27, 1972, in Gainesville, FL; daughter of Richard Rudolph (a songwriter and music producer) and Minnie Riperton (a singer). *Education:* University of California-Santa Cruz, BA, photography, 1994.

Career: The Rentals (music group), keyboard player and backup singer, 1994-96; the Groundlings (comedy troupe), Los Angeles, CA, cast member, 1996-99; actor and comedienne, 1999–.

Addresses: *Office—Saturday Night Live*, 30 Rockefeller Plaza, New York, NY 10112.

Alanis Morissette and for the Red Hot Chili Peppers. Rudolph played synthesizer and sang back-up in the band, which *Boston Globe* music critic Jim Sullivan described as a quirky mix of "killer pop sensibility and hard-rock guitar edge" similar to that of such 1970's-era bands as the Cars and Ultravox.

Drawn to Acting

Rudolph stayed with the Rentals for two years, quitting in 1996 to join the Groundlings, the noted comedy improvisation troupe in Los Angeles. She also landed a small part on the television series *Chicago Hope*, playing Nurse Leah Martine in several episodes in 1996 and 1997. She also played the delivery room nurse in the 1997 film *Gattaca*. In 2000, Rudolph took a regular role on the series *City of Angels*, the first predominantly black medical drama on network television. She played Nurse Grace Patterson. Though the series was hailed as one of the most significant new shows of the season—especially after much criticism had been leveled at the entertainment media for failing to create roles and programming for African Americans—it was canceled after one season because of poor ratings.

In 2000, Rudolph made her first appearance on *Saturday Night Live*, impersonating former MTV veejay Ananda Lewis. She continued as a featured performer through the remainder of that season, becoming a regular cast member in 2001. "The truth is I had always felt most comfortable doing comedy," she recalled in *Interview*. "My dream since I was a little girl was to be on *Saturday Night Live*." One of her most important comic inspirations was Gilda Radner, a member of *SNL*'s original cast. "I used to do impressions of her when I was five," Rudolph said in *Interview*, "because I had hair that looked like [Radner's character] Roseanne Roseannadanna."

On the program, Rudolph has drawn on both her comedic talents and her musical background to create a wide range of acclaimed sketches. Among them are a skit featuring a hip-hop version of the "Oompa Loompa" song from the children's film *Willie Wonka & the Chocolate Factory*, and several involving "Wake Up Wakefield," a high school television talk-show co-hosted by Rudolph's awkward and love-smitten character, Megan. *New York Times* writer Emily Nussbaum described Rudolph's performance in a February 2003 "Wakefield" skit as a "great bit of giggle-inducing character work—a screen grab of a young girl's self-dramatization." Rudolph has also appeared as "Britannica," half of the fictitious musical group Gemini's Twin—a satirical reference to the group Destiny's Child—and has created spoofs of such superstars as Liza Minnelli, Christina Aguilera, Macy Gray, and Halle Berry.

Perhaps Rudolph's most famous creation is her parody of Donatella Versace, the Italian diva of fashion and style. Nussbaum considered this satiric portrayal to be one of the most notable examples of Rudolph's "wide, outrageous range" as a comic actor. Donatella is usually drunk on champagne, imperious, and vulgar. She lounges in her luxurious villa surrounded by fabulous jewels and other luxurious trappings. As *Newsweek* writer Susannah Meadows noted, the Donatella sketches are written from a woman's point of view: "Rudolph's Versace regularly goes cross-eyed in her Jacuzzi, ordering her male slaves around. 'It bores me to tears to show up in a short skirt and say some lines probably some guy wrote because you're his fantasy,' [Rudolph] says."

Building on her success with *SNL*, Rudolph has gone on to appear in films starring former castmates, including *50 First Dates*, with Adam Sandler, and *Anchorman*, with Will Ferrell. Among the most notable of Rudolph's recent films is *Chuck and Buck*, an independent production about the relationship between a successful man and a boyhood friend who is mentally ill. Rudolph plays Chuck's assistant, Jamila, one of three female supporting characters whose strong performances, according to *New York Times* writer A.O. Wilson, accentuate the plight of the emotionally fragile Buck and help to make the movie "a strange, intense and moving film about friendship and loss."

Rudolph, who is single and is a vegetarian, continues to garner positive reviews for her work on *Saturday Night Live*. In fact, she has jokingly described *SNL* as her boyfriend. She lives in Los Angeles and New York City.

Selected works

Films

Gattaca, 1997.
As Good as It Gets, 1997.

Chuck & Buck, 2000.
Duets, 2000.
Frank's Book, 2001.
50 First Dates, 2004.
Anchorman, 2004.

Television

Chicago Hope, CBS, 1994.
City of Angels, CBS, 2000.

Sources

Periodicals

Boston Globe, December 2, 1995.
Interview, October 2002.
Los Angeles Times, October 8, 2002.
New York Times, July 14, 2000; May 11, 2003.
Newsweek, April 8, 2002.
People Weekly, January 21, 2002.

—E. Shostak

Pernessa Seele

1954—

AIDS activist

Seele, Pernessa, photograph. AP/Wide World Photos.

Pernessa Seele is the founder and chief executive officer of The Balm in Gilead, Inc. This secular, not-for-profit organization mobilizes black churches in the United States, the Caribbean, and Africa to work toward preventing further transmission of HIV/AIDS within black communities and to care for those infected with HIV, the cause of AIDS.

In 1989, shocked by the lack of community and church support for the AIDS victims dying at Harlem Hospital, Seele recruited local religious leaders to participate in the first Harlem Week of Prayer for the Healing of AIDS. That same year Seele founded The Balm in Gilead with the motto "Healing Through Prayer, Education, Advocacy and Service." It became the world's largest nongovernmental AIDS awareness organization directed toward the black community and the only such organization to specifically engage churches in the struggle. As The Balm in Gilead grew, Seele expanded its mission to include the entire African Diaspora.

Became a Scientist

Pernessa C. Seele was born on October 15, 1954, the daughter of Luella and Charles Seele of Lincolnville,

South Carolina, a rural black township northwest of Charleston. Weekly prayer meetings were the basis for community and political action in Lincolnville, and the local church reached out to everyone, regardless of religious affiliation. Seele attended public schools and studied biology at Clark College (now Clark Atlanta University), a historically black school. She later studied immunology at Atlanta University, earning her master's degree in 1979.

Upon completing her education Seele moved to New York City, where she became a research assistant in immunology at the City University of New York (CUNY). In 1987 Seele became the first AIDS coordinator at the Interfaith Medical Center's methadone clinics. Two years later she became the drug addiction program administrator for the New York City Health and Hospitals Corporation, working at Harlem Hospital's AIDS Initiative Program. In 1992 Seele became vice president of the corporation.

While working in New York hospitals, Seele became keenly aware of the terrible toll the AIDS epidemic was taking on the black community. By the turn of the twenty-first century, blacks accounted for more than 50 percent of new AIDS cases in the United States and more than 60 percent of new cases among teenagers. It was the number one cause of death among blacks aged 25 to 44. One in 50 American black men and one in 160 black women were infected with HIV.

Appalled by the Devastation of HIV/AIDS

On The Balm in Gilead Web site Seele wrote that, while working at Harlem Hospital, "I was stunned by the sight of people and families suffering from AIDS amid a seemingly heartless community, that neither understood the reasons for their pain, nor sought to alleviate their suffering. How could Black America, for the first time in its history, turn away from brothers and sisters caught in a crisis that could destroy the community at its very roots? Why was the response to the AIDS crisis different from previous crises—enslavement, discrimination, and lynching?"

Although black churches historically had served as centers of social and political activism, most had been silent on the issue of HIV/AIDS. Seele told *Essence* magazine in 1996, "as I watched young Black folks die from AIDS, I wondered, Where were their families, where was their church?...Black folks have always been able to pray. We successfully prayed Harriet Tubman through the Underground Railroad, and I was convinced we could pray our people through this devastating epidemic."

Seele had lived in Harlem for only one week when she began to enlist local religious leaders for a Harlem Week of Prayer for the Healing of AIDS. In 1989 hundreds of leaders from 50 churches, representing all major religions and Christian denominations, participated in the prayer march around Harlem Hospital for AIDS awareness.

Established Black Church Week of Prayer

The success of the Harlem Week of Prayer led Seele to found The Balm in Gilead. Its purpose was to involve black churches in the fight against HIV/AIDS. The organization's name, from a biblical reference in the book of Jeremiah, was familiar to blacks from the popular hymn, "Let there be balm in Gilead, and let it begin with me," and from the spiritual: "There is a balm in Gilead // To make the wounded whole // There is a balm in Gilead // To heal the sin-sick soul." For Seele, HIV/AIDS was Gilead and black churches were the balm.

Seele found that the black community was so busy fighting on other fronts, including gang violence and police brutality, church burnings, hospital closings, blighted inner-city schools, and affirmative action reversals, that for almost 20 years the community and the black media had ignored the scourge of AIDS. Seele found that many black churches refused to address the HIV/AIDS crisis because they viewed it as a disease of homosexuals. She asked church leaders to put aside their feelings on sexual issues.

Seele's Harlem Week of Prayer served as the prototype for the annual Black Church Week of Prayer for the Healing of AIDS, a cornerstone of The Balm in Gilead. By 2004 more than 15,000 black churches were participating in the program, distributing information, hosting workshops on AIDS, or devoting a sermon or song to AIDS victims. The Balm in Gilead gave the churches free resource kits.

Developed New Initiatives

Under Seele's leadership, The Balm in Gilead has developed a number of initiatives to support HIV/AIDS understanding. The Black Church HIV/AIDS Training Institute, initiated in 1998, holds annual three-day seminars and workshops for black church leaders engaged in HIV/AIDS education and support. The institute provides in-depth education from specialists about HIV/AIDS prevention and treatment, and techniques for integrating HIV/AIDS education into church programs. The institute also promotes the understanding of biblical texts that encourage church activism on issues such as HIV/AIDS, develops techniques for churches to address the social, economic, and psychological impacts of AIDS, and teaches about the politics of the disease. The institute is partnered with the Interdenominational Theological Center in Atlanta, the nation's largest institution of black religious education. Seele also developed the National Certification and Capacity Building Conference to assist community-based organizations in partnering with black churches.

The Black Church Lights the Way program encourages black churches to participate in The Balm in Gilead's annual June campaign for HIV testing. The campaign includes television, radio, and newspaper advertisements directed at the black community. It asks churches to encourage their congregations to be tested for HIV and provides resources. The campaign cooperates with local public health departments and other community-based organizations to provide on-site HIV testing to congregations and the larger community.

In conjunction with the Centers for Disease Control and Prevention, The Balm in Gilead established the Faith-Based HIV/AIDS National Technical Assistance Center. It is the only program in the nation that is designed to assist black churches—and public agencies and community-based organizations that want to work with churches—on AIDS issues within African American, African, and Caribbean communities. Seele also developed and implemented the African American National Clergy Task Force, consisting of 60 religious leaders and scholars who serve as advisors to The Balm in Gilead.

Made Use of the Media

Seele has been adept at using the media to draw attention to the issues promoted by The Balm in Gilead. She was the force behind the Black Clergy Declaration of War against HIV and AIDS, signed by leaders from every major denomination at a White House ceremony in 1995. In 1998 Seele began hosting a radio program—"A Message of Hope in This Time of AIDS"—that targeted black communities in large cities. In 2003 The Balm in Gilead launched a national magazine for the Black Church Week of Prayer. The magazine addressed AIDS issues in the black community, including stories relating to teens, women, and the elderly. The Balm in Gilead produces other publications as well as educational and training products.

Seele produced numerous fundraisers for The Balm in Gilead, including a 1996 production at Manhattan's Riverside Church and the resulting Emmy-award-winning video. She was an AIDS consultant for the

Narcotic Drug and Research Institute and has worked closely with the CDC, Memorial Sloan-Kettering Cancer Center, Rockefeller University, and the Research Foundation for the City of New York. Seele has been a consultant to the Congressional Black Caucus' Health Brain Trust. She is an adjunct professor of Ethics and AIDS at New York Theological Seminary and a consultant with the Harlem Center for Health Promotion and Disease Prevention of Columbia University School of Public Health. Seele also served a term as vice president of the Harlem Congregation for Community Improvement.

Although Seele's organization has involved thousands of churches and millions of congregants in the struggle against HIV/AIDS, many churches and mosques continue to avoid the issue because of its association with homosexuality, promiscuity, and drug addiction, and prohibitions against the use of condoms and needle exchanges. But Seele has made headway. In 1999 she gave the *New York Times* a typical scenario: "A pastor who has never said anything about H.I.V. decides to do a special prayer, even though he thinks, 'I know no one in my church has AIDS.' After church, somebody thanks him for the prayer, saying, 'I have AIDS' or 'I am taking care of my grandkids because my daughter has AIDS.' The pastor is shocked and calls an AIDS service organization that helps him begin educational work."

Seele told the *American Journal of Public Health* in 2003 about her model: "We don't come to the church and put the issues in their face. We talk about people, get them to understand that HIV is in their church, it's in the mosque, these are the people they love. There are mothers in the church whose sons have died. AIDS awareness training and education provides them with an opportunity to say something that makes sense. People want to share their burdens with their pastor, or their imam, so it's about educating the leadership so they can engage their congregations in appropriate ways."

Expanded into Africa

Over time, Seele has expanded The Balm in Gilead, first into the Caribbean, and then into sub-Saharan Africa, where HIV/AIDS has reached epidemic proportions and is threatening an already fragile social infrastructure. Seele's goals were broad: to fight the stigma associated with HIV/AIDS; to educate about HIV/AIDS and its prevention; to provide counseling and testing; to intervene to reduce high-risk behaviors and prevent mother-to-child transmission of the disease; to provide long-term care and support for those living with HIV/AIDS and for children orphaned by the epidemic. Seele led missions to Cote d'Ivoire, Nigeria, Kenya, Tanzania, and Zimbabwe. The Balm in Gilead also expanded into South Africa and reached out to Ugandan women.

By 2004 The Balm in Gilead had a staff of 22 and over $3 million in annual expenditures. It had endorsements from 17 major church denominations, caucuses, and coalitions, as well as independent churches.

Selected writings

Periodicals

"Creating Positive Change with the Power of Prayer," *About …Time* (Rochester, NY), February 28, 1999, p. 36.

On-line

"Welcome: A Message from Pernessa C. Seele," *The Balm in Gilead, Inc.* www.balmingilead.org/about/welcome.asp (June 28, 2004).

Sources

Periodicals

American Journal of Public Health, August 2003, p. 1207.
Essence, October 1996, p. 42.
Los Angeles Times, June 7, 2003, p. B20.
New Pittsburgh Courier, February 15, 2003, p. A1.
New York Times, March 2, 1999, p. F7.

On-line

The Balm in Gilead, Inc., www.balmingilead.org/home.asp (June 5, 2004).

—Margaret Alic

Marvin and Morgan Smith

1910-2003 and 1910-1993

Photographers

Photographers Morgan and Marvin Smith documented Harlem, the singular and vibrant African-American community of New York City, during the thirties and forties. The Smiths were twin brothers and ran a photography studio next door to the fabled Apollo Theater for nearly thirty years. Their clients ranged from pillars of the civil rights movement to ordinary Harlem families. The Smiths also ventured outside their studio to capture the rhythm and beauty of everyday life in this northern quadrant of Manhattan. "Their subjects are presented quietly and affectionately, without fanfare, and most often with great dignity," wrote James A. Miller in the introduction to *Harlem: The Vision of Morgan and Marvin Smith.* "In an era before 'Black Is Beautiful' became the watchword for a generation, the Smiths quietly and effectively launched their own cultural revolution, creating in the process a visual legacy that stands the test of time."

The Smiths were identical twins born on February 16, 1910, in Nicholasville, Kentucky, a rural area near Lexington. Their parents, Charles and Allena, were sharecroppers. As youngsters, the Smiths attended a local one-room schoolhouse, but also missed many days of class when they helped their parents to plant and harvest tobacco, corn, and sugarcane during peak times. Artistically gifted from an early age, the twins honed their drawing skills by copying images from the ubiquitous Sears, Roebuck catalog of the day. Around 1928 the family moved to Lexington's black community, where their father had been able to build a house for them on Roosevelt Street.

Encouraged by Community

The Smiths enrolled at Paul Laurence Dunbar High School, the city's only high school open to African-American students. Their parents encouraged their artistic ambitions and provided them with what materials they could, but the boys were also ingenious in their quest for art supplies. Once, they read a magazine article about soap carving. "So we both got involved in making figures out of cakes of Ivory soap," Marvin once recalled, according to the *Harlem* book. "The principal at Dunbar High was impressed, so he put them on display in the lobby at school...which was uplifting, which encouraged us."

Eager to earn their own way, both brothers took jobs for wealthy white Lexington citizens while still teenagers. Morgan served as a chauffeur and yardman for a private school headmaster, while Marvin was a helper for an elderly woman whose family were well-known landowners. The headmaster let Morgan use an art studio at his school, since Dunbar High did not have one; the widow, in turn, introduced Marvin to a prominent local artist, who gave him art lessons in exchange for doing chores at her home. When they became interested in photography, they went to visit the city's best-known society portrait photographer, who was also impressed by their quiet, earnest determination. He gave them their first camera, an unwieldy box device that needed powder to ignite the flash. At home, they set up a darkroom in the basement and taught themselves the rest.

At a Glance . . .

Born on February 16, 1910, in Nicholasville, KY; Morgan died of cancer on November 17, 1993, in New York, NY; Marvin died on November 9, 2003, in New York, NY; sons of Charles (a sharecropper) and Allena (a sharecropper; maiden name, Hutchinson) Smith; Morgan married Anna McLean, 1936 (divorced), and Monica Mais (a soprano), 1950; children: (with Mais) Monica; Marvin married Florence McLean, 1936 (divorced). *Education:* Marvin attended the U.S. Naval Air Station School of Photography and Motion Pictures, and studied painting in Paris under Fernand Léger, early 1950s. *Military Service:* Marvin Smith served in the U.S. Navy, World War II.

Career: Marvin Smith: New York City Parks Department, gardener, 1930s; television networks, propmaster, set decorator, and freelance sound technician, 1960s. Morgan Smith: Works Progress Administration, muralist, 1930s; *Amsterdam News,* staff photographer, 1937-39; *People's Voice,* photographer, 1942, photo news syndicate, c. World War II (1939-45); ABC Television, sound technician, c. 1950-60. Marvin and Morgan Smith: M & M Smith, Harlem, 1939-68.

In 1933 the Smiths became the first in their family to earn high school diplomas. They were offered football scholarships from leading black colleges, Fisk and Howard among them, but decided to pursue their artistic ambitions instead. They first moved to Cincinnati because, as Marvin recalled in the *Harlem* book, "There was no art for blacks in Kentucky," but they were disappointed by the unspoken racism that seemed to hinder opportunities for them there. They made a new friend, however, who encouraged them to join the artistic migration to New York City. They bought bus tickets and left with a hundred dollars between them. "After a slight disagreement, we went to the back of the bus," Marvin told *New York Times* writer Tracie Rozhon in 1997. "We really didn't have a choice." The bus dropped them off in Times Square on a September day in 1933, but the brothers were baffled, as Marvin recalled in the same interview. "We looked and looked, and then we asked, 'Where are all the black people?'"

Opened Studio in 1939

They soon found their way to Harlem, the epicenter of black life in New York. A decade earlier, the area had served as home base to a flourishing new movement that celebrated African-American art and culture. Writers like Langston Hughes and Zora Neale Hurston chronicled black life, and a vibrant musical scene lured audiences of all colors. But the heady days of the Harlem Renaissance were mostly over by the time the Smiths arrived. The Great Depression had taken hold, and times were tough for artists. Opportunity came in the form of a large-scale government jobs program that was the idea of a newly elected Democratic president, Franklin D. Roosevelt. Both brothers found jobs with the Civil Works Administration, which later evolved into the Works Progress Administration (WPA). The WPA built post offices, bridges, and other government projects. The Smiths, with their farm experience, were offered a slot on a team that created the Shakespeare Garden in Central Park. Morgan later worked on a mural for the Harlem Hospital, while Marvin stayed with New York Parks Department.

Both Morgan and Marvin also enrolled in a free school run by sculptor Augusta Savage on West 126th Street. There they met many leading black artists, among them Jacob Lawrence and Romare Bearden. They began taking street photographs, and decided to concentrate on the medium exclusively around 1937. A boost came when Morgan entered a local newspaper photography contest, which helped him land steady work at the *Amsterdam News,* the city's leading black newspaper, as its first-ever staff photographer in 1937. Two years later, the Smiths opened their own photography studio at 141 West 125th Street. Within a year they took a lease on a second-floor space at 243 West 125th Street, next door to Apollo Theater. They used the ground-floor windows for displays of their work, and since the Apollo was one of Harlem's most lively entertainment venues, it proved a shrewd marketing move. Soon, a steady stream of customers came to book portrait-sitting appointments.

The Smiths took studio portraits of ordinary folk with backgrounds much like their own. These portraits, usually sent to families back home, displayed the former Southerners' new urban affluence. Apollo Theater chorus dancers came to have publicity stills taken, as did aspiring models, and for these, the Smiths deployed their considerable artistic talents to create imaginative sets. Local figures and politicians also sat for portraits, and both inside and outside the studio the Smiths photographed a long list of African-American celebrities, from James Weldon Johnson and George Washington Carver to Billie Holiday and Fats Waller. They shot Nat King Cole at his wedding and Maya Angelou when she was a dancer. They knew prizefighter Joe Louis and went to his training camp to take photos of him—since black photographers were barred from the press box at his bouts—and caught baseball pioneer Jackie Robinson teaching his young son how to hold the bat. Their scenes of street life in Harlem were not a moneymaker by any stretch: the *Amsterdam News* and papers like it struggled financially, and could pay just a $1.50 or so for an image.

Photographs Were Collaborative Effort

All of their images bore the stamp "M & M Smith." "Sometimes I held the camera, sometimes he did," Marvin explained to the *New York Times'* Rozhon. Whether together or solo, the Smiths captured many scenes from Harlem life of the time, but never sought out the shocking or sensational, unlike some other photographers. Disdaining scenes that showed poverty, hardship, or overt racism, they instead tried to show the rhythm of life in Harlem. Their images captured acrobatic Lindy-hoppers in mid-air at dances, anti-lynching protests, a boycott campaign organized by Adam Clayton Powell Jr. that urged Harlem's blacks "Don't Buy Where You Can't Work," and crowds of Easter Sunday churchgoers. Their work became "a pictorial record of an era marked by chaos," wrote photographer and Smith protégé Gordon Parks Sr. in the foreword to *Harlem.* "They caught the smell of the streets, and they showed the social and political change that took place within Harlem's black intelligentsia."

During World War II, Marvin left New York City to serve in the U.S. Navy, and was the first African-American student to enroll at the Naval Air Station School of Photography and Motion Pictures in Pensacola, Florida. Back in New York, Morgan set up a commercial news service that provided photographs to several leading black newspapers across the United States. In 1942 he began working for a radical newspaper based in Harlem, the *People's Voice,* which was owned by Powell. Morgan was once invited to photograph the street gangs of Harlem for *Life* magazine, the preeminent publication of the day and read by millions, but he turned it down, not wishing to promote stereotypes of African-American urban life.

After the war, Marvin traveled to France with Bearden, and studied there with renowned artist Fernand Léger. Morgan ventured in another direction, setting up a sound studio in his photography building. There, he recorded well-known orators, such as W.E.B. DuBois, as well as bands, and eventually went on to a job as a sound technician with a fledgling new television network, ABC. Both brothers worked in television for a number of years, and finally closed their Harlem studio in 1968. They retired at age 65 in 1975. In the 1970s they took up needlework and created knitting and crochet patterns which they sold to popular women's magazines like *McCall's.*

Led Visitors Through Bygone Harlem

In 1936, the Smiths had married identical twins, Anna and Florence McLean, but were divorced on the same day just a few years later. Morgan remarried a soprano from Jamaica, with whom he had a daughter. He died of cancer in 1993, and Marvin passed away ten years later. In the early 1990s, the unusual photographer-twins were the subject of a documentary film, *M & M Smith: For Posterity's Sake,* that aired on public television stations in the United States. Their photographs were featured prominently in a 1996 Smithsonian Institution exhibit, *Visual Journal: Harlem and D.C. in the Thirties and Forties.* It went on to the Schomburg Center for Research in Black Culture in Harlem, where Marvin gave personal tours. "I mean, it's kind of only fair of me," he told Rozhon in the *New York Times* interview. "To share with people what I can, to tell them about the photographs."

Sources

Books

Harlem: The Vision of Morgan and Marvin Smith, foreword by Gordon Parks Sr., introductions by James A. Miller, University Press of Kentucky, 1998.

Periodicals

Art in America, June 1998, p. 111.
New York Times, February 25, 1993, p. B8; December 12, 1997; December 25, 1997; November 12, 2003, p. C13.

—Carol Brennan

Ruben Studdard

1978—

Singer

Studdard, Ruben, photograph. AP/Wide World Photos.

Dubbed the "Velvet Teddy Bear" by soul singer Gladys Knight and described as "honey-voiced" in *Jet,* this bear-like singer-with-a-dream was crowned the Fox Network's "American Idol" by viewers across the nation in May of 2003. Wooing audiences and *Idol* judges with his gentle, satiny renditions of "Ribbon in the Sky," "A House Is Not a Home," "Imagine," and his signature "Flying without Wings," the six-foot-four, 300-plus-pound Ruben Studdard emerged as king from among 70,000 other American dreamers who auditioned for the popular television talent show. Because he jumped so quickly from amateur singer to professional recording artist, music-industry insiders are not yet convinced that Studdard's talent and star quality are enduring. "Studdard doesn't have the range of most soul singers," Gemma Tarlach, music critic for the *Milwaukee Journal Sentinel,* wrote in April of 2004. "And as a songwriter he's an unknown quantity, without a single credit to his name. But what the 25-year old does have is an easy, earnest charm, which goes a long way when too many performers treat fans with surly indifference."

Dreamed of Stardom

Born Christopher Ruben Studdard on July 14, 1978, in Frankfurt am Main, West Germany, Studdard—known to family as Chris—grew up in Birmingham, Alabama. His parents, Kevin and Emily, were both teachers, secondary and elementary, respectively. His father also owned the Kevin Studdard & Sons Body Shop.

According to Studdard and his family, he began singing as early as memories begin— when he was about three years old. In a 2004 interview with CBS's *The Early Show,* Studdard described his mother as a strong encourager of his professional singing goals. "Mom did a lot," Studdard said. "She really was active in my career, you know, with making sure that I got to places I needed to be, like choir concerts and musicals and plays." "I kind of took his lead with things," Mrs. Studdard explained. "If he said that he wanted to be in something and I knew that it was legit, I would take him and just be there for him and with him." Studdard's grandmother, Hattie Williams, also supported Studdard's pursuit of a singing career. "He always said he had a dream," Williams told *The*

Early Show. "He loved to sing, and he said one day his dream will come true."

Studdard trained his voice with the school's music teacher and landed a place in several school performances during his four years at Huffman High School. He also performed in his church choir and participated in the gospel group God's Gift. He also joined with friends to form the jazz and soul group Just a Few Cats. After high school, Studdard began attending Alabama A&M University on a football scholarship. After his freshman year, he abandoned football to dedicate his studies and time to developing his voice for a professional singing career. Without completing his degree, Studdard left the university after three and a half years in December of 2002 to audition in Nashville, Tennessee, for Fox's *American Idol* show, a televised talent contest judged by a celebrity panel and the national viewing audience. The winner is awarded a recording contract with a major record label, complete with promotional image and touring support.

Became American Idol

Studdard made the Nashville cuts and found himself on Fox's televised competition. *All Music Guide*'s Stephen Thomas Erlewine described Studdard's presence on the Fox stage as distinct from the other *Idol* hopefuls, writing, "Where most of his competitors were pop star wannabes hungry to win the competition, Ruben was quiet and exceedingly laid-back, impressing audiences and judges alike with his large voice and easy confidence." Studdard's *American Idol* rival, Clay Aiken, was really a good friend, though at a glance, the large, African-American Studdard appeared to be a polar opposite to the slight, Caucasian Aiken. Yet, the competing singers were essentially quite similar in

background and perspective. They both grew up in the South, both were church going and spiritually grounded, and both seemed to harbor only the best wishes for the other. Reporting on how Aiken and Studdard were coping with the hype prior to the final *Idol* showdown, *Newsweek*'s Marc Peyser and Sean M. Smith observed, "Despite all the insanity, Aiken and Studdard appear to have kept their egos in check and their friendship intact. They still have a prayer circle before every show, and they still goof off backstage."

On May 21, 2003, Studdard was crowned American Idol before nearly 40 million voters, about 600,000 more than those who tuned in for the 2003 Academy Awards program. According to Nielsen Media Research, roughly 27 million American Idol viewers had judged the sing-off between Aiken and Studdard the evening before, casting about 260 million phone votes. Studdard won by a mere 134,400 votes. Determined to remain humble even after his big win, Studdard told *USA Today* only days after his Idol inauguration, "I'm still the same Ruben—just with extra people hanging around."

The jerseys Studdard sported on the American Idol stage—featuring his hometown area code of 205—became the subject of a lawsuit in August of 2003, when Studdard filed suit against jersey-maker 205 Flava Inc. Studdard claimed that 205 Flava profited from using his image to sell its shirts. The company's owners, brothers Frederick and Will Jenkins, explained that they had paid Studdard to wear the jerseys on American Idol, a practice expressly banned by Fox. By December of 2003, Studdard and Flava 205 had settled the lawsuit for an undisclosed sum.

After his *Idol* coronation, Studdard was an instant celebrity, just as the show promised. On June 8, 2003, Studdard began shooting his first music video in Birmingham, Alabama. The "Flying without Wings" video offered Studdard's fans images of his pre-*Idol* life, complete with his mother Emily and several of her students who appeared as extras, shots of his home church, Rising Star Baptist, and the home of his grandmother. Studdard's hometown embraced his new celebrity status. "Everyone has been 'Rubenized' as we call it," Studdard's cousin Demetra Studdard told *Jet* in June 2003. "It has brought the whole state together. No matter what race. It's not a Black or White thing.... He has really shown a big light on Alabama."

Life after 'American Idol"

When Studdard was nominated for a Grammy Award in 2003 for his cover of "Superstar," he chose to take his mother to the ceremony as his guest. Studdard told *The Early Show,* "I took my mom to the Grammys because, I think, for her it was kind of like a graduation. I never finished college." About the same time, Studdard bought his mother a brand new Ford Thunderbird.

Although he won a NAACP Image Award in 2004, Studdard recognized that his success emerged from a mixture of his talent and plain good luck. "My hat's off to the people that get a recording deal," Studdard told National Public Radio's *All Things Considered* in April of 2004. "I mean, it really is about who you know, 'cause it's really about who can get that tape to that person who really needs to hear it, you know. Because I believe if God's Gift would have ever gotten a tape to somebody who could really do something for them, we probably would be one of the largest gospel groups in the country right now."

Time's Josh Tyrangiel supported Studdard's statement about the industry in the same NPR interview, explaining that *American Idol* made singers famous not just for their talent but also for their personal stories. "Had [Studdard] made it, it would have been a really tough sell because it would have been just another guy with a nice voice coming out," Tryangiel said. "And the fact is that the market is flooded with people like that. What we don't have on the market are people who have theses great stories...." What's more, *American Idol* captured a market audience who "prefer[s] an innocent love song to today's sexually explicit lyrics," Tryangiel observed.

After *American Idol,* runner-up Aiken was in the spotlight as much, or more than, the first-place Studdard. Aiken's debut album, *Measure of a Man,* appeared in stores eight weeks before Studdard's *Soulful.* And Aiken's sales were stronger, landing him on magazine covers and television shows. Studdard and Aiken nonetheless insisted that they maintained a rivalry free friendship, despite rumors to the contrary. "He's my friend," Studdard told freelance journalist Gary Graff in the *Plain Dealer.* "I personally think it's just the media trying to perpetuate a competition spirit between me and him."

RCA, parent company to Studdard's recording label, J Records, preordered 1.3 million copies of Studdard's first solo release, *Soulful,* which appeared on store shelves on December 9, 2003. Produced by the label's legendary founder Clive Davis, the album featured emotionally upbeat tracks, some covers, and some original sings, with celebrity guest appearances by Fred Hammond, Fat Joe, R. Kelly, and Missy Elliott. "I was just trying to get some records that people would have fun listening to," Studdard told *USA Today*'s Steve Jones. "I didn't want to have a melancholy record."

Soulful reaped mixed reviews. *Rolling Stone*'s Barry Walters called the album "very poor," writing "This has little to do with Studdard himself, although, like the other idols, he's essentially an imitative singer; he hasn't learned how to fill his pretty tenor pipes with convincing emotion, something painfully clear on his ill-advised cover of the Bee Gees' 'How Can You Mend a Broken Heart.'" *People*'s Chuck Arnold called Studdard's rendition of the Bee Gee's cover "exquisite" in his largely positive review of *Soulful*, writing "the album does a good job of translating to record the cuddly Velvet Teddy Bear charm that won over *Idol* fans, resulting in a likable if unspectacular set."

The album's first-released single, "Sorry 2004," which was widely played on Top 40 and R&B radio stations across the nation during the spring of 2004, was a lyric of apology that a man might express to a woman he has wronged. The track sold more than 300,000 copies as a single in its first week. Studdard took the entire *Soulful* playlist with him on the road for a national tour. His touring band included band mates from Just a Few Cats.

In the fall of 2003 Studdard told *Ebony* that all that changed with his stardom was that "a lot of people know me now." Other than that, he said he remained the same person. About his career, Studdard said, "I want to be around for a long time. I don't want to be a one-hit wonder. I want to make sure I continue to make good music that my mom and everybody around me can be proud of." At the close of 2003, Studdard launched his own record label, Real Music Records. He immediately signed Chicago rapper Gutta and Alabama singer Kevin Bennett. In 2004, Studdard began looking into opening a restaurant. A lyric from Studdard's "Flying Without Wings" captures the moral of his inspirational story: "So impossible as they may seem, you've got to fight for every dream, 'cause who's to know which one you let go would have made you complete."

Selected discography

Soulful, J Records, 2003.

Sources

Periodicals

Chicago Sun Times, December 24, 2003, p. 62.
Ebony, September 2003, p. 24.
Jet, June 9, 2003, p. 58; June 30, 2003, p. 40.
Milwaukee Journal Sentinel, April 12, 2004, p. 6B.
Newsweek, May 26, 2003, p. 53.
People, June 23, 2003, p. 22; December, 22, 2003, p. 63; January 12, 2004, p. 43.
Plain Dealer (Cleveland), April 9, 2004, p. 4.
Rolling Stone, January 26, 2003, p. 16; January, 22, 2004, p. 70.
Time, October 5, 2003.
Us Weekly, July 7-14, 2003, p. 38.
USA Today, May 22, 2003, p. D1; December 8, 2003, p. D1.

On-line

American Idol, www.fox.com/idol2/home.htm (June 2, 2004).

E! Online, www.eonline.com (June 2, 2004).

"MTV News Archive: Ruben Studdard," *MTV.com,* www.mtv.com/news/bands/studdard_ruben.jhtml (June 29, 2004).

"Ruben Studdard's Big Career," *All Things Considered,* April 4, 2004, www.npr.org/features/feature.php?wfld=1832619 (June 29, 2004).

"Ruben Studdard's Big Love," *The Early Show,* www.cbsnews.com/stories/2004/05/07/earlyshow/saturday/main616271.shtml (June 2, 2004).

—Melissa Walsh

Regina Taylor

1959(?)—

Playwright, actor

As the star of the television series *I'll Fly Away,* Regina Taylor has successfully established herself as a dramatic actress. Through her role on the award-winning television show, she has helped dispel myths about black domestic servants during the early days of the civil rights struggle in the South. *Emerge* magazine contributor Mary Helen Washington noted Taylor's *I'll Fly Away* character was "one of the most intelligent, independent and courageous women on American TV."

Taylor echoed that opinion in an *Essence* interview when she said: "In terms of fully exploring a female character, I believe I have the best television role for a woman, black or white." Yet few people in any walk of life will say less about themselves than Regina Taylor. In interviews she refuses to discuss her private life and will not give her age, preferring, instead, to talk about the characters she portrays and their lives as she has imagined them.

Prior to landing the coveted part, Taylor had worked principally on stage, doing everything from one-woman shows to Shakespeare. "I wanted to be the [opera great] Leontyne Price of classical theater," she told *People* magazine. The role of Lilly Harper in *I'll Fly Away* provided Taylor with her first national exposure. First aired by the National Broadcasting Company (NBC), *I'll Fly Away* made its premier as a two-hour movie in 1991, and then aired weekly in hour-long episodes. The show was an instant success with the television critics, and it garnered numerous nominations for Emmy Awards, Golden Globe Awards, and even the Peabody Prize. Taylor was nominated

twice for the best-actress Emmy Award, and she won the 1993 Golden Globe Award for best actress in a dramatic series.

Encouraged by Her Mother

An only child, Taylor was born in Dallas, Texas, and was raised by her mother, a Social Security Administration employee. A job transfer resulted in mother and daughter moving to Oklahoma when Regina was in the second grade. Asked about her childhood, Taylor told *People:* "I developed an active imagination very young and was always writing plays and musicals." Her mother was an inspiration. "She taught me never to set limits on who I could be."

Taylor's mother also instilled pride and a sense of justice in her young daughter. Regina needed that pride when, in 1972, she became a seventh grader at a school that had only recently been integrated. On her first day of class she was seated next to a white girl who promptly told the teacher: "I do not want to sit next to this nigger." Taylor was completely stunned by the pronouncement and taken aback by the girl's seething hatred. "I thought, 'How can she hate me when she doesn't know me?,'" Taylor recalled in *People.* The memory of that incident stayed with Taylor, helping her to understand the people of her mother's generation who lived with that kind of intolerance every day.

After high school, Taylor enrolled at Southern Methodist University in Dallas, planning to study journalism and creative writing. On a whim she took an acting class and found that she liked it much better than her journalism classes. She also had recognizable talent. While she was still a student she earned her first important role, in a made-for-television movie called *Crisis at Central High*. In that show, produced in 1981, Taylor appeared as one of the black students affected by the landmark integration of a Little Rock, Arkansas, high school.

Taylor earned her bachelor's degree in 1981, and immediately left for New York City with the goal of becoming a professional actress. Joining the ranks of the struggling artists, she found herself sharing a two-room flat with three other people and using a makeshift bed on a rotating basis. "I fell in love with the city," she told *People*. She made ends meet by working as a housekeeper and later found employment with a firm that refurbished homes and apartments. At every opportunity she auditioned for stage roles, and very slowly, she began making her way into important parts.

Taylor's big break came in the mid-1980s, when she was accepted into New York City-based Shakespeare Festival Company, a prestigious group that stages classical plays under the guidance of important American directors. One of these directors was the late Joseph Papp, an innovator who believed in nontraditional casting for the well-known dramas of Shakespeare. It was Papp who assigned Taylor the part of Juliet in a 1987 staging of *Romeo and Juliet* on Broadway. The actress thus became the first woman of color to appear as Juliet on Broadway, a significant professional achievement.

The stage work led to television roles as well. Taylor portrayed an attorney in the starring role of the made-for-television movie *Howard Beach: Making a Case*

for *Murder* in 1989. She then proved her range as an actress by appearing in the feature film *Lean on Me* as a recovering crack addict. She had returned to New York City and her theater work when she was called to audition for the role of Lillian Harper in *I'll Fly Away* in 1990.

Starred in "I'll Fly Away"

Taylor immediately recognized the Lilly character as that rarest of opportunities—the chance to play a well-drawn black woman on television. "Lilly is a composite of many women," the actress told *Essence*. "The role has connection to my relatives and others who had to sit at the back of the bus or drink from a water fountain marked 'FOR COLOREDS.' I refuse to let her slip into somebody's mammy myth" (a reference to the derogatory name for a white child's black nanny.) Although Lilly is a housekeeper responsible for three white children, the show also explores Lilly's family life and her personal sacrifices in the quest for civil rights. An aspiring writer, Lilly begins and ends each episode quoting from entries in her journal, and the show addresses such sensitive topics as white supremacist Ku Klux Klan activities, legal injustices, and lynching.

Taylor told *USA Today* that portraying Lilly was very educational to her. "I knew something about the time," she said. "But it's one thing to have second-hand knowledge and another to take on the character. In a sense, I live her life. But when I go home, I go in the front door. I'm afforded certain rights that Lillian could only dream about." She added that *I'll Fly Away* is "film quality. All of us are challenged by it." *New York* media critic John Leonard wrote of the series: "*I'll Fly Away* doesn't so much transcend as it accretes, by scruple and witness. We're watching...Lilly think her way to heroism. In this incremental history of America—a story about something else besides what white men do in the daytime—Lilly's is the defining intelligence."

Unfortunately, *I'll Fly Away* failed to attract a large enough audience to sustain it. Mary Helen Washington, for one, felt that the show spent too much time developing the white characters and not enough time on Lilly and her peers. The critic asked: "Isn't it ironic that black people, who produced, directed, cast, and starred in the original Civil Rights Movement, have become minor players in its dramatic reenactment? Isn't it tragic that after all the protests, all the freedom songs, and all the marches against white domination, black images in media are still largely controlled by whites?" Although the show finally did attract a sizeable black viewership in its second season, it was moved from time period to time period, sent on "hiatus," and finally dropped by NBC in 1993.

I'll Fly Away did not just disappear, however. While Taylor went back to New York City and her stage work, a small but loyal group of viewers mounted a letter-writing campaign on behalf of the show. The Virginia-based Viewers for Quality Television lobbied NBC to resume the series, and an astounding 80,651 fans voted for *I'll Fly Away* in *TV Guide'* s annual "Save Our Shows" poll. This ground swell of popularity led producers at the Corporation for Public Broadcasting to buy the 39 existing segments of the series and to create a new made-for-television movie as a denouement. In *I'll Fly Away: Then and Now,* first broadcast in 1993, Taylor reprised her role as Lilly, showing how the former maid became a successful writer and lecturer in the wake of the civil rights movement advances.

Developed as Actress, Playwright

Having bid Lilly farewell, Taylor continued her work as an actress and a playwright. She has appeared in several feature films, including *Clockers, Courage Under Fire,* and *The Negotiator,* and she has also made several television appearances, including roles in the 1997 series *Feds,* and the 2001-02 series *The Education of Max Bickford.* In 1999 she played the role of Anita Hill in the Showtime original film *Strange Justice,* about the Supreme Court nomination hearings of Clarence Thomas. Increasingly, however, Taylor has devoted most of her time to the stage, both as actress and playwright. A regular performer on the stage in Chicago and New York, she has increasingly acted in her own plays Early in 1994 she appeared Off-Broadway in *Escape from Paradise,* a one-woman show she wrote herself. In a review of the production, *New York Times* critic Ben Brantley wrote: "As a whole, *Escape from Paradise* emanates an appealing wistfulness that lingers. Ms. Taylor has yet to find the theatrical polish to match her ambitions. But the pursuit of those ambitions bears watching." Taylor has since had several of her plays appear on Broadway, including *Crowns* in 2002 and *Drowning Crow* in 2004. Both plays explore, in different ways, the relationships between African Americans and the images they have of themselves.

Taylor told *Back Stage West* writer Anne Louise Bannon that her acting and writing go hand in hand. "I think one informs the other," she said. "As an actor, I feel like I can write very good dialogue. I know that the actors can fill moments around the words. As an actor, I learned how to break apart a script. On the other hand, going back [to being a playwright] helps me in being able to figure out or plot my character in a piece, filling in a piece." She has been able to nurture both sides of her career at Chicago's Goodman Theatre, where she has worked as an artistic associate since 1995.

Regina Taylor remains mute on the subject of her romantic attachments and her home life in general. She splits her time between New York City, Chicago, and wherever her plays are running, and she is always willing to relocate for movie or television work. Unde-

niably, *I'll Fly Away* has enhanced Taylor's marketability as a serious, committed artist; it's also made her a celebrity. Asked how she feels about the fame she has reaped from her work on *I'll Fly Away,* the actress admitted that she was startled by it and not entirely comfortable being so well-known. "People are starting to come up and start conversations," she told *USA Today.* "I still wonder why they're talking to me." She added, "It's hard for me to give up my bohemian status. Ten years from now, I'll still be exploring."

Selected works

Films

Lean on Me, 1989.
Jersey Girl, 1992.
Losing Isaiah, 1995.
Courage Under Fire, 1996.
The Negotiator, 1998.

Plays

Watermelon Rinds, 1991.
Escape from Paradise, 1994.
Ties That Bind: A Pair of One-Act Plays, 1995.
Oo-Bla-Dee, 2000.
Urban Zulu Mambo, 2001.
Crowns, 2002.
Drowning Crow, 2003.

Television

Crisis at Central High, 1981.
Howard Beach: Making a Case for Murder, 1989.
I'll Fly Away, 1991.
I'll Fly Away: Then and Now, 1993.
Feds, 1997.
Strange Justice, 1999.
Cora Unashamed, 2000.
The Education of Max Bickford, 2001.

Sources

Periodicals

Back Stage West, November 9, 2000, p. 12.
Emerge, September 1992, p. 35.
Essence, March 1992, p. 42; March 2004, p. 128.
New York, September 28, 1992, p. 61; October 11, 1993, p. 79.
New Yorker, December 16, 2002, p. 104.
New York Times, October 11, 1993, p. C16; February 18, 1994, p. C19.
People, March 23, 1992, pp. 75-6.
Time, October 11, 1993, pp. 82-3.
USA Today, December 24, 1991, p. D3.

—Anne Janette Johnson and Tom Pendergast

Cleopatra Vaughns

1940—

Nurse, businesswoman, and business management consultant

When Cleopatra Vaughns grew up during the 1940s and 1950s, few career opportunities were offered to women. African-American women could expect even less in the way of higher education and advancement in the business world. But Vaughns had an advantage: she grew up with the example of her hardworking mother who managed to conduct a successful career while raising her daughter on her own. Both to please her mother and to prove her own skills and abilities, Vaughns worked hard to overcome barriers and achieve success and respect in her own career.

Born on September 2, 1940, in Houston, Texas, Vaughns was the only child of Ferdinand and Helen Lucas. Her parents divorced when young Cleopatra was a child, and she and her mother moved to Oakland, California. Ferdinand Lucas was a barber who not only owned his own barber shop, but also ran several eating and entertainment establishments, called nightclubs. Helen Lucas worked as an interior decorator for several major department stores, designing the artistic displays that were meant to attract customers and encourage them to buy the stores' merchandise. She was a college graduate and taught her daughter to place great importance on schoolwork. Vaughns adored and respected her mother, and one way she showed it was to pay close attention to her studies at her Catholic co-ed boarding school, St. Peter Claver Academy in Texas.

She graduated when she was only fifteen years old with grades high enough to qualify for a full scholarship to a private college. However, when she went with her mother for an interview at the school, the administrators were surprised and dismayed to see that the excellent student they had accepted had brown skin. They withdrew the scholarship, giving Vaughns one of her first bitter lessons in racial discrimination.

Vaughns did not abandon her plans for higher education. With her mother's continued encouragement, she applied and was accepted in a three-year program of study at the Providence College of Nursing. After graduating from Providence, Vaughns took her first job as a registered nurse at Camp Timberlock, a California Girl Scout camp. The job had sounded appealing until the city-bred Vaughns learned that she was expected to sleep in the woods with the campers. She declined, and spent the summer living in the camp infirmary.

Vaughns continued her education at the University of California at Berkeley, where she earned a bachelor's of science degree in nursing education. While attending the University of California at Berkeley, she worked as a private duty nurse and as a house-call screening nurse, speaking to patients on the phone, helping those she could and setting up house visits from doctors for those who needed them. Though she could do the work ably, she did not find it challenging or rewarding. She had entered the field of nursing chiefly because it was one of the occupations thought to be acceptable for women at the time. However, she began to think that her real skills lay elsewhere—in the world of business.

At a Glance . . .

Born Cleopatra Lucas on September 2, 1940, in Houston, Texas; married (divorced); children: Phillip. *Education:* Providence College of Nursing, RN, 1958; University of California at Berkley, BS, nursing education, 1960.

Career: Private duty nursing; screening nurse for house calls; The Ivy Shoppe, owner and operator apparel store; Blue Shield of California, claims examiner; Blue Shield of California, claims processing manager; Blue Shield of California, sales and marketing manager; Blue Shield of California, government relations manager; Blue Shield of California, marketing relations manager; Blue Shield of California, community relations manager; Vaughns and Vaughns Associates, management and community relations consultant.

Selected memberships: Internationational Museum of Women, board of directors; San Francisco Giants Community Fund; San Francisco Convention and Visitors Bureau; The National Association of Negro Business and Professional Women's Clubs, national president, 1999-2003.

Selected awards: Sojourner Truth Award, 1990; United Way Shepherd Award, 1991; Woman Who Could Be President, San Francisco League of Women Voters, 2000; Cleopatra Vaughns Day proclaimed by mayor of San Francisco, 2000; Soroptimists Woman of Distinction Award, 2004.

Addresses: 6114 La Salle Avenue, Suite 289, Oakland, CA 94611.

Inspired by her mother's experiences working in department stores, and aided by her new husband, who was a Certified Public Accountant, Vaughns opened her own business in Oakland, a clothing store called the Ivy Shoppe. She and her husband ran their "ready-to-wear" business for six years. The Ivy Shoppe was very successful, and Vaughns had ambitions to expand the business when city development brought bad news. A new rapid transit system would be built in the area, forcing Vaughns' shop to move. It is often hard for small businesses to survive such displacement, and Vaughns found herself once again looking for a job as a nurse.

While looking through employment advertisements, she saw that Blue Shield of California, a healthcare insurance organization, was seeking nurses to work examining claims. Claims are like bills for medical expenses, sent to an insurance company by doctors' offices and hospitals. The company evaluates the claim and decides if it will pay the bill. Vaughns was hired as a claims examiner, and she hoped that when she showed the company how well she worked that she would be promoted to higher positions.

However, as she well knew from her early experience of losing her scholarship, sometimes it takes more than hard work to achieve success. Sometimes it takes white skin. Vaughns worked for Blue Sheild of California for thirty years, often feeling that it was only her resilience, that is, her persistence and her ability to adjust to difficult situations, that kept her there. She was promoted to supervisor of the Claims Processing Unit, but though she worked hard and held several responsible positions with the company, she received no more promotions to a higher position.

After working as manager of Claims Processing, Vaughns moved into the Sales and Marketing section of the company, then into Government Relations where she became the link between company policy and government regulations. She then worked in Marketing Relations and finally in Community Relations. However, these job changes were not promotions, but what are called "lateral" or sideways moves, where she moved into a similar job in another department.

Through her years of working for Blue Shield of California, Vaughns learned how deeply racial bias can be embedded in corporate institutions. Even though she had a fairly secure position with the company, Vaughns felt that she had to fight for each gain she made, and she strongly believed that this was because she was African American. She observed many white employees rise to higher positions much more easily than she had been able to do. She had learned the value of hard work from her mother, but her own experience had taught her that hard work did not always bring respect. In fact, as she began to work in professional organizations, charitable organizations, and clubs, she often felt she was more respected outside the workplace that in it.

During the 1990s, Blue Shield of California underwent a major reorganization, and Vaughns' position was eliminated. Rather than move to another city for a job within the corporation, she retired. However, she continued to show the same energy and enjoyment of hard work that had marked her business career. She established her own company, Vaughns and Vaughns Associates, to help and advise companies in the areas of business management and community relations. Motivated by her work in government and community relations while involved in healthcare services, she became involved in several local business and government groups. In the late 1990s she became the first woman chair of the San Francisco Convention and Visitors Bureau, and in 2000 Mayor Willie Brown of San Francisco named her to the board of directors of the Municipal Transportation Agency, where she became chair in 2004.

Vaughns also became involved in the National Association of Negro Business and Professional Women's Clubs (NANBPWC). The NANBPWC was formed during the mid 1930s by black businesswomen Emma Odessa Young and Ollie Chin Porter, who both belonged to the New York Club of Business and Professional Women. Many cities in the United States had clubs where black women in business could meet to gain support and share business opportunities. In 1934 Young had the idea of uniting the many regional clubs in one national organization which could have more influence, and in 1935, Porter began the work of reaching out to clubs across the nation. By the beginning of the twenty-first century there were more than 200 Negro Business and Professional Women's Clubs, not only in the United States, but also in the Caribbean and in the African nations of Ghana and Nigeria. NANBPWC still provide a place for black women

professionals to meet and support each other, and they also organize education and leadership programs and perform many other social services. Vaughns served as national president of the NANBPWC from 1999 to 2003. Vaughns continues to search for ways to encourage and support other black women as they navigate their own ways through the business world.

Sources

On-line

The National Association of Negro Business and Professional Women's Clubs, www.nanbpwc.org (May 29, 2004).
"2000 MTA Board Nominees," *Rescue Muni Riders Transit Association,* www.rescuemuni.org/mta_0200.html (May 29, 2004).

Other

Information for this profile was obtained through an interview with Cleopatra Vaughns on May 29, 2004.

—Tina Gianoulis

Joscelyn Wainwright

1941—

Art show producer

Joscelyn Wainwright spent a career fighting crime as a detective in the New York City Police Department. Then when he retired, he launched a new career fighting for African-American art. As founding director of the National Black Fine Art Show (NBFAS), Wainwright has shed light on an art that was long-hidden from view—fine art by black artists. According to the *NBFAS* Web site, "The intent was not only to showcase the work to the African-American community, but also, to awaken the broader American community to the richness, vitality, and vision of the Black fine art movements."

Joined the NYPD after Vietnam

Joscelyn Wainwright, Jr., was born on November 2, 1941, in New York City and grew up in Brooklyn with a younger sister. His father Joscelyn Wainwright, Sr., was a laborer; his mother Lillian Huffstead was a housewife. As a child, Wainwright's hobby was photography. "My whole family had a camera," Wainwright told *Contemporary Black Biography* (*CBB*). "It was thrust into your hand as soon as you could hold anything. Everyone in my family took photos, my mother, father, sister." After graduating from Wingate High School where he was a photographer for the school paper, Wainwright attended New York's Hunter College, earning a degree in English in 1963. The following year he was tapped to go to Vietnam. "I was drafted into the army and served from 1964 to '67," Wainwright told *CBB*. "I was on my way to Vietnam, but when I got to California, my orders were changed

and instead I was sent to Korea." There Wainwright worked as a transportation specialist. "Whatever needed to get into [Vietnam], I helped get it there."

After being honorably discharged from the army, Wainwright moved to New York and joined the New York City police force. "I was always interested in helping people and it seemed like a good thing to do," he told *CBB*. He steadily moved up the ranks from sergeant to supervising detective sergeant to executive officer of the Manhattan robbery squad by the time of his retirement in April of 1989. "I think I was lucky and very successful in that career," Wainwright told *CBB*.

Meanwhile, in 1981 Wainwright had begun to moonlight for Sanford Smith and Associates, an art show production company. "I started there as a security guard, and honestly I wasn't interested in the job at all. The idea of sitting around for hours doing security work didn't appeal to me at all. But a friend of mine who was providing security really needed the help, so I decided to do it," he told *CBB*. "At the first show I worked I began to look around and to think, 'This is really interesting.' So I started asking questions, and learning, and asking more questions, and getting more and more involved, and getting more and more responsibility." By 1987 Wainwright had moved from security detail to operations management. "I had a chance to experience the ins and outs of getting shows up and running, from hiring security to interfacing with dealers," he told *Black Enterprise*.

Frustrated at Lack of Black Art

At a Glance . . .

Born on November 2, 1941, in New York, NY; married, Sandy Keeling (second marriage); children: Margo. *Education:* Hunter College, BA, English, 1963.

Career: New York City Police Department, detective, 1968-89; Sanford Smith and Associates, New York, NY, operations manager, 1987-97; Wainwright/Smith Associates, Ltd., New York, NY, president, 1997-2001; Keeling Wainwright Associates, Cabin John, MD, president, 2001–.

Addresses: *Office*—The National Black Fine Art Show, Keeling Wainwright Associates, P.O. Box 333. Cabin John, MD 20818.

When he retired from the NYPD, Wainwright began working full-time with Sanford Smith and soon became interested in fine art by African-American artists. "Occasionally I'd see a piece or two by a black artist, but nothing more," he told *CBB*. "I tried to see more work by black artists and couldn't. It was appalling; there was just no exposure for black artists." Though there were a few mom-and-pop galleries showcasing black art as well as a couple of notable dealers, the work was virtually invisible. "I began to look into that problem and it occurred to me—there was no conspiracy to prevent the work of black artists from appearing in major shows, it was just a result of the fact that most of the major galleries were owned by whites and had white clientele. They didn't feel that presenting black art would appeal to their clients and therefore they didn't push to represent black artists," he told *CBB*. With that realization he became determined to create a venue for not only black artists and black art, but for the black public as well.

Wainwright began actively working on what would become the National Black Fine Art Show in the early 1990s. "There were days along the way when it seemed almost impossible to bring together the right mix of galleries and private dealers who would bring the fine artwork that a historic event such as this deserves," he told *The Philadelphia Tribune*. He spent over three years crisscrossing the country, visiting galleries and dealers, and trumpeting the need for the show. "But it was a vicious circle," he told *CBB*. "They had been kept out of mainstream shows for so long; they just didn't see the value of participating." Wainwright persisted in part because he was angry. "I had really fallen in love with the work and became upset that work by black artists had existed and all my life I was completely

unaware of it," he told *CBB*. "There were no galleries in my neighborhood. Yes, there were some fabulous museums, but a black kid from Brooklyn did not feel comfortable going there. So there was a whole portion of my life that I feel I was denied. I feel like I missed out on this work. Me, my family, my neighborhood. All of us."

First Show Struck Chord with African Americans

Wainwright's hard work paid off and the first annual National Black Fine Art Show opened on January 30, 1997. "That first show was the most nerve-wracking of my life," he told *CBB*. "I didn't know what to expect, nor did anyone else. We didn't know if ten people or a thousand would show up." *Essence* wrote of the show, "For three days, a line stretched down the block as Black folks—from babies to baby boomers, hip-hoppers to old-timers—crowded into the mazelike exhibition space, hungry for some reflection of themselves." And that is what over 40 galleries and hundreds of artists provided. In painting, sculpture, textile, and photography, the over 6,000 visitors to that first show found great art, but the African-American community, as Wainwright explained to *CBB*, "came and saw themselves." He continued, "They came for the preview on Thursday night, and they came back Friday, Saturday, and Sunday, with their families, their friends, their children. It was very moving. I knew that what I had hoped for with the show had happened. The African-American audience who had never seen fine art by black artists, they saw themselves, they saw us. It was definitely the proudest moment of my career so far."

The show was also well-received by art dealers and art industry insiders. Art dealer Sheryl Sutton from Chicago told *The Philadelphia Tribune*, "What is happening here is a defining moment in the dawning of a new era. To have this many works together in one place gives people the opportunity to search the breadth and depth of our artistic senses. Hopefully, this is the beginning of a new awareness. This is a bold move." Photographer Gordon Parks, famous for his 1960s photographs of civil rights icons, enthusiastically agreed. "This is a great exposure to wonderful art that a lot of people do not get a chance to see," he told *New York Amsterdam News*. "I discovered tonight, an art that I have never had a chance to see before."

Over the next several years, the NBFAS grew in stature and prestige. "More and more galleries wanted to join," Wainwright told *CBB*. "It became easier to raise the quality level of the art in the show." He explained in a press release on the NBFAS website, "We strive to include galleries representing challenging, thought-provoking and interesting work and not just those who are limited to Afro-centric or popular imagery." The eighth annual show held in 2004 featured Caribbean, African, and European galleries in addition to many prestigious American dealers.

The show also picked up several impressive sponsors including Merrill Lynch, FedEx, *Essence, The New York Times,* and *Black Enterprise.* "With the corporate sponsorships we have we are able to do a lot more in terms of education and promotion of the show," Wainwright told *CBB.* "The idea is to reach the African-American community and also to give exposure to African-American artists. The reality still is that the people who are most unaware of the power and beauty of black art is the African-American community itself." To that end the show has always highlighted both established masters such as painter Romare Bearden, photographer James Van Der Zee, and sculptor Augusta Savage as well as work by up-and-coming contemporary artists and self-taught artists. At a typical show work has ranged in price from a few hundred to nearly a million dollars. "By making available a range of art in terms of costs, we're providing a service that can satisfy all. I think it is important that people are able to come and acquire work," Wainwright told *American Visions.*

The educational component of the NBFAS has been an integral part of the show since its inception. The NBFAS Educational Series offers seminars on art collection, framing, archival methods, and investing. "As African Americans haven't had exposure to this work before, they also haven't had the opportunity to learn how to appreciate, buy, and collect art," Wainright told *CBB.* The NBFAS also works hard to expose African-American children to the art. Each year elementary and middle school children are invited to view the work and meet many of the artists. "It is a real tearjerker to see how much the work intrigues [the children]," Wainwright told *CBB.* In addition, since its beginnings the show has also featured an opening night preview party as a fundraiser for charity. Past charities have included the Boys and Girls Clubs of America,

The Studio Museum in Harlem, and the Johnnie L. Cochran Jr. Art Fund.

Despite naming the exhibition the National Black Fine Art Show, Wainwright has often dismissed the label. "The reality is that there is no such thing as black art, Asian art, Latin art. Art is art and it is good or bad," he told *CBB.* "So why have a black art show? Because what has happened, is because of politics, economics, social factors, black artists have not had exposure and black audiences have been unexposed to black art. So we have this show, to expose these artists that are not being exposed. This is not about separatism, but exactly the opposite. We want to bring this whole genre to the world." With the NBFAS growing steadily every year—over 10,000 visitors per show, international exposure, sales in the tens of millions—Wainwright has made incredible strides towards achieving that goal.

Sources

Periodicals

American Visions, December 1988.
Black Enterprise, February 2000.
Essence, July 1, 1997.
New York Amsterdam News, February 8, 1997.
The Philadelphia Tribune, February 4, 1997.

On-line

"Black Fine Art Show Mixes Business and Pleasure," *BET,* www.bet.com/articles/1,,c5gb1745-2411,00.html (May 30, 2004).
National Black Fine Art Show, www.nationalblack-fineartshow.com (May 30, 2004).
"The National Black Fine Art Show-Evolving and Educating," *Maine Antique Digest,* www.maineantique-digest.com/articles/blac0499.htm (May 30, 2004).

Other

Additional information for this profile was obtained through an interview with Joscelyn Wainwright on June 8, 2004.

—Candace LaBalle

Lloyd Ward

1949—

Corporate executive

During a 1998 interview with *Brandweek*, Lloyd Ward issued this statement. "I challenge people to act differently, think differently. If better is possible, then good is not enough. You have to reach beyond what you think you can do." throughout his illustrious career, Ward has challenged himself and those around him to exceed their own expectations. In the process, he has established himself as a rising star among business leaders.

Lloyd Ward was born on January 22, 1949, in Romulus, Michigan. One of five children, he learned the value of hard work early on from his parents, Sadie and Rubert Ward. His father supported the family by working three jobs: letter carrier, movie house janitor, and minister. When people accuse Ward of working too hard, he is quick to point out that his efforts pale in comparison to his father's. "I'm still not working nearly as hard as my father did, and I will make in one year more than he made in a lifetime," Ward was quoted as saying in a 1995 *Black Enterprise* profile.

Inspired by Parents to Succeed

Although Rubert Ward died when Lloyd was 18 years old, he still received plenty of inspiration. At the age of 50, his mother returned to school and earned her bachelor's degree. She eventually received a master's degree in social work. Through their example, Ward's parents laid the foundation for his development into an individual who was willing to set lofty goals and expend the time and effort needed to attain them.

After graduating from high school, Ward enrolled at Michigan State University, where he honed his competitive edge as a standout member of the varsity basketball team. He received his B.S. in mechanical engineering from Michigan State in 1970, then signed on as a design engineer for paper products and packaging technology at Procter & Gamble. Ward spent 18 years at Procter & Gamble and rose steadily through the corporate ranks. Along the way, he earned an MBA from Xavier University in 1984. In 1988, Ward was named general manager of Procter & Gamble's dish care products section. As general manager, he was responsible for the engineering, manufacturing, product development, advertising, and brand management of the company's well-known dish care line.

"At P&G, I learned the importance and value of understanding the consumer and being market-driven," Ward remarked in a 1998 *Brandweek* article. "It was about what was underneath the want and need, the 'why' beneath the want and need....Innovation should come from the consumer." Although working at Procter & Gamble provided Ward with valuable learning experiences, the company ultimately did not offer the long-term opportunities that Ward desired. As a result, he never felt that he could become a true leader at Procter & Gamble.

Climbed the Corporate Ladder

At a Glance . . .

Born on January 22, 1949, in Romulus, MI; son of Rubert (a letter carrier, janitor, and minister) and Sadie (a social worker) Ward; married Estralita "Lita" Ward, c. 1970; children: Lloyd II and Lance. *Education:* Michigan State University, BS, 1970; Xavier University, MBA, 1984.

Career: Procter & Gamble, various positions, including design engineer, group leader, engineering manager, 1970-88, general manager for dish care products, 1988; PepsiCo., vice president of operations for Pepsi Cola East, 1988-91, president, Frito-Lay Western Division, 1991-92, president, Frito-Lay Central Division, 1992-96; Maytag Appliances, president and chief operating officer, 1996-99; Maytag Corp., chief executive officer, 1999–; iMotors.com, chief executive officer, 2001; U.S. Olympic Committee, chairman and chief executive officer, 2002-03, BodyBlocks, chairman and chief executive officer, 2004–.

Awards: *Black Enterprise,* Executive of the Year, 1995; America's Best and Brightest Business and Professional Men and Women list, *Dollars and Sense;* Michigan State University, Jack Breslin Lifetime Achievement Award, 1996; Michigan State University, Alumni of the Year, 1998; *Business Week* Magazine, "Top 25 Executives," 1998; *BrandWeek* Magazine, "Marketer of the Year," 1998.

Addresses: *Office*—BodyBlocks, 3340 Peachtree St., NE, Suite 1800, Atlanta, GA 30326.

In 1988, Ward left Proctor & Gamble and accepted a position with the Pepsi-Cola Co. as vice president of operations for Pepsi-Cola East. At Pepsi, he found plenty of room to build on his leadership aspirations. After only two years at the company, Ward was promoted to president of PepsiCo's Frito-Lay Western Division in 1991. The following year, he advanced to president of Frito-Lay's Central Division, its largest division. At the Central Division, Ward oversaw the operations of an entity that sold more than $1.3 billion dollars worth of snacks per year. Comprised of 12 midwestern and south-central states, the Central Division employed 8,500 people in manufacturing, distribution, sales, and marketing.

In 1995, Ward was named *Black Enterprise* Executive of the Year. The magazine spoke lavishly of the energy and charisma he brings to every position he occupies. Frito-Lay CEO Steven Reinemund was quoted as saying in *Black Enterprise,* "He's done a wonderful job with his team.... Lloyd's a very effective leader—charismatic, and energetic and very principled. People respond to that."

As president of the Central Division, Ward was committed to working with the African American community in Dallas, the division's home base. He and other members of his division adopted A. C. Maceo Smith High School, a predominantly African American school with a large number of "at-risk" students. His work with the school included recruiting members of the Dallas Cowboys football team and Dallas Mavericks basketball team to give motivational speeches to the students. Ward also became a board member of Paul Quinn College, a historically black institution, and was instrumental in persuading Frito-Lay to donate $1 million in scholarship money to the school.

Joined Maytag

Although PepsiCo provided Ward with unique challenges, he still desired the opportunity to hold the top post at a large company. In 1996, Ward accepted the position as president of Maytag's Appliances Division, a newly consolidated $2 billion-a-year unit of Maytag Corporation that encompassed the Maytag, Jenn-Air, Magic Chef, and Admiral home appliance brands. Generally, it was understood that Ward was being groomed as the heir apparent to Maytag chairman and chief executive officer Leonard A. Hadley. He also became Maytag's only African American executive.

As a newcomer to the appliance industry, Ward brought a new set of expectations and a different approach to brand development from his years at P&G and Frito-Lay. Upon arriving at Maytag's Newton, Iowa headquarters he found that the company, while maintaining strong brand recognition as a leader in quality, was losing market share on most of its products. Ward believed that the only way to improve Maytag's market share was to convince consumers that appliances bearing the Maytag label were a good buy, even if they were more expensive than competing brands.

Ward quickly began the daunting task of bringing a more creative atmosphere to Maytag. He realigned the company's management structure, shifting more responsibility to brand managers in charge of entire product segments. He also built a war room where company leaders could meet regularly to strategize. In 1997, under Ward's guidance, Maytag launched its new Neptune water and energy-saving laundry system. Departing from the company's low-key style, Ward organized a high-profile media event at New York's Lincoln Center to unveil the Neptune line. The glitzy event featured appearances by four generations of TV moms, including Barbara Billingsley of *Leave It to Beaver* and Florence Henderson of *The Brady Bunch*. The Neptune, priced at $999, reversed a long-standing industry trend toward lower priced appliances. With the success of the Neptune washers, Ward succeeded in convincing consumers to replace other appliances with high-end replacements, including a double-oven range and an oven that cooks as fast as a microwave while maintaining traditional oven-cooked crispness.

Marked "Watershed Moments" for African Americans

In 1999 Lloyd Ward became the ninth chief executive of Maytag to fulfill his dream to head a Fortune 500 company. At the same time Ward became the second African American in history to lead a Fortune 500 company. *Black Enterprise* reported Ward's appointment as a "watershed moment in the history of African Americans in corporate America." At every stop along his climb—a climb that has by no means reached its peak—he has found ways to energize and motivate those around him. Colleagues continually comment on his ability to inspire others to set and achieve higher goals. Drawing on a metaphor from the basketball court, Ward summed up his approach to life in a 1995 interview in *Black Enterprise*: "I am a winner who understands that winning is important—it is critical.... I believe in playing above the rim on the court, and in my career." Indeed, upon his acceptance of the helm at Maytag, Ward declared that his objective would be "to be the best CEO on the planet," according to *Black Enterprise*.

After fifteen months leading Maytag, Ward was offered a severance packet when revenues dropped. He soon became the chairman and CEO of the used car Web site *iMotors.com*, where his business unit brought in $100 million in sales but eventually went broke. By November 2001, Ward had moved again; this time to become the first African-American CEO of the U.S. Olympic Committee (USOC). Ward's career took a sudden turn in December of 2002 when allegations of preferential treatment and misuse of funds by USOC officials surfaced. After three months of investigations, a senate hearing, and the resignation of several Committee officials, Ward also resigned because of the ethics controversy in March of 2003. Ward told *Jet* that "In the hope that we can shift the focus back to the athletes and the ideals of the Olympic movement, I have decided to resign," adding that "I do so with a deeply ingrained belief that I have served the USOC and the Olympic movement constructively and with integrity." The controversy did not defeat Ward's resolve. In May of 2004, he became chairman of Body-Blocks Nutrition Systems, a maker of nutrition bars and energy drinks sold under the N Motion brand.

Sources

Periodicals

Appliance Manufacturer, August 1997, p. AHAM2.
Black Enterprise, June 1995, p. 214; August 1999; January 1, 2004; March 2, 2003, p. 61.
Brandweek, March 10, 1997, p. 38; March 24, 1997, p. 12; October 12, 1998, p. 88.
Jet, April 29, 1996, p. 11.
Wall Street Journal, November 26, 1996, p. B1.

On-line

BodyBlocks.com, www.bodyblocks.com (July 27, 2004).
"The Saga of Maytag's Lloyd Ward," *BusinessWeek*, www.businessweek.com/1999/99_32/b3641001. htm?scriptFramed (July 27, 2004).

—Robert R. Jacobson and Sara Pendergast

Kerry Washington

1977—

Actor

In interviews, actor Kerry Washington has revealed her ambition to perform in a variety of genres, from comedy to historical films, from action movies to stage musicals. Not only does she strive to appear before more audiences as an actor, singer, and dancer, she hopes to find success behind the scenes as a screenwriter. Washington is serious about her art, continually studying her craft and eager to perform in all genres. "I want longevity in my career," she told *Essence* in 2002, "so I keep the focus on my craft." An article in *Film Comment* lauded Washington's propensity for showmanship and dexterity, citing the young actor as having a knack for "playing characters who each in a different way attempt to balance the demands of friends, family, and children."

Born with the "Acting Bug"

Kerry Washington was born in the Bronx, New York, in 1977. As a child, she experienced the thrill of the stage while dancing with the New York Negro Ballet. Her grandmother called her Sarah Bernhardt (after the acting legend), because theater was central to her dreams even as a young child. "I think I was born with the acting bug. I was always 'dramatic' as a child," Washington offered in a 2001 interview with the *Girl's World* Web site. She began acting as the youngest performer in a troupe that gave performances in schools to stress positive self-esteem and safe sex. Washington credited this experience, along with her involvement with the local Bronx Boys and Girls Club, for "cultivating my singing, acting and dancing skills."

As a teen, she landed several acting jobs, including an appearance on NBC's popular television series *Law & Order* in 2001.

Also as a teen, Washington took the Bronx's Number 6 train into Manhattan each day to attend high school at the elite Spence School, which she attended on scholarship. The daughter of a college professor mother and real-estate broker father, Washington was raised in perhaps the wealthiest household on her block in the Bronx; yet at Spence she experienced "a real culture shock" being immersed in "real wealth," she told Carla Meyer of the *San Francisco Chronicle*. The school is also alma mater to many of New York's wealthiest residents, including Gwyneth Paltrow and Soon-Ye Previn. Washington too grew a star quality at Spence. "People have said I'm like a cross between Jennifer Lopez and Gwyneth Paltrow," Washington told Meyer.

Since childhood, Washington has been a fan of performers who can "do it all," such as Barbara Streisand and Rita Moreno, she told *Film Comment* in 2001. Washington too has sought to build a long, multifaceted performing career. She earnestly began her trek to performing prowess by earning a bachelor's degree in the performing arts at George Washington University in 1998.

Debuted on Screen in 'Our Song'

Washington made her screen debut in 2000, starring in the independent film *Our Song* playing 15-year old

At a Glance . . .

Born in the Bronx, NY, in 1977. *Education:* George Washington University, BA, 1998.

Career: Actor, 2000–. Substitute teacher, New York City, 2001.

Addresses: *Agent*—Abrams Artists Agency, 9200 Sunset Blvd., Ste. 1130, Los Angeles, CA 90069.

Lanisha, a half-black, half-Cuban girl living in Brooklyn's Crown Heights neighborhood. "My character is very good at making herself fit in," Washington was quoted in the *San Francisco Chronicle.* "In the same way, I was trying to negotiate being a Spence girl and growing up in the Bronx, and trying to feel like I belonged in both of those places." In the same article, *Our Song* writer and director Jim McKay said that he immediately recognized Washington's talent. "Kerry blended well with the other actors," he said, "even though she is really trained, and would be just as comfortable doing Shakespeare." *Our Song* qualified as a finalist for the Grand Jury Prize at the 2000 Sundance Film Festival.

Washington too was cited for a winning performance. In his review of *Our Song*, *New York Times* film critic A.O. Scott called Washington "simply, a miracle." Film critic Michael Atkinson also praised Washington's breakout performance, writing in *Interview,* "Certainly, no other young African-American actress is quite as believable, as touchable." The 22-year old also explained how she developed her young character. "I worked on her walk, how she stands, how she looks people in the eye," she said. "While working it out I had lunch with a cousin of mine who's 16. Listening to her, I thought, 'You couldn't pay me to be a teenager again.' Then I realized—I was being paid."

Washington told *Girl's World* that she tapped into her "culture shock" experience at Spence to transition herself to the emotional journey Lanisha undertakes. "[Lanisha] is exploring love, she is trying to make responsible and independent decisions—these were things that I can definitely relate to...." She added, "I think *Our Song* helped me to learn that the most important elements to bring to my work are integrity, generosity, and truth."

Our Song appeared in theaters between the showing of Washington's second film, *Save the Last Dance,* and her third, *Lift,* both released in 2001. She played a teen again in *Save the Last Dance.* This time she was a teen mom, Chenille—a character Washington called her "most real" in her *Girl's World* interview. At 24-years old, Washington got her first taste of big-budget studio filmmaking. "On *Our Song* there were days I was on the set not to act," Washington explained to *Interview,* "but to watch for cops because we didn't have a permit to shoot on the subway. On the other hand, one morning on *Save the Last Dance,* I found a new DVD player in my trailer, with a stack of DVDs."

In another highly lauded independent film, *Lift,* which won honors at the 2001 Sundance Film Festival, Washington played Niecy, a 24-year old professional shoplifter with big ambition and a troubled relationship with her mother. "Having grown up in the Bronx and gone to the Spence School," Washington admitted in *Film Comment,* "I really understand Niecy's need to negotiate all kinds of socio-economic environments and her ability to do so with grace and fluidity." Film reviewers agreed that Washington was right for the role, including Phil Rosenthal of the *Chicago Sun Times,* who wrote, "Kerry Washington absolutely steals the film as the thief whose world unravels...."

Balanced Hollywood with Simple Living

After filming *Save the Last Dance,* Washington worked as a substitute teacher in Harlem. "Being recognized as Chenille and trying to be somebody's math teacher was a challenge," Washington remarked to *Entertainment Weekly.* She also appeared in *NYPD Blue* and on several episodes of *100 Centre Street* and landed roles in the films *3D, Take the A Train,* and as Chris Rock's girlfriend, Julie, in *Bad Company.* She gained recognition in Hollywood for her performance in the 2003 drama, *The Human Stain.* Also in 2003, Washington was noticed for her work in *Against the Ropes: The Jackie Kallen Story.* *New York Times* film critic A.O. Scott wrote, "It is always a pleasure to see Kerry Washington, even in the underwritten role of Jackie's sidekick and Luther's love interest." In 2004, Washington appeared in the bio-drama *Ray,* the story of musician Ray Charles.

Like many successful screen actors, Washington maintains residences in New York and Los Angeles. She prefers to fly the no-frills JetBlue Airways, where "we are all one people on [the] plane." "My favorite thing to do in L.A.," she told *Organic Style's* Jamie Diamond in 2004, "is to feed the fish in our courtyard. They swim up to the corner of the pond and are so happy to see me." Washington defined her personal goals in *Organic Style* as going "my own way, to be my own person, to make and follow my own rules." She begins each day by writing a journal entry, and regularly works on developing screenplays, hoping to wow Hollywood with her writer's vision as well as her actor's intuition.

Washington told Diamond that as a statement in simple living she wears her mother's simple diamond-studded earrings on a daily basis. "They're simple and elegant and understated—like my mom," she said. "Now that I'm working in movies, I guess I should wear fancier, big diamonds, but I love wearing these in the loud, in-your-face lifestyle of Los Angeles."

Selected works

Films

Our Song, 2000.
3D, 2000.
Save the Last Dance, 2001.
Lift, 2001.
Take the Train, 2002.
Bad Company, 2002.
The United States of Leland, 2003.
The Human Stain, 2003.
Sin, 2003.
Against the Ropes: The Jackie Kallen Story, 2004.
She Hate Me, 2004.
Ray (also known as *Unchain My Heart: The Ray Charles Story*), 2004.
Sexual Life, 2004.
Mr. and Mrs. Smith, 2004.

Television

Magical Makeover, 1994.

Other

Washington has also appeared in episodes of *NYPD Blue* (2001), *100 Centre Street* (2001), *Law & Order* (2001), *The Guardian* (2001), and *Wonderfalls* (2004).

Sources

Periodicals

Chicago Sun Times, June 26, 2002, p. 51.
Ebony, Sept. 2002, p. 174.
Entertainment Weekly, June 27/July 4, 2003, 2003, p. 50.
Esquire, Dec. 2003, p. 171.
Essence, Dec. 2002, p. 110.
Film Comment, March/April 2001, p. 6.
Interview, June 2001, p. 56.
New York Times, March 23, 2001, E5; February 20, 2004, E24.
Organic Style, March 2004, p. 32.
San Francisco Chronicle, August 8, 2001, D1.

On-line

"We're Hangin' with 'Save the Last Dance's" Chenille: Kerry Washington," *A Girl's World,* www.agirls world.com/rachel/hangin-with/Kerrywashington.ht ml (May 27, 2004).

—Melissa Walsh

Robert C. Weaver

1907-1997

Government official, scholar

Robert C. Weaver remains one of the least known of the civil rights pioneers who struggled throughout the middle half of the twentieth century to obtain rights for black Americans. *Ebony* magazine called him "one of the direct action pioneers" for picketing Washington, DC, stores as early as the 1930s. Primarily, however, his activities were within the context of his governmental jobs; he held various federal positions under Franklin D. Roosevelt's New Deal administration in the 1930s and 1940s, and then again under the John F. Kennedy and Lyndon B. Johnson presidential administrations in the early 1960s. In 1961 he received the highest federal appointment then assigned to any African American when he became Administrator of the Housing and Home Finance Agency. Four years later, he became the first African American on the presidential cabinet, when President Johnson appointed him to the top position at the newly formed U.S. Department of Housing and Urban Development.

While many have considered Weaver's achievements to be exceptional, he never considered his actions extraordinary. He was raised in a middle-class family in Washington, DC, by parents who stressed education and achievement. "They worked [and] they struggled," he told *Ebony* magazine, "and their one ambition was to send us to New England schools." The family's vision of success was rooted in its lineage. Weaver's grandfather, Robert Tanner Freeman, was the first Black person to graduate from Harvard with a degree in dentistry. His parents realized their goal, for Weaver attended Harvard from 1925 until 1934, earning

bachelor's, master's, and doctorate degrees in economics.

Weaver dedicated most of his life to fighting discrimination and improving race relations. He held a succession of assignments for a variety of departments under the New Deal administration of the 1930s and 1940s, frequently serving as advisor for minority affairs and race relations. He advised the Secretary of the Interior Harold L. Ickes from 1934 to 1938; acted as special assistant to Nathan Straus of the Housing Authority from 1938 to 1940; assisted Sidney Hillman of the National Defense Advisory Commission in 1940; and was chief of the Negro employment and training branch of the labor division in the Office of Production Management from 1942 to 1943. After the United States joined World War II, he served on the War Manpower Commission as director of Negro Manpower Services.

Simeon Booker wrote in *Ebony* magazine, "[Weaver's] race relations service was an innovation for government [at that time]." Not satisfied with fighting discrimination on the job, Weaver spent his free time fighting the battle, too; during his first year in government, he and some friends desegregated the employee cafeteria.

Throughout his life, Weaver felt the sting of discrimination personally. Shortly after he finished his work at Harvard, he was recommended for a position with the Federal Reserve Board in New York City. He did not get the job because of his race. Years later, when he

At a Glance . . .

Born Robert Clifton Weaver on December 29, 1907, in Washington, DC; died on July 17, 1997, in New York City; son of Mortimer Grover and Florence Freeman Weaver; married Ella V. Haith, 1935; children: Robert (deceased). *Education:* Harvard University, BA, 1929; Harvard University, MA, 1931; Harvard University, PhD, 1934.

Career: Advisor to U.S. Secretary of Interior, 1934-38; U.S. Housing Authority, special assistant, 1938-40; National Defense Advisory Commission, administrative assistant, 1940-42; Office of Production Management, Labor Division, chief of Negro employment and training, 1942-43; War Manpower Commission, director of the Negro Manpower Service, 1943-44; Chicago Mayor's Commission on Race Relations, director, 1944-45; American Council on Race Relations, director of community services, 1945-48; John Hay Whitney Foundation, director of Opportunity Fellowships, 1949-54; New York State Rent Administration, 1955-59; U.S. Housing and Home Finance Agency, administrator, 1961-66; Chief of U.S. Department of Housing and Urban Development, 1966-68; Baruch College, president, 1969-70; Hunter College, distinguished professor, 1971-78.

Selected memberships: Metro Life Insurance Company, board of directors, 1969-78; Bowery Savings Bank, board of trustees, 1969-80; U.S. Controller General, consulting panel, 1973-97; New York City Conciliation and Appeals Board, 1973-84; Harvard University School of Design, visiting commission, 1978-83; NAACP Legal Defense Fund, executive committee of the board, 1978-97.

Selected awards: Spingarn Medal, National Association for the Advancement of Colored People (NAACP), 1962; Russworm Award, 1963; Albert Einstein Commemorative Award, 1968; Merrick Moore Spaulding Achievement Award, 1968; U.S. General Accounting Office, Public Service Award, 1975; New York City Urban League, Frederick Douglass Award, 1977; Schomburg Collection Award, 1978; American Academy of Arts and Sciences, inductee, 1985; National Urban League, Equal Opportunity Day Award, 1987; received more than 30 honorary degrees.

became Housing and Home Finance Administrator, he had a problem with his own housing. After he and his wife moved into an apartment building on Connecticut Avenue in Washington, DC, both suffered cold shoulders from the tenants. "There was the coolness," he told *Ebony*, "and [the] management wasn't too happy with the integration idea."

Weaver left Washington in the 1940s because he felt that the anti-discriminatory programs he had helped to put in place were moving too slowly. He served on the first Mayor's race relation board in Chicago from 1944 to 1945, and then moved to New York, where he taught at Columbia University and New York University. From 1949 to 1954 he worked with the John Hay Whitney Foundation as director of Opportunity Fellowships, distributing money to fund projects that would not otherwise have received support; he distributed at least $600,000 to promising young African-American scholars. During the 1950s he served on various housing boards for the city and state of New York.

Weaver's scholarly work during the 1940s and 1950s reflected his interest in the economics and housing problems of the African-American population. In 1946 he published *Negro Labor: A National Problem*, and two years later finished *The Negro Ghetto*, a book about housing segregation in the North.

Weaver's scholarly and administrative work quietly attracted attention, and on December 31, 1960, President John F. Kennedy appointed him as the administrator of the Housing and Home Finance Agency, making him the first black to achieve such a high position in the federal government. His agency had an estimated annual budget of more than $300 million, and oversaw such subsidiary agencies as the Federal Housing Administration, Public Housing Administration, Community Facilities Administration, and the Urban Renewal Administration. In 1966, *Ebony* magazine reported, "How the...poker-faced scholar [Weaver] took over the...[Housing and Home Finance Agency] in 1961 and brought direction and morale to the sprawling agency is a sterling example of his ability. For the first time, administrators of five agencies in the network met, worked out common problems and developed programs. New projects were conceived, including moderate-income housing, rent supplement assistance for low income families, open space preservation, urban beautification, mass transit assistance, rehabilitation assistance, relocation aids, grants for basic public facilities, [and] advanced acquisition of sites and land development assistance."

In 1961 President Kennedy attempted to raise Weaver's agency to cabinet level but was blocked by Congress because of his plans to put Weaver, a black man, at the head. Four years later President Johnson succeeded, and the Department of Housing and Urban Development was established. On January 13, 1966, Weaver became the first African American appointed to a cabinet position. As President Johnson made the appointment, he told the country, according to an *Ebony* account, that "Bob Weaver's performance as administrator of the Housing and Home Finance Agency has been marked by the highest level of integrity and [an] ability to stimulate a genuine team spirit. I have found him to be a deep thinker but a quiet and articulate man of action. He is as well versed in the urban needs of America as any man I know."

When the President Richard Nixon's administration took over in 1968, Weaver left government for good, and returned to academe. He served as the President of Baruch College for two years and then became a Distinguished Professor at Hunter College until he retired in 1978. Even after his retirement, Weaver was famous for never wasting time and always working. Shortly after he joined the cabinet, in fact, an aide of his told *Ebony* that "Weaver never wastes time. He reads, writes, and constantly researches. When he makes a trip, he carries books and reports to read."

In addition to both his academic and government work, Weaver kept busy on many boards and committees. He was on the board of directors of Metro Life Insurance Company, the Bowery Savings Bank, and Mount Sinai Hospital and Medical School; he served as president of the National Committee against Discrimination in Housing, as a member of the commission on law and social action of the American Jewish Congress, the Citizens Committee for Children, the New York Civil Liberties Union, and for many years was active in the National Association for the Advancement of Colored People (NAACP). He kept busy until he no longer could. At age 89, Weaver died in New York City on July 17, 1997.

Despite his success and the praise of others, Weaver always refused to spread his own fame. "Bob believes in getting the work done, not publicity on what he plans to do," Clarence Mitchell of the NAACP told *Ebony* magazine. Even when he was waiting to be nominated to the cabinet, he refused to ask black groups to recommend him or campaign in his behalf, knowing that his qualifications would secure him the position.

While he may never have blown his own horn, many others recognized Weaver's worth and awarded him honors accordingly. In addition to the nearly 30 honorary degrees from such institutions as the University of Michigan, Howard, Harvard, Morehouse, Rutgers, Amherst, and Columbia, he received the Spingarn Medal from the NAACP in 1962, the Russworm Award in 1963, delivered the annual Godkin Lectures at Harvard in 1965, and received the Albert Einstein Commemorative Award in 1968. In 1992 the Con-

gressional Black Caucus honored him at a special party during their annual Weekend Production.

The nation commemorated Weaver's greatest legacy in 2000, when the HUD headquarters building in Washington, DC, was dedicated in his honor. Fittingly, Weaver's name became the first of any African American to grace a cabinet building in the capitol. Harlem Representative Charles Rangel, who had introduced the bill honoring Weaver to Congress told *Jet* that "This is a long overdue expression of the nation's gratitude for Robert Weaver's contributions." The HUD Secretary Andrew Cuomo praised Weaver in *Jet,* saying that he "put the bricks and mortar on President Johnson's blueprint for a Great Society. Robert Weaver got real urban legislation on the books and nurtured our country's first commitment to improve the quality of life in our nation's cities. All of us who work at HUD and all who believe we can build an even greater society, are forever in his debt." Indeed many of the "bricks and mortar" Weaver put in place continue to benefit the nation.

Selected writings

The Negro Ghetto, Russell & Russell, 1948, reprinted, 1967.
Negro Labor: A National Problem, Kennikat Press, 1946, reprinted, 1969.
Dilemmas of Urban America, Harvard University Press, 1965.
The Urban Complex; Human Values in Urban Life, Doubleday, 1966.
(With William E. Zisch and Paul H. Douglas) *The Urban Environment: How It Can Be Improved,* New York University Press, 1969.

Sources

Black Enterprise, April 1971, p. 44.
Ebony, April 1966, p. 83; April 1972, p. 182; August 1975, p. 7; March 1982, p. 129.
Jet, October 12, 1992, p. 8.; August 4, 1997, p. 57; December 13, 1999, p. 31; June 5, 2000, p. 16; January 19, 2004, p. 36.
Look, April 11, 1961, p. 33.
Newsweek, January 9, 1961, p. 23; February 20, 1961, p. 25; March 5, 1962, p. 27; January 24, 1966, p. 26.
Time, January 6, 1961, p. 15; May 14, 1961, p. 16; January 21, 1966, p. 19; March 4, 1966, p. 87.

—Robin Armstrong and Sara Pendergast

Cumulative Nationality Index

Volume numbers appear in **bold**

Cary, Mary Ann Shadd **30**
Cash, Rosalind **28**
CasSelle, Malcolm **11**
Catchings, Tamika **43**
Catlett, Elizabeth **2**
Cayton, Horace **26**
Cedric the Entertainer **29**
Chamberlain, Wilt **18**
Chambers, Julius **3**
Chapman, Nathan A. Jr. **21**
Chapman, Tracy **26**
Chappell, Emma **18**
Charles, Ray **16**
Charleston, Oscar **39**
Chase-Riboud, Barbara **20**, **46**
Chatard, Peter **44**
Chavis, Benjamin **6**
Cheadle, Don **19**
Checker, Chubby **28**
Chenault, John **40**
Chenault, Kenneth I. **4**, **36**
Cherry, Deron **40**
Chesnutt, Charles **29**
Chestnut, Morris **31**
Chideya, Farai **14**
Childress, Alice **15**
Chinn, May Edward **26**
Chisholm, Samuel **32**
Chisholm, Shirley **2**
Christian, Barbara T. **44**
Christian, Spencer **15**
Christian-Green, Donna M. **17**
Christie, Angella **36**
Chuck D **9**
Claiborne, Loretta **34**
Clark, Celeste **15**
Clark, Joe **1**
Clark, Kenneth B. **5**
Clark, Patrick **14**
Clark, Septima **7**
Clarke, Cheryl **32**
Clarke, Hope **14**
Clarke, John Henrik **20**
Clarke, Kenny **27**
Clark-Sheard, Karen **22**
Clash, Kevin **14**
Clay, William Lacy **8**
Clayton, Constance **1**
Clayton, Eva M. **20**
Clayton, Xernona **3**, **45**
Claytor, Helen **14**
Cleage, Pearl **17**
Cleaver, Eldridge **5**
Cleaver, Emanuel **4**, **45**
Cleaver, Kathleen **29**
Clements, George **2**
Clemmons, Reginal G. **41**
Clemons, Clarence **41**
Clendenon, Donn **26**
Cleveland, James **19**
Cliff, Michelle **42**
Clifton, Lucille **14**
Clinton, George **9**
Clyburn, James **21**
Coachman, Alice **18**
Cobb, Jewel Plummer **42**
Cobb, W. Montague **39**
Cobbs, Price M. **9**
Cochran, Johnnie L., Jr. **11**, **39**
Cohen, Anthony **15**
Colbert, Virgis William **17**
Cole, Johnnetta B. **5**, **43**
Cole, Nat King **17**
Cole, Natalie Maria **17**
Cole, Rebecca **38**

Coleman, Bessie **9**
Coleman, Donald A. **24**
Coleman, Gary **35**
Coleman, Leonard S., Jr. **12**
Coleman, Mary **46**
Coleman, Michael B. **28**
Coleman, Ornette **39**
Colemon, Johnnie **11**
Collins, Albert **12**
Collins, Barbara-Rose **7**
Collins, Bootsy **31**
Collins, Cardiss **10**
Collins, Janet **33**
Collins, Marva **3**
Colter, Cyrus J. **36**
Coltrane, John **19**
Combs, Sean "Puffy" **17**, **43**
Comer, James P. **6**
Common **31**
Cone, James H. **3**
Connerly, Ward **14**
Conyers, John, Jr. **4**
Conyers, Nathan G. **24**, **45**
Cook, (Will) Mercer **40**
Cook, Charles "Doc" **44**
Cook, Samuel DuBois **14**
Cook, Suzan D. Johnson **22**
Cook, Toni **23**
Cook, Will Marion **40**
Cooke, Marvel **31**
Cooper Cafritz, Peggy **43**
Cooper, Andrew W. **36**
Cooper, Anna Julia **20**
Cooper, Barry **33**
Cooper, Cynthia **17**
Cooper, Edward S. **6**
Cooper, Evern **40**
Cooper, J. California **12**
Cooper, Margaret J. **46**
Cooper, Michael **31**
Corbi, Lana **42**
Cornelius, Don **4**
Cortez, Jayne **43**
Corthron, Kia **43**
Cortor, Eldzier **42**
Cosby, Bill **7**, **26**
Cosby, Camille **14**
Cose, Ellis **5**
Cotter, Joseph Seamon, Sr. **40**
Cottrell, Comer **11**
Cowans, Adger W. **20**
Cox, Ida **42**
Craig, Carl **31**
Craig-Jones, Ellen Walker **44**
Crawford, Randy **19**
Cray, Robert **30**
Creagh, Milton **27**
Crew, Rudolph F. **16**
Crite, Alan Rohan **29**
Crocker, Frankie **29**
Crockett, George Jr. **10**
Cross, Dolores E. **23**
Crothers, Scatman **19**
Crouch, Andraé **27**
Crouch, Stanley **11**
Crowder, Henry **16**
Cullen, Countee **8**
Culpepper, Daunte **32**
Cummings, Elijah E. **24**
Cuney, William Waring **44**
Cunningham, Evelyn **23**
Cunningham, Randall **23**
Currie, Betty **21**
Curry, George E. **23**
Curry, Mark **17**

Curtis, Christopher Paul **26**
Curtis-Hall, Vondie **17**
Daly, Marie Maynard **37**
Dandridge, Dorothy **3**
Dandridge, Ray **36**
Dandridge, Raymond Garfield **45**
D'Angelo **27**
Daniels, Lee Louis **36**
Daniels-Carter, Valerie **23**
Darden, Calvin **38**
Darden, Christopher **13**
Dash, Damon **31**
Dash, Julie **4**
David, Keith **27**
Davidson, Jaye **5**
Davidson, Tommy **21**
Davis, Allison **12**
Davis, Angela **5**
Davis, Anthony **11**
Davis, Arthur P. **41**
Davis, Artur **41**
Davis, Benjamin O., Jr. **2**, **43**
Davis, Benjamin O., Sr. **4**
Davis, Chuck **33**
Davis, Danny K. **24**
Davis, Ed **24**
Davis, Gary **41**
Davis, George **36**
Davis, Guy **36**
Davis, Mike **41**
Davis, Miles **4**
Davis, Nolan **45**
Davis, Ossie **5**
Davis, Piper **19**
Davis, Ruth **37**
Davis, Terrell **20**
Davis, Viola **34**
Dawes, Dominique **11**
Dawkins, Wayne **20**
Dawson, Matel "Mat," Jr. **39**
Dawson, William Levi **39**
Day, Leon **39**
Days, Drew S., III **10**
de Passe, Suzanne **25**
De Veaux, Alexis **44**
Dean, Mark E. **35**
DeBaptiste, George **32**
DeCarava, Roy **42**
Dee, Ruby **8**
DeFrantz, Anita **37**
Delaney, Beauford **19**
Delaney, Joseph **30**
Delany, Bessie **12**
Delany, Martin R. **27**
Delany, Sadie **12**
Delany, Samuel R., Jr. **9**
Delco, Wilhemina **33**
DeLille, Henriette **30**
Dellums, Ronald **2**
DeLoach, Nora **30**
Delsarte, Louis **34**
Dennard, Brazeal **37**
DePriest, James **37**
Devers, Gail **7**
Devine, Loretta **24**
Dickens, Helen Octavia **14**
Dickenson, Vic **38**
Dickerson, Eric **27**
Dickerson, Ernest R. **6**, **17**
Dickey, Eric Jerome **21**
Diddley, Bo **39**
Diesel, Vin **29**
Diggs, Charles C. **21**
Diggs, Taye **25**
Diggs-Taylor, Anna **20**

Cumulative Occupation Index

Volume numbers appear in **bold**

McCarty, Osceola **16**
McKay, Nellie Yvonne **17**
McMillan, Terry **4, 17**
McMurray, Georgia L. **36**
McWhorter, John **35**
Meek, Carrie **6**
Memmi, Albert **37**
Meredith, James H. **11**
Millender-McDonald, Juanita **21**
Mitchell, Corinne **8**
Mitchell, Sharon **36**
Mofolo, Thomas Mokopu **37**
Mollel, Tololwa **38**
Mongella, Gertrude **11**
Mooney, Paul **37**
Moore, Harry T. **29**
Moore, Melba **21**
Morrison, Keith **13**
Morrison, Toni **15**
Moses, Robert Parris **11**
Mphalele, Es'kia (Ezekiel) **40**
Mullen, Harryette **34**
Murray, Pauli **38**
N'Namdi, George R. **17**
Naylor, Gloria **10, 42**
Neal, Larry **38**
Norman, Maidie **20**
Norton, Eleanor Holmes **7**
Ogletree, Charles Jr. **12**
Onwueme, Tess Osonye **23**
Onwurah, Ngozi **38**
Owens, Major **6**
Page, Alan **7**
Paige, Rod **29**
Painter, Nell Irvin **24**
Palmer, Everard **37**
Parker, Kellis E. **30**
Parks, Suzan-Lori **34**
Patterson, Frederick Douglass **12**
Patterson, Orlando **4**
Payton, Benjamin F. **23**
Peters, Margaret and Matilda **43**
Pickett, Cecil **39**
Pinckney, Bill **42**
Player, Willa B. **43**
Porter, James A. **11**
Poussaint, Alvin F. **5**
Price, Florence **37**
Price, Glenda **22**
Primus, Pearl **6**
Prophet, Nancy Elizabeth **42**
Puryear, Martin **42**
Quarles, Benjamin Arthur **18**
Rahman, Aishah **37**
Ramphele, Mamphela **29**
Reagon, Bernice Johnson **7**
Reddick, Lawrence Dunbar **20**
Redding, J. Saunders **26**
Redmond, Eugene **23**
Reid, Irvin D. **20**
Ringgold, Faith **4**
Robinson, Sharon **22**
Robinson, Spottswood **22**
Rogers, Joel Augustus **30**
Rollins, Charlemae Hill **27**
Russell-McCloud, Patricia **17**
Salih, Al-Tayyib **37**
Sallee, Charles Louis, Jr. **38**
Satcher, David **7**
Schomburg, Arthur Alfonso **9**
Senior, Olive **37**
Shabazz, Betty **7, 26**
Shange, Ntozake **8**
Shipp, E. R. **15**
Shirley, George **33**

Simmons, Ruth J. **13, 38**
Sinkford, Jeanne C. **13**
Sisulu, Sheila Violet Makate **24**
Sizemore, Barbara A. **26**
Smith, Anna Deavere **6**
Smith, Barbara **28**
Smith, Jessie Carney **35**
Smith, John L. **22**
Smith, Mary Carter **26**
Smith, Tubby **18**
Sowande, Fela **39**
Soyinka, Wole **4**
Spikes, Dolores **18**
Stanford, John **20**
Steele, Claude Mason **13**
Steele, Shelby **13**
Stephens, Charlotte Andrews **14**
Stewart, Maria W. Miller **19**
Stone, Chuck **9**
Sudarkasa, Niara **4**
Sullivan, Louis **8**
Swygert, H. Patrick **22**
Tanksley, Ann **37**
Tatum, Beverly Daniel **42**
Taylor, Helen (Lavon Hollingshed) **30**
Taylor, Susie King **13**
Terrell, Mary Church **9**
Thomas, Alma **14**
Thurman, Howard **3**
Tillis, Frederick **40**
Tolson, Melvin **37**
Tribble, Israel, Jr. **8**
Tucker, Rosina **14**
Turnbull, Walter **13**
Tutu, Desmond **6**
Tutuola, Amos **30**
Tyson, Andre **40**
Tyson, Asha **39**
Tyson, Neil de Grasse **15**
Usry, James L. **23**
van Sertima, Ivan **25**
Wade-Gayles, Gloria Jean **41**
Walcott, Derek **5**
Walker, George **37**
Wallace, Michele Faith **13**
Wallace, Phyllis A. **9**
Washington, Booker T. **4**
Watkins, Shirley R. **17**
Wattleton, Faye **9**
Weaver, Afaa Michael **37**
Wedgeworth, Robert W. **42**
Wells, James Lesesne **10**
Wells-Barnett, Ida B. **8**
Welsing, Frances Cress **5**
Wesley, Dorothy Porter **19**
West, Cornel **5, 33**
Wharton, Clifton R., Jr. **7**
White, Charles **39**
White, Lois Jean **20**
Wilkens, J. Ernest, Jr. **43**
Wilkins, Roger **2**
Williams, Fannie Barrier **27**
Williams, Gregory **11**
Williams, Patricia J. **11**
Williams, Sherley Anne **25**
Williams, Walter E. **4**
Wilson, William Julius **22**
Woodruff, Hale **9**
Woodson, Carter G. **2**
Worrill, Conrad **12**
Yancy, Dorothy Cowser **42**
Young, Jean Childs **14**

Fashion

Bailey, Xenobia **11**
Banks, Jeffrey **17**
Banks, Tyra **11**
Barboza, Anthony **10**
Beals, Jennifer **12**
Beckford, Tyson **11**
Berry, Halle **4, 19**
Boateng, Ozwald **35**
Bridges, Sheila **36**
Brown, Joyce F. **25**
Burrows, Stephen **31**
Campbell, Naomi **1, 31**
Dash, Damon **31**
Davidson, Jaye **5**
Henderson, Gordon **5**
Iman **4, 33**
Jay-Z **27**
John, Daymond **23**
Johnson, Beverly **2**
Jones, Carl **7**
Kodjoe, Boris **34**
Kani, Karl **10**
Kelly, Patrick **3**
Lars, Byron **32**
Malone, Maurice **32**
Michele, Michael **31**
Onwurah, Ngozi **38**
Powell, Maxine **8**
Rhymes, Busta **31**
Robinson, Patrick **19**
Rochon, Lela **16**
Rowell, Victoria **13**
Sims, Naomi **29**
Smaltz, Audrey **12**
Smith, B(arbara) **11**
Smith, Willi **8**
Steele, Lawrence **28**
Taylor, Karin **34**
Walker, T. J. **7**
Webb, Veronica **10**
Wek, Alek **18**

Film

Aaliyah **30**
Akomfrah, John **37**
Alexander, Khandi **43**
Allen, Debbie **13, 42**
Amos, John **8**
Anderson, Eddie "Rochester" **30**
Awoonor, Kofi **37**
Babatunde, Obba **35**
Baker, Josephine **3**
Banks, Tyra **11**
Barclay, Paris **37**
Bassett, Angela **6, 23**
Beach, Michael **26**
Beals, Jennifer **12**
Belafonte, Harry **4**
Bellamy, Bill **12**
Berry, Halle **4, 19**
Blackwood, Maureen **37**
Bogle, Donald **34**
Braugher, Andre **13**
Breeze, Jean "Binta" **37**
Brooks, Hadda **40**
Brown, Jim **11**
Brown, Tony **3**
Burnett, Charles **16**
Byrd, Michelle **19**
Byrd, Robert **11**
Calloway, Cab **14**
Campbell, Naomi **1, 31**
Campbell Martin, Tisha **8, 42**
Carroll, Diahann **9**

Thurman, Wallace **16**
Tillman, George, Jr. **20**
Torry, Guy **31**
Toussaint, Lorraine **32**
Townsend, Robert **4, 23**
Tucker, Chris **13, 23**
Turner, Tina **6, 27**
Tyler, Aisha N. **36**
Tyrese **27**
Tyson, Cicely **7**
Uggams, Leslie **23**
Underwood, Blair **7, 27**
Union, Gabrielle **31**
Usher **23**
Van Peebles, Mario **2**
Van Peebles, Melvin **7**
Vance, Courtney B. **15**
Vereen, Ben **4**
Walker, Eamonn **37**
Ward, Douglas Turner **42**
Warfield, Marsha **2**
Warner, Malcolm-Jamal **22, 36**
Warren, Michael **27**
Warwick, Dionne **18**
Washington, Denzel **1, 16**
Washington, Fredi **10**
Washington, Kerry **46**
Waters, Ethel **7**
Wayans, Damon **8, 41**
Wayans, Keenen Ivory **18**
Wayans, Marlon **29**
Wayans, Shawn **29**
Weathers, Carl **10**
Webb, Veronica **10**
Whitaker, Forest **2**
Whitfield, Lynn **18**
Williams, Billy Dee **8**
Williams, Clarence, III **26**
Williams, Samm-Art **21**
Williams, Saul **31**
Williams, Vanessa **32**
Williams, Vanessa L. **4, 17**
Williamson, Mykelti **22**
Wilson, Debra **38**
Winfield, Paul **2, 45**
Winfrey, Oprah **2, 15**
Witherspoon, John **38**
Woodard, Alfre **9**
Yoba, Malik **11**

Government and politics--international
Abacha, Sani **11**
Abbott, Diane **9**
Achebe, Chinua **6**
Ali Mahdi Mohamed **5**
Amadi, Elechi **40**
Amin, Idi **42**
Amos, Valerie **41**
Annan, Kofi Atta **15**
Aristide, Jean-Bertrand **6, 45**
Arthur, Owen **33**
Awoonor, Kofi **37**
Azikiwe, Nnamdi **13**
Babangida, Ibrahim **4**
Baker, Gwendolyn Calvert **9**
Banda, Hastings Kamuzu **6**
Bedie, Henri Konan **21**
Berry, Mary Frances **7**
Biko, Steven **4**
Bishop, Maurice **39**
Biya, Paul **28**
Bizimungu, Pasteur **19**
Bongo, Omar **1**
Boye, Madior **30**
Bunche, Ralph J. **5**

Buthelezi, Mangosuthu Gatsha **9**
Charlemagne, Manno **11**
Charles, Mary Eugenia **10**
Chissano, Joaquim **7**
Christophe, Henri **9**
Conté, Lansana **7**
Curling, Alvin **34**
da Silva, Benedita **5**
Dadié, Bernard **34**
Davis, Ruth **37**
Déby, Idriss **30**
Diop, Cheikh Anta **4**
Diouf, Abdou **3**
dos Santos, José Eduardo **43**
Ekwensi, Cyprian **37**
Eyadéma, Gnassingbé **7**
Fela **1, 42**
Gbagbo, Laurent **43**
Gordon, Pamela **17**
Habré, Hissène **6**
Habyarimana, Juvenal **8**
Haile Selassie **7**
Haley, George Williford Boyce **21**
Hani, Chris **6**
Houphouët-Boigny, Félix **4**
Ifill, Gwen **28**
Ingraham, Hubert A. **19**
Isaac, Julius **34**
Jagan, Cheddi **16**
Jammeh, Yahya **23**
Jawara, Sir Dawda Kairaba **11**
Ka Dinizulu, Mcwayizeni **29**
Kabbah, Ahmad Tejan **23**
Kabila, Joseph **30**
Kabila, Laurent **20**
Kabunda, Kenneth **2**
Kenyatta, Jomo **5**
Kerekou, Ahmed (Mathieu) **1**
King, Oona **27**
Liberia-Peters, Maria Philomena **12**
Lumumba, Patrice **33**
Luthuli, Albert **13**
Maathai, Wangari **43**
Mabuza, Lindiwe **18**
Machel, Samora Moises **8**
Mamadou, Tandja **33**
Mandela, Nelson **1, 14**
Mandela, Winnie **2, 35**
Masekela, Barbara **18**
Masire, Quett **5**
Mbeki, Thabo Mvuyelwa **14**
Mbuende, Kaire **12**
Meles Zenawi **3**
Mkapa, Benjamin **16**
Mobutu Sese Seko **1**
Mogae, Festus Gontebanye **19**
Moi, Daniel **1, 35**
Mongella, Gertrude **11**
Mugabe, Robert Gabriel **10**
Muluzi, Bakili **14**
Museveni, Yoweri **4**
Mutebi, Ronald **25**
Mwinyi, Ali Hassan **1**
Ndadaye, Melchior **7**
Neto, António Agostinho **43**
Ngubane, Ben **33**
Nkomo, Joshua **4**
Nkrumah, Kwame **3**
Ntaryamira, Cyprien **8**
Nujoma, Samuel **10**
Nyanda, Siphiwe **21**
Nyerere, Julius **5**
Nzo, Alfred **15**
Obasanjo, Olusegun **5, 22**
Obasanjo, Stella **32**

Okara, Gabriel **37**
Oyono, Ferdinand **38**
Pascal-Trouillot, Ertha **3**
Patterson, P. J. **6, 20**
Pereira, Aristides **30**
Perkins, Edward **5**
Perry, Ruth **15**
Pitt, David Thomas **10**
Pitta, Celso **17**
Poitier, Sidney **36**
Ramaphosa, Cyril **3**
Rawlings, Jerry **9**
Rawlings, Nana Konadu Agyeman **13**
Rice, Condoleezza **3, 28**
Robinson, Randall **7, 46**
Sampson, Edith S. **4**
Sankara, Thomas **17**
Savimbi, Jonas **2, 34**
Sawyer, Amos **5**
Senghor, Léopold Sédar **12**
Smith, Jennifer **21**
Soglo, Nicephore **15**
Soyinka, Wole **4**
Taylor, Charles **20**
Taylor, John (David Beckett) **16**
Touré, Sekou **6**
Toure, Amadou Toumani **18**
Tsvangirai, Morgan **26**
Tutu, Desmond (Mpilo) **6, 44**
Vieira, Joao **14**
Wharton, Clifton Reginald, Sr. **36**
Wharton, Clifton R., Jr. **7**
Zuma, Jacob G. **33**
Zuma, Nkosazana Dlamini **34**

Government and politics--U.S.
Adams, Floyd, Jr. **12**
Alexander, Archie Alphonso **14**
Alexander, Clifford **26**
Ali, Muhammad **2, 16**
Allen, Ethel D. **13**
Archer, Dennis **7, 36**
Arrington, Richard **24**
Avant, Clarence **19**
Baker, Thurbert **22**
Ballance, Frank W. **41**
Barden, Don H. **9, 20**
Barrett, Andrew C. **12**
Barrett, Jacqueline **28**
Barry, Marion S(hepilov, Jr.) **7, 44**
Bell, Michael **40**
Belton, Sharon Sayles **9, 16**
Berry, Mary Frances **7**
Berry, Theodore M. **31**
Bethune, Mary McLeod **4**
Blackwell, Unita **17**
Bond, Julian **2, 35**
Bosley, Freeman, Jr. **7**
Boykin, Keith **14**
Bradley, Jennette B. **40**
Bradley, Thomas **2**
Braun, Carol Moseley **4, 42**
Brazile, Donna **25**
Brimmer, Andrew F. **2**
Brooke, Edward **8**
Brown, Cora **33**
Brown, Corrine **24**
Brown, Elaine **8**
Brown, Jesse **6, 41**
Brown, Lee Patrick **24**
Brown, Les **5**
Brown, Ron **5**
Brown, Willie L., Jr. **7**
Bruce, Blanche K. **33**
Bryant, Wayne R. **6**

Wheat, Alan **14**
White, Jesse **22**
White, Michael R. **5**
Wilder, L. Douglas **3**
Wilkins, Roger **2**
Williams, Anthony **21**
Williams, Eddie N. **44**
Williams, George Washington **18**
Williams, Hosea Lorenzo **15, 31**
Williams, Maggie **7**
Wilson, Sunnie **7**
Wynn, Albert **25**
Young, Andrew **3**

Law
Alexander, Clifford **26**
Alexander, Joyce London **18**
Alexander, Sadie Tanner Mossell **22**
Allen, Samuel W. **38**
Archer, Dennis **7, 36**
Arnwine, Barbara **28**
Bailey, Clyde **45**
Banks, William **11**
Barrett, Andrew C. **12**
Barrett, Jacqueline **28**
Baugh, David **23**
Bell, Derrick **6**
Berry, Mary Frances **7**
Berry, Theodore M. **31**
Bishop Jr., Sanford D. **24**
Bolin, Jane **22**
Bolton, Terrell D. **25**
Bosley, Freeman, Jr. **7**
Boykin, Keith **14**
Bradley, Thomas **2**
Braun, Carol Moseley **4, 42**
Brooke, Edward **8**
Brown, Cora **33**
Brown, Janice Rogers **43**
Brown, Joe **29**
Brown, Lee Patrick **1, 24**
Brown, Ron **5**
Brown, Willie L., Jr. **7**
Bryant, Wayne R. **6**
Burke, Yvonne Braithwaite **42**
Burris, Roland W. **25**
Butler, Paul D. **17**
Bynoe, Peter C.B. **40**
Campbell, Bill **9**
Carter, Stephen L. **4**
Chambers, Julius **3**
Cleaver, Kathleen Neal **29**
Clendenon, Donn **26**
Cochran, Johnnie L., Jr. **11, 39**
Colter, Cyrus J. **36**
Conyers, John, Jr. **4, 45**
Crockett, George, Jr. **10**
Darden, Christopher **13**
Davis, Artur **41**
Days, Drew S., III **10**
DeFrantz, Anita **37**
Diggs-Taylor, Anna **20**
Dillard, Godfrey J. **45**
Dinkins, David **4**
Dixon, Sharon Pratt **1**
Edelman, Marian Wright **5, 42**
Edley, Christopher **2**
Ellington, E. David **11**
Ephriam, Mablean **29**
Espy, Mike **6**
Farmer-Paellmann, Deadria **43**
Fields, Cleo **13**
Frazier-Lyde, Jacqui **31**
Freeman, Charles **19**
Gary, Willie E. **12**

Gibson, Johnnie Mae **23**
Glover, Nathaniel, Jr. **12**
Gomez-Preston, Cheryl **9**
Graham, Lawrence Otis **12**
Gray, Fred **37**
Gray, Willie **46**
Grimké, Archibald H. **9**
Guinier, Lani **7, 30**
Haley, George Williford Boyce **21**
Hall, Elliott S. **24**
Harris, Patricia Roberts **2**
Harvard, Beverly **11**
Hassell, Leroy Rountree, Sr. **41**
Hastie, William H. **8**
Hastings, Alcee L. **16**
Hatchett, Glenda **32**
Hawkins, Steven **14**
Haywood, Margaret A. **24**
Higginbotham, A. Leon, Jr. **13, 25**
Hill, Anita **5**
Hillard, Terry **25**
Hills, Oliver W. **24**
Holder, Eric H., Jr. **9**
Holton, Hugh, Jr. **39**
Hooks, Benjamin L. **2**
Houston, Charles Hamilton **4**
Hubbard, Arnette Rhinehart **38**
Hunter, Billy **22**
Hurtt, Harold **46**
Isaac, Julius **34**
Jackson Lee, Sheila **20**
Jackson, Maynard **2, 41**
Johnson, James Weldon **5**
Johnson, Norma L. Holloway **17**
Jones, Elaine R. **7, 45**
Jones, Star **10, 27**
Jordan, Vernon E. **3, 35**
Kearse, Amalya Lyle **12**
Keith, Damon J. **16**
Kennard, William Earl **18**
Kennedy, Florynce **12, 33**
Kennedy, Randall **40**
King, Bernice **4**
Kirk, Ron **11**
Lafontant, Jewel Stradford **3**
Lewis, Delano **7**
Lewis, Reginald F. **6**
Majette, Denise **41**
Mallett, Conrad, Jr. **16**
Mandela, Nelson **1, 14**
Marsh, Henry, III **32**
Marshall, Thurgood **1, 44**
Mathis, Greg **26**
McDonald, Gabrielle Kirk **20**
McDougall, Gay J. **11, 43**
McKinnon, Isaiah **9**
McKissick, Floyd B. **3**
McPhail, Sharon **2**
Meek, Kendrick **41**
Meeks, Gregory **25**
Moose, Charles **40**
Morial, Ernest "Dutch" **26**
Motley, Constance Baker **10**
Muhammad, Ava **31**
Murray, Pauli **38**
Napoleon, Benny N. **23**
Noble, Ronald **46**
Norton, Eleanor Holmes **7**
Nunn, Annetta **43**
O'Leary, Hazel **6**
Ogletree, Charles, Jr. **12**
Ogunlesi, Adebayo O. **37**
Oliver, Jerry **37**
Page, Alan **7**
Paker, Kellis E. **30**

Parks, Bernard C. **17**
Parsons, James **14**
Parsons, Richard Dean **11, 33**
Pascal-Trouillot, Ertha **3**
Patrick, Deval **12**
Payne, Ulice **42**
Perry, Lowell **30**
Philip, Marlene Nourbese **32**
Powell, Michael **32**
Ramsey, Charles H. **21**
Redding, Louis L. **26**
Richie, Leroy C. **18**
Robinson, Malcolm S. **44**
Robinson, Randall **7, 46**
Russell-McCloud, Patricia **17**
Sampson, Edith S. **4**
Schmoke, Kurt **1**
Sears-Collins, Leah J. **5**
Solomon, Jimmie Lee **38**
Steele, Michael **38**
Stokes, Carl B. **10**
Stokes, Louis **3**
Stout, Juanita Kidd **24**
Sutton, Percy E. **42**
Taylor, John (David Beckett) **16**
Thomas, Clarence **2, 39**
Thomas, Franklin A. **5**
Thompson, Larry D. **39**
Tubbs Jones, Stephanie **24**
Vanzant, Iyanla **17**
Wagner, Annice **22**
Wainwright, Joscelyn **46**
Washington, Harold **6**
Watkins, Donald **35**
Watt, Melvin **26**
Wharton, Clifton Reginald, Sr. **36**
Wilder, L. Douglas **3**
Wilkins, Roger **2**
Williams, Evelyn **10**
Williams, Gregory **11**
Williams, Patricia J. **11**
Williams, Willie L. **4**
Wilson, Jimmy **45**
Wright, Bruce McMarion **3**
Wynn, Albert **25**

Military
Abacha, Sani **11**
Adams Early, Charity **13, 34**
Adams-Ender, Clara **40**
Alexander, Margaret Walker **22**
Amin, Idi **42**
Babangida, Ibrahim **4**
Bolden, Charles F., Jr. **7**
Brashear, Carl **29**
Brown, Erroll M. **23**
Brown, Jesse **6, 41**
Brown, Jesse Leroy **31**
Brown, Willa **40**
Bullard, Eugene **12**
Cadoria, Sherian Grace **14**
Chissano, Joaquim **7**
Christophe, Henri **9**
Clemmons, Reginal G. **41**
Conté, Lansana **7**
Davis, Benjamin O., Jr. **2, 43**
Davis, Benjamin O., Sr. **4**
Europe, James Reese **10**
Eyadéma, Gnassingbé **7**
Fields, Evelyn J. **27**
Flipper, Henry O. **3**
Gravely, Samuel L., Jr. **5**
Gregory, Frederick D. **8**
Habré, Hissène **6**
Habyarimana, Juvenal **8**

Stallings, George A., Jr. **6**
Steinberg, Martha Jean "The Queen" **28**
Sullivan, Leon H. **3, 30**
Thurman, Howard **3**
Turner, Henry McNeal **5**
Tutu, Desmond (Mpilo) **6, 44**
Vanzant, Iyanla **17**
Waddles, Charleszetta (Mother) **10**
Walker, Hezekiah **34**
Waters, Ethel **7**
Weems, Renita J. **44**
West, Cornel **5, 33**
White, Reggie **6**
Williams, Hosea Lorenzo **15, 31**
Wilson, Natalie **38**
Winans, BeBe **14**
Winans, CeCe **14, 43**
Winans, Marvin L. **17**
Wright, Jeremiah A., Jr. **45**
X, Malcolm **1**
Youngblood, Johnny Ray **8**

Science and technology

Adkins, Rod **41**
Adkins, Rutherford H. **21**
Alexander, Archie Alphonso **14**
Allen, Ethel D. **13**
Anderson, Charles Edward **37**
Anderson, Michael P. **40**
Anderson, Norman B. **45**
Auguste, Donna **29**
Auguste, Rose-Anne **13**
Bacon-Bercey, June **38**
Banda, Hastings Kamuzu **6**
Bath, Patricia E. **37**
Benjamin, Regina **20**
Benson, Angela **34**
Black, Keith Lanier **18**
Bluford, Guy **2, 35**
Bluitt, Juliann S. **14**
Bolden, Charles F., Jr. **7**
Brown, Willa **40**
Brown, Vivian **27**
Bullard, Eugene **12**
Callender, Clive O. **3**
Canady, Alexa **28**
Cargill, Victoria A. **43**
Carroll, L. Natalie **44**
Carruthers, George R. **40**
Carson, Benjamin **1, 35**
Carter, Joye Maureen **41**
Carver, George Washington **4**
CasSelle, Malcolm **11**
Chatard, Peter **44**
Chinn, May Edward **26**
Christian, Spencer **15**
Cobb, W. Montague **39**
Cobbs, Price M. **9**
Cole, Rebecca **38**
Coleman, Bessie **9**
Comer, James P. **6**
Cooper, Edward S. **6**
Daly, Marie Maynard **37**
Davis, Allison **12**
Dean, Mark **35**
Delany, Bessie **12**
Delany, Martin R. **27**
Dickens, Helen Octavia **14**
Diop, Cheikh Anta **4**
Drew, Charles Richard **7**
Dunham, Katherine **4**
Elders, Joycelyn **6**
Ellington, E. David **11**
Ellis, Clarence A. **38**
Emeagwali, Dale **31**

Emeagwali, Philip **30**
Ericsson-Jackson, Aprille **28**
Fields, Evelyn J. **27**
Fisher, Rudolph **17**
Flipper, Henry O. **3**
Foster, Henry W., Jr. **26**
Freeman, Harold P. **23**
Fulani, Lenora **11**
Fuller, A. Oveta **43**
Fuller, Arthur **27**
Fuller, Solomon Carter, Jr. **15**
Gates, Sylvester James, Jr. **15**
Gayle, Helene D. **3, 46**
Gibson, Kenneth Allen **6**
Gibson, William F. **6**
Gourdine, Meredith **33**
Granville, Evelyn Boyd **36**
Gray, Ida **41**
Gregory, Frederick D. **8**
Griffin, Bessie Blout **43**
Hall, Lloyd A. **8**
Hannah, Marc **10**
Harris, Mary Styles **31**
Henderson, Cornelius Langston **26**
Henson, Matthew **2**
Hinton, William Augustus **8**
Imes, Elmer Samuel **39**
Irving, Larry, Jr. **12**
Jackson, Shirley Ann **12**
Jawara, Sir Dawda Kairaba **11**
Jemison, Mae C. **1, 35**
Jenifer, Franklyn G. **2**
Johnson, Eddie Bernice **8**
Johnson, Lonnie G. **32**
Jones, Randy **35**
Julian, Percy Lavon **6**
Just, Ernest Everett **3**
Knowling, Robert E., Jr. **38**
Kountz, Samuel L. **10**
Latimer, Lewis H. **4**
Lawless, Theodore K. **8**
Lawrence, Robert H., Jr. **16**
Leevy, Carrol M. **42**
Leffall, LaSalle, Jr. **3**
Lewis, Delano **7**
Logan, Onnie Lee **14**
Lyttle, Hulda Margaret **14**
Madison, Romell **45**
Manley, Audrey Forbes **16**
Massey, Walter E. **5, 45**
Massie, Samuel P., Jr. **29**
Maxey, Randall **46**
Mays, William G. **34**
Mboup, Souleymane **10**
McCoy, Elijah **8**
McNair, Ronald **3**
Millines Dziko, Trish **28**
Morgan, Garrett **1**
Murray, Pauli **38**
Neto, António Agostinho **43**
O'Leary, Hazel **6**
Person, Waverly **9**
Peters, Lenrie **43**
Pickett, Cecil **39**
Pierre, Percy Anthony **46**
Pitt, David Thomas **10**
Poussaint, Alvin F. **5**
Prothrow-Stith, Deborah **10**
Quarterman, Lloyd Albert **4**
Riley, Helen Caldwell Day **13**
Robeson, Eslanda Goode **13**
Robinson, Rachel **16**
Roker, Al **12**
Samara, Noah **15**
Satcher, David **7**

Shabazz, Betty **7, 26**
Shavers, Cheryl **31**
Sigur, Wanda **44**
Sinkford, Jeanne C. **13**
Staples, Brent **8**
Staupers, Mabel K. **7**
Stewart, Ella **39**
Sullivan, Louis **8**
Terrell, Dorothy A. **24**
Thomas, Vivien **9**
Tyson, Neil de Grasse **15**
Wambugu, Florence **42**
Washington, Patrice Clarke **12**
Watkins, Levi, Jr. **9**
Welsing, Frances Cress **5**
Wilkens, J. Ernest, Jr. **43**
Williams, Daniel Hale **2**
Williams, O. S. **13**
Witt, Edwin T. **26**
Woods, Granville T. **5**
Wright, Louis Tompkins **4**
Young, Roger Arliner **29**

Social issues

Aaron, Hank **5**
Abbot, Robert Sengstacke **27**
Abbott, Diane **9**
Abdul-Jabbar, Kareem **8**
Abernathy, Ralph David **1**
Abu-Jamal, Mumia **15**
Achebe, Chinua **6**
Adams, Sheila J. **25**
Agyeman, Jaramogi Abebe **10**
Ake, Claude **30**
Al-Amin, Jamil Abdullah **6**
Alexander, Clifford **26**
Alexander, Sadie Tanner Mossell **22**
Ali, Muhammad, **2, 16**
Allen, Ethel D. **13**
Andrews, Benny **22**
Angelou, Maya **1, 15**
Annan, Kofi Atta **15**
Anthony, Wendell **25**
Archer, Dennis **7**
Aristide, Jean-Bertrand **6, 45**
Arnwine, Barbara **28**
Asante, Molefi Kete **3**
Ashe, Arthur **1, 18**
Auguste, Rose-Anne **13**
Azikiwe, Nnamdi **13**
Ba, Mariama **30**
Baisden, Michael **25**
Baker, Ella **5**
Baker, Gwendolyn Calvert **9**
Baker, Houston A., Jr. **6**
Baker, Josephine **3**
Baker, Thurbert **22**
Baldwin, James **1**
Baraka, Amiri **1, 38**
Bass, Charlotta Spears **40**
Bates, Daisy **13**
Beals, Melba Patillo **15**
Belafonte, Harry **4**
Bell, Derrick **6**
Bell, Ralph S. **5**
Bennett, Lerone, Jr. **5**
Berry, Bertice **8**
Berry, Mary Frances **7**
Bethune, Mary McLeod **4**
Betsch, MaVynee **28**
Biko, Steven **4**
Blackwell, Unita **17**
Bolin, Jane **22**
Bond, Julian **2, 35**
Bonga, Kuenda **13**

King, B. B. **7**
King, Bernice **4**
King, Coretta Scott **3**
King, Dexter **10**
King, Martin Luther, III **20**
King, Martin Luther, Jr. **1**
King, Preston **28**
King, Yolanda **6**
Kitt, Eartha **16**
Ladner, Joyce A. **42**
LaGuma, Alex **30**
Lampkin, Daisy **19**
Lane, Charles **3**
Lane, Vincent **5**
Lee, Canada **8**
Lee, Spike **5, 19**
Leland, Mickey **2**
Lester, Julius **9**
Lewis, Ananda **28**
Lewis, Delano **7**
Lewis, John **2, 46**
Lewis, Thomas **19**
Lewis-Thornton, Rae **32**
Little, Robert L. **2**
Logan, Rayford W. **40**
Long, Eddie L. **29**
Lorde, Audre **6**
Louis, Errol T. **8**
Lowery, Joseph **2**
Lucas, John **7**
Lucy Foster, Autherine **35**
Maathai, Wangari **43**
Mabuza-Suttle, Felicia **43**
Madhubuti, Haki R. **7**
Madison, Joseph E. **17**
Makeba, Miriam **2**
Malveaux, Julianne **32**
Mandela, Nelson **1, 14**
Mandela, Winnie **2, 35**
Manley, Audrey Forbes **16**
Marable, Manning **10**
Marley, Bob **5**
Marshall, Paule **7**
Marshall, Thurgood **1, 44**
Martin, Louis E. **16**
Masekela, Barbara **18**
Masekela, Hugh **1**
Mason, Ronald **27**
Mathabane, Mark **5**
Maynard, Robert C. **7**
Mays, Benjamin E. **7**
McCabe, Jewell Jackson **10**
McCarty, Osceola **16**
McDaniel, Hattie **5**
McDougall, Gay J. **11, 43**
McKay, Claude **6**
McKenzie, Vashti M. **29**
McKissick, Floyd B. **3**
McMurray, Georgia L. **36**
McQueen, Butterfly **6**
McWhorter, John **35**
Meek, Carrie **6, 36**
Meredith, James H. **11**
Mfume, Kweisi **6, 41**
Micheaux, Oscar **7**
Millines Dziko, Trish **28**
Millender-McDonald, Juanita **21**
Mkapa, Benjamin **16**
Mongella, Gertrude **11**
Moore, Harry T. **29**
Morial, Ernest "Dutch" **26**
Morrison, Toni **2**
Moses, Robert Parris **11**
Mosley, Walter **5, 25**
Mossell, Gertrude Bustill **40**

Motley, Constance Baker **10**
Moutoussamy-Ashe, Jeanne **7**
Mowry, Jess **7**
Muhammad, Elijah **4**
Muhammad, Khallid Abdul **10, 31**
Murphy, Laura M. **43**
Murray, Pauli **38**
Ndadaye, Melchior **7**
Nelson, Jill **6**
Newton, Huey **2**
Nkrumah, Kwame **3**
Norman, Pat **19**
Norton, Eleanor Holmes **7**
Nzo, Alfred **15**
O'Leary, Hazel **6**
Obasanjo, Olusegun **5**
Oglesby, Zena **12**
Owens, Major **6**
Page, Alan **7**
Page, Clarence **4**
Paige, Satchel **7**
Parker, Kellis E. **30**
Parker, Pat **19**
Parks, Rosa **1, 35**
Patterson, Frederick Douglass **12**
Patterson, Louise **25**
Patterson, Orlando **4**
Patterson, P. J. **6, 20**
Perkins, Edward **5**
Pitt, David Thomas **10**
Pleasant, Mary Ellen **9**
Plessy, Homer Adolph **31**
Poussaint, Alvin F. **5**
Powell, Adam Clayton, Jr. **3**
Powell, Kevin **31**
Pratt, Geronimo **18**
Pressley, Condace L. **41**
Price, Hugh B. **9**
Primus, Pearl **6**
Pritchard, Robert Starling **21**
Prothrow-Stith, Deborah **10**
Quarles, Benjamin Arthur **18**
Ramaphosa, Cyril **3**
Ramphele, Mamphela **29**
Ramsey, Charles H. **21**
Rand, A. Barry **6**
Randolph, A. Philip **3**
Rangel, Charles **3**
Rawlings, Nana Konadu Agyeman **13**
Reagon, Bernice Johnson **7**
Reed, Ishmael **8**
Rice, Norm **8**
Riggs, Marlon **5**
Riley, Helen Caldwell Day **13**
Ringgold, Faith **4**
Robeson, Eslanda Goode **13**
Robeson, Paul **2**
Robinson, Jackie **6**
Robinson, Rachel **16**
Robinson, Randall **7, 46**
Robinson, Sharon **22**
Robinson, Spottswood **22**
Rowan, Carl T. **1, 30**
Rustin, Bayard **4**
Sampson, Edith S. **4**
Sané, Pierre Gabriel **21**
Sapphire **14**
Saro-Wiwa, Kenule **39**
Satcher, David **7**
Savimbi, Jonas **2, 34**
Sawyer, Amos **2**
Sayles Belton, Sharon **9, 16**
Schomburg, Arthur Alfonso **9**
Seale, Bobby **3**
Seele, Pernessa **46**

Senghor, Léopold Sédar **12**
Shabazz, Attallah **6**
Shabazz, Betty **7, 26**
Shakur, Assata **6**
Shinhoster, Earl **32**
Sifford, Charlie **4**
Simone, Nina **15, 41**
Simpson, Carole **6, 30**
Sister Souljah **11**
Sisulu, Sheila Violet Makate **24**
Sleet, Moneta, Jr. **5**
Smith, Anna Deavere **6**
Smith, Barbara **28**
Smith, Greg **28**
Soyinka, Wole **4**
Stallings, George A., Jr. **6**
Staupers, Mabel K. **7**
Steele, Claude Mason **13**
Steele, Shelby **13**
Stewart, Alison **13**
Stewart, Ella **39**
Stewart, Maria W. Miller **19**
Stone, Chuck **9**
Sullivan, Leon H. **3, 30**
Sutton, Percy E. **42**
Tate, Eleanora E. **20**
Taulbert, Clifton Lemoure **19**
Taylor, Mildred D. **26**
Taylor, Susan L. **10**
Terrell, Mary Church **9**
Thomas, Franklin A. **5**
Thomas, Isiah **7, 26**
Thompson, Bennie G. **26**
Thurman, Howard **3**
Thurman, Wallace **16**
Till, Emmett **7**
Toomer, Jean **6**
Tosh, Peter **9**
Tribble, Israel, Jr. **8**
Trotter, Donne E. **28**
Trotter, Monroe **9**
Tsvangirai, Morgan **26**
Tubman, Harriet **9**
Tucker, C. DeLores **12**
Tucker, Cynthia **15**
Tucker, Rosina **14**
Tutu, Desmond **6**
Tyree, Omar Rashad **21**
Underwood, Blair **7, 27**
Van Peebles, Melvin **7**
Vanzant, Iyanla **17**
Vincent, Marjorie Judith **2**
Waddles, Charleszetta (Mother) **10**
Walcott, Derek **5**
Walker, A'lelia **14**
Walker, Alice **1, 43**
Walker, Cedric "Ricky" **19**
Walker, Madame C. J. **7**
Wallace, Michele Faith **13**
Wallace, Phyllis A. **9**
Washington, Booker T. **4**
Washington, Fredi **10**
Washington, Harold **6**
Waters, Maxine **3**
Wattleton, Faye **9**
Wells-Barnett, Ida B. **8**
Wells, James Lesesne **10**
Welsing, Frances Cress **5**
West, Cornel **5, 33**
White, Michael R. **5**
White, Reggie **6**
White, Walter F. **4**
Wideman, John Edgar **5**
Wilkins, Roger **2**
Wilkins, Roy **4**

Jones, Roy Jr. **22**
Jordan, Michael **6, 21**
Joyner-Kersee, Jackie **5**
Justice, David **18**
Kaiser, Cecil **42**
Kennedy-Overton, Jayne Harris **46**
Kerry, Leon G. **46**
Kimbro, Henry A. **25**
King, Don **14**
Lacy, Sam **30, 46**
Lanier, Willie **33**
Lankford, Ray **23**
Larkin, Barry **24**
Lassiter, Roy **24**
Lee, Canada **8**
Lennox, Betty **31**
Leonard, Sugar Ray **15**
Leslie, Lisa **16**
Lester, Bill **42**
Lewis, Carl **4**
Lewis, Denise **33**
Lewis, Lennox **27**
Lewis, Ray **33**
Liston, Sonny **33**
Littlepage, Craig **35**
Lloyd, Earl **26**
Lloyd, John Henry "Pop" **30**
Lofton, James **42**
Lofton, Kenny **12**
Lott, Ronnie **9**
Louis, Joe **5**
Love, Nat **9**
Lucas, John **7**
Malone, Karl A. **18**
Manigault, Earl "The Goat" **15**
Mariner, Jonathan **41**
Master P **21**
Mayers, Jamal **39**
Mays, Willie **3**
McBride, Bryant **18**
McCray, Nikki **18**
McGriff, Fred **24**
McKegney, Tony **3**
McNabb, Donovan **29**
McNair, Steve **22**
McNeil, Lori **1**
Metcalfe, Ralph **26**
Milla, Roger **2**
Miller, Cheryl **10**
Miller, Reggie **33**
Milton, DeLisha **31**
Mills, Sam **33**
Minor, DeWayne **32**
Monk, Art **38**
Montgomery, Tim **41**
Moon, Warren **8**
Moorer, Michael **19**
Morgan, Joe Leonard **9**
Moses, Edwin **8**
Mosley, Shane **32**
Moss, Randy **23**
Motley, Marion **26**
Mourning, Alonzo **17, 44**
Murray, Eddie **12**
Murray, Lenda **10**
Mutola, Maria **12**
Mutombo, Dikembe **7**
Nakhid, David **25**
Newcombe, Don **24**
Newsome, Ozzie **26**
Noah, Yannick **4**
O'Neal, Shaquille **8, 30**
O'Neil, Buck **19**
O'Ree, Willie **5**
Olajuwon, Hakeem **2**

Owens, Jesse **2**
Pace, Orlando **21**
Page, Alan **7**
Paige, Satchel **7**
Parish, Robert **43**
Patterson, Floyd **19**
Payne, Ulice **42**
Payton, Walter **11, 25**
Peck, Carolyn **23**
Peete, Calvin **11**
Pelé **7**
Perrot, Kim **23**
Perry, Lowell **30**
Peters, Margaret and Matilda **43**
Phillips, Teresa L. **42**
Pickett, Bill **11**
Pippen, Scottie **15**
Powell, Mike **7**
Powell, Renee **34**
Pride, Charley **26**
Puckett, Kirby **4**
Quirot, Ana **13**
Rashad, Ahmad **18**
Ready, Stephanie **33**
Reese, Pokey **28**
Rhodes, Ray **14**
Ribbs, Willy T. **2**
Rice, Jerry **5**
Richardson, Donna **39**
Richardson, Nolan **9**
Richmond, Mitch **19**
Rivers, Glenn "Doc" **25**
Robertson, Oscar **26**
Robinson, David **24**
Robinson, Eddie G. **10**
Robinson, Frank **9**
Robinson, Jackie **6**
Robinson, Sugar Ray **18**
Rodman, Dennis **12, 44**
Rudolph, Wilma **4**
Rubin, Chanda **37**
Russell, Bill **8**
Sampson, Charles **13**
Sanders, Barry **1**
Sanders, Deion **4, 31**
Sapp, Warren **38**
Sayers, Gale **28**
Scott, Stuart **34**
Scott, Wendell Oliver, Sr. **19**
Scurry, Briana **27**
Sharper, Darren **32**
Sheffield, Gary **16**
Shell, Art **1**
Shippen, John **43**
Showers, Reggie **30**
Sifford, Charlie **4**
Silas, Paul **24**
Simmons, Bob **29**
Simpson, O. J. **15**
Singletary, Mike **4**
Smith, Emmitt **7**
Smith, Hilton **29**
Smith, Tubby **18**
Solomon, Jimmie Lee **38**
Sosa, Sammy **21, 44**
St. Julien, Marlon **29**
Stackhouse, Jerry **30**
Stargell, Willie **29**
Stearns, Norman "Turkey" **31**
Steward, Emanuel **18**
Stewart, Kordell **21**
Stone, Toni **15**
Strahan, Michael **35**
Strawberry, Darryl **22**

Stringer, C. Vivian **13**
Stringer, Korey **35**
Swann, Lynn **28**
Swoopes, Sheryl **12**
Taylor, Lawrence **25**
Thomas, Debi **26**
Thomas, Derrick **25**
Thomas, Frank **12**
Thomas, Isiah **7, 26**
Thompson, Tina **25**
Thrower, Willie **35**
Thugwane, Josia **21**
Tyson, Mike **28, 44**
Unseld, Wes **23**
Upshaw, Gene **18**
Ussery, Terdema, II **29**
Vick, Michael **39**
Walker, Herschel **1**
Ware, Andre **37**
Washington, MaliVai **8**
Watson, Bob **25**
Watts, J. C., Jr. **14, 38**
Weathers, Carl **10**
Webber, Chris **15, 30**
Westbrook, Peter **20**
Whitaker, Pernell **10**
White, Bill **1**
White, Jesse **20**
White, Reggie **6**
Whitfield, Fred **23**
Wilkens, Lenny **11**
Williams, Doug **22**
Williams, Serena **20, 41**
Williams, Natalie **31**
Williams, Venus Ebone **17, 34**
Willingham, Tyrone **43**
Wilson, Sunnie **7**
Winfield, Dave **5**
Winkfield, Jimmy **42**
Woods, Tiger **14, 31**

Television
Alexander, Khandi **43**
Allen, Byron **3**
Allen, Debbie **13, 42**
Allen, Marcus **20**
Amos, John **8**
Anderson, Eddie "Rochester" **30**
Arkadie, Kevin **17**
Babatunde, Obba **35**
Banks, William **11**
Barclay, Paris **37**
Barden, Don H. **9**
Bassett, Angela **6, 23**
Beach, Michael **26**
Beaton, Norman **14**
Beauvais, Garcelle **29**
Belafonte, Harry **4**
Bellamy, Bill **12**
Berry, Bertice **8**
Berry, Halle **4, 19**
Blackwood, Maureen **37**
Blake, Asha **26**
Boston, Kelvin E. **25**
Bowser, Yvette Lee **17**
Bradley, Ed **2**
Brady, Wayne **32**
Brandy **14, 34**
Braugher, Andre **13**
Bridges, Todd **37**
Brooks, Avery **9**
Brooks, Hadda **40**
Brown, James **22**
Brown, Joe **29**
Brown, Les **5**

Shange, Ntozake **8**
Smith, Anjela Lauren **44**
Smith, Anna Deavere **6, 44**
Smith, Roger Guenveur **12**
Snipes, Wesley **3, 24**
Soyinka, Wole **4**
St. Jacques, Raymond **8**
Talbert, David **34**
Taylor, Meshach **4**
Taylor, Regina **9, 46**
Taylor, Ron **35**
Thigpen, Lynne **17, 41**
Thompson, Tazewell **13**
Thurman, Wallace **16**
Toussaint, Lorraine **32**
Townsend, Robert **4, 23**
Tyson, Cicely **7**
Uggams, Leslie **23**
Underwood, Blair **7, 27**
Van Peebles, Melvin **7**
Vance, Courtney B. **15**
Vereen, Ben **4**
Walcott, Derek **5**
Walker, Eamonn **37**
Ward, Douglas Turner **42**
Washington, Denzel **1, 16**
Washington, Fredi **10**
Waters, Ethel **7**
Whitaker, Forest **2**
Whitfield, Lynn **18**
Williams, Bert **18**
Williams, Billy Dee **8**
Williams, Clarence, III **26**
Williams, Samm-Art **21**
Williams, Vanessa L. **4, 17**
Williamson, Mykelti **22**
Wilson, August **7, 33**
Winfield, Paul **2, 45**
Wolfe, George C. **6, 43**
Woodard, Alfre **9**

Writing
Abrahams, Peter **39**
Abu-Jamal, Mumia **15**
Achebe, Chinua **6**
Adams-Ender, Clara **40**
Aidoo, Ama Ata **38**
Ake, Claude **30**
Al-Amin, Jamil Abdullah **6**
Alexander, Margaret Walker **22**
Allen, Debbie **13, 42**
Allen, Robert L. **38**
Allen, Samuel W. **38**
Amadi, Elechi **40**
Ames, Wilmer **27**
Andrews, Raymond **4**
Angelou, Maya **1, 15**
Ansa, Tina McElroy **14**
Anthony, Michael **29**
Aristide, Jean-Bertrand **6, 45**
Arkadie, Kevin **17**
Asante, Molefi Kete **3**
Ashe, Arthur **1, 18**
Ashley-Ward, Amelia **23**
Atkins, Cholly **40**
Atkins, Russell **45**
Aubert, Alvin **41**
Awoonor, Kofi **37**
Azikiwe, Nnamdi **13**
Ba, Mariama **30**
Baiocchi, Regina Harris **41**
Baisden, Michael **25**
Baker, Augusta **38**
Baker, Houston A., Jr. **6**
Baldwin, James **1**

Ballard, Allen Butler, Jr. **40**
Bambara, Toni Cade **10**
Bandele, Asha **36**
Baraka, Amiri **1, 38**
Barnett, Amy Du Bois **46**
Barrax, Gerald William **45**
Barrett, Lindsay **43**
Bass, Charlotta Spears **40**
Bates, Karen Grigsby **40**
Beals, Melba Patillo **15**
Bebey, Francis **45**
Beckham, Barry **41**
Bell, Derrick **6**
Bell, James Madison **40**
Bennett, George Harold "Hal" **45**
Bennett, Lerone, Jr. **5**
Benson, Angela **34**
Berry, James **41**
Berry, Mary Frances **7**
Beti, Mongo **36**
Bishop, Maurice **39**
Bland, Eleanor Taylor **39**
Blassingame, John Wesley **40**
Blockson, Charles L. **42**
Bluitt, Juliann S. **14**
Bolden, Tonya **32**
Bontemps, Arna **8**
Booker, Simeon **23**
Borders, James **9**
Boston, Lloyd **24**
Boyd, Gerald M. **32**
Bradley, David Henry, Jr. **39**
Bradley, Ed **2**
Branch, William Blackwell **39**
Brand, Dionne **32**
Brathwaite, Kamau **36**
Brawley, Benjamin **44**
Breeze, Jean "Binta" **37**
Bridges, Sheila **36**
Brimmer, Andrew F. **2**
Briscoe, Connie **15**
Britt, Donna **28**
Brooks, Gwendolyn **1, 28**
Brown, Cecil M. **46**
Brown, Claude **38**
Brown, Elaine **8**
Brown, Les **5**
Brown, Llyod Louis **42**
Brown, Marie Dutton **12**
Brown, Sterling **10**
Brown, Tony **3**
Brown, Wesley **23**
Brutus, Dennis **38**
Bryan, Ashley F. **41**
Buckley, Gail Lumet **39**
Bullins, Ed **25**
Bunche, Ralph J. **5**
Bunkley, Anita Richmond **39**
Burroughs, Margaret Taylor **9**
Butler, Octavia **8, 43**
Bynum, Juanita **31**
Campbell, Bebe Moore **6, 24**
Carby, Hazel **27**
Carmichael, Stokely **5, 26**
Carroll, Vinnette **29**
Cartíer, Xam Wilson **41**
Carter, Joye Maureen **41**
Carter, Stephen L. **4**
Cary, Lorene **3**
Cary, Mary Ann Shadd **30**
Cayton, Horace **26**
Chamberlain, Wilt **18**
Channer, Colin **36**
Chase-Riboud, Barbara **20, 46**
Chenault, John **40**

Cheney-Coker, Syl **43**
Chesnutt, Charles **29**
Chideya, Farai **14**
Childress, Alice **15**
Christian, Barbara T. **44**
Clark, Kenneth B. **5**
Clark, Septima **7**
Clark-Bekedermo, J. P. **44**
Clarke, Austin C. **32**
Clarke, Cheryl **32**
Clarke, George **32**
Cleage, Pearl **17**
Cleaver, Eldridge **5**
Cliff, Michelle **42**
Clifton, Lucille **14**
Cobbs, Price M. **9**
Cohen, Anthony **15**
Cole, Johnnetta B. **5, 43**
Colter, Cyrus J. **36**
Comer, James P. **6**
Cone, James H. **3**
Cook, Suzan D. Johnson **22**
Cooke, Marvel **31**
Coombs, Orde M. **44**
Cooper, Andrew W. **36**
Cooper, Anna Julia **20**
Cooper, J. California **12**
Cortez, Jayne **43**
Cosby, Bill **7, 26**
Cosby, Camille **14**
Cose, Ellis **5**
Cotter, Joseph Seamon, Sr. **40**
Couto, Mia **45**
Creagh, Milton **27**
Crouch, Stanley **11**
Cullen, Countee **8**
Cuney, William Waring **44**
Cunningham, Evelyn **23**
Curry, George E. **23**
Curtis, Christopher Paul **26**
Curtis-Hall, Vondie **17**
Dadié, Bernard **34**
Damas, Léon-Gontran **46**
Dandridge, Raymond Garfield **45**
Danticat, Edwidge **15**
Davis, Allison **12**
Davis, Angela **5**
Davis, George **36**
Davis, Miles **4**
Davis, Nolan **45**
Davis, Ossie **5**
Dawkins, Wayne **20**
de Passe, Suzanne **25**
De Veaux, Alexis **44**
Delany, Martin R. **27**
Delany, Samuel R., Jr. **9**
DeLoach, Nora **30**
Dickey, Eric Jerome **21**
Diesel, Vin **29**
Diop, Cheikh Anta **4**
Dodson, Howard, Jr. **7**
Dodson, Owen Vincent **38**
Dove, Rita **6**
Draper, Sharon Mills **16, 43**
Driskell, David C. **7**
Driver, David E. **11**
Drummond, William J. **40**
Du Bois, David Graham **45**
Du Bois, W. E. B. **3**
DuBois, Shirley Graham **21**
Due, Tananarive **30**
Dumas, Henry **41**
Dunbar, Paul Laurence **8**
Dunbar-Nelson, Alice Ruth Moore **44**
Dunham, Katherine **4**

Cumulative Subject Index

Volume numbers appear in **bold**

A Better Chance
Lewis, William M., Jr. **40**

A Harvest Biotech Foundation International
Wambugu, Florence **42**

AA
See Alcoholics Anonymous

AAAS
See American Association for the Advancement of Science

Aaron Gunner series
Haywood, Gar Anthony **43**

AARP
Dixon, Margaret **14**

ABC
See American Broadcasting Company

Abstract expressionism
Lewis, Norman **39**

A. C. Green Youth Foundation
Green, A. C. **32**

Academy awards
Austin, Patti **24**
Freeman, Morgan **2, 20**
Goldberg, Whoopi **4, 33**
Gooding, Cuba, Jr. **16**
Gossett, Louis, Jr. **7**
Jean-Baptiste, Marianne **17, 46**
McDaniel, Hattie **5**
Poitier, Sidney **11, 36**
Prince **18**
Richie, Lionel **27**
Washington, Denzel **1, 16**
Wonder, Stevie **11**

Academy of Praise
Kenoly, Ron **45**

A cappella
Cooke, Sam **17**
Reagon, Bernice Johnson **7**

Access Hollywood
Robinson, Shaun **36**

ACDL
See Association for Constitutional Democracy in Liberia

ACLU
See American Civil Liberties Union

Acquired Immune Deficiency Syndrome (AIDS)
Ashe, Arthur **1, 18**
Broadbent, Hydeia **36**
Cargill, Victoria A. **43**
Gayle, Helene D. **3, 46**
Hale, Lorraine **8**
Johnson, Earvin "Magic" **3, 39**
Lewis-Thornton, Rae **32**
Mboup, Souleymane **10**
Moutoussamy-Ashe, Jeanne **7**
Norman, Pat **10**
Pickett, Cecil **39**
Riggs, Marlon **5, 44**
Satcher, David **7**
Seele, Pernessa **46**
Wilson, Phill **9**

Act*1 Personnel Services
Howroyd, Janice Bryant **42**

ACT-SO
See Afro-Academic Cultural, Technological, and Scientific Olympics

Acting
Aaliyah **30**
Adams, Osceola Macarthy **31**
Ailey, Alvin **8**
Alexander, Khandi **43**
Allen, Debbie **13, 42**
Amos, John **8**
Anderson, Eddie "Rochester" **30**
Angelou, Maya **1, 15**
Armstrong, Vanessa Bell **24**
Ashanti **37**
Babatunde, Obba **35**
Baker, Josephine **3**
Banks, Tyra **11**
Bassett, Angela **6, 23**
Beach, Michael **26**

Beals, Jennifer **12**
Beaton, Norman **14**
Beauvais, Garcelle **29**
Berry, Halle **4, 19**
Blanks, Billy **22**
Blige, Mary J. **20, 34**
Borders, James **9**
Brady, Wayne **32**
Branch, William Blackwell **39**
Braugher, Andre **13**
Bridges, Todd **37**
Brooks, Avery **9**
Brown, Jim **11**
Caesar, Shirley **19**
Calloway, Cab **14**
Cameron, Earl **44**
Campbell, Naomi **1, 31**
Campbell-Martin, Tisha **8, 42**
Carroll, Diahann **9**
Carson, Lisa Nicole **21**
Carey, Mariah **32**
Cash, Rosalind **28**
Cedric the Entertainer **29**
Cheadle, Don **19**
Chestnut, Morris **31**
Childress, Alice **15**
Clarke, Hope **14**
Cliff, Jimmy **28**
Cole, Nat King **17**
Cole, Natalie Maria **17**
Coleman, Gary **35**
Combs, Sean "Puffy" **17, 43**
Cosby, Bill **7, 26**
Crothers, Scatman **19**
Curry, Mark **17**
Curtis-Hall, Vondie **17**
Dandridge, Dorothy **3**
David, Keith **27**
Davidson, Jaye **5**
Davis, Guy **36**
Davis, Ossie **5**
Davis, Sammy Jr. **18**
Davis, Viola **34**
Dee, Ruby **8**
Devine, Loretta **24**
Diesel, Vin **29**
Diggs, Taye **25**
DMX **28**
Dourdan, Gary **37**
Duke, Bill **3**
Duncan, Michael Clarke **26**
Dutton, Charles S. **4, 22**

Elise, Kimberly **32**
Emmanuel, Alphonsia **38**
Epps, Omar **23**
Esposito, Giancarlo **9**
Everett, Francine **23**
Falana, Lola **42**
Fields, Kim **36**
Fetchit, Stepin **32**
Fishburne, Larry **4, 22**
Fox, Rick **27**
Fox, Vivica A. **15**
Foxx, Jamie **15**
Foxx, Redd **2**
Freeman, Al, Jr. **11**
Freeman, Morgan **2, 20**
Freeman, Yvette **27**
Gibson, Althea **8, 43**
Ginuwine **35**
Givens, Robin **4, 25**
Glover, Danny **1, 24**
Goldberg, Whoopi **4, 33**
Gooding, Cuba, Jr. **16**
Gordon, Dexter **25**
Gossett, Louis, Jr. **7**
Greaves, William **38**
Grier, David Alan **28**
Grier, Pam **9, 31**
Guillaume, Robert **3**
Gunn, Moses **10**
Guy, Jasmine **2**
Hammer, M. C. **20**
Hammond, Fred **23**
Hardison, Kadeem **22**
Harper, Hill **32**
Harris, Robin **7**
Harvey, Steve **18**
Hawkins, Screamin' Jay **30**
Hayes, Isaac **20**
Haysbert, Dennis **42**
Hemsley, Sherman **19**
Henry, Lenny **9**
Hill, Dulé **29**
Hill, Lauryn **20**
Hines, Gregory **1, 42**
Horne, Lena **5**
Hounsou, Djimon **19, 45**
Houston, Whitney **7, 28**
Howard, Sherri **36**
Hughley, D.L. **23**
Hyman, Earle **25**
Ice Cube **8, 30**
Iman **4, 33**
Ingram, Rex **5**
Ja Rule **35**
Jackson, Janet **6, 30**
Jackson, Michael **19**
Jackson, Millie **25**
Jackson, Samuel L. **8, 19**
Jean-Baptiste, Marianne **17, 46**
Johnson, Dwayne "The Rock" **29**
Johnson, Rafer **33**
Johnson, Rodney Van **28**
Jones, James Earl **3**
Jones, Orlando **30**
Kennedy-Overton, Jayne Harris **46**
King, Regina **22, 45**
King, Woodie, Jr. **27**
Kirby, George **14**
Kitt, Eartha **16**
Knight, Gladys **16**
Knowles, Beyoncé **39**
Kodhoe, Boris **34**
Kotto, Yaphet **7**
L. L. Cool J **16**
LaBelle, Patti **13, 30**

La Salle, Eriq **12**
Lampley, Oni Faida **43**
Lane, Charles **3**
Lassiter, Roy **24**
Lathan, Sanaa **27**
Lawrence, Martin **6, 27**
Lee, Canada **8**
Lee, Joie **1**
Lee, Spike **5, 19**
Lemmons, Kasi **20**
LeNoire, Rosetta **37**
Lester, Adrian **46**
Lewis, Emmanuel **36**
(Lil') Bow Wow **35**
Lil' Kim **28**
Lincoln, Abbey **3**
Lindo, Delroy **18, 45**
LisaRaye **27**
Love, Darlene **23**
Mabley, Jackie "Moms" **15**
Mac, Bernie **29**
Marrow, Queen Esther **24**
Martin, Helen **31**
Martin, Jesse L. **31**
Master P **21**
Mayo, Whitman **32**
McDaniel, Hattie **5**
McDonald, Audra **20**
Mckee, Lonette **12**
McKinney, Nina Mae **40**
McQueen, Butterfly **6**
Meadows, Tim **30**
Michele, Michael **31**
Mitchell, Brian Stokes **21**
Mo'Nique **35**
Moore, Chante **26**
Moore, Melba **21**
Moore, Shemar **21**
Morris, Garrett **31**
Morris, Greg **28**
Morton, Joe **18**
Mos Def **30**
Moten, Etta **18**
Murphy, Eddie **4, 20**
Muse, Clarence Edouard **21**
Nash, Johnny **40**
Neal, Elise **29**
Newton, Thandie **26**
Nicholas, Fayard **20**
Nicholas, Harold **27**
Nichols, Nichelle **11**
Norman, Maidie **20**
Notorious B.I.G. **20**
O'Neal, Ron **46**
Orlandersmith, Dael **42**
Payne, Allen **13**
Peete, Holly Robinson **20**
Perry, Tyler **40**
Phifer, Mekhi **25**
Pinkett Smith, Jada **10, 41**
Poitier, Sidney **11, 36**
Premice, Josephine **41**
Prince **18**
Pryor, Richard **3, 24**
Queen Latifah **1, 16**
Randle, Theresa **16**
Rashad, Phylicia **21**
Raven, **44**
Reese, Della **6, 20**
Reuben, Gloria **15**
Rhames, Ving **14**
Rhymes, Busta **31**
Ribeiro, Alfonso **17**
Richards, Beah **30**
Richards, Lloyd **2**

Robeson, Paul **2**
Robinson, Shaun **36**
Rock, Chris **3, 22**
Rodgers, Rod **36**
Rolle, Esther **13, 21**
Ross, Diana **8, 27**
Ross, Tracee Ellis **35**
Roundtree, Richard **27**
Rowell, Victoria **13**
Rudolph, Maya **46**
Shakur, Tupac **14**
Sinbad **1, 16**
Sisqo **30**
Smith, Anjela Lauren **44**
Smith, Anna Deavere **6, 44**
Smith, Barbara **11**
Smith, Roger Guenveur **12**
Smith, Will **8, 18**
Snipes, Wesley **3, 24**
Snoop Dogg **35**
St. Jacques, Raymond **8**
St. John, Kristoff **25**
Tamia **24**
Tate, Larenz **15**
Taylor, Meshach **4**
Taylor, Regina **9, 46**
Taylor, Ron **35**
Thomas, Sean Patrick **35**
Thompson, Tazewell **13**
Torry, Guy **31**
Toussaint, Lorraine **32**
Townsend, Robert **4, 23**
Tucker, Chris **13, 23**
Turner, Tina **6, 27**
Tyler, Aisha N. **36**
Tyrese **27**
Tyson, Cicely **7**
Uggams, Leslie **23**
Underwood, Blair **7, 27**
Union, Gabrielle **31**
Usher **23**
Van Peebles, Mario **2**
Van Peebles, Melvin **7**
Vance, Courtney B. **15**
Vereen, Ben **4**
Walker, Eamonn **37**
Ward, Douglas Turner **42**
Warfield, Marsha **2**
Warner, Malcolm-Jamal **22, 36**
Warren, Michael **27**
Washington, Denzel **1, 16**
Washington, Fredi **10**
Washington, Kerry **46**
Waters, Ethel **7**
Wayans, Damon **8, 41**
Wayans, Keenen Ivory **18**
Wayans, Marlon **29**
Wayans, Shawn **29**
Weathers, Carl **10**
Webb, Veronica **10**
Whitaker, Forest **2**
Whitfield, Lynn **18**
Williams, Bert **18**
Williams, Billy Dee **8**
Williams, Clarence, III **26**
Williams, Joe **5, 25**
Williams, Samm-Art **21**
Williams, Saul **31**
Williams, Vanessa **32**
Williams, Vanessa L. **4, 17**
Williamson, Mykelti **22**
Wilson, Debra **38**
Wilson, Flip **21**
Winfield, Paul **2, 45**
Winfrey, Oprah **2, 15**

Witherspoon, John **38**
Woodard, Alfre **9**
Yoba, Malik **11**

Active Ministers Engaged in Nurturance (AMEN)
King, Bernice **4**

Actors Equity Association
Lewis, Emmanuel **36**

Actuarial science
Hill, Jessie, Jr. **13**

ACT UP
See AIDS Coalition to Unleash Power

Acustar, Inc.
Farmer, Forest **1**

ADC
See Agricultural Development Council

Addiction Research and Treatment Corporation
Cooper, Andrew W. **36**

Adoption and foster care
Baker, Josephine **3**
Clements, George **2**
Gossett, Louis, Jr. **7**
Hale, Clara **16**
Hale, Lorraine **8**
Oglesby, Zena **12**

Adventures in Movement (AIM)
Morgan, Joe Leonard **9**

Advertising
Barboza, Anthony **10**
Burrell, Thomas J. **21**
Campbell, E. Simms **13**
Chisholm, Samuel J. **32**
Coleman, Donald A. **24**
Johnson, Beverly **2**
Jones, Caroline R. **29**
Jordan, Montell **23**
Lewis, Byron E. **13**
Mingo, Frank **32**
Olden, Georg(e) **44**
Roche, Joyce M. **17**

Advocates Scene
Seale, Bobby **3**

AFCEA
See Armed Forces Communications and Electronics Associations

Affirmative action
Arnwine, Barbara **28**
Berry, Mary Frances **7**
Carter, Stephen L. **4**
Higginbotham, A. Leon Jr. **13, 25**
Maynard, Robert C. **7**
Norton, Eleanor Holmes **7**
Rand, A. Barry **6**
Thompson, Bennie G. **26**
Waters, Maxine **3**

AFL-CIO
See American Federation of Labor and Congress of Industrial Organizations

African/African-American Summit
Sullivan, Leon H. **3, 30**

African American Catholic Congregation
Stallings, George A., Jr. **6**

African American Dance Ensemble
Davis, Chuck **33**

African American folklore
Bailey, Xenobia **11**
Brown, Sterling **10**
Driskell, David C. **7**
Ellison, Ralph **7**
Gaines, Ernest J. **7**
Hamilton, Virginia **10**
Hughes, Langston **4**
Hurston, Zora Neale **3**
Lester, Julius **9**
Morrison, Toni **2, 15**
Primus, Pearl **6**
Tillman, George, Jr. **20**
Williams, Bert **18**
Yarbrough, Camille **40**

African American folk music
Cuney, William Waring **44**
Handy, W. C. **8**
House, Son **8**
Johnson, James Weldon **5**
Lester, Julius **9**

African American history
Angelou, Maya **1, 15**
Ashe, Arthur **1, 18**
Bennett, Lerone, Jr. **5**
Berry, Mary Frances **7**
Blockson, Charles L. **42**
Burroughs, Margaret Taylor **9**
Camp, Kimberly **19**
Chase-Riboud, Barbara **20, 46**
Cheadle, Don **19**
Clarke, John Henrik **20**
Coombs, Orde M. **44**
Cooper, Anna Julia **20**
Dodson, Howard, Jr. **7**
Douglas, Aaron **7**
Du Bois, W. E. B. **3**
DuBois, Shirley Graham **21**
Dyson, Michael Eric **11, 40**
Feelings, Tom **11**
Franklin, John Hope **5**
Gaines, Ernest J. **7**
Gates, Henry Louis, Jr. **3, 38**
Haley, Alex **4**
Harkless, Necia Desiree **19**
Hine, Darlene Clark **24**
Hughes, Langston **4**
Johnson, James Weldon **5**
Jones, Edward P. **43**
Lewis, David Levering **9**
Madhubuti, Haki R. **7**
Marable, Manning **10**
Morrison, Toni **2**
Painter, Nell Irvin **24**
Pritchard, Robert Starling **21**
Quarles, Benjamin Arthur **18**
Reagon, Bernice Johnson **7**
Ringgold, Faith **4**
Schomburg, Arthur Alfonso **9**
Wilson, August **7, 33**
Woodson, Carter G. **2**
Yarbrough, Camille **40**

African American Images
Kunjufu, Jawanza **3**

African American literature
Andrews, Raymond **4**
Angelou, Maya **1, 15**
Baisden, Michael **25**
Baker, Houston A., Jr. **6**
Baldwin, James **1**
Bambara, Toni Cade **1**
Baraka, Amiri **1, 38**
Bennett, George Harold "Hal" **45**
Bontemps, Arna **8**
Briscoe, Connie **15**
Brooks, Gwendolyn **1, 28**
Brown, Claude **38**
Brown, Wesley **23**
Burroughs, Margaret Taylor **9**
Campbell, Bebe Moore **6, 24**
Cary, Lorene **3**
Childress, Alice **15**
Cleage, Pearl **17**
Cullen, Countee **8**
Curtis, Christopher Paul **26**
Davis, Arthur P. **41**
Davis, Nolan **45**
Dickey, Eric Jerome **21**
Dove, Rita **6**
Du Bois, W. E. B. **3**
Dunbar, Paul Laurence **8**
Ellison, Ralph **7**
Evans, Mari **26**
Fauset, Jessie **7**
Feelings, Tom **11**
Fisher, Rudolph **17**
Ford, Nick Aaron **44**
Fuller, Charles **8**
Gaines, Ernest J. **7**
Gates, Henry Louis, Jr. **3, 38**
Gayle, Addison, Jr. **41**
Gibson, Donald Bernard **40**
Giddings, Paula **11**
Giovanni, Nikki **9, 39**
Goines, Donald **19**
Golden, Marita **19**
Guy, Rosa **5**
Haley, Alex **4**
Hansberry, Lorraine **6**
Harper, Frances Ellen Watkins **11**
Heard, Nathan C. **45**
Himes, Chester **8**
Holland, Endesha Ida Mae **3**
Hughes, Langston **4**
Hull, Akasha Gloria **45**
Hurston, Zora Neale **3**
Iceberg Slim **11**
Joe, Yolanda **21**
Johnson, Charles **1**
Johnson, James Weldon **5**
Jones, Gayl **37**
Jordan, June **7, 35**
July, William **27**
Kitt, Sandra **23**
Larsen, Nella **10**
Lester, Julius **9**
Little, Benilde **21**
Lorde, Audre **6**
Madhubuti, Haki R. **7**
Major, Clarence **9**
Marshall, Paule **7**
McKay, Claude **6**
McKay, Nellie Yvonne **17**
McKinney-Whetstone, Diane **27**
McMillan, Terry **4, 17**
Morrison, Toni **2, 15**

Civil rights

Abbott, Diane **9**
Abernathy, Ralph **1**
Agyeman, Jaramogi Abebe **10**
Al-Amin, Jamil Abdullah **6**
Alexander, Clifford **26**
Ali, Muhammad **2, 16**
Angelou, Maya **1, 15**
Anthony, Wendell **25**
Aristide, Jean-Bertrand **6, 45**
Arnwine, Barbara **28**
Baker, Ella **5**
Baker, Houston A., Jr. **6**
Baker, Josephine **3**
Ballance, Frank W. **41**
Bass, Charlotta Spears **40**
Bates, Daisy **13**
Baugh, David **23**
Beals, Melba Patillo **15**
Belafonte, Harry **4**
Bell, Derrick **6**
Bell, James Madison **40**
Bennett, Lerone, Jr. **5**
Berry, Mary Frances **7**
Berry, Theodore M. **31**
Biko, Steven **4**
Bishop, Sanford D. Jr. **24**
Bond, Julian **2, 35**
Booker, Simeon **23**
Boyd, John W., Jr. **20**
Bradley, David Henry, Jr. **39**
Brown, Elaine **8**
Brown, Tony **3**
Brown, Wesley **23**
Brown, Willa **40**
Burks, Mary Fair **40**
Campbell, Bebe Moore **6, 24**
Carmichael, Stokely **5, 26**
Carter, Mandy **11**
Carter, Rubin **26**
Carter, Stephen L. **4**
Cary, Mary Ann Shadd **30**
Cayton, Horace **26**
Chambers, Julius **3**
Chavis, Benjamin **6**
Clark, Septima **7**
Clay, William Lacy **8**
Cleaver, Eldridge **5**
Cleaver, Kathleen Neal **29**
Clyburn, James **21**
Cobb, W. Montague **39**
Cobbs, Price M. **9**
Cooper, Anna Julia **20**
Cosby, Bill **7, 26**
Crockett, George, Jr. **10**
Cunningham, Evelyn **23**
Davis, Angela **5**
Davis, Artur **41**
Days, Drew S., III **10**
Dee, Ruby **8**
Diallo, Amadou **27**
Diggs, Charles C. **21**
Diggs-Taylor, Anna **20**
Divine, Father **7**
Dodson, Howard, Jr. **7**
Du Bois, W. E. B. **3**
Dumas, Henry **41**
Edelman, Marian Wright **5, 42**
Ellison, Ralph **7**
Evers, Medgar **3**
Evers, Myrlie **8**
Farmer, James **2**
Farmer-Paellmann, Deadria **43**
Fauntroy, Walter E. **11**
Fletcher, Bill, Jr. **41**

Forman, James **7**
Fortune, T. Thomas **6**
Franklin, John Hope **5**
Gaines, Ernest J. **7**
George, Zelma Watson **42**
Gibson, William F. **6**
Gray, Fred **37**
Gregory, Dick **1**
Grimké, Archibald H. **9**
Guinier, Lani **7, 30**
Haley, Alex **4**
Haley, George Williford Boyce **21**
Hall, Elliott S. **24**
Hamer, Fannie Lou **6**
Hampton, Fred **18**
Hampton, Henry **6**
Hansberry, Lorraine **6**
Harper, Frances Ellen Watkins **11**
Harris, Patricia Roberts **2**
Hastie, William H. **8**
Hawkins, Steven **14**
Hedgeman, Anna Arnold **22**
Height, Dorothy I. **2, 23**
Henderson, Wade J. **14**
Henry, Aaron **19**
Higginbotham, A. Leon Jr. **13, 25**
Hill, Jessie, Jr. **13**
Hill, Oliver W. **24**
Hilliard, David **7**
Hobson, Julius W. **44**
Holland, Endesha Ida Mae **3**
Hooks, Benjamin L. **2**
hooks, bell **5**
Horne, Lena **5**
Houston, Charles Hamilton **4**
Howard, M. William, Jr. **26**
Hughes, Langston **4**
Innis, Roy **5**
Jackson, Alexine Clement **22**
Jackson, Jesse **1, 27**
James, Daniel, Jr. **16**
Jarret, Vernon D. **42**
Johnson, Eddie Bernice **8**
Johnson, Georgia Douglas **41**
Johnson, James Weldon **5**
Johnson, Norma L. Holloway **17**
Johns, Vernon **38**
Jones, Elaine R. **7, 45**
Jordan, Barbara **4**
Jordan, June **7, 35**
Jordan, Vernon E. **3, 35**
Julian, Percy Lavon **6**
Kennedy, Florynce **12, 33**
Kenyatta, Jomo **5**
Kidd, Mae Street **39**
King, Bernice **4**
King, Coretta Scott **3**
King, Martin Luther, Jr. **1**
King, Martin Luther, III **20**
King, Preston **28**
King, Yolanda **6**
Ladner, Joyce A. **42**
Lampkin, Daisy **19**
Lee, Spike **5, 19**
Lester, Julius **9**
Lewis, John **2, 46**
Logan, Rayford W. **40**
Lorde, Audre **6**
Lowery, Joseph **2**
Lucy Foster, Autherine **35**
Makeba, Miriam **2**
Mandela, Nelson **1, 14**
Mandela, Winnie **2, 35**
Martin, Louis E. **16**
Mayfield, Curtis **2, 43**

Mays, Benjamin E. **7**
Mbeki, Thabo Mvuyelwa **14**
McDonald, Gabrielle Kirk **20**
McDougall, Gay J. **11, 43**
McKissick, Floyd B. **3**
Meek, Carrie **6**
Meredith, James H. **11**
Metcalfe, Ralph **26**
Moore, Harry T. **29**
Morial, Ernest "Dutch" **26**
Morrison, Toni **2, 15**
Moses, Robert Parris **11**
Motley, Constance Baker **10**
Mowry, Jess **7**
Murphy, Laura M. **43**
Murray, Pauli **38**
Ndadaye, Melchior **7**
Nelson, Jill **6**
Newton, Huey **2**
Nkomo, Joshua **4**
Norman, Pat **10**
Norton, Eleanor Holmes **7**
Nunn, Annetta **43**
Nzo, Alfred **15**
Parker, Kellis E. **30**
Parks, Rosa **1, 35**
Patrick, Deval **12**
Patterson, Louise **25**
Patterson, Orlando **4**
Perkins, Edward **5**
Pinchback, P. B. S. **9**
Player, Willa B. **43**
Pleasant, Mary Ellen **9**
Plessy, Homer Adolph **31**
Poitier, Sidney **11, 36**
Powell, Adam Clayton, Jr. **3**
Price, Hugh B. **9**
Ramaphosa, Cyril **3**
Randolph, A. Philip **3**
Reagon, Bernice Johnson **7**
Redding, Louis L. **26**
Riggs, Marlon **5, 44**
Robeson, Paul **2**
Robinson, Jackie **6**
Robinson, Rachel **16**
Robinson, Randall **7, 46**
Robinson, Sharon **22**
Robinson, Spottswood W. III **22**
Rowan, Carl T. **1, 30**
Rush, Bobby **26**
Rustin, Bayard **4**
Sané, Pierre Gabriel **21**
Saro-Wiwa, Kenule **39**
Seale, Bobby **3**
Shabazz, Attallah **6**
Shabazz, Betty **7, 26**
Shakur, Assata **6**
Shinhoster, Earl **32**
Simone, Nina **15, 41**
Sisulu, Sheila Violet Makate **24**
Sleet, Moneta, Jr. **5**
Smith, Barbara **28**
Staupers, Mabel K. **7**
Sullivan, Leon H. **3, 30**
Sutton, Percy E. **42**
Thompson, Bennie G. **26**
Thurman, Howard **3**
Till, Emmett **7**
Trotter, Monroe **9**
Tsvangirai, Morgan **26**
Turner, Henry McNeal **5**
Tutu, Desmond Mpilo **6, 44**
Underwood, Blair **7**
Washington, Booker T. **4**
Washington, Fredi **10**

Watt, Melvin **26**
Weaver, Robert C. **8, 46**
Wells-Barnett, Ida B. **8**
Wells, James Lesesne **10**
West, Cornel **5**
White, Walter F. **4**
Wideman, John Edgar **5**
Wilkins, Roy **4**
Williams, Evelyn **10**
Williams, Fannie Barrier **27**
Williams, Hosea Lorenzo **15, 31**
Williams, Robert F. **11**
Williams, Walter E. **4**
Wilson, August **7, 33**
Wilson, Sunnie **7**
Wilson, William Julius **22**
Woodson, Robert L. **10**
X, Malcolm **1**
Yoba, Malik **11**
Young, Andrew **3**
Young, Jean Childs **14**
Young, Whitney M., Jr. **4**

Civilian Pilots Training Program
Brown, Willa **40**

Classical music
Adams, Leslie **39**
Baiocchi, Regina Harris **41**
Bonds, Margaret **39**
Brown, Uzee **42**
Cook, Will Marion **40**
Dawson, William Levi **39**
DePriest, James **37**
Dunner, Leslie B. **45**
Freeman, Paul **39**
Kay, Ulysses **37**
Lewis, Henry **38**
Moore, Dorothy Rudd **46**
Pratt, Awadagin **31**
Price, Florence **37**
Sowande, Fela **39**
Still, William Grant **37**
Tillis, Frederick **40**
Walker, George **37**
Williams, Denise **40**

Classical singers
Anderson, Marian **2, 33**
Bumbry, Grace **5**
Hayes, Roland **4**
Hendricks, Barbara **3**
Norman, Jessye **5**
Price, Leontyne **1**
Three Mo' Tenors **35**
Williams, Denise **40**

Clearview Golf Club
Powell, Renee **34**

Cleo Parker Robinson Dance Ensemble
Robinson, Cleo Parker **38**

Clergy
Anthony, Wendell **25**
Austin, Junius C. **44**
Burgess, John **46**
Caesar, Shirley **19**
Cleveland, James **19**
Cook, Suzan D. Johnson **22**
Dyson, Michael Eric **11, 40**
Gilmore, Marshall **46**
Gomes, Peter J. **15**
Gregory, Wilton **37**

Howard, M. William, Jr. **26**
Jakes, Thomas "T.D." **17, 43**
James, Skip **38**
Johns, Vernon **38**
Kelly, Leontine **33**
King, Barbara **22**
Kobia, Rev. Dr. Samuel **43**
Lincoln, C. Eric **38**
Long, Eddie L. **29**
McClurkin, Donnie **25**
McKenzie, Vashti M. **29**
Reese, Della **6, 20**
Weems, Renita J. **44**
Winans, Marvin L. **17**

Cleveland Browns football team
Brown, Jim **11**
Hill, Calvin **19**
Motley, Marion **26**
Newsome, Ozzie **26**

Cleveland Cavaliers basketball team
Brandon, Terrell **16**
Wilkens, Lenny **11**

Cleveland city government
Stokes, Carl B. **10**
White, Michael R. **5**

Cleveland Foundation
Adams, Leslie **39**

Cleveland Indians baseball team
Belle, Albert **10**
Bonds, Bobby **43**
Carter, Joe **30**
Doby, Lawrence Eugene Sr. **16, 41**
Justice, David **18**
Lofton, Kenny **12**
Murray, Eddie **12**
Paige, Satchel **7**
Robinson, Frank **9**

Cleveland Rockers basketball team
Jones, Merlakia **34**

CLIO Awards
Lewis, Emmanuel **36**

Clothing design
Bailey, Xenobia **11**
Burrows, Stephen **31**
Henderson, Gordon **5**
John, Daymond **23**
Jones, Carl **7**
Kani, Karl **10**
Kelly, Patrick **3**
Lars, Byron **32**
Malone, Maurice **32**
Pinkett Smith, Jada **10, 41**
Robinson, Patrick **19**
Smith, Willi **8**
Walker, T. J. **7**

CNBC
Thomas-Graham, Pamela **29**

CNN
See Cable News Network

CNU
See Cameroon National Union

Coaching
Ashley, Maurice **15**
Baker, Dusty **8, 43**
Baylor, Don **6**
Bickerstaff, Bernie **21**
Bonds, Bobby **43**
Campanella, Roy **25**
Carew, Rod **20**
Carter, Butch **27**
Cooper, Michael **31**
Davis, Mike **41**
Dungy, Tony **17, 42**
Dunn, Jerry **27**
Ellerbe, Brian **22**
Freeman, Marianna **23**
Gaither, Alonzo Smith (Jake) **14**
Gentry, Alvin **23**
Gibson, Althea **8, 43**
Gibson, Bob **33**
Green, Dennis **5, 45**
Greene, Joe **10**
Haskins, Clem **23**
Heard, Gar **25**
Lofton, James **42**
Miller, Cheryl **10**
O'Neil, Buck **19**
Parish, Robert **43**
Phillips, Teresa L. **42**
Rhodes, Ray **14**
Richardson, Nolan **9**
Rivers, Glenn "Doc" **25**
Robinson, Eddie G. **10**
Russell, Bill **8**
Shell, Art **1**
Silas, Paul **24**
Simmons, Bob **29**
Smith, Tubby **18**
Stringer, C. Vivian **13**
White, Jesse **22**
Williams, Doug **22**
Willingham, Tyrone **43**

Coca-Cola Company
Ware, Carl T. **30**

Coca-Cola Foundation
Jones, Ingrid Saunders **18**

COHAR
See Committee on Appeal for Human Rights

Collage
Andrews, Benny **22**
Bearden, Romare **2**
Driskell, David C. **7**

College and University Administration
Archie-Hudson, Marguerite **44**
Barnett, Marguerite **46**
Christian, Barbara T. **44**
Ford, Nick Aaron **44**
Hill, Leslie Pinckney **44**
Horne, Frank **44**
Lee, Joe A. **45**

Colorado Rockies baseball team
Baylor, Don **6**

Colorado state government
Rogers, Joe **27**

Roche, Joyce M. **17**
Walker, A'lelia **14**
Walker, Madame C. J. **7**

Cotton Club Revue
Johnson, Buddy **36**

**Council for a Black Economic Agenda
(CBEA)**
Woodson, Robert L. **10**

**Council for Social Action of the Congre-
gational Christian Churches**
Julian, Percy Lavon **6**

**Council for the Economic Development
of Black Americans (CEDBA)**
Brown, Tony **3**

**Council on Legal Education Opportuni-
ties (CLEO)**
Henderson, Wade J. **14**
Henry, Aaron **19**

Count Basie Orchestra
Eldridge, Roy **37**
Johnson, J.J. **37**
Rushing, Jimmy **37**
Williams, Joe **5, 25**
Young, Lester **37**

Country music
Bailey, DeFord **33**
Pride, Charley **26**
Randall, Alice **38**

Covad Communications
Knowling, Robert **38**

Cowboy
Love, Nat **9**
Pickett, Bill **11**

CPB
See Corporation for Public Broadcasting

CPDM
See Cameroon People's Democratic
Movement

CPP
See Convention People's Party

Credit Suisse First Boston, Inc.
Ogunlesi, Adebayo **37**

**Cress Theory of Color-Confrontation
and Racism**
Welsing, Frances Cress **5**

Crisis
Du Bois, W. E. B. **3**
Fauset, Jessie **7**
Wilkins, Roy **4**

Critic's Choice Award
Channer, Colin **36**

Crown Media
Corbi, Lana **42**

Cross Colours
Jones, Carl **7**
Kani, Karl **10**
Walker, T. J. **7**

Crucial Films
Henry, Lenny **9**

Crusader
Williams, Robert F. **11**

CTRN
See Transitional Committee for National
Recovery (Guinea)

Cuban League
Charleston, Oscar **39**
Day, Leon **39**

Cuban music
Ferrer, Ibrahim **41**

CubeVision
Ice Cube **8, 30**

Cubism
Bearden, Romare **2**

Culinary arts
Clark, Patrick **14**

Cultural pluralism
Locke, Alain **10**

Cumulative voting
Guinier, Lani **7, 30**

Curator/exhibition designer
Camp, Kimberly **19**
Campbell, Mary Schmidt **43**
Golden, Thelma **10**
Hutson, Jean Blackwell **16**
Sanders, Joseph R., Jr. **11**
Sims, Lowery Stokes **27**
Stewart, Paul Wilbur **12**

Cytogenetics
Satcher, David **7**

Dallas city government
Johnson, Eddie Bernice **8**
Kirk, Ron **11**

Dallas Cowboys football team
Hill, Calvin **19**
Jones, Ed "Too Tall" **46**
Sanders, Deion **4, 31**
Smith, Emmitt **7**

Dallas Mavericks basketball team
Ussery, Terdema **29**

Dallas Police Department
Bolton, Terrell D. **25**

DanceAfrica
Davis, Chuck **33**

Dance Theatre of Harlem
Johnson, Virginia **9**
King, Alonzo **38**
Mitchell, Arthur **2**

Nicholas, Fayard **20**
Nicholas, Harold **20**
Tyson, Cicely **7**

Darell Green Youth Life Foundation
Green, Darrell **39**

Darkchild Records
Jerkins, Rodney **31**

DAV
See Disabled American Veterans

David M. Winfield Foundation
Winfield, Dave **5**

Daytona Institute
See Bethune-Cookman College

Dayton Philharmonic Orchestra
Jackson, Isaiah **3**

D.C. Black Repertory Theater
Reagon, Bernice Johnson **7**

D.C. Sniper
Moose, Charles **40**

Death Row Records
Dre, Dr. **14, 30**
Hammer, M. C. **20**
Knight, Suge **11, 30**
Shakur, Tupac **14**

De Beers Botswana
See Debswana
Allen, Debbie **13, 42**

Debswana
Masire, Quett **5**

Decca Records
Hardin Armstrong, Lil **39**

Defense Communications Agency
Gravely, Samuel L., Jr. **5**

Def Jam Records
Brown, Foxy **25**
DMX **28**
Gotti, Irv **39**
Jay-Z **27**
Jordan, Montell **23**
L.L. Cool J **16**
Liles, Kevin **42**
Simmons, Russell **1, 30**

Def Jam South Records
Ludacris **37**

Def Poetry Jam
Letson, Al **39**

Democratic National Committee (DNC)
Brown, Ron **5**
Brown, Willie L., Jr. **7**
Dixon, Sharon Pratt **1**
Fattah, Chaka **11**
Hamer, Fannie Lou **6**
Jackson, Maynard **2, 41**
Jordan, Barbara **4**
Joyner, Marjorie Stewart **26**

Dr. Martin Luther King Boys and Girls Club
Gaines, Brenda **41**

Drama Desk Awards
Carter, Nell **39**
Taylor, Ron **35**

Dreamland Orchestra
Cook, Charles "Doc" **44**

Drug abuse prevention
Brown, Les **5**
Clements, George **2**
Creagh, Milton **27**
Hale, Lorraine **8**
Harris, Alice **7**
Lucas, John **7**
Rangel, Charles **3**

Drug synthesis
Julian, Percy Lavon **6**
Pickett, Cecil **39**

Drums
Blakey, Art **37**
Locke, Eddie **44**

DSA
See Democratic Socialists of America

Dub poetry
Breeze, Jean "Binta" **37**
Johnson, Linton Kwesi **37**

Duke Ellington School of Arts
Cooper Cafritz, Peggy **43**

Duke Records
Bland, Bobby "Blue" **36**

Dunham Dance Company
Dunham, Katherine **4**

DuSable Museum of African American History
Burroughs, Margaret Taylor **9**

E Street Band
Clemons, Clarence **41**

Earthquake Early Alerting Service
Person, Waverly **9**

East Harlem School at Exodus House
Hageman, Hans **36**
Hageman, Ivan **36**

East St. Louis city government
Powell, Debra A. **23**

Ebenezer Baptist Church
King, Bernice **4**

Ebonics
Cook, Toni **23**

Ebony magazine
Bennett, Lerone, Jr. **5**
Branch, William Blackwell **39**
Fuller, Hoyt **44**
Johnson, John H. **3**

Massaquoi, Hans J. **30**
Rice, Linda Johnson **9, 41**
Sleet, Moneta, Jr. **5**

Ebony Museum of African American History
See DuSable Museum of African American History

E.C. Reems Women's International Ministries
Reems, Ernestine Cleveland **27**

Economic Community of West African States (ECOWAS)
Sawyer, Amos **2**

Economic Regulatory Administration
O'Leary, Hazel **6**

Economics
Ake, Claude **30**
Arthur, Owen **33**
Boyd, T. B. III **6**
Brimmer, Andrew F. **2**
Brown, Tony **3**
Divine, Father **7**
Dodson, Howard, Jr. **7**
Gibson, William F. **6**
Hamer, Fannie Lou **6**
Hampton, Henry **6**
Machel, Graca Simbine **16**
Malveaux, Julianne **32**
Masire, Quett **5**
Raines, Franklin Delano **14**
Robinson, Randall **7, 46**
Sowell, Thomas **2**
Sullivan, Leon H. **3, 30**
Van Peebles, Melvin **7**
Wallace, Phyllis A. **9**
Wharton, Clifton R., Jr. **7**
White, Michael R. **5**
Williams, Walter E. **4**

ECOWAS
See Economic Community of West African States

Edelman Public Relations
Barrett, Andrew C. **12**

Editing
Aubert, Alvin **41**
Bass, Charlotta Spears **40**
Brown, Llyod Louis **42**
Curry, George E. **23**
Delany, Martin R. **27**
Dumas, Henry **41**
Murphy, John H. **42**
Schuyler, George Samuel **40**

Edmonds Entertainment
Edmonds, Kenneth "Babyface" **10, 31**
Edmonds, Tracey **16**
Tillman, George, Jr. **20**

Edmonton Oilers hockey team
Fuhr, Grant **1**
Grier, Mike **43**

Educational Testing Service
Stone, Chuck **9**

EEC
See European Economic Community

EEOC
See Equal Employment Opportunity Commission

Egyptology
Diop, Cheikh Anta **4**

Elder Foundation
Elder, Lee **6**

Electronic music
Craig, Carl **31**

Elektra Records
McPherson, David **32**

Emerge (Savoy) **magazine**
Ames, Wilmer **27**
Curry, George E. **23**

Emmy awards
Allen, Debbie **13, 42**
Amos, John **8**
Ashe, Arthur **1, 18**
Barclay, Paris **37**
Belafonte, Harry **4**
Bradley, Ed **2**
Branch, William Blackwell **39**
Brown, James **22**
Brown, Les **5**
Carter, Nell **39**
Clayton, Xernona **3, 45**
Cosby, Bill **7, 26**
Curtis-Hall, Vondie **17**
Dee, Ruby **8**
Foxx, Redd **2**
Freeman, Al, Jr. **11**
Goldberg, Whoopi **4, 33**
Gossett, Louis, Jr. **7**
Guillaume, Robert **3**
Gumbel, Greg **8**
Hunter-Gault, Charlayne **6, 31**
Jones, James Earl **3**
La Salle, Eriq **12**
Mabrey, Vicki **26**
McQueen, Butterfly **6**
Moore, Shemar **21**
Parks, Gordon **1, 35**
Pinkston, W. Randall **24**
Quarles, Norma **25**
Richards, Beah **30**
Robinson, Max **3**
Rock, Chris **3, 22**
Rolle, Esther **13, 21**
St. John, Kristoff **25**
Stokes, Carl B. **10**
Taylor, Billy **23**
Thigpen, Lynne **17, 41**
Tyson, Cicely **7**
Uggams, Leslie **23**
Wayans, Damon **8, 41**
Whack, Rita Coburn **36**
Whitfield, Lynn **18**
Williams, Montel **4**
Williams, Sherley Anne **25**
Winfrey, Oprah **2, 15**
Woodard, Alfre **9**

Emory University
Cole, Johnnetta B. **5, 43**

Benson, Angela **34**
Berry, James **41**
Bland, Eleanor Taylor **39**
Bolden, Tonya **32**
Bradley, David Henry, Jr. **39**
Brand, Dionne **32**
Briscoe, Connie **15**
Brown, Cecil M. **46**
Brown, Llyod Louis **42**
Bunkley, Anita Richmond **39**
Butler, Octavia **8, 43**
Campbell, Bebe Moore **6, 24**
Cartíer, Xam Wilson **41**
Chase-Riboud, Barbara **20, 46**
Cheney-Coker, Syl **43**
Chesnutt, Charles **29**
Clarke, Austin **32**
Cleage, Pearl **17**
Cliff, Michelle **42**
Creagh, Milton **27**
Curtis, Christopher Paul **26**
Danticat, Edwidge **15**
Draper, Sharon Mills **16, 43**
Due, Tananarive **30**
Dumas, Henry **41**
Dunbar-Nelson, Alice Ruth Moore **44**
Emecheta, Buchi **30**
Farah, Nuruddin **27**
Files, Lolita **35**
Ford, Nick Aaron **44**
Forrest, Leon **44**
Gomez, Jewelle **30**
Harris, E. Lynn **12, 33**
Haywood, Gar Anthony **43**
Hercules, Frank **44**
Hill, Donna **32**
Holton, Hugh, Jr. **39**
Horne, Frank **44**
Jackson, Sheneska **18**
Jakes, Thomas "T.D." **17, 43**
Jasper, Kenji **39**
Jenkins, Beverly **14**
Johnson, Georgia Douglas **41**
Johnson, Mat **31**
Jones, Edward P. **43**
Jones, Gayl **37**
Kamau, Kwadwo Agymah **28**
Kay, Jackie **37**
Kayira, Legson **40**
Laferriere, Dany **33**
LaGuma, Alex **30**
Lamming, George **35**
Marechera, Dambudzo **39**
Markham, E.A. **37**
Mason, Felicia **31**
Mbaye, Mariétou **31**
McFadden, Bernice L. **39**
McKinney-Whetstone, Diane **27**
McMillan, Terry **4, 17**
Memmi, Albert **37**
Monroe, Mary **35**
Mosley, Walter **5, 25**
Mossell, Gertrude Bustill **40**
Mphalele, Es'kia (Ezekiel) **40**
Mwangi, Meja **40**
Naylor, Gloria **10, 42**
Nkosi, Lewis **46**
Nugent, Richard Bruce **39**
Okara, Gabriel **37**
Peters, Lenrie **43**
Philip, Marlene Nourbese **32**
Randall, Alice **38**
Saro-Wiwa, Kenule **39**
Schuyler, George Samuel **40**
Senior, Olive **37**

Smith, Danyel **40**
Tate, Eleanora E. **20**
Taylor, Mildred D. **26**
Thomas-Graham, Pamela **29**
Tutuola, Amos **30**
Vera, Yvonne **32**
Verdelle, A. J. **26**
wa Thiong'o, Ngugi **29**
Walker, Margaret **29**
Weaver, Afaa Michael **37**
Whitfield, Van **34**
Williams, Sherley Anne **25**
Williams, Stanley "Tookie" **29**
Yarbrough, Camille **40**
Youngblood, Shay **32**

Figure skating
Bonaly, Surya **7**
Thomas, Debi **26**

Film direction
Akomfrah, John **37**
Allen, Debbie **13, 42**
Blackwood, Maureen **37**
Burnett, Charles **16**
Byrd, Robert **11**
Campbell-Martin, Tisha **8, 42**
Cortez, Jayne **43**
Curtis-Hall, Vondie **17**
Dash, Julie **4**
Davis, Ossie **5**
Dickerson, Ernest **6, 17**
Diesel, Vin **29**
Duke, Bill **3**
Franklin, Carl **11**
Freeman, Al, Jr. **11**
Fuqua, Antoine **35**
Gerima, Haile **38**
Gray, F. Gary **14**
Greaves, William **38**
Harris, Leslie **6**
Hayes, Teddy **40**
Henriques, Julian **37**
Hines, Gregory **1, 42**
Hudlin, Reginald **9**
Hudlin, Warrington **9**
Hughes, Albert **7**
Hughes, Allen **7**
Jackson, George **19**
Julien, Isaac **3**
Lane, Charles **3**
Lee, Spike **5, 19**
Lemmons, Kasi **20**
Lewis, Samella **25**
Martin, Darnell **43**
Micheaux, Oscar **7**
Morton, Joe **18**
Moses, Gilbert **12**
Moss, Carlton **17**
Mwangi, Meja **40**
Onwurah, Ngozi **38**
Peck, Raoul **32**
Poitier, Sidney **11, 36**
Prince-Bythewood, Gina **31**
Riggs, Marlon **5, 44**
Schultz, Michael A. **6**
Sembène, Ousmane **13**
Singleton, John **2, 30**
Smith, Roger Guenveur **12**
St. Jacques, Raymond **8**
Tillman, George, Jr. **20**
Townsend, Robert **4, 23**
Tyler, Aisha N. **36**
Underwood, Blair **7**
Van Peebles, Mario **2**

Van Peebles, Melvin **7**
Ward, Douglas Turner **42**
Wayans, Damon **8, 41**
Wayans, Keenen Ivory **18**

Film production
Daniels, Lee Louis **36**
Gerima, Haile **38**
Greaves, William **38**
Hines, Gregory **1, 42**
Lewis, Emmanuel **36**
Martin, Darnell **43**
Onwurah, Ngozi **38**
Poitier, Sidney **11, 36**
Randall, Alice **38**
Tyler, Aisha N. **36**
Ward, Douglas Turner **42**

Film scores
Blanchard, Terence **43**
Crouch, Andraé **27**
Hancock, Herbie **20**
Jean-Baptiste, Marianne **17, 46**
Jones, Quincy **8, 30**
Prince **18**

Finance
Adams, Eula L. **39**
Banks, Jeffrey **17**
Boston, Kelvin E. **25**
Bryant, John **26**
Chapman, Nathan A. Jr. **21**
Doley, Harold, Jr. **26**
Ferguson, Roger W. **25**
Fletcher, Alphonse, Jr. **16**
Funderburg, I. Owen **38**
Gaines, Brenda **41**
Griffith, Mark Winston **8**
Hobson, Mellody **40**
Jones, Thomas W. **41**
Lawless, Theodore K. **8**
Lewis, William M., Jr. **40**
Louis, Errol T. **8**
Marshall, Bella **22**
Rogers, John W., Jr. **5**
Ross, Charles **27**
Thompson, William C. **35**

Firefighters
Bell, Michael **40**

First Data Corporation
Adams, Eula L. **39**

Fisk University
Harvey, William R. **42**
Imes, Elmer Samuel **39**
Johnson, Charles S. **12**
Phillips, Teresa L. **42**
Smith, John L. **22**

Fitness
Richardson, Donna **39**

FlipMode Entertainment
Rhymes, Busta **31**

Florida A & M University
Gaither, Alonzo Smith (Jake) **14**
Humphries, Frederick **20**
Meek, Kendrick **41**

Florida International baseball league
Kaiser, Cecil **42**

Multimedia art
Bailey, Xenobia **11**
Simpson, Lorna **4, 36**

Multiple Sclerosis
Falana, Lola **42**

Muppets, The
Clash, Kevin **14**

Murals
Alston, Charles **33**
Biggers, John **20, 33**
Douglas, Aaron **7**
Lee-Smith, Hughie **5**
Walker, Kara **16**

Murder Inc.
Ashanti **37**
Gotti, Irv **39**
Ja Rule **35**

Music Critics Circle
Holt, Nora **38**

Music One, Inc.
Majors, Jeff **41**

Music publishing
Combs, Sean "Puffy" **17, 43**
Cooke, Sam **17**
Edmonds, Tracey **16**
Gordy, Berry, Jr. **1**
Handy, W. C. **8**
Holland-Dozier-Holland **36**
Humphrey, Bobbi **20**
Ice Cube **8, 30**
Jackson, George **19**
Jackson, Michael **19**
James, Rick **17**
Knight, Suge **11, 30**
Lewis, Emmanuel **36**
Master P **21**
Mayfield, Curtis **2, 43**
Prince **18**
Redding, Otis **16**
Ross, Diana **8, 27**

Music Television (MTV)
Bellamy, Bill **12**
Chideya, Farai **14**
Powell, Kevin **31**

Musical composition
Armatrading, Joan **32**
Ashford, Nickolas **21**
Baiocchi, Regina Harris **41**
Ballard, Hank **41**
Bebey, Francis **45**
Blanchard, Terence **43**
Blige, Mary J **20, 34**
Bonds, Margaret **39**
Bonga, Kuenda **13**
Braxton, Toni **15**
Brown, Uzee **42**
Burke, Solomon **31**
Caesar, Shirley **19**
Carter, Warrick L. **27**
Chapman, Tracy **26**
Charlemagne, Manno **11**
Charles, Ray **16**
Cleveland, James **19**
Cole, Natalie Maria **17**
Coleman, Ornette **39**

Collins, Bootsy **31**
Combs, Sean "Puffy" **17, 43**
Cook, Will Marion **40**
Davis, Anthony **11**
Davis, Miles **4**
Davis, Sammy Jr. **18**
Dawson, William Levi **39**
Diddley, Bo **39**
Ellington, Duke **5**
Elliott, Missy "Misdemeanor" **31**
Europe, James Reese **10**
Evans, Faith **22**
Fats Domino **20**
Freeman, Paul **39**
Fuller, Arthur **27**
Gaynor, Gloria **36**
George, Nelson **12**
Gillespie, Dizzy **1**
Golson, Benny **37**
Gordy, Berry, Jr. **1**
Green, Al **13**
Hailey, JoJo **22**
Hailey, K-Ci **22**
Hammer, M. C. **20**
Handy, W. C. **8**
Harris, Corey **39**
Hathaway, Donny **18**
Hayes, Isaac **20**
Hayes, Teddy **40**
Hill, Lauryn **20**
Holland-Dozier-Holland **36**
Holt, Nora **38**
Humphrey, Bobbi **20**
Isley, Ronald **25**
Jackson, Fred James **25**
Jackson, Michael **19**
Jackson, Randy **40**
James, Rick **17**
Jean-Baptiste, Marianne **17, 46**
Jean, Wyclef **20**
Jerkins, Rodney **31**
Jones, Jonah **39**
Jones, Quincy **8, 30**
Johnson, Buddy **36**
Johnson, Georgia Douglas **41**
Joplin, Scott **6**
Jordan, Montell **23**
Jordan, Ronny **26**
Kay, Ulysses **37**
Kee, John P. **43**
Kelly, R. **18, 44**
Keys, Alicia **32**
King, B. B. **7**
León, Tania **13**
Lincoln, Abbey **3**
Little Milton **36**
Little Walter **36**
Lopes, Lisa "Left Eye" **36**
Majors, Jeff **41**
Marsalis, Delfeayo **41**
Marsalis, Wynton **16**
Master P **21**
Maxwell **20**
Mayfield, Curtis **2, 43**
McClurkin, Donnie **25**
Mills, Stephanie **36**
Mitchell, Brian Stokes **21**
Mo', Keb' **36**
Monica **21**
Moore, Chante **26**
Moore, Dorothy Rudd **46**
Moore, Undine Smith **28**
Muse, Clarence Edouard **21**
Nash, Johnny **40**
Ndegéocello, Me'Shell **15**

Osborne, Jeffrey **26**
Pratt, Awadagin **31**
Price, Florence **37**
Prince **18**
Pritchard, Robert Starling **21**
Reagon, Bernice Johnson **7**
Redding, Otis **16**
Reed, A. C. **36**
Reid, Antonio "L.A." **28**
Roach, Max **21**
Run-DMC **31**
Rushen, Patrice **12**
Sangare, Oumou **18**
Silver, Horace **26**
Simone, Nina **15, 41**
Simpson, Valerie **21**
Sowande, Fela **39**
Still, William Grant **37**
Strayhorn, Billy **31**
Sweat, Keith **19**
Tillis, Frederick **40**
Usher **23**
Van Peebles, Melvin **7**
Walker, George **37**
Warwick, Dionne **18**
Washington, Grover, Jr. **17, 44**
Williams, Deniece **36**
Winans, Angie **36**
Winans, Debbie **36**

Musicology
George, Zelma Watson **42**

Muslim Mosque, Inc.
X, Malcolm **1**

The Mystery
Delany, Martin R. **27**

Mysteries
Bland, Eleanor Taylor **39**
Creagh, Milton **27**
DeLoach, Nora **30**
Himes, Chester **8**
Holton, Hugh, Jr. **39**
Mickelbury, Penny **28**
Mosley, Walter **5, 25**
Thomas-Graham **29**
Wesley, Valerie Wilson **18**

Mystic Seaport Museum
Pinckney, Bill **42**

NAACP
See National Association for the Advancement of Colored People

NAACP Image Awards
Fields, Kim **36**
Lawrence, Martin **6, 27**
Warner, Malcolm-Jamal **22, 36**

NAACP Legal Defense and Educational Fund (LDF)
Bell, Derrick **6**
Chambers, Julius **3**
Edelman, Marian Wright **5, 42**
Guinier, Lani **7, 30**
Jones, Elaine R. **7, 45**
Julian, Percy Lavon **6**
Marshall, Thurgood **1, 44**
Motley, Constance Baker **10**

Larsen, Nella **10**
Lyttle, Hulda Margaret **14**
Riley, Helen Caldwell Day **13**
Robinson, Rachel **16**
Robinson, Sharon **22**
Shabazz, Betty **7, 26**
Staupers, Mabel K. **7**
Taylor, Susie King **13**

Nursing agency
Daniels, Lee Louis **36**

Nutrition
Clark, Celeste **15**
Gregory, Dick **1**
Watkins, Shirley R. **17**

NWBL
See National Women's Basketball
League

NYA
See National Youth Administration

Nyasaland African Congress (NAC)
Banda, Hastings Kamuzu **6**

Oakland Athletics baseball team
Baker, Dusty **8, 43**
Baylor, Don **6**
Henderson, Rickey **28**
Jackson, Reggie **15**
Morgan, Joe Leonard **9**

Oakland Oaks baseball team
Dandridge, Ray **36**

Oakland Raiders football team
Howard, Desmond **16**
Upshaw, Gene **18**

Oakland Tribune
Maynard, Robert C. **7**

OAR
See Office of AIDS Research

OAU
See Organization of African Unity

Obie awards
Carter, Nell **39**
Freeman, Yvette **27**
Orlandersmith, Dael **42**
Thigpen, Lynne **17, 41**

OBSSR
See Office of Behavioral and Social Sciences Research

OECS
See Organization of Eastern Caribbean States

Office of AIDS Research (OAR)
Cargill, Victoria A. **43**

Office of Behavioral and Social Science Research
Anderson, Norman B. **45**

Office of Civil Rights
See U.S. Department of Education

Office of Management and Budget
Raines, Franklin Delano **14**

Office of Public Liaison
Herman, Alexis M. **15**

Ohio House of Representatives
Stokes, Carl B. **10**

Ohio state government
Brown, Les **5**
Ford, Jack **39**
Stokes, Carl B. **10**
Williams, George Washington **18**

Ohio State Senate
White, Michael R. **5**

Ohio Women's Hall of Fame
Craig-Jones, Ellen Walker **44**
Stewart, Ella **39**

OIC
See Opportunities Industrialization Centers of America, Inc.

OKeh record label
Brooks, Hadda **40**
Mo', Keb' **36**

Oklahoma Hall of Fame
Mitchell, Leona **42**

Oklahoma House of Representatives
Ross, Don **27**

Oklahoma Eagle
Ross, Don **27**

Olatunji Center for African Culture
Olatunji, Babatunde **36**

Olympics
Abdur-Rahim, Shareef **28**
Ali, Muhammad **2, 16**
Beamon, Bob **30**
Bonaly, Surya **7**
Bowe, Riddick **6**
Carter, Vince **26**
Christie, Linford **8**
Coachman, Alice **18**
Dawes, Dominique **11**
DeFrantz, Anita **37**
Devers, Gail **7**
Edwards, Harry **2**
Edwards, Teresa **14**
Ewing, Patrick A. **17**
Flowers, Vonetta **35**
Ford, Cheryl **45**
Freeman, Cathy **29**
Garrison, Zina **2**
Gourdine, Meredith **33**
Greene, Maurice **27**
Griffith, Yolanda **25**
Griffith-Joyner, Florence **28**
Hardaway, Anfernee (Penny) **13**
Hardaway, Tim **35**
Harrison, Alvin **28**
Harrison, Calvin **28**
Hill, Grant **13**

Hines, Garrett **35**
Holyfield, Evander **6**
Howard, Sherri **36**
Iginla, Jarome **35**
Johnson, Ben **1**
Johnson, Michael **13**
Johnson, Rafer **33**
Jones, Randy **35**
Joyner-Kersee, Jackie **5**
Leslie, Lisa **16**
Lewis, Carl **4**
Malone, Karl A. **18**
Metcalfe, Ralph **26**
Miller, Cheryl **10**
Montgomery, Tim **41**
Moses, Edwin **8**
Mutola, Maria **12**
Owens, Jesse **2**
Pippen, Scottie **15**
Powell, Mike **7**
Quirot, Ana **13**
Robertson, Oscar **26**
Rudolph, Wilma **4**
Russell, Bill **8**
Scurry, Briana **27**
Swoopes, Sheryl **12**
Thomas, Debi **26**
Thugwane, Josia **21**
Ward, Lloyd **21, 46**
Westbrook, Peter **20**
Whitaker, Pernell **10**
Wilkens, Lenny **11**

On A Roll Radio
Smith, Greg **28**

Oncology
Leffall, LaSalle, Jr. **3**

One Church, One Child
Clements, George **2**

100 Black Men of America
Dortch, Thomas W., Jr. **45**

One Way-Productions
Naylor, Gloria **10, 42**

Ontario Legislature
Curling, Alvin **34**

Onyx Opera
Brown, Uzee **42**

OPC
See Ovambo People's Congress

Opera
Adams, Leslie **39**
Anderson, Marian **2, 33**
Arroyo, Martina **30**
Brooks, Avery **9**
Brown, Uzee **42**
Bumbry, Grace **5**
Davis, Anthony **11**
Dobbs, Mattiwilda **34**
Estes, Simon **28**
Freeman, Paul **39**
Graves, Denyce **19**
Greely, M. Gasby **27**
Hendricks, Barbara **3**
Joplin, Scott **6**
Joyner, Matilda Sissieretta **15**
Maynor, Dorothy **19**

U.S. Department of Commerce
Brown, Ron **5**
Irving, Larry, Jr. **12**
Person, Waverly **9**
Shavers, Cheryl **31**
Wilkins, Roger **2**

U.S. Department of Defense
Tribble, Israel, Jr. **8**

U.S. Department of Education
Hill, Anita **5**
Hill, Bonnie Guiton **20**
Paige, Rod **29**
Thomas, Clarence **2, 39**
Tribble, Israel, Jr. **8**

U.S. Department of Energy
O'Leary, Hazel **6**

U.S. Department of Health and Human Services (HHS)
See also U.S. Department of Health, Education, and Welfare

U.S. Department of Health, Education, and Welfare (HEW)
Bell, Derrick **6**
Berry, Mary Frances **7**
Harris, Patricia Roberts **2**
Johnson, Eddie Bernice **8**
Sullivan, Louis **8**

U.S. Department of Housing and Urban Development (HUD)
Gaines, Brenda **41**
Harris, Patricia Roberts **2**
Weaver, Robert C. **8, 46**

U.S. Department of Justice
Bell, Derrick **6**
Campbell, Bill **9**
Days, Drew S., III **10**
Guinier, Lani **7, 30**
Holder, Eric H., Jr. **9**
Lafontant, Jewel Stradford **3**
Lewis, Delano **7**
Patrick, Deval **12**
Thompson, Larry D. **39**
Wilkins, Roger **2**

U.S. Department of Labor
Crockett, George, Jr. **10**
Herman, Alexis M. **15**

U.S. Department of Social Services
Little, Robert L. **2**

U.S. Department of State
Bethune, Mary McLeod **4**
Bunche, Ralph J. **5**
Keyes, Alan L. **11**
Lafontant, Jewel Stradford **3**
Perkins, Edward **5**
Powell, Colin **1, 28**
Rice, Condoleezza **3, 28**
Wharton, Clifton Reginald, Sr. **36**
Wharton, Clifton R., Jr. **7**

U.S. Department of the Interior
Person, Waverly **9**

U.S. Department of Transportation
Davis, Benjamin O., Jr. **2, 43**

U.S. Department of Veterans Affairs
Brown, Jesse **6, 41**

U.S. Diplomatic Corps
Grimké, Archibald H. **9**
Haley, George Williford Boyce **21**
Harris, Patricia Roberts **2**
Stokes, Carl B. **10**

U.S. District Court judge
Diggs-Taylor, Anna **20**
Keith, Damon J. **16**
Parsons, James **14**

USFL
See United States Football League

U.S. Foreign Service
Davis, Ruth **37**

U.S. Geological Survey
Person, Waverly **9**

U.S. House of Representatives
Archie-Hudson, Marguerite **44**
Ballance, Frank W. **41**
Bishop, Sanford D., Jr. **24**
Brown, Corrine **24**
Burke, Yvonne Braithwaite **42**
Carson, Julia **23**
Chisholm, Shirley **2**
Clay, William Lacy **8**
Clayton, Eva M. **20**
Clyburn, James **21**
Collins, Barbara-Rose **7**
Collins, Cardiss **10**
Conyers, John, Jr. **4, 45**
Crockett, George, Jr. **10**
Cummings, Elijah E. **24**
Davis, Artur **41**
Dellums, Ronald **2**
Diggs, Charles C. **21**
Dixon, Julian C. **24**
Dymally, Mervyn **42**
Espy, Mike **6**
Fauntroy, Walter E. **11**
Fields, Cleo **13**
Flake, Floyd H. **18**
Ford, Harold Eugene **42**
Ford, Harold E., Jr., **16**
Franks, Gary **2**
Gray, William H. III **3**
Hastings, Alcee L. **16**
Hilliard, Earl F. **24**
Jackson, Jesse, Jr. **14, 45**
Jackson Lee, Sheila **20**
Jefferson, William J. **25**
Jordan, Barbara **4**
Kilpatrick, Carolyn Cheeks **16**
Lee, Barbara **25**
Leland, Mickey **2**
Lewis, John **2, 46**
Majette, Denise **41**
Meek, Carrie **6**
Meek, Kendrick **41**
Meeks, Gregory **25**
Metcalfe, Ralph **26**
Mfume, Kweisi **6, 41**
Millender-McDonald, Juanita **21**
Mitchell, Parren J. **42**
Norton, Eleanor Holmes **7**

Owens, Major **6**
Payne, Donald M. **2**
Pinchback, P. B. S. **9**
Powell, Adam Clayton, Jr. **3**
Rangel, Charles **3**
Rush, Bobby **26**
Scott, David **41**
Scott, Robert C. **23**
Stokes, Louis **3**
Towns, Edolphus **19**
Tubbs Jones, Stephanie **24**
Washington, Harold **6**
Waters, Maxine **3**
Watson, Diane **41**
Watt, Melvin **26**
Watts, J.C. **14, 38**
Wheat, Alan **14**
Wynn, Albert R. **25**
Young, Andrew **3**

U.S. Information Agency
Allen, Samuel **38**

U.S. Joint Chiefs of Staff
Howard, Michelle **28**
Powell, Colin **1, 28**
Rice, Condoleezza **3, 28**

U.S. Marines
Bolden, Charles F., Jr. **7**
Brown, Jesse **6, 41**
Petersen, Franke E. **31**
Von Lipsey, Roderick K. **11**

U.S. Navy
Brashear, Carl **29**
Brown, Jesse Leroy **31**
Doby, Lawrence Eugene Sr. **16, 41**
Fields, Evelyn J. **27**
Gravely, Samuel L., Jr. **5**
Howard, Michelle **28**
Miller, Dorie **29**
Pinckney, Bill **42**
Reason, J. Paul **19**
Wright, Lewin **43**

U.S. Olympic Committee (USOC)
DeFrantz, Anita **37**

U.S. Open golf tournament
Shippen, John **43**
Woods, Tiger **14, 31**

U.S. Open tennis tournament
Williams, Venus **17, 34**

U.S. Peace Corps
Days, Drew S., III **10**
Johnson, Rafer **33**
Lewis, Delano **7**

U.S. Register of the Treasury
Bruce, Blanche Kelso **33**

U.S. Senate
Braun, Carol Moseley **4, 42**
Brooke, Edward **8**
Bruce, Blanche Kelso **33**
Dodson, Howard, Jr. **7**
Johnson, Eddie Bernice **8**
Pinchback, P. B. S. **9**

Cumulative Name Index

Volume numbers appear in **bold**

Bosley, Freeman (Robertson), Jr. 1954—
7
Boston, Kelvin E. 1955(?)— **25**
Boston, Lloyd 1970(?)— **24**
Bowe, Riddick (Lamont) 1967— **6**
Bowser, Yvette Lee 1965(?)— **17**
Boyd, Gerald M. 1950— **32**
Boyd, John W., Jr. 1965— **20**
Boyd, T(heophilus) B(artholomew), III
1947— **6**
Boye, Madior 1940— **30**
Boykin, Keith 1965— **14**
Bradley, David Henry, Jr. 1950— **39**
Bradley, Ed(ward R.) 1941— **2**
Bradley, Jennette B. 1952— **40**
Bradley, Thomas 1917— **2, 20**
Brady, Wayne 1972— **32**
Branch, William Blackwell 1927— **39**
Brand, Dionne 1953— **32**
Brand, Elton 1979— **31**
Brandon, Barbara 1960(?)— **3**
Brandon, Thomas Terrell 1970— **16**
Brandy 1979— **14, 34**
Brashear, Carl Maxie 1931— **29**
Brashear, Donald 1972— **39**
Brathwaite, Fred 1972— **35**
Brathwaite, Kamau 1930— **36**
Brathwaite, Lawson Edward
See Kamau Brathwaite
Braugher, Andre 1962(?)— **13**
Braun, Carol (Elizabeth) Moseley
1947— **4, 42**
Brawley, Benjamin 1882-1939 **44**
Braxton, Toni 1968(?)— **15**
Brazile, Donna 1959— **25**
Breedlove, Sarah
See Walker, Madame C. J.
Breeze, Jean "Binta" 1956— **37**
Bridges, Christopher
See Ludacris
Bridges, Sheila 1964— **36**
Bridges, Todd 1965— **37**
Bridgewater, Dee Dee 1950— **32**
Bridgforth, Glinda 1952— **36**
Brimmer, Andrew F(elton) 1926— **2**
Briscoe, Connie 1952— **15**
Briscoe, Marlin 1946(?)— **37**
Britt, Donna 1954(?)— **28**
Broadbent, Hydeia 1984— **36**
Brock, Louis Clark 1939— **18**
Bronner, Nathaniel H., Sr. 1914-1993
32
Brooke, Edward (William, III) 1919— **8**
Brooks, Aaron 1976— **33**
Brooks, Avery 1949— **9**
Brooks, Derrick 1973— **43**
Brooks, Gwendolyn 1917-2000 **1, 28**
Brooks, Hadda 1916-2002 **40**
Brown Bomber, The
See Louis, Joe
Brown, Andre
See Dr. Dre
Brown, Charles 1922-1999 **23**
Brown, Claude 1937-2002 **38**
Brown, Cora 1914-1972 **33**
Brown, Corrine 1946— **24**
Brown, Donald 1963— **19**
Brown, Eddie C. 1940— **35**
Brown, Elaine 1943— **8**
Brown, Erroll M. 1950(?)— **23**
Brown, Foxy 1979— **25**
Brown, H. Rap
See Al-Amin, Jamil Abdullah
Brown, Hubert Gerold
See Al-Amin, Jamil Abdullah

Brown, James 1933— **15**
Brown, James 1951— **22**
Brown, James Nathaniel
See Brown, Jim
Brown, James Willie, Jr.
See Komunyakaa, Yusef
Brown, Janice Rogers 1949— **43**
Brown, Jesse 1944-2003 **6, 41**
Brown, Jesse Leroy 1926-1950 **31**
Brown, Jim 1936— **11**
Brown, Joe 19(?)(?)— **29**
Brown, Joyce F. 1946— **25**
Brown, Lee P(atrick) 1937— **1, 24**
Brown, Les(lie Calvin) 1945— **5**
Brown, Lloyd Louis 1913-2003 **42**
Brown, Ron(ald Harmon) 1941— **5**
Brown, Sterling (Allen) 1901— **10**
Brown, Tony 1933— **3**
Brown, Uzee, Jr. 1950— **42**
Brown, Vivian 1964— **27**
Brown, Wesley 1945— **23**
Brown, Willa Beatrice 1906-1992 **40**
Brown, Willard 1911(?)-1996 **36**
Brown, William Anthony
See Brown, Tony
Brown, Willie L., Jr. 1934— **7**
Brown, Zora Kramer 1949— **12**
Bruce, Blanche Kelso 1849-1898 **33**
Bruce, Isaac 1972— **26**
Brunson, Dorothy 1938— **1**
Brutus, Dennis 1924— **38**
Bryan, Ashley F. 1923— **41**
Bryant, John 1966— **26**
Bryant, John R. 1943— **45**
Bryant, Kobe 1978— **15, 31**
Bryant, Wayne R(ichard) 1947— **6**
Buchanan, Ray 1971— **32**
Buckley, Gail Lumet 1937— **39**
Buckley, Victoria (Vikki) 1947-1999 **24**
Bullard, Eugene Jacques 1894-1961 **12**
Bullins, Ed 1935— **25**
Bullock, Anna Mae
See Turner, Tina
Bullock, Steve 1936— **22**
Bumbry, Grace (Ann) 1937— **5**
Bunche, Ralph J(ohnson) 1904-1971 **5**
Bunkley, Anita Richmond 19(?)(?)— **39**
Burke, Selma Hortense 1900-1995 **16**
Burke, Solomon 1936— **31**
Burke, Yvonne Braithwaite 1932— **42**
Burks, Mary Fair 1920-1991 **40**
Burley, Mary Lou
See Williams, Mary Lou
Burnett, Charles 1944— **16**
Burnett, Chester Arthur
See Howlin' Wolf
Burnett, Dorothy 1905-1995 **19**
Burns, Eddie 1928— **44**
Burrell, Orville Richard
See Shaggy
Burrell, Stanley Kirk
See Hammer, M. C.
Burrell, Thomas J. 1939— **21**
Burris, Chuck 1951— **21**
Burris, Roland W. 1937— **25**
Burroughs, Margaret Taylor 1917— **9**
Burrows, Stephen 1943— **31**
Burrus, William Henry "Bill" 1936— **45**
Burton, LeVar(dis Robert Martyn)
1957— **8**
Busby, Jheryl 1949(?)— **3**
Buthelezi, Mangosuthu Gatsha 1928—
9
Butler, Jerry 1939— **26**
Butler, Jonathan 1961— **28**

Butler, Leroy, III 1968— **17**
Butler, Octavia (Estelle) 1947— **8, 43**
Butler, Paul D. 1961— **17**
Butts, Calvin O(tis), III 1950— **9**
Bynoe, Peter C.B. 1951— **40**
Bynum, Juanita 1959— **31**
Byrd, Donald 1949— **10**
Byrd, Michelle 1965— **19**
Byrd, Robert (Oliver Daniel, III) 1952—
11
Byron, JoAnne Deborah
See Shakur, Assata
Cade, Toni
See Bambara, Toni Cade
Cadoria, Sherian Grace 1940— **14**
Caesar, Shirley 1938— **19**
Cain, Herman 1945— **15**
Calhoun, Cora
See Austin, Lovie
Callender, Clive O(rville) 1936— **3**
Calloway, Cabell, III 1907-1994 **14**
Cameron, Earl 1917— **44**
Camp, Georgia Blanche Douglas
See Johnson, Georgia Douglas
Camp, Kimberly 1956— **19**
Campanella, Roy 1921-1993 **25**
Campbell, Bebe Moore 1950— **6, 24**
Campbell, Bill 1954— **9**
Campbell, Charleszetta Lena
See Waddles, Charleszetta (Mother)
Campbell, E(lmer) Simms 1906-1971 **13**
Campbell, Mary Schmidt 1947— **43**
Campbell, Milton
Little Milton
Campbell, Naomi 1970— **1, 31**
Campbell, Tisha
See Campbell-Martin, Tisha
Campbell-Martin, Tisha 1969— **8, 42**
Canada, Geoffrey 1954— **23**
Canady, Alexa 1950— **28**
Canegata, Leonard Lionel Cornelius
See Lee, Canada
Cannon, Katie 1950— **10**
Carby, Hazel 1948— **27**
Cardozo, Francis L. 1837-1903 **33**
Carew, Rod 1945— **20**
Carey, Mariah 1970— **32**
Carmichael, Stokely 1941-1998 **5, 26**
Carnegie, Herbert 1919— **25**
Carroll, Diahann 1935— **9**
Carroll, L. Natalie 1950— **44**
Carroll, Vinnette 1922— **29**
Carruthers, George R. 1939— **40**
Carson, Benjamin 1951— **1, 35**
Carson, Josephine
See Baker, Josephine
Carson, Julia 1938— **23**
Carson, Lisa Nicole 1969— **21**
Carter, Anson 1974— **24**
Carter, Ben
See Ben-Israel, Ben Ami
Carter, Betty 1930— **19**
Carter, Butch 1958— **27**
Carter, Cris 1965— **21**
Carter, Joe 1960— **30**
Carter, Joye Maureen 1957— **41**
Carter, Mandy 1946— **11**
Carter, Nell 1948-2003 **39**
Carter, Regina 1966(?)— **23**
Carter, Rubin 1937— **26**
Carter, Shawn
See Jay-Z
Carter, Stephen L(isle) 1954— **4**
Carter, Vince 1977— **26**

See Carroll, Diahann
Johnson, Caryn E.
  See Goldberg, Whoopi
Johnson, Charles 1948— **1**
Johnson, Charles Arthur
  See St. Jacques, Raymond
Johnson, Charles Spurgeon 1893-1956
  12
Johnson, Dwayne "The Rock" 1972—
  29
Johnson, Earvin "Magic" 1959— **3, 39**
Johnson, Eddie Bernice 1935— **8**
Johnson, George E. 1927— **29**
Johnson, Georgia Douglas 1880-1966
  41
Johnson, Harvey Jr. 1947(?)— **24**
Johnson, Hazel 1927— **22**
Johnson, J. J. 1924-2001 **37**
Johnson, Jack 1878-1946 **8**
Johnson, James Louis
  See Johnson, J. J.
Johnson, James Weldon 1871-1938 **5**
Johnson, James William
  See Johnson, James Weldon
Johnson, Jeh Vincent 1931— **44**
Johnson, John Arthur
  See Johnson, Jack
Johnson, John H(arold) 1918— **3**
Johnson, Larry 1969— **28**
Johnson, Linton Kwesi 1952— **37**
Johnson, Lonnie G. 1949— **32**
Johnson, Mamie "Peanut" 1932— **40**
Johnson, Marguerite
  See Angelou, Maya
Johnson, Mat 1971(?)— **31**
Johnson, Michael (Duane) 1967— **13**
Johnson, Norma L. Holloway 1932—
  17
Johnson, R. M. 1968— **36**
Johnson, Rafer 1934— **33**
Johnson, Robert 1911-1938 **2**
Johnson, Robert L. 1946(?)— **3, 39**
Johnson, Robert T. 1948— **17**
Johnson, Rodney Van 19(?)(?)— **28**
Johnson, Taalib
  See Musiq
Johnson, Virginia (Alma Fairfax) 1950—
  9
Johnson, William Henry 1901-1970 **3**
Johnson, Woodrow Wilson
  See Johnson, Buddy
Johnson-Brown, Hazel W.
  See, Johnson, Hazel
Jolley, Willie 1956— **28**
Jones, Bill T. 1952— **1**
Jones, Bobby 1939(?)— **20**
Jones, Carl 1955(?)— **7**
Jones, Caroline R. 1942— **29**
Jones, Cobi N'Gai 1970— **18**
Jones, Donell 1973— **29**
Jones, E. Edward, Sr. 1931— **45**
Jones, Edward P. 1950— **43**
Jones, Elaine R. 1944— **7, 45**
Jones, Elvin 1927— **14**
Jones, Etta 1928-2001 **35**
Jones, Gayl 1949— **37**
Jones, Ingrid Saunders 1945— **18**
Jones, James Earl 1931— **3**
Jones, Jonah 1909-2000 **39**
Jones, Kimberly Denise
  See Lil' Kim
Jones, Le Roi
  See Baraka, Amiri
Jones, Lillie Mae
  See Carter, Betty

Jones, Lois Mailou 1905— **13**
Jones, Marion 1975— **21**
Jones, Merlakia 1973— **34**
Jones, Nasir
  See Nas
Jones, Orlando 1968— **30**
Jones, Quincy (Delight) 1933— **8, 30**
Jones, Randy 1969— **35**
Jones, Robert Elliott
  See Jones, Jonah
Jones, Roy Jr. 1969— **22**
Jones, Ruth Lee
  See Washington, Dinah
Jones, Sarah 1974— **39**
Jones, Sissieretta
  See Joyner, Matilda Sissieretta
Jones, Star(let Marie) 1962(?)— **10, 27**
Jones, Thomas W. 1949— **41**
Joplin, Scott 1868-1917 **6**
Jordan, Barbara (Charline) 1936— **4**
Jordan, Eric Benét
  See Benét, Eric
Jordan, June 1936— **7, 35**
Jordan, Michael (Jeffrey) 1963— **6, 21**
Jordan, Montell 1968(?)— **23**
Jordan, Ronny 1962— **26**
Jordan, Vernon E(ulion, Jr.) 1935— **3, 35**
Josey, E. J. 1924— **10**
Joyner, Jacqueline
  See Joyner-Kersee, Jackie
Joyner, Marjorie Stewart 1896-1994 **26**
Joyner, Matilda Sissieretta 1869(?)-1933
  15
Joyner, Tom 1949(?)— **19**
Joyner-Kersee, Jackie 1962— **5**
Julian, Percy Lavon 1899-1975 **6**
Julien, Isaac 1960— **3**
July, William II 19(?(?)— **27**
Just, Ernest Everett 1883-1941 **3**
Justice, David Christopher 1966— **18**
Ka Dinizulu, Israel
  See Ka Dinizulu, Mcwayizeni
Ka Dinizulu, Mcwayizeni 1932-1999
  29
Kabbah, Ahmad Tejan 1932— **23**
Kabila, Joseph 1968(?)— **30**
Kabila, Laurent 1939— **20**
Kaiser, Cecil 1916— **42**
Kamau, Johnstone
  See Kenyatta, Jomo
Kamau, Kwadwo Agymah 1960(?)— **28**
Kani, Karl 1968(?)— **10**
Karenga, Maulana 1941— **10**
Kaunda, Kenneth (David) 1924— **2**
Kay, Jackie 1961— **37**
Kay, Ulysses 1917-1995 **37**
Kayira, Legson 1942— **40**
Kearse, Amalya Lyle 1937— **12**
Kee, John P. 1962— **43**
Keith, Damon Jerome 1922— **16**
Kelly, Leontine 1920— **33**
Kelly, Patrick 1954(?)-1990 **3**
Kelly, R(obert) 1969(?)— **18, 44**
Kelly, Sharon Pratt
  See Dixon, Sharon Pratt
Kendricks, Eddie 1939-1992 **22**
Kennard, William Earl 1957— **18**
Kennedy, Adrienne 1931— **11**
Kennedy, Florynce Rae 1916-2000 **12, 33**
Kennedy, Lelia McWilliams Robinson
  1885-1931 **14**
Kennedy, Randall 1954— **40**
Kenoly, Ron 1944— **45**

Kenyatta, Jomo 1891(?)-1978 **5**
Kerekou, Ahmed (Mathieu) 1933— **1**
Keyes, Alan L(ee) 1950— **11**
Keys, Alicia 1981— **32**
Khan, Chaka 1953— **12**
Khanga, Yelena 1962— **6**
Kidd, Mae Street 1904-1995 **39**
Kilpatrick, Carolyn Cheeks 1945— **16**
Kilpatrick, Kwame 1970— **34**
Kimbro, Dennis (Paul) 1950— **10**
Kimbro, Henry A. 1912-1999 **25**
Kincaid, Bernard 1945— **28**
Kincaid, Jamaica 1949— **4**
King, Alonzo 19(?)(?)— **38**
King, B. B. 1925— **7**
King, Barbara 19(?)(?)— **22**
King, Bernice (Albertine) 1963— **4**
King, Coretta Scott 1929— **3**
King, Dexter (Scott) 1961— **10**
King, Don 1931— **14**
King, Gayle 1956— **19**
King, Martin Luther, III 1957— **20**
King, Martin Luther, Jr. 1929-1968 **1**
King, Oona 1967— **27**
King, Preston 1936— **28**
King, Regina 1971— **22, 45**
King, Riley B.
  See King, B. B.
King, Woodie Jr. 1937— **27**
King, Yolanda (Denise) 1955— **6**
Kirby, George 1924-1995 **14**
Kirk, Ron 1954— **11**
Kitt, Eartha Mae 1928(?)— **16**
Kitt, Sandra 1947— **23**
Knight, Etheridge 1931-1991 **37**
Knight, Gladys Maria 1944— **16**
Knight, Marion, Jr.
  See Knight, Suge
Knight, Suge 1966— **11, 30**
Knowles, Beyoncé 1981— **39**
Knowling, Robert Jr. 1955(?)— **38**
Knuckles, Frankie 1955— **42**
Kobia, Rev. Dr. Samuel 1947— **43**
Kodjoe, Boris 1973— **34**
Komunyakaa, Yusef 1941— **9**
Kone, Seydou
  See Blondy, Alpha
Kool DJ Red Alert
  See Alert, Kool DJ Red
Kool Moe Dee 1963— **37**
Kotto, Yaphet (Fredrick) 1944— **7**
Kountz, Samuel L(ee) 1930-1981 **10**
Kravitz, Lenny 1964— **10, 34**
Kravitz, Leonard
  See Kravitz, Lenny
KRS-One 1965— **34**
Krute, Fred
  See Alert, Kool DJ Red
Kunjufu, Jawanza 1953— **3**
Kuti, Fela Anikulapo
  See Fela
Kyles, Cedric
  See Cedric the Entertainer
L. L. Cool J 1968— **16**
La Menthe, Ferdinand Joseph
  See Morton, Jelly Roll
La Salle, Eriq 1962— **12**
LaBelle, Patti 1944— **13, 30**
Lacy, Sam 1903— **30**
Ladner, Joyce A. 1943— **42**
Laferriere, Dany 1953— **33**
Lafontant, Jewel Stradford 1922— **3**
LaGuma, Alex 1925-1985 **30**
Lamming, George 1927— **35**
Lampkin, Daisy 1883(?)-1965 **19**

Massenburg, Kedar 1964(?)— **23**
Massey, Brandon 1973— **40**
Massey, Walter E(ugene) 1938— **5, 45**
Massie, Samuel Proctor, Jr. 1919— **29**
Master P 1970— **21**
Mathabane, Johannes
  See Mathabane, Mark
Mathabane, Mark 1960— **5**
Mathis, Greg 1960— **26**
Mathis, Johnny 1935— **20**
Mauldin, Jermaine Dupri
  See Dupri, Jermaine
Maxwell 1973— **20**
May, Derrick 1963— **41**
Mayers, Jamal 1974— **39**
Mayfield, Curtis (Lee) 1942-1999 **2, 43**
Mayhew, Richard 1924— **39**
Maynard, Robert C(lyve) 1937-1993 **7**
Maynor, Dorothy 1910-1996 **19**
Mayo, Whitman 1930-2001 **32**
Mays, Benjamin E(lijah) 1894-1984 **7**
Mays, Leslie A. 19(?)(?)— **41**
Mays, William G. 1946— **34**
Mays, William Howard, Jr.
  See Mays, Willie
Mays, Willie 1931— **3**
Mazrui, Ali Al'Amin 1933— **12**
Mbaye, Mariétou 1948— **31**
Mbeki, Thabo Mvuyelwa 1942— **14**
Mboup, Souleymane 1951— **10**
Mbuende, Kaire Munionganda 1953— **12**
MC Lyte 1971— **34**
McBride, Bryant Scott 1965— **18**
McBride, James C. 1957— **35**
McCabe, Jewell Jackson 1945— **10**
McCall, H. Carl 1938(?)— **27**
McCall, Nathan 1955— **8**
McCann, Renetta 1957(?)— **44**
McCarty, Osceola 1908— **16**
McClurkin, Donnie 1961— **25**
McCoy, Elijah 1844-1929 **8**
McCray, Nikki 1972— **18**
McDaniel, Hattie 1895-1952 **5**
McDaniels, Darryl
  See DMC
McDonald, Audra 1970— **20**
McDonald, Erroll 1954(?)— **1**
McDonald, Gabrielle Kirk 1942— **20**
McDougall, Gay J. 1947— **11, 43**
McEwen, Mark 1954— **5**
McFadden, Bernice L. 1966— **39**
McGee, Charles 1924— **10**
McGriff, Fred 1963— **24**
McGruder, Aaron Vincent 1974— **28**
McGruder, Robert 1942— **22, 35**
McIntosh, Winston Hubert
  See Tosh, Peter
McIntyre, Natalie
  See Gary, Macy
McKay, Claude 1889-1948 **6**
McKay, Festus Claudius
  See McKay, Claude
McKay, Nellie Yvonne 194(?)— **17**
McKee, Lonette 1952— **12**
McKegney, Tony 1958— **3**
McKenzie, Vashti M. 1947— **29**
McKinney, Cynthia Ann 1955— **11**
McKinney, Nina Mae 1912-1967 **40**
McKinney-Whetstone, Diane 1954(?)— **27**
McKinnon, Ike
  See McKinnon, Isaiah
McKinnon, Isaiah 1943— **9**
McKissick, Floyd B(ixler) 1922-1981 **3**

McKnight, Brian 1969— **18, 34**
McLeod, Gus 1955(?)— **27**
McLeod, Gustavus
  See McLeod, Gus
McMillan, Rosalynn A. 1953— **36**
McMillan, Terry 1951— **4, 17**
McMurray, Georgia L. 1934-1992 **36**
McNabb, Donovan 1976— **29**
McNair, Ronald (Ervin) 1950-1986 **3**
McNair, Steve 1973— **22**
McNeil, Lori 1964(?)— **1**
McPhail, Sharon 1948— **2**
McPherson, David 1968— **32**
McQueen, Butterfly 1911— **6**
McQueen, Thelma
  See McQueen, Butterfly
McWhorter, John 1965— **35**
Meadows, Tim 1961— **30**
Meek, Carrie (Pittman) 1926— **6, 36**
Meek, Kendrick 1966— **41**
Meeks, Gregory 1953— **25**
Meles Zenawi 1955(?)— **3**
Memmi, Albert 1920— **37**
Memphis Minnie 1897-1973 **33**
Mercado-Valdes, Frank 1962— **43**
Meredith, James H(oward) 1933— **11**
Messenger, The
  See Divine, Father
Metcalfe, Ralph 1910-1978 **26**
Meyer, June
  See Jordan, June
Mfume, Kweisi 1948— **6, 41**
Micheaux, Oscar (Devereaux) 1884-1951 **7**
Michele, Michael 1966— **31**
Mickelbury, Penny 1948— **28**
Milla, Roger 1952— **2**
Millender-McDonald, Juanita 1938— **21**
Miller, Bebe 1950— **3**
Miller, Cheryl 1964— **10**
Miller, Dorie 1919-1943 **29**
Miller, Doris
  See Miller, Dorie
Miller, Maria 1803-1879 **19**
Miller, Percy
  See Master P
Miller, Reggie 1965— **33**
Millines Dziko, Trish 1957— **28**
Mills, Florence 1896-1927 **22**
Mills, Sam 1959— **33**
Mills, Stephanie 1957— **36**
Milner, Ron 1938— **39**
Milton, DeLisha 1974— **31**
Mingo, Frank L. 1939-1989 **32**
Mingus, Charles Jr. 1922-1979 **15**
Minor, DeWayne 1956— **32**
Mitchell, Arthur 1934— **2**
Mitchell, Brian Stokes 1957— **21**
Mitchell, Corinne 1914-1993 **8**
Mitchell, Leona 1949— **42**
Mitchell, Loften 1919-2001 **31**
Mitchell, Parren J. 1922— **42**
Mitchell, Russ 1960— **21**
Mitchell, Sharon 1962— **36**
Mizell, Jason
  See Jay, Jam Master
Mkapa, Benjamin William 1938— **16**
Mo', Keb' 1952— **36**
Mo'Nique 1967— **35**
Mobutu Sese Seko (Nkuku wa za Banga) 1930— **1**
Mobutu, Joseph-Desire
  See Mobutu Sese Seko (Nkuku wa za Banga)

Mofolo, Thomas (Mokopu) 1876-1948 **37**
Mogae, Festus Gontebanye 1939— **19**
Mohamed, Ali Mahdi
  See Ali Mahdi Mohamed
Mohammed, W. Deen 1933— **27**
Mohammed, Warith Deen
  See Mohammed, W. Deen
Moi, Daniel (Arap) 1924— **1, 35**
Mollel, Tololwa 1952— **38**
Mongella, Gertrude 1945— **11**
Monica 1980— **21**
Monk, Art 1957— **38**
Monk, Thelonious (Sphere, Jr.) 1917-1982 **1**
Monroe, Mary 19(?)(?)— **35**
Montgomery, Tim 1975— **41**
Moody, Ronald 1900-1984 **30**
Moon, (Harold) Warren 1956— **8**
Mooney, Paul 19(?)(?)— **37**
Moore, Alice Ruth
  See Dunbar-Nelson, Alice Ruth Moore
Moore, Bobby
  See Rashad, Ahmad
Moore, Chante 1970(?)— **26**
Moore, Harry T. 1905-1951 **29**
Moore, Jessica Care 1971— **30**
Moore, Johnny B. 1950— **38**
Moore, Kevin
  See Mo', Keb'
Moore, Melba 1945— **21**
Moore, Minyon 19??— **45**
Moore, Shemar 1970— **21**
Moore, Undine Smith 1904-1989 **28**
Moorer, Lana
  See MC Lyte
Moorer, Michael 1967— **19**
Moose, Charles 1953— **40**
Morgan, Garrett (Augustus) 1877-1963 **1**
Morgan, Joe Leonard 1943— **9**
Morgan, Rose (Meta) 1912(?)— **11**
Morganfield, McKinley
  See Muddy Waters
Morial, Ernest "Dutch" 1929-1989 **26**
Morial, Marc 1958— **20**
Morris, Garrett 1937— **31**
Morris, Greg 1934-1996 **28**
Morris, Stevland Judkins
  See Wonder, Stevie
Morrison, Keith 1942— **13**
Morrison, Toni 1931— **2, 15**
Morton, Jelly Roll 1885(?)-1941 **29**
Morton, Joe 1947— **18**
Mos Def 1973— **30**
Moseka, Aminata
  See Lincoln, Abbey
Moseley-Braun, Carol
  See Braun, Carol (Elizabeth) Moseley
Moses, Edwin 1955— **8**
Moses, Gilbert, III 1942-1995 **12**
Moses, Robert Parris 1935— **11**
Mosley, "Sugar" Shane 1971— **32**
Mosley, Tim
  See Timbaland
Mosley, Walter 1952— **5, 25**
Moss, Carlton 1909-1997 **17**
Moss, Randy 1977— **23**
Moss, Shad Gregory
  See (Lil') Bow Wow
Mossell, Gertrude Bustill 1855-1948 **40**
Moten, Emma Barnett 1901— **18**
Motley, Archibald, Jr. 1891-1981 **30**
Motley, Constance Baker 1921— **10**
Motley, Marion 1920-1999 **26**

Perry, Rainford Hugh
   See Perry, Lee "Scratch"
Perry, Ruth 1936— **19**
Perry, Ruth Sando 1939— **15**
Perry, Tyler 1969— **40**
Person, Waverly (J.) 1927— **9**
Peters, Lenrie 1932— **43**
Peters, Margaret and Matilda **43**
Peters, Maria Philomena 1941— **12**
Petersen, Frank E. 1932— **31**
Peterson, Hannibal
   See, Peterson, Marvin "Hannibal"
Peterson, James 1937— **38**
Peterson, Marvin "Hannibal" 1948—
   27
Petry, Ann 1909-1997 **19**
Phifer, Mekhi 1975— **25**
Philip, M. Nourbese
   See Philip, Marlene Nourbese
Philip, Marlene Nourbese 1947— **32**
Phillips, Teresa L. 1958— **42**
Pickett, Bill 1870-1932 **11**
Pickett, Cecil 1945— **39**
Pierre, Andre 1915— **17**
Pinchback, P(inckney) B(enton) S(tewart) 1837-1921 **9**
Pinckney, Bill 1935— **42**
Pinkett Smith, Jada 1971— **10, 41**
Pinkett, Jada
   See Pinkett Smith, Jada
Pinkney, Jerry 1939— **15**
Pinkston, W. Randall 1950— **24**
Pippen, Scottie 1965— **15**
Pippin, Horace 1888-1946 **9**
Pitt, David Thomas 1913-1994 **10**
Pitta, (do Nascimento), Celso (Roberto) 19(?)(?)— **17**
Player, Willa B. 1909-2003 **43**
Pleasant, Mary Ellen 1814-1904 **9**
Plessy, Homer Adolph 1862-1925 **31**
Poitier, Sidney 1927— **11, 36**
Poole, Elijah
   See Muhammad, Elijah
Porter, Countee Leroy
   See, Cullin, Countee
Porter, James A(mos) 1905-1970 **11**
Potter, Myrtle 1958— **40**
Poussaint, Alvin F(rancis) 1934— **5**
Powell, Adam Clayton, Jr. 1908-1972 **3**
Powell, Bud 1924-1966 **24**
Powell, Colin (Luther) 1937— **1, 28**
Powell, Debra A. 1964— **23**
Powell, Kevin 1966— **31**
Powell, Maxine 1924— **8**
Powell, Michael Anthony
   See Powell, Mike
Powell, Michael K. 1963— **32**
Powell, Mike 1963— **7**
Powell, Renee 1946— **34**
Pratt Dixon, Sharon
   See Dixon, Sharon Pratt
Pratt, Awadagin 1966— **31**
Pratt, Geronimo 1947— **18**
Premice, Josephine 1926-2001 **41**
Pressley, Condace L. 1964— **41**
Preston, Billy 1946— **39**
Preston, William Everett
   See Preston, Billy
Price, Florence 1887-1953 **37**
Price, Frederick K.C. 1932— **21**
Price, Glenda 1939— **22**
Price, Hugh B. 1941— **9**
Price, Kelly 1973(?)— **23**
Price, Leontyne 1927— **1**
Pride, Charley 1938(?)— **26**

Primus, Pearl 1919— **6**
Prince 1958— **18**
Prince-Bythewood, Gina 1968— **31**
Pritchard, Robert Starling 1927— **21**
Procope, Ernesta 19(?)(?)— **23**
Prophet, Nancy Elizabeth 1890-1960 **42**
Prothrow, Deborah Boutin
   See Prothrow-Stith, Deborah
Prothrow-Stith, Deborah 1954— **10**
Pryor, Richard (Franklin Lennox Thomas) 1940— **3, 24**
Puckett, Kirby 1961— **4**
Puff Daddy
   See Combs, Sean "Puffy"
Puryear, Martin 1941— **42**
Quarles, Benjamin Arthur 1904-1996 **18**
Quarles, Norma 1936— **25**
Quarterman, Lloyd Albert 1918-1982 **4**
Queen Latifah 1970(?)— **1, 16**
Quirot, Ana (Fidelia) 1963— **13**
Rahman, Aishah 1936— **37**
Raines, Franklin Delano 1949— **14**
Rainey, Ma 1886-1939 **33**
Ralph, Sheryl Lee 1956— **18**
Ramaphosa, (Matamela) Cyril 1952— **3**
Ramphele, Mamphela 1947— **29**
Ramsey, Charles H. 1948— **21**
Rand, A(ddison) Barry 1944— **6**
Randall, Alice 1959— **38**
Randall, Dudley (Felker) 1914— **8**
Randle, Theresa 1967— **16**
Randolph, A(sa) Philip 1889-1979 **3**
Rangel, Charles (Bernard) 1930— **3**
Ras Tafari
   See Haile Selassie
Rashad, Ahmad 1949— **18**
Rashad, Phylicia 1948— **21**
Raspberry, William 1935— **2**
Raven, 1985— **44**
Raven-Symone
   See Raven
Rawlings, Jerry (John) 1947— **9**
Rawls, Lou 1936— **17**
Raymond, Usher, IV,
   See Usher
Razaf, Andy 1895-1973 **19**
Razafkeriefo, Andreamentania Paul
   See Razaf, Andy
Ready, Stephanie 1975— **33**
Reagon, Bernice Johnson 1942— **7**
Reason, Joseph Paul 1943— **19**
Reddick, Lawrence Dunbar 1910-1995 **20**
Redding, J. Saunders 1906-1988 **26**
Redding, Louis L. 1901-1998 **26**
Redding, Otis, Jr. 1941— **16**
Redman, Joshua 1969— **30**
Redmond, Eugene 1937— **23**
Reed, A. C. 1926— **36**
Reed, Ishmael 1938— **8**
Reed, Jimmy 1925-1976 **38**
Reems, Ernestine Cleveland 1932— **27**
Reese, Calvin
   See Reese, Pokey
Reese, Della 1931— **6, 20**
Reese, Pokey 1973— **28**
Reeves, Dianne 1956— **32**
Reeves, Rachel J. 1950(?)— **23**
Reeves, Triette Lipsey 1963— **27**
Reid, Antonio "L.A." 1958(?)— **28**
Reid, Irvin D. 1941— **20**
Reid, L.A.
   See Reid, Antonio "L.A."

Reid, Vernon 1958— **34**
Reuben, Gloria 19(?)(?)— **15**
Rhames, Ving 1961— **14**
Rhoden, Dwight 1962— **40**
Rhodes, Ray 1950— **14**
Rhone, Sylvia 1952— **2**
Rhymes, Busta 1972— **31**
Ribbs, William Theodore, Jr.
   See Ribbs, Willy T.
Ribbs, Willy T. 1956— **2**
Ribeiro, Alfonso 1971— **17**
Rice, Condoleezza 1954— **3, 28**
Rice, Jerry 1962— **5**
Rice, Linda Johnson 1958— **9, 41**
Rice, Norm(an Blann) 1943— **8**
Richards, Beah 1926-2000 **30**
Richards, Lloyd 1923(?)— **2**
Richardson, Desmond 1969— **39**
Richardson, Donna 1962— **39**
Richardson, Elaine Potter
   See Kincaid, Jamaica
Richardson, Nolan 1941— **9**
Richardson, Pat
   See Norman, Pat
Richie, Leroy C. 1941— **18**
Richie, Lionel 1949— **27**
Richmond, Mitchell James 1965— **19**
Ridenhour, Carlton
   See Chuck D.
Riggs, Marlon 1957-1994 **5, 44**
Riley, Helen Caldwell Day 1926— **13**
Ringgold, Faith 1930— **4**
Riperton, Minnie 1947-1979 **32**
Rivers, Glenn "Doc" 1961— **25**
Roach, Max 1924— **21**
Roberts, Deborah 1960— **35**
Roberts, James
   See Lover, Ed
Roberts, Marcus 1963— **19**
Roberts, Marthaniel
   See Roberts, Marcus
Roberts, Robin 1960— **16**
Roberts, Roy S. 1939(?)— **14**
Robertson, Oscar 1938— **26**
Robeson, Eslanda Goode 1896-1965 **13**
Robeson, Paul (Leroy Bustill) 1898-1976 **2**
Robinson, Bill "Bojangles" 1878-1949 **11**
Robinson, Cleo Parker 1948(?)— **38**
Robinson, David 1965— **24**
Robinson, Eddie G. 1919— **10**
Robinson, Fatima 19(?)(?)— **34**
Robinson, Fenton 1935-1997 **38**
Robinson, Frank 1935— **9**
Robinson, Jack Roosevelt
   See Robinson, Jackie
Robinson, Jackie 1919-1972 **6**
Robinson, Luther
   See Robinson, Bill "Bojangles"
Robinson, Malcolm S. 1948— **44**
Robinson, Max 1939-1988 **3**
Robinson, Rachel 1922— **16**
Robinson, Randall 1942(?)— **7**
Robinson, Sharon 1950— **22**
Robinson, Shaun 19(?)(?)— **36**
Robinson, Smokey 1940— **3**
Robinson, Spottswood W., III 1916-1998 **22**
Robinson, Sugar Ray 1921— **18**
Robinson, William, Jr.
   See Robinson, Smokey
Roche, Joyce M. 1947— **17**
Rochester
   See Anderson, Eddie "Rochester"